Cliff + Helen Pease
Sept. '96

RIVERS, RAILWAYS, AND ROADS

A HISTORY OF

HENDERSON COUNTY

ROBERT P. SUTTON

HENDERSON COUNTY HISTORICAL SOCIETY
RARITAN, ILLINOIS

© 1988 Henderson County Historical Society and Robert P. Sutton. All rights reserved. No part of this book may be reproduced in any form without the written permission of the Henderson County Historical Society.

Printed in the United States of America

Published with technical assistance from the
Illinois Heritage Association
602-604 E. Green Street
Champaign, IL 61820

Library of Congress Cataloging-in-Publication Data
88-16538
ISBN 0-9620376-0-5

CONTENTS

Preface	v
Acknowledgements	vii
Introduction	ix

RIVERS, RAILWAYS AND ROADS

The People and The Land 1820-1832	1
The Community Building Years 1832-1858	25
The Civil War 1858-1865	51
The Golden Years 1865-1900	77
Complacency and War 1900-1920	105
The Twenties	129
The Great Depression and The New Deal 1929-1940	159
World War II 1940-1947	185
Henderson County 1948-1984	211
List of Illustrations	245
Index	247

Representative Neff, Judge Evans, Cindy Pence and Senator Railsback

PREFACE

The State of Illinois celebrated its bicentennial in 1968. This activity generated a good deal of interest in historical events and many historical societies throughout the state considered or published some revision of their respective county histories. The fervor for a better grasp of our local histories was accelerated by the celebration of the 1976 bicentennial of the United States.

This heightened desire and interest sowed the seeds for this volume. During the early 1970's the Henderson County Historical Society experienced an increased level of activity. One of these interests was the compilation of a current Henderson County history. Reprints of the Henderson County portion of the 1882 volume and Gordon's 1911 work had been commissioned and sold by the Historical Society during the bicentennial celebration. Interest continued to mount and publication of a new history was a regular agenda item at the Historical Society meetings. The nature and scope of the proposed history were frequently discussed.

With respect to scope, there was some discussion of publishing a book that covered only the period from 1911 to approximately 1980; however, it was ultimately decided that the history should go back as far as possible.

The nature of the proposed publication was an issue which the Historical Society debated for some time. The two prior histories (1882 and 1911) consist substantially of biographies of subscribers. While these are valuable and interesting, the Historical Society did not believe that they constituted "history" in the strict sense. In Webster's definition of history, consisting of approximately twelve column lines, history is, for our purposes, "a systematic account of what has happened in the life or development of a people, country, or institution, usually with an analysis and explanation." The Henderson County Historical Society wanted this kind of perspective for the current writing. The goal was to have a volume that contained more than a collection of events and persons; rather, historical perspective, world, national, state, and local events, and their relationships were to be the content of the book.

In planning for this publication the Henderson County Historical Society determined that it would be best to hire a professional historian. It was felt that to achieve the type of history work which we wished, it would be better to have a professional with a different view of the events than that which we might have. We recognized that an outside author might miss some of the insight of residents, but would also have a point of view that would differ from those persons who live in Henderson County. The 1882 and 1911 histories were written by local residents: perhaps the history to be written in twenty, forty, sixty or 100 years may again be authored locally.

On behalf of the Henderson County Historical Society and the History Book Committee, I hope that reading this volume will be a catalyst to your memory of significant events and will bring you much enjoyment.

                Stephen G. Evans
                For the History Book Committee
                of the Henderson County Historical Society

Sheep on Lomax Township farm

ACKNOWLEDGEMENTS

In a project of this nature where the historian must start his research from scratch into unmined primary sources and then must interpret the development of a community over a century-and-a-half of time the interest and assistance of many other individuals is invaluable. To the Henderson County Historical Society goes my appreciation for their vision and support over a five year undertaking. From beginning to end several individuals in particular have come to my aid on countless requests: John H. Allaman, Mildred Anderson, and Jim Cook were indispensable. Judge Stephen G. Evans of the Ninth Judicial Circuit served with painstaking care as chair of the Committee on Publication. John Lee Allaman, a member of the Society, whom I first met when he was finishing his Master of Arts degree in History at Western Illinois University, stopped by my office on numerous occasions to share vital bits of new information on the county's history. He was also helpful in my gaining access to the mountain of data on the economic and social history of the area contained in the computer print out of the Federal Land Records available from the Illinois State Archives.

I am especially appreciative of the work done for me in the census manuscripts by two graduate assistants, Qi Wang and Anthony J. Karlson, both of whom have since completed their Master of Arts in History at Western Illinois University. Gordana Rezab and the staff of the Archives and Special Collections of the Western Illinois University Libraries were more than willing to aid in my continual requests for information. Marjorie Dreher of the Henderson County District Library was extremely helpful in the critical early days of research as was Rodney O. Davis, Professor of History at Knox College, who led me to materials housed in the Finely Collection at that institution's library. The staff of the public libraries at Monmouth, Illinois and Burlington, Iowa were likewise eager to help every time I visited them. My friends John Daly, Director of the Illinois State Archives, and Roger D. Bridges, Assistant State Historian and Editor of the Lincoln Legal Papers Project at the Illinois State Historical Library, took time out from their cramped schedules to give me assistance throughout the research and writing. Lastly, I am indebted to the countless residents of the county who, in cooperation with the Historical Society, typed and retyped, read and reread the manuscript and to Yvonne Knapp who dependably and safely served as my courier back and forth to these typists. Any errors of omission or commission in the final product are, despite the efforts of others, mine alone.

                                          Robert P. Sutton
                                          Macomb, Illinois
                                          November, 1987

Burg Home-Dallas City

INTRODUCTION

Over twenty-five years ago, as a graduate student at the College of William and Mary, the eminent scholar Lester Cappon had advised me: "if you want to write history you have to do as the first generation of historians did, you must go back to the place, get a real personal sense of the setting and the people." Sure, I said, those first American historians of the last century, such as the great Francis Parkman or Henry Adams, *could* tromp virgin territory. After all no one before them had written about the Oregon Trail, the French in North America, or the presidencies of Jefferson and Madison. But those opportunities by the 1960s were long gone. By then it was apparent that chances for research and writing lay in revising and reinterpreting what had been published already; many historians had become reduced to charwomen, taking in one another's wash. And so it was, because professional historians for a variety of legitimate reasons, had overlooked the only available chunk of America's past that had not been defiled by overuse: local history.

For over a hundred years almost all local and county histories have been done by amateur historians—dentists, lawyers, and businessmen, largely. Their volumes served an invaluable purpose of preserving information that otherwise would have been lost. Yet there was no historical analysis in their books, no effort to deal with causation or the relation of local happenings to larger events. It was as if each locality were created and existed in a vacuum. Local history was of interest to those who already were interested. And so for a combination of reasons—being ignored by university professors and being trivialized by well meaning amateur writers—local history in America is a neglected field.

These were the circumstances when, in late 1981, I agreed to write a history of Henderson County. Many of my professional associates asked "Why are you doing *that*?" I would answer "Because no one else has done it." And so it was, just as I had been told to do, I found myself in my car traveling the township roads of a county I had never visited to meet people I had never seen in my life. I became in my own mind a latter-day Francis Parkman, in miniature of course. The county highways over the next five years were my Oregon Trail. What I would discover in this journey I had no idea; the only evidence I had to start with was a state road map.

What I found in Henderson County was a story of a people who shared a journey in time themselves (since most of the original descendants have progeny still living there) through a unique historical landscape of intersecting rivers, railways, and roads. Each feature on the landscape marked a change from one way of life to another. First they came and settled on the Mississippi and its tributaries. Then new social patterns grew up as towns were created along the arteries of two national railroads that crisscrossed the county after the Civil War. Finally, by the 1920s, the "paved roads" arrived and rearranged the economy and the social life of this rural, small town western Illinois community.

Yet even though the historical landscape was a unique combination of major river, rail, and concrete communication lines the political, economic, social, and intellectual life of Henderson County was interlocked with that of the state and the nation. Sometimes the connection was obvious, to those living at the time and to the historian, sometimes the link was more subtle and unnoticed by contemporaries but nonetheless discernable a century or so later. In simple terms, the history of Henderson County is a history in miniature of the region and the nation. It is a sort of historical cell of the larger body politic. And through a detailed and careful study of this cell historians can learn a good deal about the historical physiology and pathology of the American people.

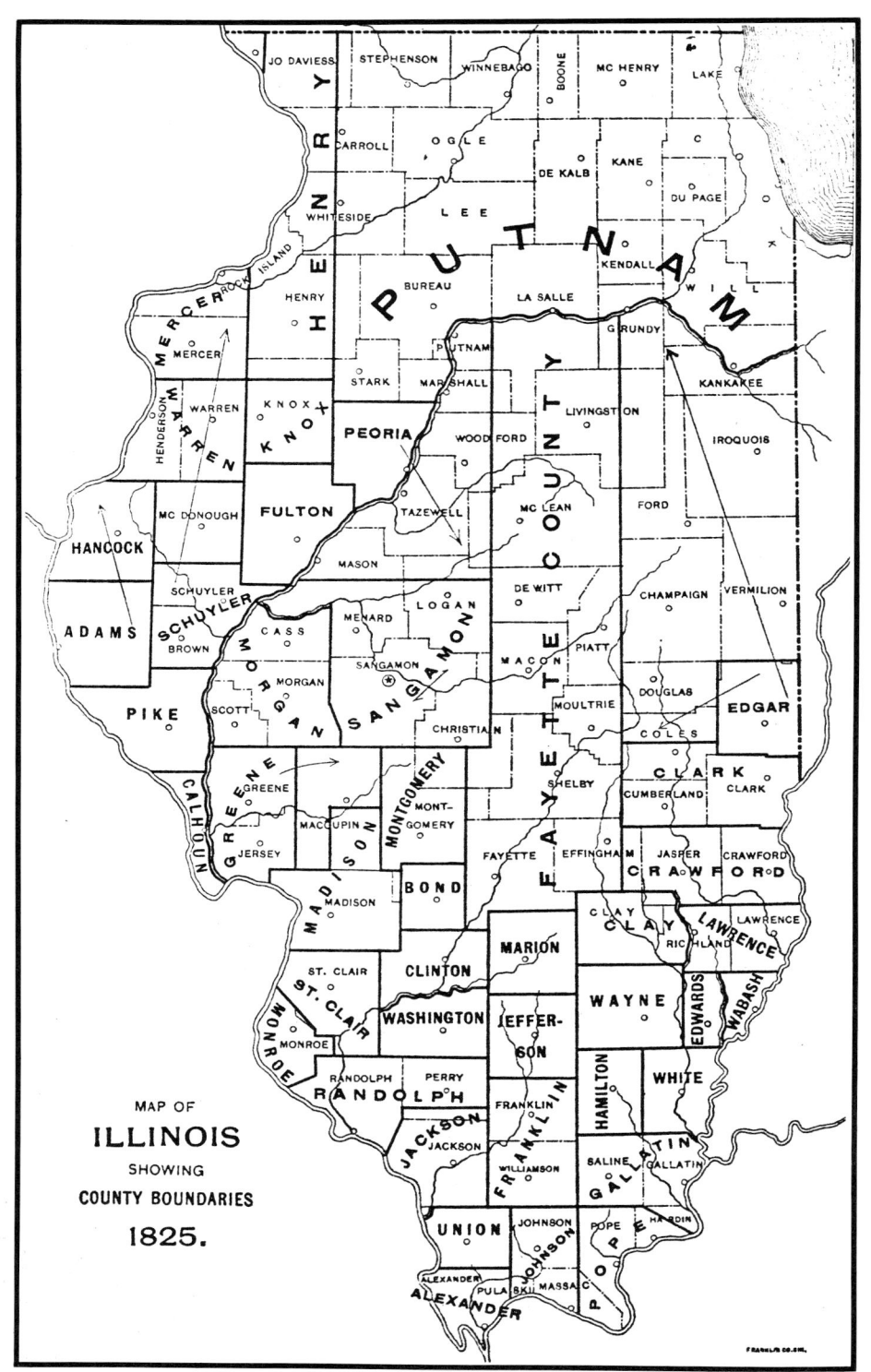

CHAPTER ONE
THE PEOPLE AND THE LAND
1820 - 1832

They came west and they settled in Henderson County, Illinois and this is what happened to them.

Across the Appalachian Mountains, down and away from Pittsburgh and into the state of Ohio they came. Other pioneers hiked from Virginia and Maryland up to the Monongahela River and they, too, floated into the Buckeye State. Still other Virginians, in the company of a few North Carolinians, followed a path made by squatters who had picked their way, with only a horse, cow, and dog in tow, through the Cumberland Gap and into Kentucky. After a while many of them, too, wound up in Ohio and still later on in Indiana. Sooner or later these pioneers came to Illinois and in these treeless lands they stopped. Some though made their way to the end of Illinois and to the area along the Mississippi River in the ancestral lands of the Sauk-Fox Indians. Here they stayed, and died, and left their progeny. The place was later called Henderson County.[1]

The pioneers were not alone in their westward trek although they often lived alone, miles from other travelers. They were a part of the great opening of the West (now called the Mid-West) of the Age of Jackson. For in 1828, three years after the first homesteader arrived in Henderson County, Andrew Jackson was elected the seventh President of the United States. His victory signaled a democratic revolution in politics because for the first time since the American Revolution the unpropertied white adult males decided the outcome of elections. And they chose Jackson, the Hero of the Battle of New Orleans in the War of 1812, by a vote of 647,286 to 508,064 over his opponent John Quincy Adams, son of the second President. It was the era of the common man. But more than politics was changing. A revolution in the old agrarian order of the seaboard states was transforming the life of the small, independent farmer who had for generations lived there. It was this transformation that pushed Americans westward.[2]

Andrew Jackson

In the years after the War of 1812 farming in the Middle Atlantic states steadily declined. The fertile acres of colonial days were worn out and the remaining marginal lands yielded discouraging returns. The Federal Census figures of 1820 and 1830 show an alarming decrease in productivity and, more specifically, its impact on farm families. Over 30 percent of that region's population emigrated during the Jacksonian era. Technological changes in farm operation exacerbated the decline in soil fertility. The new eastern cities demanded that farmers switch from grain to the cultivation of fruits and vegetables. Railroad owners insisted that farmers ship crops which sold in urban markets. As a consequence, farmers in New York, for example, started to raise great quantities of apples. In New Jersey, they grew peaches. In Pennsylvania, they marketed vegetables and fruits like beans, peas, cherries and strawberries.

Some farmers tried scientific innovations to adapt their land to the changed production. For the first time they used manure as a fertilizer rather than throw it away as a stinking nuisance. Others attempted crop rotation, now feasible with the planting of diverse crops. Grasses and clover and a variety of new plants were advertised, and tried out, in handbooks like the *Farmer's Register* and the *Cultivator*. For the farmers

Opposite page: Map of Illinois, 1825

who were willing and able to change and to adapt to the new demands of marginal acreage cultivation, diversified crop production, and a scientific approach to soil fertility the improved farming meant increased output and profits. Put simply, for those farmers who adapted it meant that by 1840 they could produce from two to four times as much in 1820.

But, as the census figures tell, many men, about one-third, could not or would not change. Some were too young to be able to borrow the capital to subsidize the changes. Unmarried men felt little compelling need to make the commitment in money (if they could get it) and in time. Middle-aged (in their thirties) farm owners were chagrined and disgruntled at the changing patterns of rural life. For instance, the time-honored practice where the local merchant accepted wood, grain, or butter as payment was replaced by his insistence upon hard cash. Other changes in daily life bothered the head of the household. He saw his wife with idle time on her hands as she was freed from such traditional homemaking responsibilities as spinning and weaving. Now peddlers brought finished cloth directly to her door. Daughters, too, were liberated from staying home with the chores of domestic manufacturing and had the option of going off to the new city mills to earn their keep, independent of father's eye.

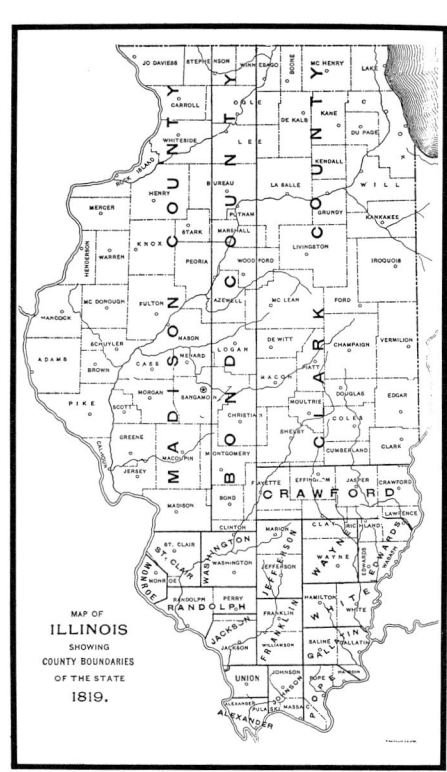

Map of Illinois Counties, 1819

Thus many eastern farmers, whether bachelor sons or heads of households, by the late 1820s felt that their world was changing—for the worse. Yet at the same time they saw some of their neighbors adapt to these changes in colonial agriculture and prosper. They themselves felt locked out or at best expected that they could just barely hold their own. As wealth inequality increased so did dissatisfaction, so did the compulsion to improve their situation by leaving for an imagined better place—west. A popular song of the Age of Jackson went like this.
"Come, all ye Yankee farmers who want to change your lot, /
Who've spunk enough to travel beyond your native spot. /
And leave behind the village where Pa and Ma do stay, /
Come, follow me, and settle in Michigan, yea, yea."[3]

The farmer of the upper South had even more troubles than his northern counterpart. The problem in Virginia and Maryland, for example, was two-fold: soil exhaustion and slave labor. The red clay soil of this region had by the War of 1812 withstood almost 200 years of a single crop production that was tied to, and inseparable from, chattel slavery. The crop, tobacco, moreover, took chemicals, mainly phosphorous, from the soil which until the advent of chemical fertilizers were impossible to replace. The soil was exhausted and the acreage was used up. The pending disaster of single-crop tobacco production had been forestalled, temporarily, in the eighteenth century by clearing what unused lands still remained from colonial days. But with the tobacco crop itself shrinking in quality and in size the number of additional acres was gone in a generation. To keep the same income from tobacco one needed more and more new acres but there was less and less uncultivated soil left. Only the large landowning families - those with 2,000 acres or more - had by 1820 any surplus land available.

For most southern farmers, those with about 100 acres or less, their way of life seemed about to disappear. Although most farmers of this region, some 75 percent of the total population, were not tobacco growers or slave owners their small farms had been carved out of the tobacco lands of the large planters. So even if they tried to raise corn and wheat, chickens, hogs, and vegetables for their own subsistence those crops were doomed by an exhausted red soil incapable of being replenished. Their household routines from year to year were grim indeed. Living in a two-room clapboard home, these families made soap, candles, coarse cloth, and whiskey. They traded eggs, hams and hand-made textiles for cash or goods, and ate their corn, wheat and vegetables. It was a drab existence. But even this bleak livelihood was threatened. Southern farmers, then, fiercely proud of their independence, felt that they had to find another place to live. They had no choice. They just were not able to pay a modest yearly property tax of about $50 per 100 acres and have enough to feed and clothe their families.

For a combination of reasons many farmers, both from North and South, were confronted with a reckoning. They could stay put and face a calamity if not for themselves then almost certainly for their children. These men believed they were living in a rapidly changing economic system which, for them, was not working out. Thus the paradox. In the Age of Jackson many a small farmer, the backbone of the Republic in the eyes of Thomas Jefferson, was being squeezed out of the opportunities of the American dream. The Era of the Common Man came to promise little to the common man "back East." So they packed up and went West.

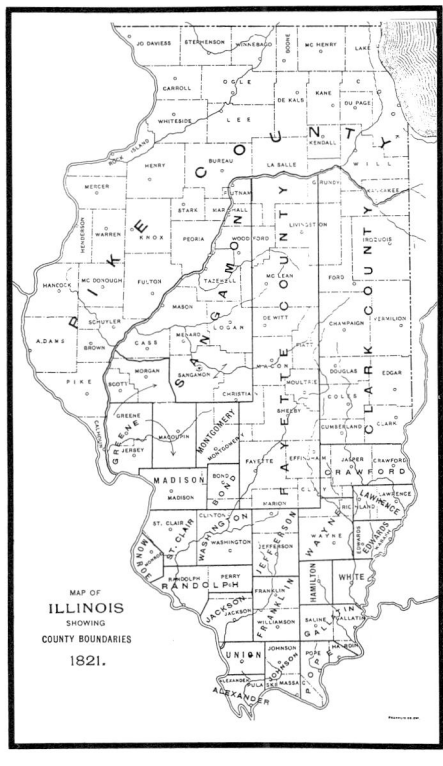

Map of Illinois Counties, 1821

James Monroe

The Prairie State, where many eastern farmers ended up, was in the 1820s second in size in the Union but had the fewest people. When Illinois was granted statehood in 1818 it had just under 35,000 souls and in 1830 counted only 157,445 inhabitants. Indiana, next door, had twice as many citizens. The physical area of Illinois out of which Henderson County would be created was called the Military Tract, a huge triangle of land between the Mississippi and Illinois rivers in the south which extended northward to the mouth of the Rock River. The Tract was created on paper in 1814 when two-thirds of the acreage was set aside as bounty land for enlisted veterans of the War of 1812. Congress provided for 160 acre warrants, called "Patents" and signed by President James Monroe in 1818, to be given to privates and corporals. Non-commissioned officers were to receive 320 acres.

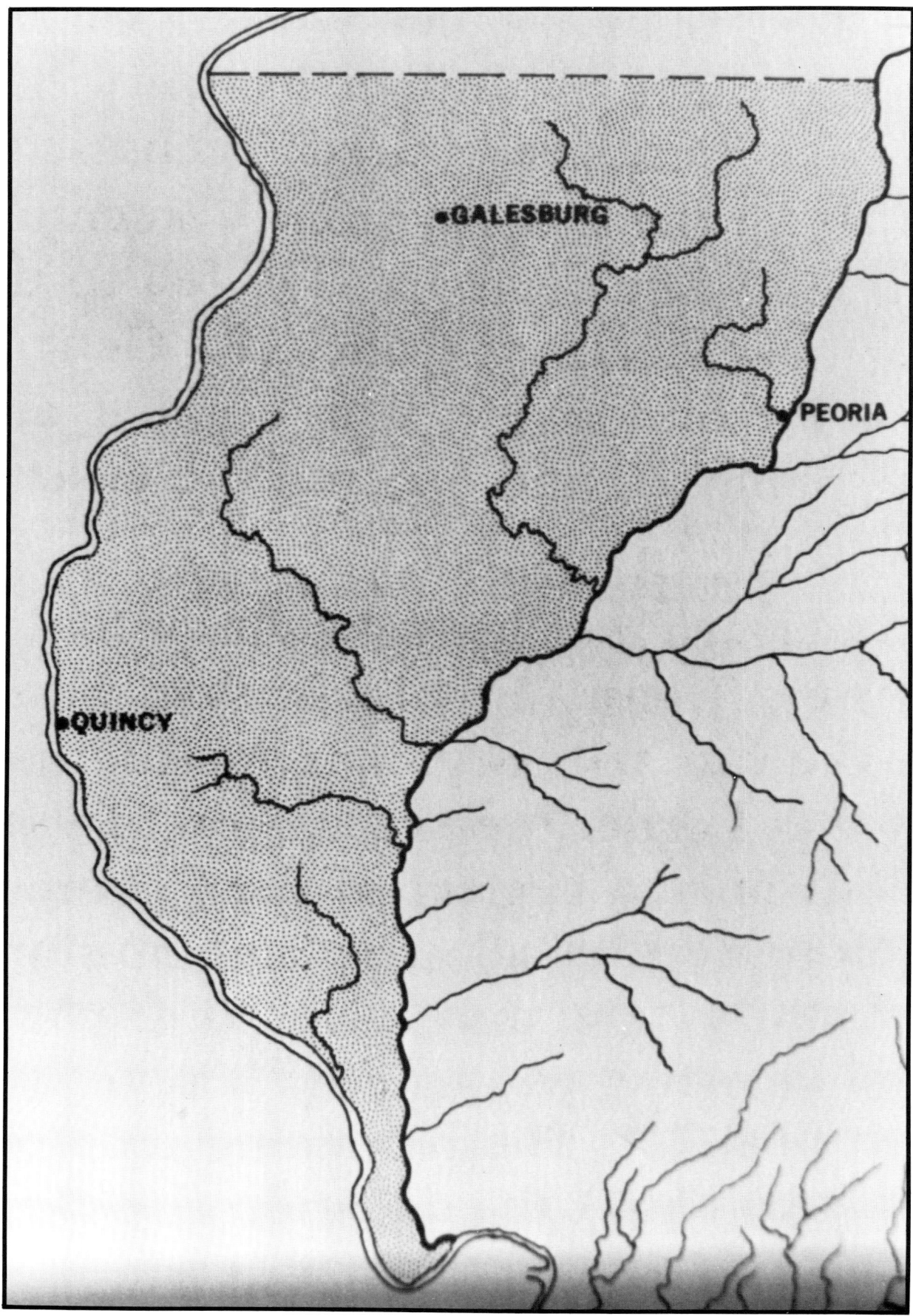

The Tract was over one-half million acres and in October, 1817 a preliminary survey began off the fourth Principle Meridian. At first all of the Tract was legally a part of Madison County and land records were kept at Edwardsville. Then from 1820 to 1824 Pike County took jurisdiction with the county seat located at Pittsfield. After 1825 the Tract was quickly carved into its permanent counties and all records were then transferred to the respective courthouses.[5]

Access to the Military Tract at first was hampered by New England and St. Louis land speculators who bought up thousands of acres from veterans or their heirs for as little as 25¢ an acre. Speculators were able to do this because the federal law did not require the patent recipient actually to settle in Illinois. So, legally, the veteran could, and most did, sell the patent the day he received it for whatever price he could get. Speculators, throughout the 1820s sold off only a handful of patents in the northern part of the Tract. They expected that the price of land would stay at least as high as the Land Act of 1796 had fixed it, at $2.00 an acre with a minimum purchase of 640 acres, reduced in 1801 to a 320 acre minimum.[6]

In 1820, however, Congress revised the statute downward to require just $1.25 an acre for a plot of only 80 acres. Compared to the situation when the Military Tract was first created—where, in order to make a purchase of any land left outside the Patent System a farmer had to have $640 just for the land alone—now after 1820, a person could buy cheaply and directly from the Beardstown or Quincy Federal Land Offices. He could acquire a warranty deed, debt free, for only $100. Speculators, anticipating little future profit, started to unload their investments. The Military Tract was finally open for settlement.

Before the crash of the land speculator market and the completion of the federal land survey off the Fourth Principle Meridian, (*ie* before about 1830) the northern half of the Military Tract was Indian country. Along the Illinois river and its tributaries lived the Kickapoo tribe. West of them, along the upper branches of the Lamoine River the Winnebago and Potawatomi camped in scattered villages. Farther to northwest lay the Sauk-Fox. These two tribes had moved into the area in the early eighteenth century from the Green Bay of Wisconsin, pushed the Potawatomis eastward, and established a confederation of villages between the Rock and Des Moines rivers. They dominated the Mississippi fur trade through contracts with the French and English and later with Astor's American Fur Company. After the War of 1812 the Sauk-Fox pelt business was further enhanced by Congress when it created two new trading ports, Edwards and Armstrong, to support Ft. Madison built in 1808, as permanent links in the Mississippi fur trade.

The first white men to enter the northern half of the Military Tract and to trespass on the Indian lands were trappers and traders. Always young and unmarried they had one primary, but transitory, interest—to make money. But soon after the wandering traders came the eastern farmers. They too were young, in their twenties, but more often than not were just married. Some had small children. As soon as possible these settlers put up a double log cabin complete with chinked walls, doors, and open windows. "The small caliber rifle, the spinning wheel, wool cards, and heavy plow," historian Theodore Pease wrote in *The Story of Illinois* "were his essential possessions."[8] Some might have brought along a piece or two of furniture, iron cooking utensils, blankets, or a clock. Many followed Josiah T. Marshall's *The Farmer's and Emigrant's Guidebook* which dealt

Opposite: Map of the Military Tract

with every facet of the pioneer's needs on the Illinois frontier.[9] It gave detailed advice on land selection, tools which the farmer would need, the time and money required for a cabin, and offered hints on land management. Under "Articles Necessary for a New Settler" Marshall listed both the items and their cost.

One span of Horses	$100.00
One yoke of oxen	50.00
One double wagon	50.00
One plough	10.00
One drag	5.00
One spade, shovel and hoe	2.50
Two log chains	8.00
One cradle, scythe and snath	7.00
One axe	2.00
Two augers - half inch and inch	1.00
One saw	1.00
Two chisels	1.00
Rake and pitchfork	1.00
One hammer & 10 lbs of nails	1.25
One cow	25.00
	$254.50

On the time to build a dwelling he tabulated:

Cutting, hewing and hauling timber	4 days work
Raising (with help)	1 day
Putting on roof	2 days
Cutting out doors, windows, and place for fireplace; making casing, doors	4 days
Laying floors & making ladder to chamber	3 days
Chinking and daubing	3 days
Building chimney	3 days
	20 days work

Marshall insisted that the farmer arrive in June. He offered, in chapter three, the following points on managing the new farm. He elaborated on what to be expected, and planned for, under seven areas. In Marshall's words:

Firstly - What proportion of the farm it is proper to preserve uncleared of wood.
Secondly - The proper division of the cleared land into fields, size of fields, manner of fencing etc.
Thirdly - The proper improvements of the soil which will include draining, manuring, etc.
Fourthly - The cultivation of various kinds of crops.
Fifthly - Seeding of land with grass seeds.
Sixthly - Raising domestic animals.
Seventhly - Necessity of barns and sheds sufficiently to store all crops, will protect domestic animals from the inclemency of weather.

Most of the first settlers walked to Henderson County. Either alone or with families, they arrived over wagon trails, more like foot paths, extending out from two embarkation points, the land office towns of Quincy and Beardstown. Leaving Quincy, they headed northeast over a ridge of land to Round Prairie and proceeded north to Carthage and Commerce (soon called Nauvoo) located at the southwest tip of the county. From Beardstown, they traveled in an elliptical arc northward to Rushville and then northwest through Littleton and Doddsville. Then they crossed the La Moine River south of Job's Landing (Blandinsville) and moved on to La Harpe. They entered the county at about the same point as their fellow pioneers coming up from Quincy. Finally, all of them headed toward their claims or homesteads along ever narrower paths treaded by the Sauk and Fox Indians.[10]

What they saw when they penetrated the county at the edge of Lomax Township was tempting. The land was well watered by creeks and streams, all of which spread as so many arteries inland from the Mississippi. Henderson Creek headed northeast. The South Henderson curved

Land Office Warrant, Henderson County, 1818

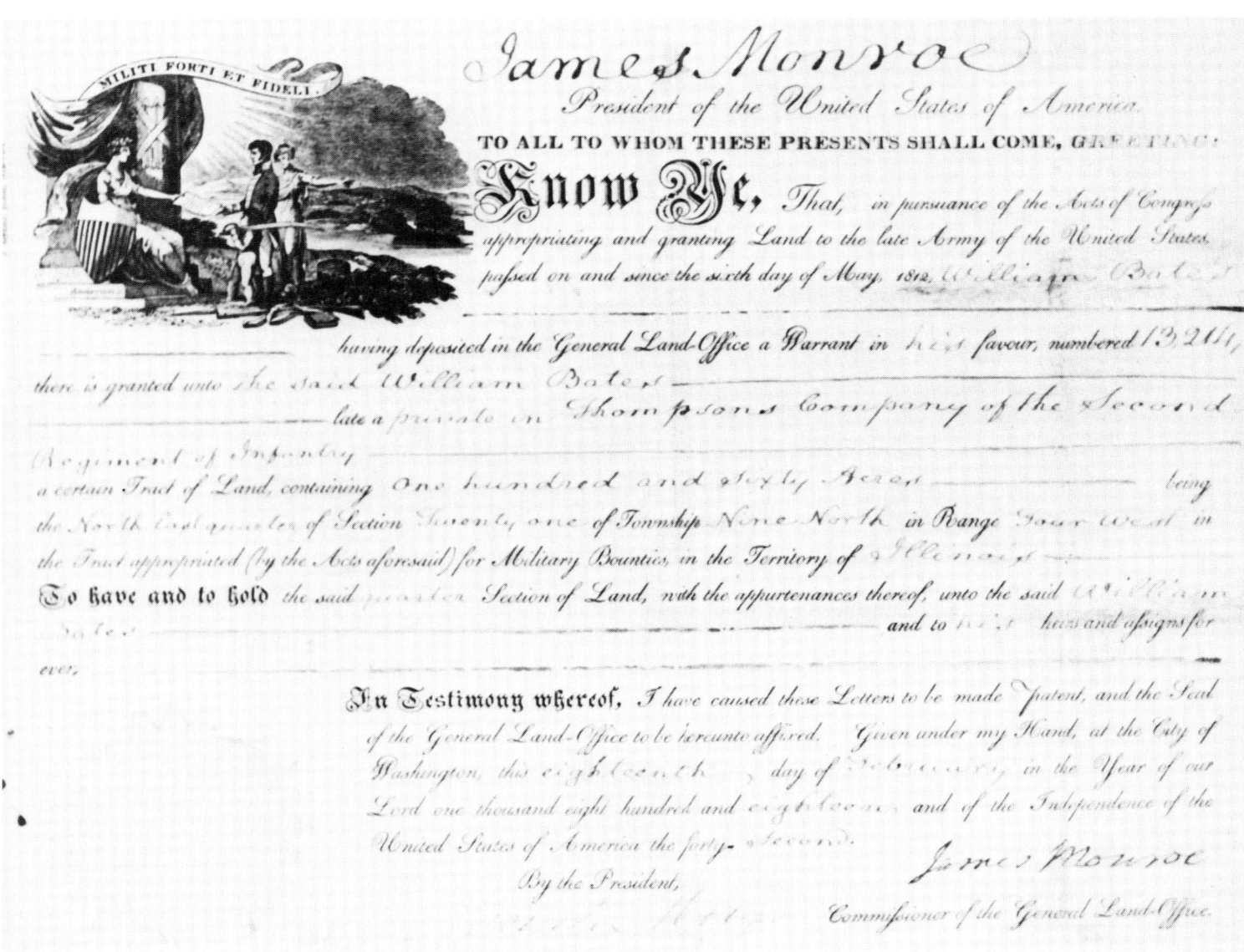

eastward, while Ellison Creek pointed southeast toward its genesis in the highlands of another county. There were other, smaller streams—the Cedar in the northeast corner, the Honey and Dugout in the southwest. Around these major waterways grew the all-important groves of timber: oak, ash, walnut and hickory. Wood was the other indispensable element, besides water, needed for survival. Pioneers used it in all aspects of daily life. They cut it for their cabins, their fuel, their animal shelters. They used it for fencing, for tools, for household utensils, for furniture. Consequently all but ignored in the beginning was the treeless prairie — about one-half the surface area of the county. It was thought uninhabitable because it had neither water nor timber. Besides, the tales of devastating prairie grass fires frightened away everyone. Lastly, numerous fresh water springs provided an abundant water supply for livestock. Even drinking water, a serious health problem in other parts of Illinois, was surprisingly pure. Full-flowing surface wells were tapped at less than ten feet. Nature combined to favor the dreams of the first pioneer settlers. Many expected that, whatever the short term hardships might be, life itself in the long run would be better and more rewarding than the future they had faced before.[11]

Early Nineteenth Century log cabin

For a while, however, life was primitive and at times discouraging. Early visitors to the Illinois frontier, such as James Haines and Ferdinand Ernst, tended to draw the same hard picture of daily life. They described settlers as unusually reticent and slow in movement. The men, they said, spent all their waking hours clearing the fields and hunting, in other words providing the food. The women filled their day working to feed their hungry family. They also made all the clothing except for the moccasins and boots which the men stitched together. Clothing was simple, functional, and poorly fitted. Women wore a frock made of wool and flax which was dyed with tints and shades made from tree bark. A "rainey day" dress was sewn from the same material, ankle-length with sleeves attached. This was put on by slipping it over their head and drawing it around the waist and neck with a cord. Men wore leather pants and shirts or the same two items woven of flax. All wore a hat of plaited rye, oats, or straw for protection in summer or a fur cap in winter.

The following account by James Haines entitled "Social Tales and Scenes" conjured up a typical interior of one of the Illinois log cabins of the 1830s.

> An elder wife-perhaps grandmother in person-sits at the small spinning wheel driving it rapidly by intermittent pressure with her right foot on the treadle, with eye and mind intent on drawing out and twisting the fine linen thread from the flax-covered distaff of even size and continuous length, while a younger wife or unmarried girl drives a big wheel to furious motion and loud hum with the wheel-pin in her right hand dashing backward to draw the roll of carded wool to proper size as the whirring spindle unites and hardens it into yarn-woof for the loom. And ever as she returns in gentle pace from the utmost stretch of the yarn she jogs with her foot the sugar-trough cradle close to her line of retreat to reunite the baby's broken slumber. Meantime the low sound of gently simmering cabbage and bacon-perchance fresh venison, fruit of the hunter's skill-from the singing iron pot on the wood fire, joins with the hum of wheel and lullaby song of the spinner. Rare fragrance from the boiling pot fills the cabin area with appetizing odors reminding all its occupants of approaching meal time. The spinner hastens her humming wheel to complete the half dozen cuts-her stint for the dinner hour, eighteen cuts or hanks being a big day's work.
>
> When at noon the simple meal is sit up and all the family gather at the table to discuss the "creature comforts" of a log cabin dinner, the graceful, health-giving exercise of the big wheel over a puncheon floor and the rugged sprinting demands of the chase or long plodding guidance of the plow, all prove their power to win a vigorous appetite. Not strictly a "dinner of herbs" yet it had the Bible element to sweeten it— "love therewith."[12]

Food of the frontier was simple, like clothing, and ample. Before gardens pioneers depended upon wild vegetables such as onions, lamb's quarter, dandelions, and varieties of dock. These were boiled with a piece of salt meat to concoct a wild pottage. The first garden produced a supply of beans, peas, squashes, mustard, lettuce, carrots, leeks, cabbage, potatoes, melons, and tomatoes (called "love apples"). Settlers always "put away" part of their vegetables for use throughout the winter. Green corn was cut and dried. Potatoes, turnips, and cabbages were buried in a root cellar or piled and covered with hay and mulch in the garden itself. Beans and peas were put in sacks to dry by hanging from tree limbs. One problem was a lack of fresh fruit because orchards and vineyards were frustratingly slow growing. So they fell back upon blackberries, dewberries, strawberries, gooseberries and currants. The women made them into pies or cobblers but, with sugar non-existent any preserves, jams, or jellies were unavailable in winter. For beverages the mainstay was tea brewed from herbs and roots.

Every male pioneer was a hunter who provided venison, quail, squirrel, and rabbit for the table. Venison, though, was the staple with deer-hams cured for the winter. Pork, by the 1830s was added to the diet. Ranging free in the woods each family hog was "earmarked" by its owner. November was hog-killing time when the meat was cut into hams, shoulders, and sides which were then trimmed and salted in barrels. Scraps were ground into sausage and stuffed into long, thin sacks or wrapped in cornhusks. Lard fat was rendered out and souse, or head cheese, was prepared. The heart and liver were eaten right away.

Finally, by the mid-1830s, pioneers began butchering some of their beefstock. It was cut and pounded into slices and then fried in hot lard. Larger pieces were boiled. What was left was then re-sliced and served with onions and potatoes as a hash. In sum, these first settlers felt well-fed with a high protein diet at the end of a day of hard work. "With such an abundant supply of pork, ham, and bacon, together with some fresh beef from time to time, and the occasional use of game," Edward E. Dale commented in his discussion of frontier food in Illinois, "it is not surprising that meat constituted a large part of the diet of the average pioneer settler."[13]

Yet life could be discouraging, especially for the women. Months of isolation from any company (except at times a Sauk or Fox brave), the feeling of the loss of friends and family left behind, the new dangers and rigors of life in the wilderness, all played upon the minds of these early settlers. One pioneer woman, a Mrs. Clark, felt continually depressed. In August 1828 she had come from Virginia to Mclean County, Illinois and then to Warsaw. Finally she ended up at Fort Armstrong. Her malaise set in right away. She had no friends close enough for her to visit. As winter descended her family's stock of provisions dwindled except for a barrel of whiskey which the captain of the small steamer that had carried Mrs. Clark up river from Warsaw had left for safe keeping until his return. Soon some Sauk-Fox Indians as well as federal soldiers at Ft. Armstrong found out about the whiskey barrel. Winter passed with repeated episodes of the woman fending off conniving soldiers and half-drunk Indians. Life by spring was "tragically lonely." Mother Clark, as she was later called, felt "cut off from all society and intercourse with other white families...living in constant dread of the Indians, with no doctor near and no one to turn to for help or sympathy in time of sickness and with scant communication with the outside world for there was no mail."[14] There was, indeed, no one.

The earliest permanent white inhabitant of Henderson County was Captain Rezin Redman. A veteran of the War of 1812, but not a recipient of a warrant in the county, Redman came up the Mississippi in 1825 and built a crude lean-to shelter on Honey Creek along a slough where it emptied into the Mississippi. The next spring he brought his family here and put up a small two-room log cabin. Not until 1834 though was Redman able to secure a deed to his homestead. In that year he purchased eighty acres on section twelve on Honey Creek for $1.25 an acre. In 1835, he bought another eighty acres at the same price about one-half mile north. Then on

January 25, 1836 he secured a deed for eighty acres adjacent to his Honey Creek farm for a total of two hundred forty acres.[15]

The next settlers were the Phelps Brothers. In the fall of 1828 Stephen Sumner Phelps arrived at Yellow Banks. When Phelps landed on the east side of the Mississippi that summer he was greeted by a mysterious, elusive figure of the Illinois frontier, Dr. Isaac Galland. Whether or not Galland was a physician is doubtful. But the self-proclaimed "doctor" first appeared in the early histories of the towns of Carthage and Hamilton and then as the land owner who sold the tract called Commerce to the Mormon Prophet Joseph Smith. Later he came in and out of accounts of fraudulent land dealing with the Indians in the 1830s in the so-called "half-breed" lands in eastern Iowa.[16]

What is known of Galland's activities in Henderson County is that he landed at Yellow Banks in 1827 with a barrel of whiskey and called the location by the Sauk-Fox name for the place, Oquawkick. That year he and a nameless companion hired some Indians living nearby to build a log cabin by giving each brave a healthy slug of whiskey for every log cut and set into place. Although the work became tougher for the six or eight braves as the sides of the cabin progressed upward, "their love of fire water," recounted an early history of Warren County, "was so great that they would always return the following day, thereby repeating the process until the house was completed."[622] In 1828, the restless, peripatetic Galland sold his homestead to Stephen Sumner Phelps.

Stephen Sumner Phelps was born in Palmyra, New York on August 1, 1805 of New England parents, Stephen and Lois, who had converted to Quakerism. Stephen Jr. was the fifth of seven children. The oldest brother, Alexis, was the first to head west, walking from New York to Kentucky after the War of 1812. Then, in 1820, he enticed Sumner to come along on a second trek, this time to Illinois, where the two brothers purchased a family homestead near the Sangamon River close to the future site of Springfield. In the fall of 1821 the rest of the Phelps family relocated to the newly-created state. The Phelps stayed along the Sangamon River until 1825 when they moved northward to Lewistown in Fulton County.

Stephen Sumner Phelps

For the next three years young Sumner wandered throughout the prairies north and east of Lewistown, trading with the Potawatomi tribes in that desolate region. In the fall of 1826 he established a log cabin trading post on the Illinois River at the old french colony of Starved Rock. While Sumner was building up a regular fur trading route to the northeast of Lewistown Alexis headed west to the Mississippi and then upriver to Galena to begin a stake in that booming lead-mining town. In 1827 he wrote to Stephen to invite him to Galena as a partner with a one-third share of the profits. The younger Sumner, who had married Phoebe Chase of Lewistown in early 1828, welcomed the chance to expand beyond the itinerant duties of fur trader and at the same time to settle into a more permanent domestic life-style with his new bride. On March 1, 1828 Sumner arrived at Galena. His first assignment was to set up a family smelting furnace nearby on the Wisconsin River. Then in the early fall he started back to Lewistown for his wife. By the time he arrived home, though, Sumner was seriously ill from what he thought was mineral poisoning from the lead smelting. Sumner and Phoebe both decided to forget about Alexis and the Galena project.

Late in the spring of 1828 Sumner received a report from a friend, Jeremiah Smith, who had just walked to Lewistown from Yellow Banks. Smith said a Dr. Galland there wanted to sell his homestead and, from all accounts, it seemed that the location would be an excellent spot for Sumner to pick up the fur trade again, this time in a better location on the Mississippi. Sumner's father backed the idea and purchased the Galland tract for his namesake for $400. Sumner and Phoebe, in September, carted their meager possessions in a small wagon to Galland's cabin. On this trip Sumner also brought along his younger brother, William and his wife, and a slave called "Nigger Dick."

Both Sumner and William, over the next four years (until Alexis joined them in 1833) carved out a trade empire in the Mississippi lands of the Sauk-Fox. In pack trains filled with goods such as tools, cloth, guns, and whiskey they wandered through western Illinois and swapped them for furs. In the fall of 1830 William ventured westward into Iowa. He crossed the river at Yellow Banks in a canoe with his wife and dog and made his way twenty-five miles north along the west bank in shallow water free from the strong down-river channel currents. At the mouth of the Iowa River, where a small natural harbor formed at the eastward bend of the Mississippi River, the pair built a log cabin.[17]

William Phelps

In October, William traded that small supply of goods and ammunition he was able to bring along to a band of passing Sauk-Fox. That winter, though, the couple almost froze to death. It was later called the "winter of the deep snow." From early November until April they saw not a soul. Snowbound on the west, ice locked on the east, they faced starvation. In January, William broke the flintlock of his rifle. Luckily, soon afterwards, their dog, as desperately hungry as his masters, cornered a deer which William then killed with a make-shift spear made from a hunting knife tied to the end of a pole. In April, with the spring thaw, the exhausted pair headed back down river to Sumner's cabin. But from then on, the Phelps operated a northern trade outpost on the Iowa River opposite William's winter ordeal at Upper Yellow Banks, later New Boston, Illinois.

In the summer of 1831 the Phelps Brothers expanded their operations southward to the rapids at Commerce (Nauvoo) and then farther westward into Indian country in the Iowa territory. With a trade license from the federal government, William built a third outpost at what would be Iowa town of Farmington, a site which gave the Phelps' access to the extensive fur trade coming down both the Skunk and Des Moines rivers. Sumner, heading the operation out of Yellow Banks, became close friends with Sauk-Fox chiefs Tama and Keokuk and developed a casual acquaintance with the warrior Black Hawk. It was they who labeled Sumner Hawk-eye (Wah-wash-e-we-qua) because of the fierce hawk-like look that came over his face when he was angry.

Sumner's temper was directed not at the Indians but at agents of the American Fur Company. Operating out of St. Louis under the name of Pratt, Shonteau & Co. and out of Ft. Armstrong under agent John Davenport. Their trappers and traders were determined to break the back of the Phelps interlopers. Approved by the head of the American Fur Company in New York City, John Jacob Astor, their men regularly tried to ambush, hijack, or destroy Phelps' pack trains and at the same time began "price wars" in bargaining with the Sauk-Fox for their pelts. Sumner took the initiative. He traveled alone on foot from Upper Yellow Banks to Farmington and then back to Yellow Banks carrying huge packs of tools and cloth on his shoulders.

Life, at best, was brutal for the young Phelps families. They lived long months separated from one another, Sumner, back-packing through the wilderness and William holding down the western outpost in Iowa. The two brides stayed at Yellow Banks by themselves with "Nigger Dick" and the dogs. Yellow Banks itself by 1831 consisted only of a single log cabin, a small storage building and, a half-mile away on Henderson Creek, a tiny sawmill that had been started in 1828 by Jeremiah Smith, the "middle man" for Galland in the Phelps purchase. The women suffered from the cold and lack of provisions. Their furniture was a crude box for a table and a bed or "couch" made up of two cut poles stuck in the side of the log house, called a "stake and rider bedstead." They baked bread from corn pounded in a tree trunk. Wild game and berries were their staples. Salt, brought up-river by traders headed to Galena, was the only store-bought luxury. Not until March 1, 1832 was Sumner himself able to purchase any land, acquiring 240 acres for $300 in section twenty-two on the site of the future town of Oquawka. Then, in 1835, he bought at the same location, another 155 acres for $193.94. And, finally, on March 25, 1836 he made his last purchase of 200 acres for $250.[18]

Before 1830 then Henderson County remained the domain of traders, squatters, and Indians. Indeed, only a handful of other white men came to the county along with the Redmans, Jeremiah Smith, and the Phelps brothers. All of them were young, small subsistence homesteaders, in their twenties, some with pregnant brides others with wives and small children. Everyone lived pretty much the same. Each family faced days on end with only the wilderness, the rivers, and the wolves. They ate dried meat and drank sassafras tea. And, for seasons at a time, they spoke to nobody, except for husbands and wives who, with a passing Indian or two, had at least each other for human companionship.

The first subsistence homesteaders remain all but nameless. Little more is known of them than was recounted over a hundred years ago when the first county history was completed in 1882 by Jonathan Simpson. The records they left only tell who they were, where they came from and what land they bought. About a dozen such faceless names appear in these early records, names such as John Pence, William Beaty, James Ryson, John Gibson, the Jamison brothers, Abner and Gabriel Short, James Ritchie, John Campbell and the first real market farmer, a transitional figure to a new stage of Henderson County history, John McKinney.[19]

Late in the fall of 1829, twenty-six year old John Pence walked from Indiana with his bride to begin his married life on a spot some three miles east of Yellow Banks. The following spring their son, John A. was born, the first white child of Henderson County. That summer Pence erected a crude log stockade which, during the next few years, served as a refuge from Indian attacks along Henderson Creek. This fort and another two-story blockhouse built in 1830 along South Henderson Creek were the only Indian defense structures in the county. Pence, in 1835 and 1836 purchased clear title to 153.54 acres for $92.73. Not far from "Pence's Fort" was the homestead of Captain William Beaty. He came there in May, 1830 from Bartholomew County, Indiana but in the spring of 1831 moved his family into Pence's Fort because of his fear of Indian harassment at his isolated homestead. There, at the fort, a second child was born in the county, Ezra Beaty, on September 9, 1831.

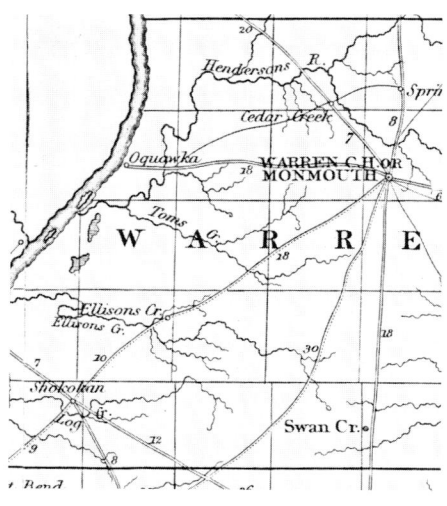

Area Waterways

About the same time, an Ohioan, James Ryson, left his wife and father-in-law in Edgar County, Illinois and traveled down the Illinois River on a flatboat loaded with whiskey bound for New Orleans. Hearing that the price of whiskey was considerably higher among the lead miners of Galena, Ryson turned northward at St. Louis. At Galena he unloaded his liquor at a large profit, loaded up with hides and lead, and floated back down-river. He stopped at Yellow Banks where he stayed a few days with the Phelps. Impressed with the commercial potential of the spot as a half-way stop between Galena and Quincy he built a log cabin on a river bluff two-and-one-half miles southwest of Phelps' near Henderson Creek. To earn more money in order to bring out his family he split fence rails and sold them to the Phelps at 50¢ a thousand. By 1830 he had purchased a team of oxen and started back to Edgar County for his wife and her father. To the south of the Ryson farm came the first pioneer on Ellison Creek, a Tennessean, John Gibson. In early 1833 he paddled up the Ellison into its Wolf Creek branch, built a split-rail lean-to, and cleared some land for plowing. By late fall Gibson had replaced the temporary shelter with a two-room log cabin where he felt more secure from marauding packs of wolves.

Further inland from the Mississippi, on a tributary of Henderson Creek called Goose Run, the brothers John and Samuel Jamison arrived in 1829. John eventually purchased forty-one acres for $51.26 and Samuel got a debt-free title for 153.87 acres for $153.76. In 1830, the Jamisons acquired their first neighbors, Samuel's sons-in-law Abner and Gabriel Short. The Shorts had left Perry County, Indiana in September of that year with one wagon, a team of horses, and a yoke of oxen. For a while they lived along the Henderson in a pole cabin where, with the family oxen, they planted corn. During these first years the Shorts survived on venison, duck, and wild turkey. They ground some corn into meal for bread and, at Yellow Banks, traded for salt. To the southeast of the Jamisons and Shorts, on the Tom Creek branch of South Henderson, James Ritchie came to set up his cabin in the spring of 1829. There, alone, he planted a few acres of corn and wheat.

The last pioneers of the early 1830s were John Campbell and John McKinney. Campbell, with his wife and nine children (itself a new phenomenon in those parts) came from Scott County, Indiana in 1829 and homesteaded on eighty acres about one-half mile east of Yellow Banks. There, five years later, he purchased a warranty deed of federal land for $100. The earliest white man in the upper reaches of South Henderson was John McKinney. He first arrived at Yellow Banks in 1831 from Kentucky and the next spring he moved his wife and two children back to the Phelps trading post. They tarried only a couple of months at Phelps' cabin before pushing inland to the upper South Henderson. McKinney purchased the entire section of number twenty-five in what became Biggsville Township from the St. Louis land speculator Romelius Rigg for $1,000. The following year he bought one-half of section twenty-six from another speculator for $500. Then in July, 1835 he purchased eighty acres in section thirteen for $100 and 160 acres in section twenty-four for $200. There, in his extensive holdings, with the help of other farmers who by then were filling up the South Henderson lands, he started an ambitious harvesting of corn and wheat.

By the time McKinney started his homestead, a sense of community had begun to replace the survival instincts of the isolated trader and settler. Now, in numbers, came other farmers who, like McKinney, grew crops not only for their families but also for markets in Oquawka and other terminal towns which had just started to develop. Soon these commercial farmers sent their corn and wheat farther eastward over traveled roads, then by railroads, to Monmouth and Galesburg or, westward, to down-river towns on the Mississippi. Along with the market-farmer came the mills, churches, schoolhouses, county government and, inevitably, social problems such as crime and violence. But before a more civilized life style could take shape on the Henderson County frontier one last vestige of the earlier period had to be removed, physically. That remnant of the primitive frontier was the Sauk-Fox Indians. And the event which brought about their removal was the Black Hawk War.

Even while white settlers were moving into the county the Sauk-Fox continued to use the land for agriculture, hunting, and for sacred burial grounds, all contrary to earlier treaty obligations with the Federal government. For example, in violation of an agreement of 1817, in which they had ceded all tribal rights east of the Mississippi River, some of the war chiefs kept families in western Illinois and harassed white settlers south of the Rock River. Keokuk and Tama, full tribal chieftains, on the other hand, were content to stay in Iowa and claim the $1,000 annuity promised by the United States Government.

Keokuk, Chief of the Sauk and Fox Indians

In 1827, one of these war chiefs, Black Hawk, confronted Keokuk and Tama on the need and the right to occupy tribal lands along the Rock River. Black Hawk, in fact, wanted to lead a war party to regain total control of the area. The head chiefs dissuaded the aging warrior from taking any precipitous action. But a year later Black Hawk was joined by other warrior chiefs such as Red Head, Bad Thunder, Ihowai, and the Winnebago Prophet. All of them opposed the public sale of their former lands, some 3,000 acres, to white settlers. Black Hawk, as their spokesman, told the Federal Indian agent of the area, Thomas Forsyth, that "... the land was theirs, that they never sold the land, that the land contained the bones of their ancestors and they would not give it up...and would defend it as long as they existed."[20] Chief Keokuk repudiated Black Hawk saying that the warrior spoke only for a small minority of his tribe. That summer there were a series of ugly incidents. "Indians were beaten by white men. White men fought with each other over Indian cornfields. Indians tore down white men's fences and sheds and broke their whiskey barrels.[21] That fall Keokuk ordered all of his warriors out of Illinois to a new village located on the Iowa River and stated emphatically that any mutinous braves who stayed east of the Mississippi River "must take their chance."[22]

Black Hawk's influence might have waned had it not been for a series of episodes over the next couple of years that gathered a momentum of tribal support around his policy of armed resistance.[23] In 1830 there was the "Warner Incident" where some sixteen chiefs on their way to a powwow summoned by the Indian agent on the upper Mississippi, Captain Wynkoop Warner, were murdered by a party of Sioux and Winnebago. The United States government, in violation of their promised justice in such cases, failed to provide adequate compensation to the relatives of the victims.

Black Hawk recruited braves from among these disgruntled relatives and crossed the Mississippi. In response, Governor John Reynolds, in May, 1831 called up the militia and ordered 700 mounted men to "remove them dead or alive over the west side of the Mississippi." He also ordered

Chief Black Hawk

General Edmund P. Gaines, commander of the federal garrison at St. Louis, to send an additional ten companies of infantry up-river to reinforce the militia. Gaines wrote back to Reynolds telling him not to give marching orders to the undisciplined militia at that time but, rather, to let him and the regulars handle the Indian problem, Reynolds complied and the militia stayed home.

At Rock Island, Gaines met with Black Hawk. The shallow-cheeked warrior refused to move out. He denied any intention to harm white settlers. He said that the land was theirs and it had never been sold. Gaines was insistent. Black Hawk and his band would have to move across the Mississippi but, if they evacuated, he promised that the Federal government would provide them with corn from lands in Illinois. It was a stalemate. In June, Reynolds decided to send out some of the militia anyhow and by the end of the month some 1,500 of them mustered in at Rock Island. Black Hawk, intimidated, submitted to Keokuk's authority and agreed to move back across the Mississippi. He crossed the river into Iowa in the fall of 1831.

In 1832, however, Black Hawk returned. The reasons behind his re-entry into Illinois are complex. The prime cause was an enticement by the Winnebago Prophet who convinced Black Hawk to come back to the Rock River since, the Prophet said, the 1831 prohibition referred only to the old Rock Island village. The Indians who followed Black Hawk into Illinois were a polygot group of about 1,000 men, women, and children made up of Sauk-Fox, Sauk-Winnebago half-breeds, and Kickapoos. These renegades in varying degrees held resentments against their own head chiefs like Keokuk, shared a hatred of white incursions on tribal burial grounds, harbored a distrust of all Federal agents, and of course had no fear of military reprisals. Some authorities saw another, hidden, motive in Black Hawk's own dread of the loss of his reputation, or personal integrity, by giving in to his opponents — either to Keokuk or to General Gaines.

There were fantasies at work, too. One fantasy was sexual. Many of Black Hawk's braves resented the rough white frontiersmen who, they believed, sexually exploited their squaws. Indeed, by 1832 lurid sexual rumors were rampant among the Sauk-Fox men. In July of that year two of the tribal chiefs, Taimah and Apenose, wrote to Indian agent William Clark in St. Louis about one of these "fables."

> "Father, we are told that the Americans were determined shortly to lay hands on all our males, both young and old, and deprive them of those parts which are said to be *essential* to courage; then, a horde of Negro men were to be brought up from the South, to whom our wives, sisters, and daughters were to be given, for the purpose of raising a stock of *Slaves* to supply the demand in this country, where negroes are scarce.[24]

These and other similar stories, the chiefs warned, had had a great influence on the band that gathered about Black Hawk. There was also the legal argument, eloquently expressed time and again by Black Hawk, that the 1817 cession was invalid and void; that the drunken, illiterate chiefs who had first agreed to that document had no idea what they had ceded. Furthermore, the right of the Sauk-Fox to hunt on any public land not purchased by whites was perpetual. Then, too, there was the unfounded assurance given to Black Hawk by a young, fanatical anti-America council chief Napope that the British in Canada and the Choctaw and Chickasaw tribes to the south would come to their aid as soon as they crossed into Illinois.

For whatever combination of motives, the Black Hawk party gathered together at Ft. Madison in early April, 1832 and on the sixth of that month they crossed the river. The women, children, and baggage were in canoes. The men, all armed, were on horseback. That evening they camped at Oquawka. Black Hawk told Sumner Phelps why they were there and what they wanted to do, namely, return up the Rock River. Sumner told him to go back to the Iowa Territory and that his continued presence in violation of tribal treaties would only mean disaster. Black Hawk, the following morning, moved further up-river and within three days reached the mouth of the Rock River.

There, at Ft. Armstrong, he talked with George Davenport, the supplier of the troops at the fort, who again told Black Hawk to turn back or the federal troops at the fort would be ordered out against his people. Black Hawk was now urged by the Prophet who told him that Black Hawk had a "right" to move north along the Rock River to the Winnebago villages. He predicted that Winnebago and Pottawatamie braves would join the Iowa warrior as he ascended the river.

For the next two weeks Black Hawk moved steadily along the Rock River. During this stage of the migration there was no bloodshed, no destruction of property, and no stealing. At this time, too, Black Hawk continually received demands from Keokuk to return before it was too late. Keokuk tried to entice the women and children to drop out of the "war party" for their own safety. Black Hawk responded by calling Keokuk a coward. By the end of April, he realized that the promises of support from the British and other Indian tribes was a dream. He knew he was isolated, running low on provisions, and was even rejected by the neighboring Winnebago villages along the Rock River. Their leaders told Black Hawk not "to go any further up."[25]

Meanwhile, the federal troops and the Illinois militia had been ordered to the field to destroy Black Hawk's "tribe" if any resistance to removal to Iowa were found. Commanding General Atkinson, on April 24, officially ordered Black Hawk back across the Mississippi "without delay." "You will be sorry," Atkinson warned, "if you do not come back."[26] At Springfield, Governor Reynolds called up 1,500 mounted militia. On April 27 the militia mustered at Beardstown and crossed the Illinois River into the Military Tract. Along with other volunteers was twenty-one year old Abraham Lincoln, who only the year before, had come to the small log cabin village of New Salem on the Sangamon River. "Being without a job at the time," he signed up on April 21 for the expedition along with sixty-eight other men from the area.[27] Lincoln first borrowed a horse for the trek and then was elected captain in the Fourth Regiment.

On April 30, the "army" left Beardstown and traveled north to Rushville. The next day they pushed on to Yellow Banks but gained only about twenty-five miles, stopping at the LaMoine River in McDonough County near Macomb. On May second they marched another twenty-five miles to a spot on the open prairie somewhere east of Stronghurst. The next day, about noon, the men crossed Henderson Creek and by sundown arrived at Oquawka. There they bivouacked for three days to await provisions coming upriver by steamboat. When the boat pulled in with supplies on the afternoon of May sixth the militia broke camp. On the morning of the seventh they moved up the east bank of the Mississippi to Ft. Armstrong where they reported that evening. General Atkinson officially swore in the militia as part of the army of the United States along with two additional militia companies from Shelby County which had joined the convoy. Sumner Phelps, although offered a position as Commissary to the government troops, stayed out of direct military involvement in the campaign. He did agree, however, to store a case of twenty-six guns along with ammunition while the militia moved on to Rock Island.

During the May bivouac, however, the aged Sauk-Fox tribal chief, Tama, a friend of Phelps, along with his wife and son, came over to Oquawka and was nearly killed by a group of drunken militiamen. Tama was spending the night in Phelp's cabin and the soldiers insisted that Sumner surrender him. Sumner refused predicting that if any harm came to Tama

The Black Hawk War

there would be a wholesale massacre of innocent settlers throughout the county. There was a brief stand-off between the militia and Sumner, who with Tama, his family, and four other civilians, armed themselves inside the cabin.

At the clapboard building next to the cabin, called the "store," Sumner met with the soldiers whose spokesman, Captain White, gave Phelps an ultimatum. Surrender the Indians within three minutes, he ordered, or "we will shoot you, throw your body into the river, burn your house and kill your men." Sumner called back, "Shoot and be damned. I will never yield the Indians to you." "The safety of all the whites in Illinois forbids it," he argued. Just in time, the Jamison and Short men arrived along with Jeremiah Smith and John Pence.

White and the militia capitulated, apologized, and even asked to shake hands with Chief Tama! Tama and his family were then escorted to their canoe and the old chief paddled over to Iowa. Following the "Tama incident" and the subsequent departure of the militia the settlers decided to construct a stockade for protection. At the Phelp's store they buried several kegs of gunpowder, called "sausage bags," linked by a fuse of linen strips buried underground to blow up the extra supplies in event of an Indian attack. Such precautions were groundless because Keokuk, nearby in Iowa, remained out of the "Black Hawk War" and the fighting which did occur was located farther to the north along the Rock River.[28]

There, Black Hawk, acutely aware of his predicament, decided to turn back down the Rock River. As early as May 4, an Indian deserter told General Atkinson that the "Sauk Indians of the Rock River were returning to the west side of the Mississippi."[29] Other intelligence revealed that they were near starvation and wanted to get across the Mississippi as quickly as possible but feared to travel the direct route of the Rock River because they believed the white troops would slaughter them. On May 14, the Illinois militia under command of Major Isiah Stillman camped within eight miles of Black Hawk's tribe. Black Hawk then sent out a three-brave peace team under a white flag to discuss his descent of the Rock River. The militia, most of them drunk, murdered one of the braves and moved armed toward Black Hawk's main camp. The Indians fired on the advancing crowd of yelling whites. The militia turned and ran, leaving their wounded and dead, and headed for Dixon's Ferry twenty-five miles away.

Black Hawk realized from this episode that any further migration down the Rock River was suicidal. He decided, instead, to turn northward into Wisconsin and then move westward, across vacant land free of troops or settlers, to final safety across the Mississippi. But the organized white force, now upwards of 4,000 regulars and militia, pursued him. The exhausted, hungry, out-numbered Indians fled the advance columns of troops who started a forced march from Dixon's Ferry on June 27. They first met up with Black Hawk at Wisconsin Heights (now Madison, Wisconsin) where the braves kept the troops held down while women and children forded the Wisconsin River. Then, meandering westward, Black Hawk finally reached the Mississippi in late July at Bad Axe Creek half way between Prairie du Chien and La Crosse. He was still hounded by General Atkinson's troops along with a party of Sioux warriors (the historic enemy of the Sauk-Fox tribes), and on August second they caught up with Black Hawk near the mouth of Bad Axe Creek. By then the military was joined by a gunboat, which, under Captain Throckmorton had steamed up the Mississippi.

The battle of Bad Axe began on August 3, 1832 at sunrise. The troops, under the field command of General James D. Henry, were deployed to the right and left of the Indian camp. A full charge was sounded. Black Hawk's warriors fought in random Indian fashion, that is without tactical organization, individually from tree to tree. They fell back under Henry's assault to the river bank. Henry then ordered a bayonet assault and drove the bewildered, outnumbered braves into the east channel. Once in the water, the General ordered a heavy barrage of musket fire that indiscriminately killed men, women, and children. What was left of the Indians waded, chest high, to a small island in midstream. There, among the willow trees, Black Hawks tribe was slaughtered. Black Hawk himself and the Winnebago Prophet escaped to Wisconsin but were soon captured. Black Hawk was imprisoned for a short while in Fort Monroe, and then spent his last years on Sauk-Fox lands in Iowa in abject submission to his tribal chief Keokuk.

The St. Louis *Globe* on September 3, 1832 gloated: "The Indian war is over."[30] And so it was. With the slaughter of Black Hawk's band all Indian presence in Illinois was removed. The war also marked the end of the fur trading, primitive pioneer settlement pattern in Henderson County. Now a new breed of settler rapidly filled up the empty spaces along and between the Henderson, Ellison, Honey, and Dugout creeks. They came not just with axe and musket in hand, but with plows, spinning wheels, porcelain plates, and glass windows. They settled on the open prairie. They built not just homesteads but also towns. They organized into church groups. They established regular county government and agencies of law enforcement. They cleared roadways to replace the pathways and, in short order, they laid the railroad lines. These steel ribbons of travel, in turn, brought in a steady wave of additional community settlers who built other new town and villages along the railroads right of way. A traveler in Henderson County in the 1850s would have found it hard to imagine that less than twenty years before this had been the land of isolated log cabins, illiterate pioneers, wild game, marauding wolves, and patrolling Sauk-Fox Indians.

END NOTES FOR CHAPTER ONE

[1] Recommended reading for the westward movement are the general standard works in the field: Ray Allen Billington, *Americas Frontier Heritage* (New York, 1966); Stuart Bruchey, *The Roots of American Economic Growth, 1607-1861* (New York, 1965); George R. Taylor, *The Transportation Revolution* (New York, 1951). For Illinois early settlement see Arthur C. Bogess, *The Settlement of Illinois 1778-1836* (Chicago, 1908) and the first chapters of Theodor Calvin Pease, *The Frontier State 1818-1848.* More recent accounts appear in Robert P. Howard, *Illinois A History of the Prairie State* (Grand Rapids MI, 1972); Robert P. Sutton *The Prairie State A Documentary History of Illinois,* 2 vols, (Grand Rapids, MI 1976); Roger D. Bridges and Rodney O. Davis, *Illinois Its History & Legacy* (St. Louis, 1984) and John E. Hallwas, *Western Illinois Heritage* (Macomb, IL, 1983). John Mack Faragher's *Sugar Creek Life on the Illinois Prairie* (New Haven, 1986). Richard J. Jensen's interpretative analysis *Illinois A History* (New York, 1978), chapters one and two, should also be consulted.

[2] Clarence Danhof, *Changes in Agriculture: The Northern United States, 1820-1870* (Cambridge, MA, 1969); Edward Pessen, *Riches, Class, and Power Before the Civil War* (Lexington, MA, 1973)

[3] For specific examples of economic and social dislocation in individual communities in the East in the Jacksonian Era see: Thomas Dublin, ed. *Farm to Factory: Women's Letters, 1830-1860* (New York, 1981); Russell Lynes, *The Domesticated Americans* (New York, 1957); Mary P. Ryan, *Cradle of the Middle Class: the Family in Oneida County, New York, 1790-1865* (Cambridge, Eng., 1981); Allen F. Davis and Mark H. Haller, eds, *The Peoples of Philadelphia* (Philadelphia, PA, 1973); Robert V. Wells, *Revolutions in American's Lives: A Demographic Perspective of the History of Americans, Their Families, and Their Society* (Westport, CN, 1982).

[4] For troubles affecting the Southern yeoman farmers see accounts in Frank Owsley, *Plain Folk in the Old South* (Baton Rouge, LA, 1949); Robert Fogel and Stanley Gutman, *Time on the Cross: The Economics of American Negro Slavery* (New York, 1976) should be read in consultation with the rebuttal viewpoint of Herbert Gutman and Richard Sutch, *Slavery and the Numbers Game* (Urbana, IL, 1975). An exhaustive study of the problem is Gavin Wright, *The Political Economy of the Cotton South: Households, Markets and Wealth in the Nineteenth Century* (New York, 1978).

[5] Theodore L. Carlson, *The Illinois Military Tract: A Study in Land Occupation, Utilization and Tenure* (Urbana, 1951) is the standard work.

[6] The Archives and Special Collections of Western Illinois University Libraries has a printout of purchases of land in the Military Tract 1818-1824 by speculators. The data was transferred to computer disc in 1977-1979 by the author from the deed books of Madison and Pike Counties (which were in those years the county seats of the Military Tract).

[7] See Wayne C. Temple, *Indian Villages of the Illinois Country: Historic Tribes* (Springfield, 1958) and Elaine A. Bluhm, *Illinois Archaeology* (Urbana, 1959).

[8] Theodore Calvin Pease's earlier monograph was consolidated, enlarged, and updated in 1949 in *The Story of Illinois* (Chicago, 1949) and a third edition, revised by his wife Marguerite Jenison Pease, was published in 1965.

[9] Josiah T. Marshall, *The Farmer's and Emigrant's Handbook* (New York, 1845).

[10] See the collection of historic maps of the region in the Map Library of Western Illinois University Library. A map of early wagon trails is also found in George W. Shadwick, Jr. *History of McDonough, County, Illinois* (Moline, IL, 1968). See also, Sutton, *The Prairie State*, vol. I, p189, for stagecoach and river routes.

[11] For other descriptions of the land see Shepard & Johnson 1882 *History of Henderson County* and James W. Gordon, ed, *Historical Encyclopedia of Illinois, History of Henderson County* (Chicago, 1911).

[12] James Haines, "Social Life and Scenes in the Early Settlement at Central Illinois," *Transactions of the Illinois State Historical Society*, (1905), 35-57.

[13] Edward E. Dale, "The Food of the Frontier," *Journal of the Illinois State Historical Society*, XL(1947), 38-62.

[14] Mrs. K.T. Anderson, "Some Reminiscences of Pioneer Rock Island Women," *Transactions of the Illinois State Historical Society*, XVII(1912), 63-76.

[15] State of Illinois, Archives Division, Public Domain Sales, Land Tract Record Listing. Henderson County by Section, Township, Range, and Meridian.

[16] See D.W. Kilbourne, *Strictures on Dr. Galland's Pamphlet...*" (Fort Madison, IA, 1850) for a contemporary view of Galland in the Finley Collection, Knox College Library and for a modern interpretation consult

John Hallwas, "The Notorious Dr. Galland," *Western Illinois Heritage* pp 145-46.

[17] Accounts of the Phelps Brothers early activities in Henderson County are found in Gordon, *History of Henderson County* and in Shephard & Johnson *History of Henderson County*. Other accounts appeared in Norman L. Patterson, "Stephen Sumner Phelps," *Journal of the Illinois State Historical Society* XII (1919-20), 252-59 and in "Captain William Phelps Story" printed in the *Henderson County Quill*, April 14, 1982, for the business records of the Phelps' trading enterprises see the "Pierre Chateaux Papers" in the Missouri Historical Society, St. Louis.

[18] The land holdings of all three brothers are listed in the computer printout of State of Illinois, Land Tract Record Listing.

[19] See Gordon, *History of Henderson County* and State of Illinois, Land Tract Record Listing. These and other first settlers also appear in the United States Census, Population Schedules, manuscript census rolls for Henderson County, 1830, 1840, 1850.

[20] Anthony F.C. Wallace, *Prelude To Disaster The Course of Indian-White Relations Which Led to the Black Hawk War of 1832* (Springfield, IL, 1970), p 31.

[21] Ibid., p 31

[22] Ibid., p 32

[23] An earlier yet full account of the events of 1830-1832 is Frank E. Stevens, *The Black Hawk War Including A Review of Black Hawk's Life* (Chicago, 1903). John Hallwas brief essays appeared on "Black Hawk's Dilemma" and "The Tragedy of Black Hawk" in *Western Illinois Heritage*, pp 13-18.

[24] Quoted in Wallace, *Prelude to Disaster,* p 42.

[25] Ibid., p 49.

[26] Ibid., p 48.

[27] Stevens, *Black Hawk War* p 278.

[28] Gordon, *Henderson County*, VII, pp 646-47

[29] Wallace, *Prelude to Disaster,* p 50.

[30] Quoted in Stevens, *Black Hawk War,* p 230.

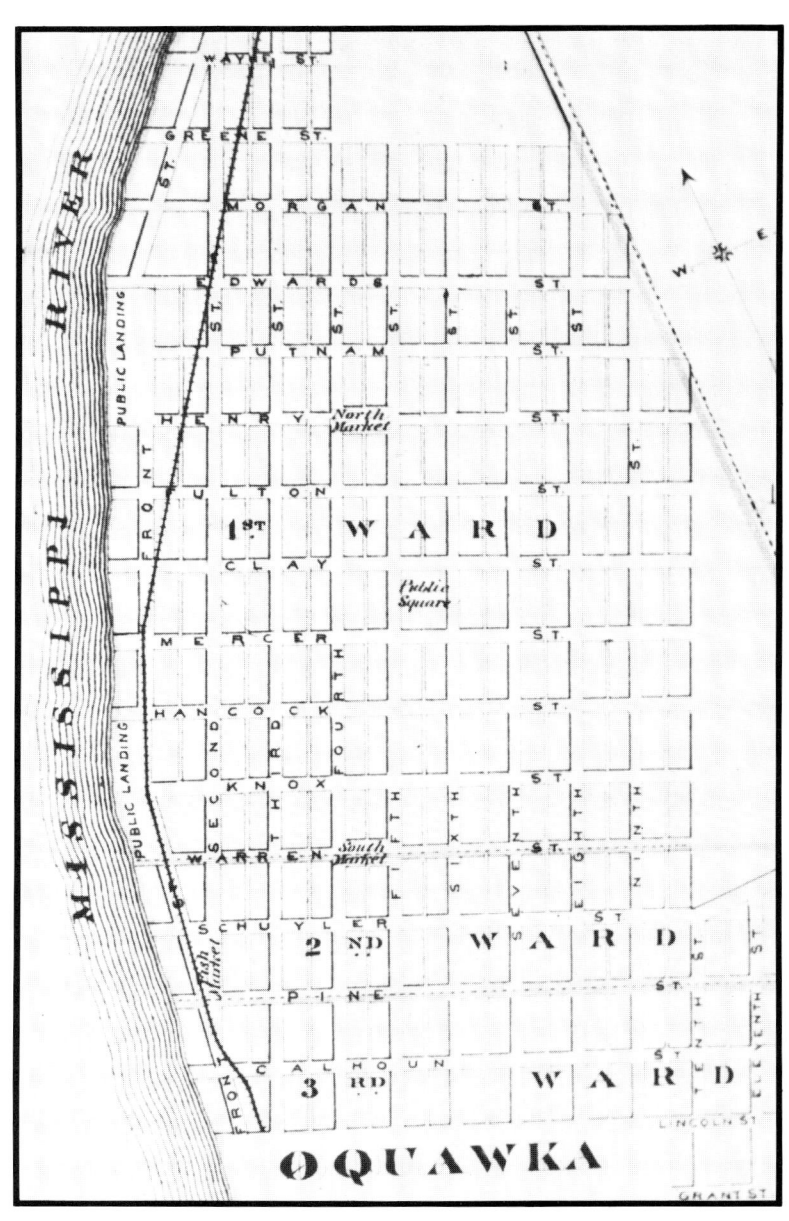

CHAPTER TWO
THE COMMUNITY BUILDING YEARS
1832-1858

Settlement patterns into Henderson County after Black Hawk's defeat in 1832 were in marked contrast to the sporadic infusion of the first log-cabin pioneers. A problem of the earlier records, however, still remains. The second wave of settlers, the farmers, left little behind for historians to reconstruct their lives except lists of names and places. But, compared to the story of the subsistence trader-hunters, two unused historical sources shed new and important insights into the lives of those individuals who laid down the basic institutions of community life -- the towns, roads and railroads, mills and shops, churches, schools, and the political institutions of county government. These historical records are the manuscripts of the federal population schedules and the county's first newspaper, the *Spectator*, established by John B. Patterson in February, 1848.

Beginning in 1790 and every ten years thereafter men hired by the Federal government, called census marshals, went from door to door enumerating the inhabitants of the United States. Traveling along the most available paths and roads they wrote down names of only heads of households until 1850. In that year the marshals listed all members of the family, or anyone else living at the place, along with vital statistics such as age, occupation, place of birth, education, and race. From such data on Henderson County during the years before the Civil War historians can determine what kind of people came into the county, where they came from, and what they did for a living.

The county census marshal in those days traveled in a south-to-north line covering ten separate polling locations. He began in the southeast corner of the county, at the source of Honey Creek, and went directly north parallel to the Fourth Principal Meridian to settlements along the upper Ellison Creek area. Then he rode on to the fork of the South Henderson and Tom Creeks and up to the fourth stop at Stringtown along Fall Creek to a northermost point on the North Henderson Creek at Bald Bluff. On the second leg of each census journey the marshal entered the county in the southwest corner and this time began at Dugout Creek. He then walked due north to the branches of Ellison Creek and Wolf Creek, went on to the fork of the Henderson and South Henderson at Sagetown, and ended the trip at Oquawka. The marshall's last stop, the tenth, was in the southwest corner of the county at what became Lomax Township.

In the first county census of 1840, 343 families lived in the ten different locations. Oquawka had the largest number of families, sixty-one, with the South Henderson and Tom Creek settlements supported by only fourteen homesteads. All settlements, from the start, exhibited a common sexual profile. The overall ratio of males to females that year was 1,033 to 809, a pattern typical of early western settlements in the preponderance of bachelors between the ages of fifteen and thirty. In this age group men outnumbered young women by 309 to 233 and constituted about one-third of the total male population of the county. In Oquawka, the disproportion was greater with almost twice as many young men as young women.

Opposite page: Early plat map of Oquawka

Illustrations depicting the progression of frontier homesteading from clearing the land to an imposing estate on the edge of a village.

The male occupational profile of this first census is also interesting. The marshal counted 428 men (included in this total were males between fifteen and twenty years of age) engaged in agriculture, seven in commerce (one in Olena, six in Oquawka), fifty in the "manufactures and trades" (meaning skilled artisans), one as a sea captain living in Bald Bluff (a riverboat captain from Oquawka), and only four adults in the "learned professions and engineers" — two men living in Oquawka and two physicians in Rozetta township and Biggsville.[1] Eighty-eight percent of the men gainfully employed, however, were farmers of some sort, or farm hands.

The unemployment figure in these early years (that is, those considered as loafers, idlers, and drifters) was just under 30 percent. In Oquawka, with more job opportunities for young men than elsewhere, the rate of unemployment was down slightly in 1840 to under 28 percent of all men over fifteen years of age. This total county figure, however, must be adjusted to subtract from the labor force those men, due to age, who were unable to work. The number of old men in the county was fifty-six. With this adjustment, the hard-core unemployed was somewhere around 23 percent. Oquawka figures, adjusted for seven elderly males out of a work force of 118, also stayed at 22 percent.

The census manuscripts of 1850 shows that basic demographic changes took place in the county during the first decade of community growth.[2] Horizontal mobility (people coming into the county, or moving from place to place within the county itself) increased. Compared to the only 343 families in the county in 1840, in 1850 there were 736 families — more that a 100 percent increase. As before, Oquawka had the largest number of new families, up from sixty-one to 141 households over a ten year period. New settlement clusters began to form. In Biggsville Township, by 1850, there were 133 families and in Olena Township there were 118. Both townships saw homesteads established in the villages of Biggsville (which had seventy homes) and Olena (which built thirteen homes). Rozetta Township, despite the absence of similar village growth, jumped in the number of farm families from forty-one in 1840 to 117 ten years later. In other areas the increase in the number of families was substantial but not as dramatic. Raritan Township, for example, still counted only thirty-three households, up from fourteen homesteads in the first county census. Lomax Township, too, went from just twenty-four to forty families during the same years.

By 1850, the sex ratio had evened out at 2,422 males to 2,121 females, indicating that the earlier frontier ratio, with its high proportion of unmar-

ried men, had passed. The community was stabilizing. In the river town of Oquawka as well as in the inland farm market villages of Biggsville and Stronghurst the frontier male sex bias had disappeared. In Oquawka, by mid-century, there were 390 men and 355 women and in Biggsville only 108 men to 192 women. In Olena, then just a community of thirteen families, there were forty-one males and thirty-six females. The same sexual equilibrium was established in the marriageable age population. The number of males between fifteen and thirty was 731 and the number of young women in that age bracket was 677. Only in Gladstone Township did the earlier inverse ratio persist. There, eighty-five bachelors still wandered about talking to only forty-five unmarried females their own age.

The occupational profile of the county had diversified considerably during the previous decade. When the community was just beginning to take shape in 1840, 88 percent of the work force was in agriculture with only a smattering number of adult males in the skilled crafts and professions. By mid-century, however, the figures showed important shifts. In 1850, there were 905 males over fifteen years of age listed as farmers or field hands. But the census marshal now listed 12 percent as skilled workers (carpenters, blacksmiths, cabinet makers, shoemakers, masons, etc), six percent as businessmen (grocer, hotelkeeper, clothier, butcher) five percent as in the professions (teaching, clerk, constable, lawyer, physician). Five percent of the work force of 1,238 men were counted as day-laborers. In 1850 there were a total of nine college students in the county. Most of the artisans and merchants were found in the villages. Collectively, the settlements of Oquawka, Olena, Sagetown, and Biggsville counted ninety-seven men in business, and fifty-three in the professions. These towns supported an unskilled labor population of forty-seven adults. Oquawka was by far the most populous and diversified town. It listed seventy-seven skilled workers, forty-six merchants, forty-one men in the professions, and twenty-seven laborers.

The overall unemployment ratio in the county in 1850 was astonishing. Compared to 1840, the phenomenon disappeared. Ten years before there were 30 percent overall umemployment or, at best, an adjusted figure of 23 percent. In 1850 there was no unemployment. There were 1,256 men over fifteen years of age that year residing in the county and of these 1,238 were listed in some gainful occupation. If one adds to the number of men employed the number of college students, which counted as a separate category, then the number of unemployed is insignificant, only one-half of one percent. The economic life of the county had hit boom proportions in growth both in terms of population increase, town development, occupational diversification, and opportunity for making a living.

The census data reveals other developments in the social structure of the county compared to its first settlement years. In 1840, the birth rate (those children listed as under five years of age) was 18 percent of the male population and 16 percent of the female population. There was that year an amazingly high number of baby boys. For example, in Gladstone Township there were thirty-five males to eighteen females under the age of five. In Stronghurst Township, thirty-six little boys were listed compared to only twenty-three girls. In Rozetta Township the ratio was thirty-four to fifteen. By 1850, though, the birth rate had dropped for both sexes, 14.6 percent for boys and 14 percent for girls. Moreover, the astonishing high number of little boys had receded. Only in one part of Stronghurst Township did the earlier, lopsided, male increase continue. There, in 1850, there were still forty-three boys to only twenty-eight girls in early childhood.

Family size though (that is the number and percentage of children within the household) changed little over the ten year period. In 1840, new families coming into this western Illinois frontier averaged 2.45 children while in 1850 the average number of children rose only slightly to 2.88 per household. The combination of steady population growth and stabilization of family size, when added to expanding economic opportunity, gives a picture of a contended community rapidly discarding its earlier rough edges (such as the unnatural number of baby boys, the high percentage of unmarried males, and the large number of men without work). It had comfortably made the transition from the primitive Indian-trapper-squatter years to a stabilized agrarian community.

Another often overlooked social variable that contributed to the rapid growth of community life in the county was the fact that while all people were, of course, immigrants to this part of western Illinois, most came from the same social backgrounds. They shared from the beginning, as new neighbors, common memories of what they left behind and what they brought with them. They had similar attitudes and values. They carried, in a word, a common cultural baggage along with the boxes of boots, blankets, plates, and livestock that they lugged to the Mississippi Valley. Almost all settlers came from the farming areas of the Middle Atlantic states or, in lesser numbers, from the southern border Commonwealths. The first figures available on origins, or place of birth, were in 1850. Those census marshals counted most heads of families as having been born in the Northeast, or 33 percent. Twenty-five percent of the household heads were born in the Upper South. Ohio and Indiana births account for 21 percent of the total. Just twelve percent of the heads of households were born in the Prairie State.

In the broadest profile analysis the whole country was overwhelmingly northern, or "Yankee." Two-thirds (excluding foreign born) were born outside of a slave state. More significantly, block clusters according to birth do not show, as is commonly thought, that the southern half of the county was settled by Southerners and the northern half by Yankee stock. It was decidedly a mixed pattern. The census of 1850, for example, reveals that southern townships such as Media and Lomax had the highest percentage of Pennsylvanians, with 15.2 and 23.3 percent respectively. At the same time southern communities like Stronghurst Township had the highest percentage of Kentuckians (25.3) along with Gladstone and its

Frank Gove, Mr. and Mrs. Gove, Cliff Harvey, Farm Home North of Raritan

South Carolinians (27.5). Raritan Township had the largest percentage of Tennessee-born heads of households and their spouses, 34.3 percent, in 1850. The southernmost township of Terre Haute, on the Hancock County line, though, had 29 percent of its inhabitants born in Ohio. Rozetta Township lying in the northern half of the county had its largest block of householders born in Kentucky, 19.3 percent. Oquawka's 1850 adult population was the most spread-out (percentage-wise) as well as the most diversified (in number of states represented). The largest cluster of Oquawka's adults were born in Ohio (23 percent) followed by New York (15 percent).

The foreign-born adults living in Henderson County in 1850 amounted to only nine percent of the total heads of households. Every township however, counted some European immigrants among its household heads, although Raritan had only one foreigner, a Scotsman, living there that year. Most immigrants came from Ireland (35 percent) or England (33 percent). Then the figures dropped off to only 16 percent German-born, just one-half of one percent from France and Scotland each and a combined figure of one-half of one percent for those born in Portugal, Sweden, Wales, and Canada. Oquawka had, as expected, the greatest concentration of foreign-born, over 13 percent of its heads of households with the following countries represented — England, France, Germany, Ireland, Scotland, Wales, and Canada.

When one examines the birth place of the county's children (under 18) in 1850 and compares it with their parents' places of birth, another intriguing pattern appears that diminishes the impact of the slave-society backgrounds of its first citizens. While one-third of Henderson County *adults* were born in the South only a small percentage of their children were born there. Of the 2,180 children in the county that year only 113 were born in a slave state. Three southern states were represented in the census of childrens' birth: Kentucky (with ninety-seven) followed by Tennessee, claiming just fourteen children, and Virginia with two. This data indicate that while one-third of Henderson County settlers might have been born in the South, they had early-on left that region, most likely with their parents or by themselves as teenagers. Either as children or young adults they had crossed the Ohio River into the free states, married and started a family in Ohio or Indiana. Then, they pulled-up stakes and headed west to their final destination in Henderson County. Only Rozetta Township broke the pattern of the early-out migration of the southern-born adults. There, 20 percent of the parents in 1850 came from Kentucky. Nine percent of their children were born in that slave state, a higher percentage of southern babies than in any other township. Other figures support this picture of early emigration of Southerners to the North. Thirteen percent of Henderson County children were born in Indiana and another twelve percent were born in Ohio. A whopping 61 percent of all the county's children that year were born in the Prairie State.

The foreign-born children in the county by mid-century were insignificant. In most areas they were nonexistent. There were only sixty-nine families of European extraction then and just sixty-seven foreign-born children. Dispersal was wide. Raritan and Media each had one family, Rozetta two, Gladstone three, Terre Haute two, and Lomax had four young immigrant families. The towns of Biggsville and Oquawka had five families apiece. The origins of the county's European immigrants were surprisingly diverse. There was no ethnic grouping of nationalities. So, one set of immigrants from a European Mother Country did not serve as a magnet to attract additional compatriots. The census marshall tabulated people born in England, Germany, Ireland, Scotland, Portugal, Canada and Mexico.

The appearance of villages and towns was the visible sign of the changeover from pioneer days to community life. Essentially they were market places for farm products, retail distribution centers for necessary items of clothing and supplies, and sources for basic services such as medicine and the law. Understandably the first railroad depots were built there. Towns became the focus of social life, a depressing rarity during the frontier era. Townspeople, for the most part, built the churches and organized the congregations. In Oquawka the first newspaper was published and an even greater literary adventure was planned. It was the towns that experienced the problems of community tension such as drifters and crime. The villages, too, were the focal point of political activities in the formation of county government and in the growth of party organization.

Two early towns were laid out in 1836 at Oquawka and Shokokon. Two years later settlers founded villages at Olena and Hopper along Ellison Creek. A second spurt of town growth started at mid-century. In 1849 Dallas City was surveyed as a river town. Terre Haute appeared along a railroad survey in 1854. Biggsville and Gulfport, also railroad towns, were laid out the following year. In 1856 Gladstone came into existence as a rail depot. Raritan was established by religious pioneers in 1856.

Oquawka was a Phelps town. Soon after the two brothers set up their fur trading headquarters at Yellow Banks, other folks moved in as neighbors. In 1831 John McKinney stayed there for a while. So did John Campbell and John Pence. William Jamison started his retail business at the site. Alexis Phelps, in 1836, abandoned his many operations at Galena and joined his brothers at Yellow Banks. He became the resident proprietor of the family store, while "Hawk Eye" and William expanded the fur trade up the Skunk and Des Moines Rivers. The log cabin store boasted a new clapboard awning of "A & S.S. Phelps" and stocked a supply of whiskey, tobacco, pipes, glass, clothes, nails, and tools. Earlier, in 1832, Alexis and Sumner had put up a four-room frame house, at about the same time that the Phelps expanded their operations to start a lumber yard.

On a steamy August day in 1832, John B. Patterson, one of the town's first entrepreneurs, set foot at Yellow Banks. Just one year younger than Sumner Phelps, J.B. was born in Virginia on January 11, 1809, the son of an English immigrant teacher. Raised at Winchester, Virginia, he, between 1827 and 1830, began two unsuccessful newspapers, the *Leesburg Observer* and the *American Argus*. In 1832, he moved west to Rock Island with his young wife, Mahala. The couple then settled at Galena where, for a third time, J.B. started another paper, the *Galenian*. It, too, went bankrupt after three months. For a while, now broke, he worked for Colonel John Davenport at his American Fur Company store back in Rock Island. Then, in 1834, he switched jobs and companies and began fur trading forays out of Yellow Banks into Iowa under Sumner Phelps.

In 1835 the two young men laid out the town then already budding with new arrivals. A carpenter, W.C. Ellet, and a tailor, D.M. Gordon, had arrived. Then came another merchant, Harry Jennings. They called the town Oquawka, the name itself a mispronunciation of the Sauk-Fox word for Yellow Banks, "Oquawkiek." Illinois Governor, the forty-year old Joseph Duncan, a Phelps family friend, was willing to put up $50,000 — an enormous sum for the time — to buy one-fourth of the proposed town lots which had been just surveyed by a Rock Island engineer. A physician from New York named Milldollare, also bought into the venture. J.B. Patterson even promised to pay $600 for a single lot — at a time when he had no money at all to pay for it! Other lots soon were going for $900 apiece with river sites bringing over $1,000. One could buy in town blocks, such as one of foot-frontage 150 feet deep in front of Alexis' property, for $3,300.[3]

Reports of the new boom city on the Mississippi were mailed to eastern newspapers by Patterson. Partially in response to the glowing promotional literature Edgar Allen Poe wrote to Patterson concerning a project the two men concocted to begin a "literary journal" in the town. Poe also forwarded to Patterson a description of Oquawka, along with a map, which had just been published by S. Augutus Mitchell in Philadelphia in the pamphlet *Illinois in 1837*. Poe wrote that he had found there "this interesting information."

> Oquawka, or "Yellow Banks" is a town recently settled. It is situated on the Mississippi River, about midway between the Des Moines and Rock Island rapids, and is the principal depot for freight between those points. The town is laid out in two sections on an extensive site. The soil is sandy, and the surface, gently undulating, is sparcely covered with a stunted growth of oaks, extending to the bluff, two miles back. Henderson River, a fine stream for milling purposes, passes along the foot of these, and is crossed by a neat and

substantial bridge. There are two large warehouses in the town, one store, one grocery, two taverns, and several dwelling houses. There is a good flouring and sawmill about two miles distant, and a steam mill is to be erected. The site of this place was sold by the original to the present proprietors for $200.[4]

The big day was set for early July, 1836. Then, a public auction under Hart Fellows of Rushville of all available lots would signal the real beginning of the city. Men arrived from as far away as New York and New Jersey for the spectacle. More lots were sold. Carpenters, now working under three construction companies of Kinton & Mackey, Young & Russell, and Young & Blackburn, set to work. A hotel-saloon went up, run by William Causland. A physician, Alpheus Russel, began his practice of medicine. A blacksmith, William Mason, appeared. D.S. Brainard opened a horse-selling business, working in partnership with his suppliers, the Sauk-Fox. Sumner and Alexis started an addition to the old cabin which later was sold to J.R. Barnes as a hotel.

Jack's Mill Bridge, Oquawka

The moon never rose. Oquawka the metropolis never appeared. A national economic depression began the following spring and lasted some eight years. Called the Panic of 1837, it caused a severe recall of outstanding loans, especially mortgages, and the investment bubble burst. Men could not meet payments on their lots in Oquawka let alone expand their business activity.

Steamboat: Oquawka

The town, however, did grow during the pre-Civil War years and it became the most important commercial center in the county. It was, first and foremost, the key Mississippi River port between Keokuk and Rock Island. Reports of river traffic, of commodities going in and out of Oquawka, in the 1840s and 1850s indicate a steady, respectable prosperity. For example, in 1847-48 the town shipped out 5,200 hogs, 130,148 bushels of wheat, 43,316 bushels of corn, 7,084 bags of flour, 2,250 barrels of pork, 12,555 pounds of butter, 21,580 pounds of hides, and 4,880 pounds of bacon. Four years later, at the heyday of steamboat commerce on the Mississippi, exports through Oquawka were valued at $441,746 retail and import commerce at $412,880. During these years Solomon Foot had the Phelps put up a steam saw-mill with local lumber from both Jack's Mill, on Henderson Creek, and imported pine from St. Louis. Clark and James Blandin built another mill to prepare house lumber from raft pine brought downriver from Wisconsin. Houses went up one after another at anywhere from $123.00 to $1,100. Its waterfront boasted 2,730 feet of graded rock wharfage.

Other merchants and businesses moved into the town. In 1846, the earliest furniture manufacturing firm of Joseph Chickering, Abner Hebbard, and C.S. Cowan began using finished lumber from the town's saw mills. Oquawka's bookstore and daguerreotype shop was started by Asa Smith who soon became another entrepreneur in the lumber and saw-mill businesses. William and James Moir built a wine distillery in 1846, the northernmost on the Mississippi river. In 1854, the pioneer millwright, W.R. Jamison moved into town and put up a brick and stone building to rival the other brick store erected in 1848 by Sumner Phelps. The town's grand hotel, The "American House" (later the "Eagle House") went up in 1849 and was run by R.W. Young. This elegant establishment quickly eclipsed the shabby services offered the year before by C. Catlin and his "Catfish House" near the wharf. Lawyers, physicians, dentists, and druggists opened their practices and stores.

Jack's Mill, Oquawka

The apex of Oquawka's prosperity came in the mid-1850s. By then, it was by all accounts one of the main river ports on the upper Mississippi. Steamboats anchored off the wharf to bring in or take away volumes of livestock, produce, household supplies, and dairy products. Warehouses crowded along the waterfront. On the eve of the Civil War it was expected that the town's prosperity would continue unabated, that investors could count on selling their town lots at at least a profit of 100 percent. The golden age was yet to come because, as it was predicted: "The proprietors of the town propose making a railroad from here to Peoria, on the Illinois river." The railroad never arrived and Oquawka in the space of a few years began to die. Business waned. Investors tried to sell out. Entrepreneurs left for Burlington, Galesburg, Monmouth or Macomb.[5]

The same year that Oquawka was incorporated a second town was started in what was then called Honey Creek Township. The Sauk Fox earlier called the place Shokokanon or Shoquokon. In 1836, three settlers moved in and put up log cabins: Robert McQueen, Harrison Barnes, and Henry Babcock. James and Robert Lomax, both veterans of the War of 1812, had been given the first titles, or warrants, to land at Shokokon in 1830, forty acres each in section 27, but neither settled there. Robert McQueen acquired land that year and secured title to another eighty acres in 1844, when on October 12 of that year he paid $99.94 for the parcel at the Quincy Federal Land office. Barnes, an auctioneer and stage driver from New York, soon moved to LaHarpe. Babcock, also a New Yorker and a veteran of the War of 1812, received a warrant for 160 acres near Carthage, in Hancock County, but instead decided to sell it and settle permanently closer to the Mississippi. In 1838 John Pence, (no relative to Virginia John Pence of Pence's Fort) came from Lycoming County in western Pennsylvania to Shokokon with his wife Hanna and eight-year old son Robert. They shared an end of a log cabin that summer with the Tull family, near the Ellison River slough. In 1839 they moved southward into Lomax Township and lived in their own cabin on section 11. Then, on 160 acres in the southeast quarter of section 15, John built a sturdy double-log house.

Shokokon itself was officially surveyed by John B. Talbott and recorded as a plat in the Warren County records in July, 1836 as situated on the N.W. 1/4 of Section 27, T. 9N R. 6W. The town, unlike Oquawka, did not grow, perhaps because of the competition from its northern neighbor up-river. It had certain geographic advantages though, especially as a log-jam stop for lumbermen floating timber down the Mississippi. The sloughs, while attractive to lumber shippers, were much too shallow for steamboat traffic. And, moreover, the natural river channel itself carried boats and barges along the Iowa shore towards Ft. Madison.[6]

In 1838, the towns of Olena and Warren (Hopper) were laid out as a result of the rapid settlement of Olena Township (later Stronghurst Township). Until about 1834, the Tennessean John Gibson and his family had lived alone along the Ellison Creek interior run on 160 acres at Wolf Creek. In the spring of that year alone, however, ten families moved in. Among them was John Dunn, who built a cabin on 160 acres in the southwest corner of section 10 and lived there until his death in 1840. Jacob Mendenhall settled just north of Gibson in section 3, coming to Illinois from North Carolina through the familiar path of southern Indiana in a small buggy with his wife.[7]

Other farmers arrived in regular progression. In 1835, for example, Abner Davis, a Vermont veteran of the War of 1812 came to Olena Township. Born in 1794, he married Lucy Oaks in 1821 and the couple moved, in 1825, to Saratoga County in western New York where their first son was born and, in 1835, on to Henderson County. There, on a military patent of 160 acres in section 33, they built a cabin and started to farm. The next year Peter Nichol came from Virginia through Ohio and Indiana to Olena Township. A miller and distiller by trade until he left Ohio, he took up corn farming on his military patent. Then in 1836 the 49 year old South Carolina veteran of the War of 1812, Alexander Marshall, on a grueling two-month overland journey brought his wife and three sons to the 160 acres he had purchased in section 16 as his prairie homestead. The third new settler in 1836 was John Curts. Born in 1786 in Pennsylvania, he was first a boatman on the Susquehanna River and then a tavern keeper. In the fall of 1835 he visited his cousin Michael Crane in Lomax Township and purchased a 450 acre tract at Gettings Mound where he erected a cabin and started a farm.[8]

In 1837, the abolitionist, Nathaniel Martin, then twenty-seven years old and a native of New Hampshire, and a cabinet maker, was attracted to the West by the glowing promotional reports of prairie farming. He came to 160 acres in the northwest corner of section 12 stopping only long enough along the way in Ohio to acquire a bride, Lois Barton. In 1839, Kentuckian William Rodman, a friend of Abraham Lincoln, moved in on 320 acres of section 13 with his wife and fifteen year old son, Robert. In 1840, Andrew Carothers came out from Cumberland County Pennsylvania, with his wife and, later, was joined by his son Andrew Jr., and grandson, Jacob. Cyrus W. Steel, born in Augusta County, Virginia, but raised in Green County, Ohio, opened a saw mill and worked as a carpenter in section 10. Another Virginia-born, Green County, Ohioan, William Black, settled in 1841 on section 3. And in 1842, Thomas Nichols, born in the Virginia County adjacent to Cyrus Shell in 1799 and a near-by neighbor in Ross County, Ohio, moved first to Abingdon and then built a small frame house in Olena Township with lumber bought at Oquawka.[9]

Sawmill at Jack's Mill

The town of Warren was begun in 1837 when Lambert Hopper opened a packing house and store and surveyed the town plat. Hopper also started a carding machine operation for wool manufacturing nearby on Ellison Creek in 1843. John Houchins built a saw and grist mill opposite Hopper's business which, in late 1836, he sold to Hopper. Several saw mills were started at or near Warren by Ohioan Wilson Kendall and others. The Strahan brothers opened a distillery in a log dwelling here in 1840. The other village, Olena, was laid out by Kendall in 1838 when he started the first retail store at the town site. In 1843, Kendall replaced the log store with a sturdy brick building that became the post office and social center of a village of skilled craftsman and merchants.[10]

By the late 1840s settlement patterns began to show a heavy increase in the number of families living in the south and southwest corner of the county. Dallas City, which lay in both Henderson and Hancock County, began with the arrival in 1844 of John M. Finch. Finch and his partner, William H. Rolloson, opened a store there on the Mississippi River and, shortly thereafter, put up a warehouse. They named their village after George M. Dallas, the newly-elected Vice President of the United States. It was not until the fall of 1848 that the deputy surveyor of the county, J. Wilson, got around to recording the plat at Oquawka although Finch operated a postoffice there from the start. To the east of Dallas City the town of Terre Haute was placed on file in March, 1854 by William C. Rice. The town originally covered 13 acres and contained a postoffice and the homesteads of William Reynolds and Joseph Genung, the latter of whom came to the area in 1842 from Terre Haute, Indiana with his father, Steven. The first store was opened by Alexander Bushnell. William P. Bryan, of Pennsylvania, began another mercantile business soon after his arrival in 1840. In 1854, V.P. Lovitt started his cooper trade in the town. Other services essential to nearby farmers soon sprang up: a blacksmith, a druggist, and two physicians took up residence in the town. Upriver from Dallas City, the town of Gulfport was laid out in 1855 from Gladstone Township by A.D. Green and Major A.W. Armstrong. The prime motive for town building at that geographical point on the Mississippi was to have a marketing terminus of a proposed railroad. A.D. Green, representing the Chicago, Burlington and Quincy Company planned to use the area for the railroad's stockyards and mercantile operations.[11]

The other town built in 1855 was Biggsville. Situated on South Henderson Creek and serving as another market point on the new CB&Q railroad, it was platted by Andrew and Samuel Douglass and surveyed by William McChesney. Biggsville, similar to the towns of Warren and Olena, was not only part of the coming of the railroads but also was a reflection of the needs of the farm families who were arriving steadily in that part of the county. Settlement started with the construction of a grist mill and dam by John Hopper and David Roberson on South Henderson Creek in the summer of 1839. John, a brother of Lambert of nearby Warren, opened it for business in the spring of 1840. In 1843, he sold out to John Biggs. Biggs was born in England in 1802 and, after the accidental death of his father in 1816, served as a cabin boy in the British navy until his embarkation to New England in 1820. He worked for a time as a day laborer in factories in Philadelphia and Texas before landing in Henderson County in 1843 with his family. Biggs, in 1844, expanded the Hopper Mill operation to service nearby farmers such as Amos Williams, Abram Hendrick, Ezekiel Smith, Andrew Graham, Samuel and George McDill, Benjamin Thompson, and Dykeman Shook. The Jamison brothers, the Shorts, and the McKinney family, of course, were already established patrons of the mill.

Almost immediately houses were built in Biggsville in rows of lots on either side of a main street between Biggs' mill on the west end and the railroad depot on the east end. The town became a shipping center for grain in the late 1850s when other businessmen like Solomon Essex, George Wax and his brother Seth, and Benjamin H. Martin (son of pioneer Preston Martin who settled in Gladstone Township in 1836) opened a grain elevator in 1857. Even though the corn was hand-shelled, ground, and weighed by each barrel on a Fairbanks scale the export business grew by impressive proportions. Daily, 389 farm wagon loads of grain were received there at harvest. Each day some twenty-six train cars were loaded with the grain and twenty-two more were filled with livestock. In 1858, Noah Purcell moved to town from Kirkwood and began a grocery store featuring tea, coffee, calico, soap, molasses and, as was common to almost all such "grocery" stores then, a stock of whiskey. Another store, this one run by H.W. Crosthwait, was opened in a room of the Martin warehouse.

A third merchant went into business in Biggsville before the Civil War. Isaac Myerstine specialized in dry goods, hardware, and medicines at his home on the south side of the main street. Next to Myerstine's store, A. Talcott built the town's hotel, mainly for the farmers, who after bringing grain and livestock to town, often had to remain overnight before returning home. The postoffice was started in 1858 in another corner of Martin's warehouse. In 1859, the fourth merchant, John McKee, established a trade in drugs and groceries. The first blacksmith was Patrick Shaw, who opened shop in 1856, followed shortly by Len Fuller and J.H. Wiley. Farmers, driving into town could, during the day, market their crops and animals, stock up on home supplies, medicine and whiskey, and have their tools repaired—all before returning homeward by evening. In the event of delays, they could, of course, spend the night comfortably at Talcott's Hotel. Compared to two decades before, when a few pioneers, alone, survived on venison and fruits in log cabins, life was civilized indeed.[12]

Main Street, Gladstone

The last two towns established before the Civil War in the county were Gladstone and Raritan. Gladstone was first known as Sagetown after George Sage, a native of New York who immigrated to western Illinois via Dearborn County, Indiana in his early fifties. His name stuck to the village until the nomenclature of Gladstone was approved in April, 1881. Sage owned land on the site of the future town and himself settled there in 1848 with some of his fourteen children. It was platted in 1856 as another market spot, along with Biggsville, along the east-west Chicago, Burlington and Quincy Railroad at the junction of another planned north-south branch of the same railroad to Oquawka. Clearly a railroad town, its sole reason for existence was to distribute farm products to the major Mississippi ports of Burlington or Oquawka. It had almost overnight three wooden stores featuring dry goods, drugs, groceries, and whiskey. Two hotels, the "Star House" and the "Commercial House" were put up. There were two saloons, a barbershop, two blacksmiths, a butcher shop, a feed mill, a carpenter shop, and a sorghum mill. Lucius Cook, in 1856, began his tenure as station master and mail agent for the CB&Q. Gideon Sage and George Sotlle both operated grain warehouses for local farmers. Unlike the other villages, Gladstone had a large percentage of foreign-born citizens. Immigrants from Ireland, Germany, Scandinavia, and Scotland were hired by the railroad as laborers and quarry hands.[13]

In the southeast corner of the county the village of Raritan was set up, also in 1856, when a group of immigrants of the Dutch Reformed denomination from New Jersey came to what was then called Bedford Precinct after a brief stop-over in Fulton County at Fairview. They called the place along the upper reaches of Honey Creek, Raritan, after the river by that name in New Jersey. Leaders of the community were Joshia Brokaw, Jacob Thorp, S.B. Van Arsdale, Peter Tharp, Henry and Jacques Voorhees, and Andrew Hageman. These farm families replaced the squatters of the earlier era such as traders John Scroggins, who had arrived there from Tennessee in 1829, and Joel Huston, also from Tennessee. Both men were drifters and lingered in Bedford Township only a couple of years before pushing on.

Raritan, 1865

The New Jerseyites, however, were permanent settlers. Josiah Brokaw, of West Somerset County, New Jersey, was their advance guard. He came to the Honey Creek prairie in 1837. The homestead he established about one mile southwest of the Honey Creek location of Raritan was known as the "Brokaw Settlement." His son, Joshia, Jr. in 1851, added eighty more acres of federal land. Then came Henry Voorhees. Also a New Jerseyite, he settled in 1855 on eighty acres of land in section one in the northwest corner of Bedford Precinct then, three years later, moved to Raritan and opened the village blacksmith shop. In April, 1856 James Hageman, thirty-two years old, arrived. A graduate of Rutgers College, he built an imposing home in Raritan, called "Prairieside Park," consisting of three acres of 500 shade trees. Peter Tharp immigrated in 1855 and bought eighty acres when the town of Raritan itself was surveyed two years later. F.A. Hixon moved out from Hunterton County, New Jersey, in 1854 and built his log cabin in a fenced-in homestead in section fifteen, also adjacent to the new town. S.B. Van Arsdale in 1856 located on 160 acres in section twenty-two, farmed it, and soon traded it for another 180 acres in section seven. Finally, Van Arsdale sold his farm and purchased a house and lot in Raritan itself. Raritan was incorporated, as the original plat shows, on the adjacent corners of sections fourteen, fifteen, ten, and eleven in January, 1857. It immediately boasted a grocery store, started by Voorhees, a blacksmith shop, a hotel put up by Charles Hartshorn, and four churches: the Bedford Christian, Raritan Baptist, St. Patrick's Chapel, and the Raritan Reformed.[14]

As towns and villages began to appear as a part of the emerging farm community of the 1840s and 1850s other basic economic improvements and social institutions developed as an integral part of town growth. Henderson County by mid-century saw new roads and railroads and, as Raritan's story indicates, the steeples of church buildings.

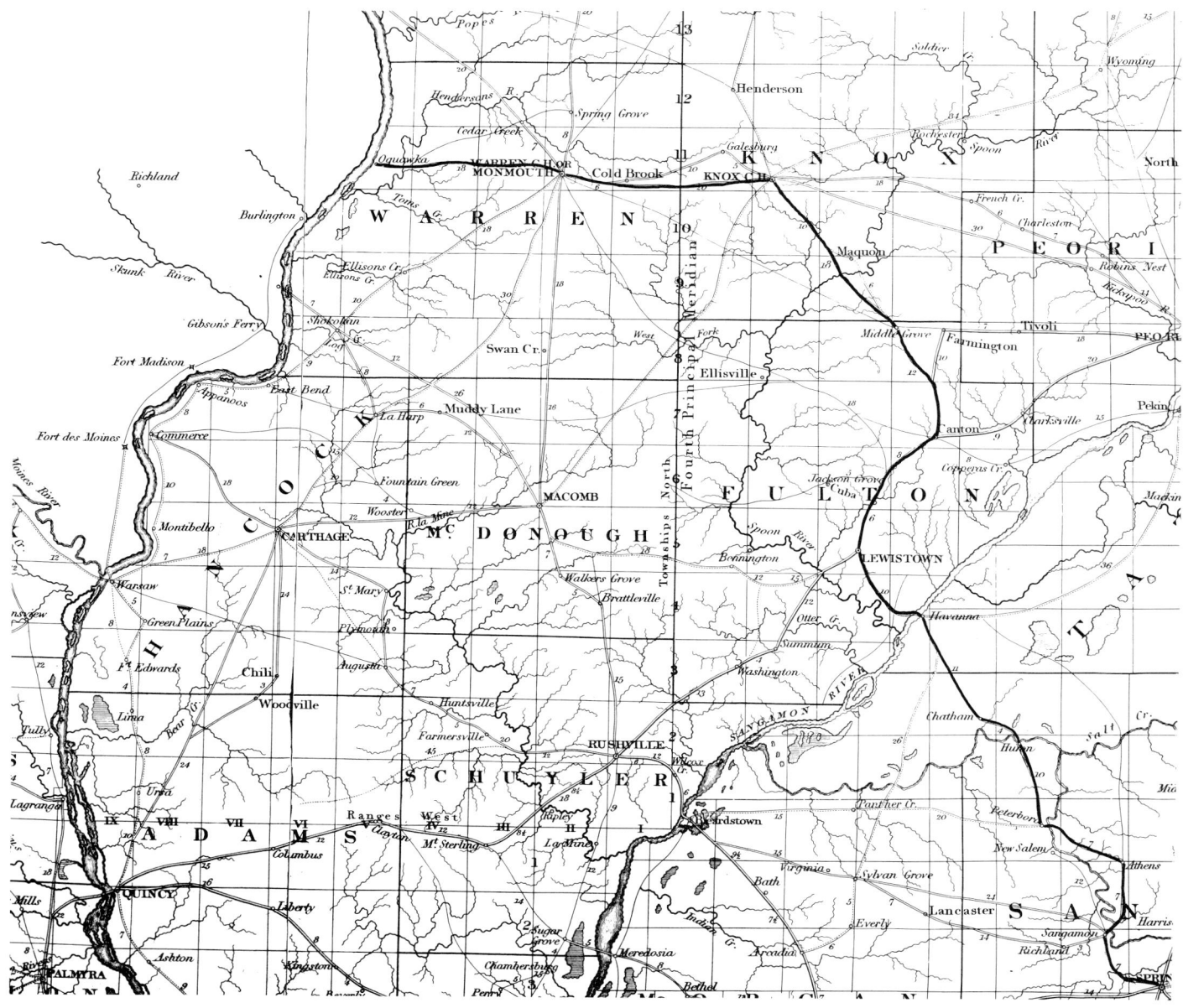

Early Stagecoach line

The first stage coach line began running in 1834 as a three-and-one-half day trip from Springfield to Oquawka. A four-horse coach left Springfield every Wednesday at six in the morning and moved northwest with stops at New Salem, Petersburg, Havana, Lewiston, Canton, and Knoxville. By Friday evening at 6:00 it pulled in at Monmouth. Then, at Saturday noon, it landed passengers and baggage on the wharf at Oquawka. A return trip, beginning each Sunday morning, brought travelers back to the Springfield landing at the state capitol by six o'clock Tuesday night. One could pay $9.00 for a full one-way ticket or log distances to any point at 6½ cents per mile. Baggage was brought along at no extra fee, as space allowed, conveyed at the owner's risk. The ride was rough and dirty. The coaches had no springs, only rockers, and passengers were jerked back and forth through the river and creek valleys. The time schedule was seldom met because drivers continually got bogged-down in mudholes or swollen streams. In the 1840s the firm of Fink and Wagner opened an identical line, in terms of speed and comfort, from Chicago which, stopping at Monmouth, crossed the county to Oquawka.

The first county railroad was the Peoria and Oquawka project. Promoters such as John McKinney, Preston Martin, Robert M. Patterson, and nine others organized as "commissioners" at a meeting on December 20, 1849, and agreed to sell stock in the enterprise at $100 a share with a down payment of only five percent. They estimated the total cost of construction would be anywhere from $6,000 to $10,000 a mile. Authorized, legally, by the state legislature as a private corporation the previous February, the first railroad ties were laid the next year. But the road never reached Oquawka. In May, 1851 the voters of the county overwhelmingly refused to approve a proposed $50,000 investment in the enterprise. As a result of this setback, the legislature changed the initial route and the corporate charter was amended to build the railroad to Monmouth (which had subscribed $100,000) through Warren County. It then would cross directly westward through what became the towns of Biggsville and Gladstone to the Mississippi at Burlington. Oquawka voters, unable or unwilling to see any value in a railroad to their river town, ignored the changed route.

Construction of the P & O went ahead without a hitch. It was completed as planned to Monmouth, in January, 1855 and linked up to another new railroad coming from Chicago, the Chicago & Quincy line. This company, in turn, finished construction of the roadbed to Burlington, absorbed the P & O, and renamed the entire operation the Chicago, Burlington & Quincy Railroad Company. Belatedly the citizens of Oquawka voted $25,000 to construct a roadbed between Gladstone and their town in the vain hope that the directors of the CB&Q would link up. The line was a waste of time and money and was never built. Oquawka ended up with nothing. Gulfport, instead, was created as the final CB&Q Illinois stopping point. Gladstone, with the CB&Q, received its economic lease on life. And Biggsville, by 1858, had enough business to warrant a railroad station of its own.

A third line envisioned before the Civil War was the Warsaw & Rockford Company. It also was charted in 1849 by the legislature to serve as a complement north-south segment to the proposed east-west Peoria & Oquawka route. The company was managed by incompetents, however, and the line was never built even though Henderson County commissioners authorized a stock subscription of $100,000, $78,000 of which was lost to the fraudulent construction spending of the managers. Oquawka residents, not learning from their mistakes, sank an additional $10,000 into the pipedream of a plank road to Washington, Iowa. In theory, the road was to be served by a ferry boat operation which would be the key link with the imaginary railroad that would run through the town from Warsaw. Nothing happened.[15]

Religion was of little or no concern to the early traders and hunter-farmers but it was indispensable to the farmers and townsmen of the 1840s and 1850s. The main Protestant denominations in the county before the Civil War were the Presbyterians, the Baptists, the Methodists, the Reformed, Dutch Reformed, and Catholic. The earliest Presbyterian congregation was organized in 1835 when two groups of settlers, one at the Jamison Settlement, the other at the Ritchie Settlement at Cedar Creek, began to hold regular Sunday meetings alternately in each location. In 1837, they built a common log-cabin church, without seats or a floor, some three miles northwest of what would be the town of Biggsville. Then, in 1855, a stone building, later known as the South Henderson Church, was erected with the work of about sixty members of the congregation.[16] In 1840, the First Presbyterian Church of Oquawka was

South Henderson Church

Cumberland Presbyterian Church, Rozetta Twp

founded at a meeting of the Presbytery at Monmouth with James Wilson and George Stebbins chosen as ministers. From time to time the Reverend W.K. Stewart of the Macomb First Presbyterian Church was their guest. A Presbyterian congregation was formed in 1837 at Ellison Creek next to John Gibson's farm and in 1850 they constructed a frame church at one corner of his tract. Over the next eight years it attracted seventy members and was renamed, in 1857, the United Presbyterian Church of Ellison. At Olena, in 1858, a thirty member United Presbyterian Church was created. In 1847, the Smith Creek Presbyterian Church appeared in Rozetta Township and shared a Minister with the Olena group. At Biggsville, in the summer of 1859, Reverend J.A.P. McGaw, of the South Henderson Church, held his first service in a wooded area just east of the railroad station. He continued a mission in the town until after the Civil War when an independent congregation was organized along with other denominations of the Presbyterian groups, such as the Cumberland branch. In Media Township, then known as Walnut Grove Precinct, Joseph and William Rankin built a Reformed Presbyterian Church north of the future town of Media, which, just before the Civil War, was reorganized into the United Presbyterian Church of Media.[17]

The Baptists organized under Benjamin C. Coghill at his home in Rozetta Township on May 10, 1837 with four families present. Not until 1849, though, did they have enough members to warrant a church. Another Baptist congregation met at Raritan on Christmas eve 1858 under the leadership of Jacques Voorhees. A declaration of faith was drawn up and signed by five men and seven women. They called their first pastor, H.B. Johnson, at a salary of $200 a year and required him to hold Sunday services in the morning and in late afternoon. Jacques Voorhees gave three town lots as a site for the church. It was erected in 1863.

The Methodists appeared as early as 1837 at Olena when they met in the home of William Gosden. For the next twenty years they met from house to house, as weather permitted, until 1857 when they constructed a fine church in the town. In the southern edge of the county, Methodists organized themselves in 1850 and four years later put up one of that denomination's earliest brick churches. It operated as a branch of the Methodist Church at LaHarpe in Hancock County until 1866. At Oquawka, in 1856, about fifty members of a "Methodist Society" met in the Court House after having gathered together for a number of years intermittently in private homes. There they agreed to construct at 44 x 64 foot church at a cost of about $4,500. In September, Episcopal Bishop Janes formally dedicated the building and inaugurated Reverend J.S. Cummings as its first pastor. In 1860, eight families started a Methodist church at Biggsville. Led by H.P. Brown, they worshipped in a school building near the railroad depot, organized a Sunday School for their children, and took steps to buy town lots. Eventually, in 1867, they put up a permanent church building.[18]

Sloan Hall, Biggsville
First Meeting Place for Biggsville Churches

The appearance of the Dutch Reformed Church in Henderson County was a phenomenon of Raritan. It was formed in August, 1855, by thirteen settlers who, under Rev. A.D. Wilson and S.A. Bumstead, met at the home of S.P. Nevius. They called themselves the Reformed Church of Honey Creek. Their first service was held in September at the home of Peter S. Tharp. In 1856, they began their Sunday School at the town's blacksmith shop. In October, their minister, Reverend C.D. Eltinge of Port Jarvis, New Jersey arrived and laid the cornerstone of the church. It was built with a $1,600 donation by fellow members in New Jersey, by $1,000 out

Dutch Reformed Church, Raritan

of Eltinge's own pocket, and by small contributions of the Raritan settlers. Materials were shipped from Oquawka. All town residents pitched in during the actual construction with one man, Aaron Johnson, building a church spire which topped at sixty-nine feet above ground. The Greek Revival structure was completed in the summer of 1858 and on the eighth of September it was formally dedicated.[19]

Biggsville Methodist Church

Raritan not only had the only antebellum Dutch Reformed Church it also claimed the county's only Roman Catholic Chapel. By the 1850s a number of Catholic families had arrived from Ireland, some as farmers others as workers on the CB&O railroad. The nearest Sunday mass was a trying twenty miles away, in Monmouth. In 1856, some thirteen families asked the Springfield dioceses to send a priest to the area to stay in local homes on Saturday night and hold Sunday services. Nothing happened. Not until 1872 were both the need and the money present for a chapel and not until four years later were John Barry, Pat McCleary, and Thomas Huston successful in their campaign to raise the requested funds for materials and land.[20]

After the churches came the schools. The first school houses, often adjacent to one of the denominational structures, were small cabins with one or two windows covered with greased oilpaper for glass. Floors were either dirt or covered with smoothed-off logs of linnwood. Each child lugged along his or her seat every morning to the cabin. They put the seat down at wooden desks, usually built around the edge of the room. The teacher stood or sat in the center. At one end of the wall was the slate slab, the school's writing blackboard. Classes started at 7:30 in the morning and, with one hour for recess and lunch at noon, continued until supper time. There were no "grades" of students by either age or ability since the teacher had to work with whatever books were available regardless of their level of difficulty. Usually, though, copies of three texts were used, the *English Reader*, the *American Preceptor*, and the New Testament. No child graduated. They came to school as long as parents wanted them to attend, which was usually until their early teens when they were able to help with farm chores and had acquired the distinction of being literate, that is able to read and to write their signature.

Teachers had only to demonstrate that they could read, write, and master arithmetic. Their salaries, on the average, ran about $13 a month for a term of twelve weeks. There were two terms each year, one after the fall harvest, the other after spring planting time. Not until 1849 was there an organized state effort behind financing and supporting education. In that year the legislature stipulated that each township could establish whatever number of districts the voters wished to create. Each district would have one schoolhouse. Within those areas voters could levy a tax of up to 25 cents on $100 worth of property evaluation. A district would have a three-member board to allocate these funds for the teacher's salary, supplies, and upkeep expenses.[21]

In 1838, eleven years before the state school law, Oquawka opened its school under the tutelage of Rhoda Greene. Two other part-time teachers helped during the next few years, Thomas McElira and the First Presbyterian minister, George Stebbins. Stebbins, about the same time, started his own private Latin School for young men interested in a college education. William H. Phelps and E.H.N. Patterson both enrolled and Patterson went on to graduate from Jubilee College. In 1848, a fourth teacher, Jonathan Simpson, advertised a private school in a room at the Court House "for the instruction of youth in all branches of English education." The fee was only $2.50 for a three-month term. It attracted about 100 students during the next two years. Simpson's Academy, though, was eclipsed by the opening, in 1850, of the town's newly-built public school. Located in the north-central part of Oquawka, the brick structure cost $1,800. So many students applied the first year that extra room had to be temporarily found in the basement of the Methodist Church and in a local warehouse until, in 1858, a second schoolhouse was put up.

Liberty School, Rozetta

Outside of the County Seat other efforts at education were underway about the same time. W.R. Jamison as early as 1829 taught his children, as well as those of the Shorts, Ritchie, Ryason, and Lynn families in the South Henderson region. A South Henderson log cabin school with a wooden hinged door and a mud chimney began about 1840. Farther south, in section twenty-eight and twenty-nine, two schools were started by Dr. William McMillan, the county's only itinerate physician. The Lynn School, on section ten just north of the town of Gladstone, opened in 1842 in a tiny cabin built by Ebenezer Russell. In 1849, complying with state laws the voters of that district approved fifteen cents per $100 tax, hired Wilson Hopkins for $13 a month and authorized the construction of the first school building in the southwest corner of that section. Within a decade, over 100 pupils attended the school from time to time. At Biggsville Township, John McKinney began a cabin school in section 26. In 1855 and in 1856 a second building was put up in section twenty-nine by directors R. Duncan, D. Rawhouser, and Samuel Stewart. White frame schoolhouses were built in Section nineteen and Section five before the Civil War. In Rozetta (or Greenville) Township, the pupils were taught by N.H. Davis over the winter of 1836-37 at a cabin called the "Subscription House." It was later replaced by a frame structure one-half mile west of the town of Rozetta. Another district school was built in 1842, another in 1845, then another in 1849. In Olena Township (later Stronghurst) a twelve foot square cabin school opened under James H. Beveridge and served about twenty children and then, in 1857, it was relocated to the town of Olena. A succession of small structures appeared in Olena Township before the Civil War. One was in the northcentral part (Section four), a second was located in the center (Section sixteen), a third in the east (Section twenty-three), and a fourth in the south near Decorra (Section thirty-two). At Walnut Grove Township (Media) the pattern continued. Small log cabins came first, then frame or brick structures were built. One was put up in the southeast (Section thirty-five), the northeast (Section eleven), the northwest (Section five) and central (Section twenty). At Raritan, a clapboard school house was erected in 1856 when Peter Tharp gave the school district directors an acre of land for that purpose.[22]

Col. John B. Patterson, Editor
Oquawka Spectator

Corresponding to the rise of churches and schools in the county were other signs of an awakened sense of community awareness, the publication of its first newspapers. On February 12, 1848 John B. Patterson, then thirty-nine years old, announced the appearance of the *Oquawka Spectator*. This venture was a weekly paper published out of a back room of a general merchandise store which Patterson had been running since 1836 while he served as the town's postmaster and bridge inspector. Patterson's editorial policy would be strictly non-partisan politically, a stance he was able to maintain until he broke with Lincoln over the Emancipation Proclamation. Thereafter, the *Spectator* was blatantly a Democratic partisan, a policy continued by his son Edwin (or E.H.N.), whom he admitted as co-editor in 1848. The other newspaper was the *Oquawka Plaindealer*, begun by Francis A. Dallam in July, 1852. Dallam operated the paper for three years when, after a series of temporary editors, M.H. Jamison moved it to Biggsville. Unlike the neutral *Spectator*, the *Plaindealer* was openly for the Whig party nationally and, after 1856, was an organ of the new Republican party and Abraham Lincoln.

In 1848, young associate editor of the *Spectator*, E.H.N. Patterson, launched the most ambitious literary venture of the county's, if not that of all of the state's, history. He wrote to the famous New York man of letters Edgar Allen Poe in January of that year proposing that the two collaborate in starting a journal on the model of *The Southern Literary Messenger* in the Mississippi Valley. Poe endorsed the idea and they exchanged letters which laid out details of their plans. The new journal, Poe suggested, should sell at $5.00 for a year's subscription. The two men could count on an annual circulation in the vicinity of 20,000 patrons, Poe thought. Poe offered to make a personal tour of the West to promote the journal and predicted that, by the end of the tour, he would have 1,000 signed subscribers. He offered to come to Oquawka to discuss the matter with Patterson. Or, if that were not convenient Poe could meet him "at any place you suggest where we can talk the matter over with deliberation." Patterson's reply was enthusiastic. He offered to print the journal, monthly, at Oquawka. He suggested a plan which, in fact, made Poe the actual editor by asking Poe to read all prospective manuscripts and then supply Patterson with edited copy by mail from New York. Lastly, Patterson fixed a tentative issue of ninety-six pages, exclusive of cover, with the first run to appear in January, 1850. Patterson eagerly anticipated Poe's reply. When the mail did come from New York it was a letter written by a friend of Poe's telling Patterson that Poe had just died. So did the literary journal.[23]

The Patterson-Poe correspondence represented the quintessence of the aspirations of the frontier community. It had emerged overnight out of unbelievable primitiveness into the civilized atmosphere of town life, railroads, churches, schools, and newspapers. It seemed destined for a time to be *the* cultural center of the Upper Mississippi Valley. With the good times, however, came the bad. For during these same first years of community building troubles started to beset the county.

The first recorded crime brought to trial in the area was an Indian murder of a white man. On August 9, 1832 while William Martin was cutting field grass for his horse on his homestead on the Cedar Creek branch of the North Henderson, five Sauk-Fox braves, apparently after his horses, shot him in the back and killed him. People then living in the block-house at nearby Little York heard the shots. Only one of the Indians was actually captured and turned over by Chief Keokuk. He soon escaped. Then

Keokuk, in compliance with Indian custom in murders, sent the relatives of all five assailants to the county sheriff, Peter Baker. These relatives were the individuals who were actually indicted and tried at the June, 1833 Circuit Court at Yellow Banks after having been confined in the Monmouth jail since March. The formal indictment, however, specifically charged five braves by name — Shash-quaw-a-shi, Neesh-wak-que, Muck-que-che-qua, Muck-qua-po-la-shah, and Was-a-wan-a-quot — but the court put the substitutes on trial. Keokuk and other chiefs attended. Colonel George Davenport acted as interpreter. The five surrogates were defended by three lawyers hired by the tribe. They moved at once for dismissal of charges on a writ of habeas corpus. Judge James Ralston agreed with the motion and reprimanded Keokuk for turning over innocent men. Keokuk, in turn, said that he acted according to Indian custom and had done what tradition compelled him to do in such matters. In other words, Keokuk felt that he had no choice. The prisoners were thereupon released.

The first crime of one white settler against another happened about the same time as the Indian trial that was going on at Yellow Banks. Daniel Harris, a veteran of the War of 1812, had just arrived in Walnut Grove Township to start his new life on a bounty of 160 acres just north of Tom Creek. He was last seen working on his log cabin. Later, he was found face-down in a bowl of hominy with a bullet hole in the back of his head. Immediately neighbors thought it was another Indian outrage. Although the real culprit was never caught, details of the murder came out some twenty years later in a signed confession which was printed in a Cincinnati newspaper. The culprit, then about to be hanged in Ohio for other murders, detailed the events at the Harris cabin. Apparently, the murderer had followed Harris all the way from New York City where, before starting out for his military bounty in Illinois, Harris had withdrawn a sizable amount of cash from his bank. Tracking Harris to the isolated cabin, the assailant disguised himself as a Sauk-Fox brave and killed Harris while he was eating his supper. But there was no money at all in the cabin, he admitted, only a quarter.[24]

Other less violent crimes also appeared during these decades. A group of couterfeiters set up operations in southern Gladstone (South Henderson) Township in a place called Bogus Hollow. There they coined half-dollars which were placed in circulation throughout the county and across the river in Iowa. Their hideout was raided and the ladles, dies, and crucibles were confiscated along with a stash of counterfeit coins. No one was arrested, however. In the 1850s, with the arrival of a large number of Irish workers to help with the CB&Q railroad, the court recorded an increasing number of assaults. The *Spectator* in January, 1857 recounted one such episode which took place at Oquawka Junction. According to this account two Irishmen got into a fight and one of them drew out a shotgun and fired at the other. The pellets hit the man in the face and the shoulder "inflicting several frightful wounds," in the words of Patterson. The wounded man survived though, and the other Irishman fled.[25]

The last crime before the Civil War was another homicide. This felony was the result of a quarrel over the ownership of a flour mill in Rozetta Township. Joseph Hollingsworth, who built and owned the mill got into a vicious fight during the winter of 1859 with his sons, Addison (who rented the operation) and Enoch (who worked there). Joseph then secured an arrest warrant for the two boys on the charge that he, the father, had been physically threatened. With warrant in hand, David Welch, a sheriff's deputy, went to the mill to apprehend the sons and arrived after dark. He entered the building and found two employees inside. One of them, for no apparent reason, shot Welch through the hip with a rifle. Soon after, Welch bled to death. The two men were tried in Mercer County on a change of venue motion by the defense. They were convicted of murder and sentenced to Joliet State Prison for the usual term of two years for unpremeditated murder.[26]

The record of only five episodes of recorded criminal conduct during the 1840s and 1850s shows that the tone of violence in the county was indeed moderate. The first farmers of Henderson County were a peaceable lot. Their energies were taken up with building their farms, their churches, and their schools. Little time was left for quarreling with one another. Even in the more congregated river town of Oquawka, with its mobile and divergent population, there were no serious crimes.

Perhaps, too, as the county-wide social data show, a degree of stability was arrived at almost right away in the community stage of development. For example, the number and percentage of unmarried young men dwindled rapidly and the sex ratio evened-out thus providing greater opportunity for family-building. Unemployment all but disappeared from the county by 1850. While the overall population more than doubled by mid-century, in itself a potential cause of dislocation and potential crime, the new arrivals brought with them a common set of values and standards of acceptable conduct. Then, too, the basic institutions of church and school appeared almost overnight in every township. Indeed, the picture of social stability as indicated by the low crime rate is all the more apparent when during and after the Civil War the number and the kinds of criminal activity surged definitely upwards.

The final stage of the establishment of the Henderson County community was the formation of institutions of local government and the appearance of regular political acitivity, i.e., political parties and elections. Until January 20, 1841 Henderson had been roughly the western half of Warren County, which, in 1830, had been created and organized for the three functions of raising taxes, transacting and recording legal business, and performing marriages. On Friday, July 9, 1830 the first elected Warren County Commissioners met temporarily at the Phelps' cabin at Yellow Banks and Daniel McNeil, Jr., was appointed County Clerk. Routine transactions were paid out by the new county to Adam Ritchie, John Pence, and John B. Talboy. A license was issued to William Causland to start an inn at Yellow Banks and to Sumner Phelps to operate the store there. The commissioners located the temporary county seat at Phelps' cabin and divided the county itself into two election precincts. At the first general election forty-seven of the fifty eligible adult males cast their votes. The commissioners, on April 7, 1831 agreed to locate the permanent county court at Monmouth and took the first survey there later that month. Simple matters occupied county officers during the next decade. They planned a courthouse and agreed upon specifications that it would be 10 x 22 and "built of logs hewn down inside and out, and finished as the County Commissioners shall direct."[27] A county jailhouse was designed in 1832. In 1833, the first taxes were collected on Military Bounty farms which, till then, had been exempt. A Probate Court for registration of wills was created in 1837.

The reasons behind the severing of Warren County in two and the creation of a separate Henderson County in 1841 are obscure. The 1886

History of Warren County only states that the "residents of the territory now embraced by Henderson County, were not satisfied with the location of the county seat at Monmouth, and made an effort to have it changed to a more central location. Failing this, they succeeded and organized themselves into a county which was called Henderson."[28] In any event, by an 1840 act of the state legislature an election had to take place in the new county on April 5, 1841. At that time Preston Martin and Benjamin C. Coghill were chosen as the first commissioners along with James C. Hutchinson, who was held over from the earlier Warren County jurisdiction. They met at Oquawka where the Phelps brothers had donated lots to be sold as a way of financing the construction of county buildings. Other newly chosen officers were John McKinney, Recorder; William Jameson, Treasurer; William D. Henderson, Sheriff; and Alfred Knowles, Clerk.

At its first meeting the Board arranged for the construction of a brick courthouse to be built by Alexis Phelps. The opening of the court was scheduled for May at a storeroom in J.B. Patterson's house. There it opened on the twenty-eighth of the month, presided over by Judge Stephen A. Douglas. They decided to locate the jail in the basement of the county poorhouse situated about one mile and-a-half east of the town. Trustees of the county school districts were appointed. The commissioners granted William H. Mauro a license to operate a ferry across the Mississippi to Burlington. They authorized John A. Lynn to operate the first saloon. And, as a last item of business they divided the county into precincts for elections.

Stephen A. Douglas

Political parties of the 1840s were called the Whigs and Democrats. The Whigs at the time supported Henry Clay and President William Henry Harrison's ("Old Tippecanoe") national program of more internal improvements (roads, canals, railroads) financed with federal money, a higher tariff on foreign imports, and a national banking system. They usually held the majority in the county before the Civil War. The Democrats claimed their followers from those coming to the county from the South and stressed cheaper federal land prices, state control of banking, and only a modest support of federal internal improvements.

Both parties squared off on the issue of territorial expansion because, linked with it, was the question of the future of slavery. In the 1840s the Whigs opposed any further acquisition of territory west of the Louisiana Purchase in the fear that most of that area could eventually be made into slave states. They particularly rejected the appeal of Texas, where slavery flourished, for annexation to the Union after winning its independence from Mexico. And subsequently, they opposed the 1848 War with Mexico for the same reasons. The Whigs thought that in such a war America was certain to win and thus not only get Texas but also add to the potential "slave block" in Congress by picking up all the rest of the Mexican Cession. Democrats in Illinois, led by Stephen Douglas, supported westward expansion. Douglas said that the slavery issue should be left to the people who went to live in the West to decide, not Congress. He and his party supported both the annexation of Texas and the war with Mexico without hesitation.

The eventual war with Mexico and its settlement, the Compromise of 1850, caused a new party, the Republican Party, to gain voters in Henderson County. By the Compromise, California was admitted as a free state and the future of slavery in New Mexico and Arizona was left hanging on future decisions of the federal courts. Some people believed this was only a ruse whereby slavery, although permanently blocked from going into California, could still extend farther westward beyond Texas. Let these areas remain free of slavery, they said, open to the small, independent, farmer who could cultivate his acres free of competition from slave labor. "Keep the soil free", argued the Free Soil Party. Over the next decade, though, disillusionment with the Compromise widened, in the nation and in the county. For a brief time, 1854-1856, another splinter party, the Know Nothing Party, mushroomed in the nation and in parts of the Prairie State built out of a combined fear of foreigners and Catholics. It had no following in Henderson County, however.

By 1854 the dissatisfied of all parties pulled together in a new coalition called the Republican Party. This party, first organized at Ripon, Wisconsin glued the economic programs of the Whig Party (internal improvements, protective tariff, central banking) on to the increasingly emotional issue of opposition to the spread of slavery. The gut issue of slavery, though, was the paste which held together the former Whigs, Democrats, and of course, a handful of Abolitionists. In the election of 1856, Henderson County voters gave this new party and its presidential candidate, John C. Fremont, a 350 vote majority. And, four years later, the same voters cast 911 votes for Democrat Stephen A. Douglas and 1,253 for the Republican nominee, Abraham Lincoln.

END NOTES FOR CHAPTER TWO

[1] United States Census, Population Schedules, 1840, Warren County, Illinois. Henderson County was not organized until 1841 when the state legislature created it out of the western half of Warren County. The marshal did, however, list his data by existing township survey boundaries off the Fourth Principle Meridian and the Base Line survey demarcation. It is possible therefore to plot accurately the 1840 data to correspond with later townships designated by name after 1841. The 1840 census listed names of heads of households, ages of household members, occupations, and "people of color." There were only twelve blacks in the county in 1840: six in Oquawka, two in Sagetown, and one each in Bald Bluff and Rozetta. The black population thereafter never numbered over four families in the county. Microfilm copy of these census manuscripts are available in the Archives and Special Collections, Western Illinois University Library and in the Illinois State Archives, Springfield as are all subsequent census data used in this study.

[2] The 1850 Population Schedules list names of the family members, their ages, occupations, whether they attended school, place of birth in the United States, by state, or foreign countries.

[3] For a detailed account of early Oquawka see Virginia Hughes, "Oquawka, A Study of the Influence of Mississippi River Trade on Oquawka 1850-1880." Hughes' paper is a Knox College Honors Thesis done in 1943 and currently in the Finley Collection, Knox College, Galesburg. Also in the Finley Collection is an 1836 Currier and Ives map of Oquawka.

[4] See galley-proof copy of Eugene Field. "Poe, Patterson, and Oquawka," Finley Collection.

[5] For details of Oquawka's early history see Gordon, *History of Henderson County* and Shephard & Johnson, *History of Henderson County*. Ralph Eckley, feature reporter, retired, of the *Monmouth Review Atlas* has an extensive collection of newspaper articles written by himself and his predecessor John Moffit organized in dozens of scrapbooks currently housed in the building of the *Monmouth Review Atlas* at Monmouth.

Eckley permitted the author to examine and to copy extensively those materials dealing with Henderson County. Also, The Chicago Sunday *Tribune* ran a feature on early Oquawka in November 22, 1953.

[6] State of Illinois, Land Track Records Listing, State Archives, Springfield.

[7] Ibid. See also Gordon and Shephard & Johnson; and Virginia Ross and Jane Evans, *Henderson County Illinois Cemeteries*, 2 vols. (Gladstone, Il., 1979).

[8] Ibid.

[9] Ibid.

[10] Ibid.

[11] Ibid.

[12] Ibid. See the sixty-three page pamphlet "Biggsville 1854-1979" published in commeration of the town's Quasquicentennial Celebration, Biggsville, Illinois (no date).

[13] State of Illinois, Land Tract Records Listing. See also Gordon, Shephard & Johnson, and United States Census. Population Schedules Henderson County, Illinois. 1850, 1860.

[14] Ibid. See also *A History of Raritan, Illinois and Community 1856-1981* (Aledo, Il., 1981); *Past and Present of the Raritan Baptist Church, Raritan Illinois 1858-1983* (N.Y. 1983) compiled by Wayne Gearhart and John Lee Allaman; *125th Anniversary of the Reformed Church Raritan Illinois, 1980* (1980). James H. Cook tape, interviewed by Rita Souther, Feb. 22, 1980, on early Raritan (WIU Archives & Special Collections).

[15] Gordon, *History of Henderson County*; Shephard & Johnson, *History of Henderson County*. See also John M. Foster tape, interviewed by Rita Souther, March 4, 1980 (WIU Archives & Special Collections). See also Raritan histories, *op cit*, above.

[16] John E. Hallwas, *Western Illinois Heritage*, "South Henderson Church," pp 60-62. Henderson County *Quill* ran two features on "The Story of South Henderson" on May 31 and June 7, 1978.

[17] Gordon, and Shepherd & Johnson, *History of Henderson County*.

[18] *Ibid*.

[19] *125th Anniversary of Reformed Church*.

[20] *History of Raritan*.

[21] Gordon, and Shepherd & Johnson, *History of Henderson County*.

[22] Ibid.

[23] Edgar Allan Poe, "Letters to E.H.N. Patterson of Oquawka," Illinois State Historical Library, Springfield. See also Eugene Field, "Poe, Patterson, and Oquawka," Finley Collection, Knox College.

[24] Gordon, and Shepherd & Johnson, *History of Henderson County*.

[25] Oquawka *Spectator*, January 17, 1857.

[26] Gordon, *History of Henderson County* p 691.

[27] *Portrait and Biographical Album of Warren County, Illinois*. (Chicago, 1886), p 681.

[28] Gordon and Shephard, *History of Henderson County* p 682.

CHAPTER THREE
THE CIVIL WAR 1858-1865

The Civil War can be said to have begun and ended in Henderson County, mentally and emotionally if not physically, with Abraham Lincoln. The grim reality of the impending, irreversible conflict first was brought to the county during the Lincoln-Douglas debates in the summer of 1858 when, in August, the two men spoke in Oquawka. And, six years later, when the news of both Lee's surrender at Appomattox and Lincoln's assassination appeared in the Oquawka *Spectator* at about the same time, the people of the county knew that the war was finished.

During the 1840s and 1850s Henderson County folks were just like Americans everywhere, they did not believe that a war between North and South over the "slavery question" was possible. They were preoccupied with getting along, making a living, fulfilling the opportunities which an expanding American society provided. But the reality of the problem would not go away, not for the citizens of Henderson County or, for that matter, for the national political parties. Democrats squeezed their imaginations dry for a compromise on slavery that would work, but none did. The Whig party went out of existence on the slavery issue and its replacement, the Republicans, were pre-occupied with it. The slavery problem, in a word, would not disappear. It had to be dealt with, one way or another. Slavery had to expand beyond its present limits and become, eventually, a national institution, legal in all states. Or, it had to be eliminated. And that is exactly what the Republican Candidate for the United States Senate, Abraham Lincoln, said in 1858.[1]

In June of that year at the state Republican Convention in Springfield, Lincoln painted a grim future of the nation that everyone could understand and, it turned out, was too clear to be ignored. In his "House Divided" speech of June 17 he warned that the slavery question would not be resolved until a crisis was reached and passed. The nation could not go on the way it was, half slave, half free. "It will become all one thing, or all the other," he said. And the tendency, if nothing were done to stop it, Lincoln predicted, was for the whole nation to legalize slavery. "Its advocates will push it forward till it shall become alike lawful in all the States," he declared, "old as well as new, North as well as South."[2]

In the remainder of that summer and fall the citizens of the nation and of the state saw Lincoln repeat the same message in a series of debates with Stephen Douglas. Both men then running for the United States Senate (Douglas for his third term) put forth and analyzed the slavery question. Beginning at Ottawa on August 21, they debated at Freeport (August 27), Jonesboro (September 15), Charleston (September 18), Galesburg (October 7), Quincy (October 13), and Alton (October 15). "The issues they expanded," Robert P. Howard has observed, "were national and monumental."[3] Douglas argued that blacks were an inferior race and that Lincoln favored Negro equality. Douglas said that popular sovereignty, or people living in the area where slavery might exist, could decide the question, not Congress. Lincoln, avoiding the issue of racial, social, and political equality, said that blacks and whites had the same natural rights. At Freeport he maneuvered Douglas into admitting that popular sovereignty was too vague to be workable and, getting Douglas to refine his definition, had him concede that unless a people passed specific territorial laws permitting slavery to exist it would be illegal. Lincoln was

Opposite: Union Army Soldier

Packet Steamboat
Steamboats were a major means of transport between Henderson County and Iowa until the construction of a railroad bridge in the early 1900's.

able to have Doulgas defeat himself by demonstrating that his key doctrine of popular sovereignty was too fuzzy to be workable and if it were refined, it excluded southern slaveholders from the territories. Douglas' position was still acceptable in Illinois, however, and he won re-election after gerrymandering the legislature.[4]

In the process of traveling throughout the seven Congressional districts where the face to face confrontations took place both men made solo excursions to nearby towns. One such visit was to Oquawka. The fourth formal debate was scheduled at Galesburg on the afternoon of Thursday, October seventh. Three days earlier, on Monday, Douglas came to town. The early crowd, of about 100, was sparce. The day was rainy and overcast according to the *Spectator*.[5] The Senator pulled in at 9:00 and an hour later a group of outside visitors arrived from down-river on the steamboat "Keokuk." There was a brief welcoming parade featuring the Oquawka and Monmouth brass bands. After lunch, at about 1:00, a contingent of local Democrats, led by I.N. Morris, escorted Douglas to a decorated platform erected in front of the Courthouse. Morris began by making a few announcements about Democratic party activities. Then, C.M. Harris officially welcomed Douglas and introduced him to a crowd by then considerably enlarged to about 1,000 citizens. Douglas spoke for a little over two hours and left right away aboard the "Keokuk" for Burlington.

On Saturday, October 9, Lincoln came over from Galesburg by rail through Galdstone. The day was bright and cool. A procession, led by the Oquawka band, escorted him to the home of his friend Sumner Phelps. From there the two men drove to a bunted platform erected near the river dock on Main street. Lincoln was appropriately introduced by J.H. Stewart to a crowd of 1,500. Lincoln used the same language as the House Divided Speech. After the speech, also about two hours long, Lincoln returned to the Phelps home where, after a brief nap, he stayed for dinner. He left that evening on the "Keokuk" to Burlington and then went on to Quincy for another scheduled face to face debate with Douglas on the thirteenth.[6]

The Lincoln Douglas Debates destroyed Douglas nationally among southern Democrats, divided his party into warring factions, one North one South, and in 1860 led to the election of Lincoln as the first Republican President. As the Union itself rapidly split into North and South during the two years following the debates, many still persisted in the attitude that nothing unusual was going on. Henderson County voters felt that way. The *Spectator*, a reliable instrument of community business during these years, was void of any mention of an on-going civil war in the Kansas Territory over the spread of slavery. There was no discussion of John Brown's raid on Harper's Ferry on October 16, 1859, nor of the reaction to his subsequent arrest, trial, and hanging for treason. There was no mention of southern threats, especially from Senators from South Carolina and Georgia, to leave the Union if a Republican were elected in 1860. Instead, the columns of the *Spectator* were replete with information about the gold rush to Pike's Peak. It reprinted at length letters from prospectors who had gone there. Indeed, in 1859, five times as much space was devoted to Pike's Peak news than to any other matter.[7]

Early in the spring of 1860 the *Spectator* started printing routine information about the forthcoming Republican convention. The acrimonious dissension among the Democrats then going on was ignored. In May, it said that the Republican convention had met in Chicago to nominate its candidates and predicted they would choose either Simon Cameron of Pennsylvania or Lincoln. At Chicago, David Wilmont, also of Pennsylvania, was selected temporary chairman. He then appointed the standing committees to draft a platform. The platform stated that slavery must be kept intact where it existed but condemned attempts by Southerners and the Democratic Party to spread the institution by violence into Kansas. On slavery, the platform further condemned "unqualified property" in persons as leading to the "dangerous political heresy that the Constitution carries slavery into all territories."[8] Plank eight applied the historical precedent of the Northwest Ordinances of 1785 and 1787 to the existing question. There, by act of Congress, slavery had been excluded from north of the Ohio River. The lesson was clear: Congress had prevented slavery from expanding before, it should do the same thing again. Other parts of the platform dealt with a demand for a transcontinental railroad and a statement for unrestricted immigration.

On the convention floor Republicans on the first ballot chose Senator William Seward of New York by 173 to Lincoln's second place of 102 votes. Simon Cameron of Pennsylvania, the anticipated front runner, came in a weak third with only 50 votes. The second ballot was indecisive, neither Seward nor Lincoln came near to the 233 majority needed to nominate. On the third ballot, Lincoln picked up enough support to move to 231, two short, with Seward trailing at 180. Then the head of the Ohio delegation, L. Carter, rose and changed four Ohio votes from its own candidate, Senator Salmon P. Chase, to give Lincoln the majority at 235 votes. With Lincoln's nomination the convention adjourned at five o'clock, then reconvened briefly that evening to select Hannibal Hamlin of Maine as Lincoln's Vice President.[9]

Six weeks passed before any further indication of the irreversible conflict was evident in Henderson County. On July 4, E.H.N. Patterson, for the first time, predicted a civil war. The union was in danger, he stated. Then Patterson asked: "Is there not now cause for patriotic fear?"[10] The language was restrained, but compared to the indifference and apathy of the past, the stand must have been alarming news to the uninformed farmers and townsmen along the Mississippi and its tributaries. Finally, the story was out, undeniable in its catastrophic consequences. War seemed by then to Patterson to be unavoidable, beyond control, moving by its own momentum on the emotional energy of the slavery question. "Behold," he wrote, "in our country two great sectional parties nearly equally divided representing the free and slave states each found almost exclusively in its own section of the country."[11] The Union was being torn apart in front of him over slavery. Each section, he said, regarded expansion of slavery or its extinction as vital to its way of life. Slavery had destroyed the national Democratic Party already, Patterson sadly observed. Now he saw the two great sections "pitched against each other in battle array and their bitterness goes to the extent of threatening disunion...."[12] Do not fall back into the old complacency, he warned. "Let us not flatter ourselves that we are secure in the possession of our great inheritance." "We must," he exhorted, in direct reference to "extremists" North and South, "prepare to meet the enemies of our common country."[13] It was, by then, too little warning, too late.

Through the rest of the summer, Republicans and Democrats in the county organized for the fall election. At Olena, the Republicans staged a meeting to ratify, in their words, the national ticket. Despite the day's drizzly weather the Oquawka Brass Band showed up. Also, along with the

Masthead, Oquawka Spectator

band on the same seventy-one car train from Oquawka, were 427 people. Captain Prentise of Quincy brought with him a caravan of between 1,500 and 2,000 party regulars.[14] Lieutenant Governor Grimes addressed the throng. The last political meeting held in Henderson County was at Oquawka on September 27 when the Republican candidate for Governor, Richard Yates, addressed his supporters.[17] The Democrats were not to be outdone. On August 11 they conducted a meeting and a "pole raising" ceremony at Terre Haute. There, Colonel William H. Rollossin of Dallas City addressed the people.[15] On August 30 he led a "Douglas Ratification Meeting" to Monmouth.[16] These Democrats met up with a party contingent from Mercer County at Pleasant Green and the two groups went on together to the Warren County seat for the meeting.

On election eve Patterson printed some advice and offered his reflections on the campaign. Not for twenty years, he said, had there been so much excitement over an election. This agitation worried him. But, he predicted, "as usual after elections the troubled waves will subside and all will become calm again." In the meantime though, all eyes were fixed on Pennsylvania and New York. In these states "all parties opposed to the Republicans" have agreed to "throw their votes together." But, Patterson found out, many of the rank and file Democrats "have repudiated their actions and threaten to go over" to the Repubican ticket. If Lincoln loses either state, he said, he will lose the Electoral College and if that happens the next president, according to Article II, section l of the Constitution, will be chosen by the House of Representatives. In any case, Patterson resigned himself to the fact that "the result, whatever it may be, will be known by the end of next week."[18]

On November 8, 1860 upper case, bold type of the *Spectator* announced: **LINCOLN ELECTED.**[19] The main cause of Republican victory, as Patterson anticipated, was their getting both Pennsylvania and New York by large majorities. This editor and publisher, who dispite his claim to nonpartisanship was a loyal Democrat, conceded his loss with a tone of resignation. "The great battle has been fought," he wrote, "the sovereign people have spoken and a change in administration of the government has been decided upon." "It is the duty of all good citizens," he admonished his Democratic subscribers, "to bow and as in former times to await the action of the new administration."[20]

The official returns show that Illinois and Henderson County joined Pennsylvania and New York in their strong vote for Lincoln. Lincoln also pulled along the Republican gubernatorial candidate and the party candidate for Congress. Lincoln won the county by an aggregate of 1,253 over Douglas' 911. The other two candidates received insignificant support. Breckenridge, the "Southern" Democrat, received only twenty-two votes and Bell of the Constitutional Union party tallied only thirty-three ballots. Yates defeated the Democrat Richard Allen by 1,259 to 931 and the Republican man for Congress, Benjamin Prentiss, won over William A. Richardson by 1,268 to 918.[21]

Township returns show interesting pockets of Douglas strength in six areas. In the southern part of the county Douglas beat Lincoln in townships of Olena (Stronghurst), Bedford (Raritan), Warren, Honey Creek (Lomax) and Dallas City. In the northern part only Bald Bluff voted for Douglas. Allen won just Honey Creek and Dallas City while Richardson pulled slim majorities in Warren, Bedford, Dallas City, and Bald Bluff. Henderson County voters felt the same way about Lincoln as their

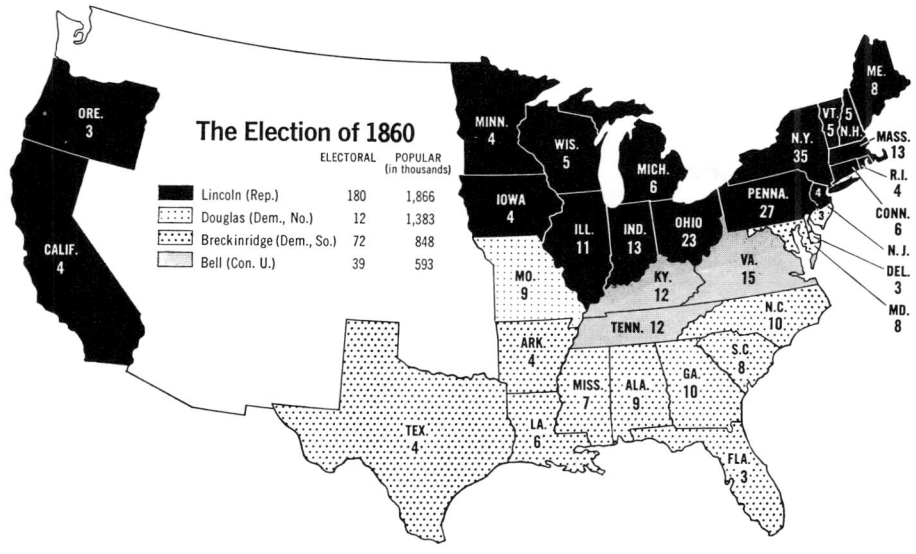

Election Results, 1860

neighbors in adjacent counties. Three of the four tallied Republican majorities (Warren, by 526, Mercer by 615, McDonough by 116). Only Hancock went for Douglas, by 400 votes.[22]

In the weeks following the election Patterson's political bias for the Democrats became more obvious. He reprinted verbatim President Buchanan's Message to Congress when, in early December, he asked the nation for understanding and conceded that while secession was illegal the President had no constitutional power to stop it. Patterson applauded Buchanan.[23] He condemned the "extremists" who were refusing to compromise. On December 20, Patterson charged that the worsening crisis (South Carolina had seceded that day declaring the "experiment" of governing people "with different pursuits and institutions" a failure) was caused by "misguided men both North and South." "It was the duty of every good citizen," he scolded, "to allay the excitement that is now spreading all over the land."[24] A week later he wrote despairingly that secession "seems to be gaining ground—all the Cotton States are determined to go with South Carolina."[25] And so they were. Six states, Mississippi, Florida, Alabama, Georgia, Louisiana, and Texas seceded. From each state, as it left the Union in January, the *Spectator* reprinted telegrams from their capitals about what was happening. The citizens of Henderson County now knew in detail why and how their federal government was falling apart.[26]

As the Union crumbled during that early winter of 1861 attention more and more was fixed on the President elect. How would he respond? Would he tolerate secession? Would he use force to hold the states? Would he attack the Confederacy? On February 14, Patterson detailed Lincoln's departure from Springfield on February 11 to Washington D.C. At the depot, betraying "much emotion" and bringing many in the crowd of over 1,000 to tears, he said to his friends.

> "No one not in my position can appreciate the sadness I feel at this parting. To this people I owe all that I am. Here I have lived more than a quarter of a century; here my children were born, and here one of them lies buried. A duty devolves upon me which is, perhaps, greater than that which has devolved upon any other man since the days of Washington."[27]

Lincoln's train chugged eastward to Indianapolis. From there Lincoln went on to speak briefly at Columbus and Cleveland, Ohio, Pittsburgh, Buffalo, New York City, Philadelphia, and Harrisburg, Pennsylvania. Then he was secretly wisked past Baltimore because of an assassination plot to the nation's capital. At every whistle stop he was unequivocal about his intentions. Lincoln promised to retain all federal property, by force if necessary. A state had no "original right" to break up and ruin the nation. He meant to leave slavery alone, free from all federal interference, where it existed.[28] That, he repeated, would be his policy after inauguration day. If the voters did not like it, well, Lincoln said, that was too bad. At Steubenville, Ohio, he had simply stated: "If anything goes wrong, however, and you find you have made a mistake, elect a better man next time. There are plenty of them."[29]

During the days following Lincoln's Inaugural Address on March 4 the *Spectator* was full of speculation about whether there would be conciliation or coercion.[30] Patterson's confusion was understandable. Lincoln's speech did leave much up in the air. The new President reiterated his intention to leave slavery alone, where it was. He would, in compliance with federal law, return all runaway slaves. He did say, again, that "no State, upon its own mere motion, can lawfully get out of the Union." What would he now do that states *had* gotten out? Lincoln said that he would be sure "that the laws of the Union be faithfully executed in all the States." But he did not say how he could do that. In any event, "there needs to be no bloodshed or violence; and there shall be none, unless it be forced upon the national authority."[31]

So, there it was. Lincoln would not fire unless fired upon. In the meantime, he declared a holding action. The President would "hold, occupy, and possess the property, and places belonging to the government." "Beyond what may be necessary for these objects," he promised, "there will be no invasion—no use of force against, or among, the people anywhere."[32] Finally, Lincoln disclaimed ultimate responsibility, and blame, for what was to happen. "In *your* hands, my dissatisfied fellow countrymen, and not in *mine*, is the momentous issue of civil war."[33]

Civil War Veterans of Raritan
John Butler, Charles Cooper, Isaac M. Smith, Wesley Michaels, S.L. Clark, Tom Garrett, Aaron Johnson, Horatio Westcott, James Staats, Peter VanArsdale

Has war already commenced? Will "Old Abe" use coercion to bring back seceding states? These were the tough questions which the Inaugural raised in Patterson's mind. He was under no illusion about the precariousness of the situation. On March 14, he wrote that "now the Union hangs upon a single shred."[34] But at least it was a shred of hope. He was thankful that Lincoln had rejected advise of men like Edwin Stanton, the Chairman of Committee on Military Affairs in the House of Representatives, to start "a war of subjugation and conquest." Patterson's advise at this juncture to Lincoln was not to acknowledge the Confederate states who had left the Union. To do that, he felt, would both alienate Southern states who were still loyal and encourage foreign governments to acknowledge them, especially England which was heavily dependent on cotton. Rather the President, wrote Patterson, should "withdraw all military forces from seceded states, allow them to try to protect themselves." "Time would work a radical change," he predicted, "and would soon bring them back to their allegiance." Patterson ought to have read more closely Lincoln's lengthy Inaugural, for the new President had said that evacuation of federal property was what he would not do. Lincoln would not surrender, for example, the two federal forts at Charleston harbor, Ft. Moltiere and Ft. Sumter.[35]

On April 11, 1861 the *Spectator* reported the arrival of "Sensational Dispatches!" about federal naval forces being ordered southward, some thought for Texas.[36] On April 18, it announced: WAR HAS COMMENCED. There was no point now in agonizing over the causes. It no longer mattered. Duty now compelled every citizen of Henderson County to be loyal, to stand by the flag in all circumstances. Still, Patterson could not stop himself from the forlorn hope that "even yet" Lincoln could come up with a policy to "retain the loyalty of the Border States and thereby bring back ... those deluded states that have seceded from the Union and thus unite and cement ... this great republic."[37]

Such serendipity was short lived. At 4:30 in the morning of April 12, 1861, acting on orders from President Jefferson Davis, General P.G.T. Beauregard, commander of Confederate troops at Charleston, opened his five batteries on Ft. Sumter. All day the Union commanding officer Major Anderson returned artillery fire while Charleston civilians lined up on the dock to watch the gala display. The next morning, at nine o'clock, the wooden barracks within the fort caught fire. By afternoon the union flag was blown away. By evening Anderson surrendered. On Sunday, April 14, the garrison evacuated.

On April 15 Lincoln issued a call for 75,000 volunteers. His justification: to suppress combinations "too powerful to be suppressed by the ordinary course of judicial proceedings," and "to cause the laws to be duly executed."[38] Besides, the Union had been attacked and, as he had promised at his inauguration, and reaffirmed privately in writing, he would strike back. The *Spectator* merely reported the rapidly arriving news dispatches without comment.[39]

With the troop call up, though, the final act of secession was played. Lincoln had forced the issue. Four states of the Upper South—Virginia, North Carolina, Tennessee, and Arkansas—joined the Confederacy by the third week of May. The slave states of Delaware, Maryland, Kentucky, and Missouri were kept in the Union by military force or threat of it. West Virginia, creating itself a new state out of the Old Dominion in 1863, also sided with the North.

The first reaction to the troop call up in Henderson County was military hoopla. The Oquawka Brass Band played its marches. Recruiting stations signed up volunteers. Businessmen closed their shops and "a constant whirl of excitement was kept up."[40] By the end of April ninety young men had enlisted for one of the six regiments ordered by Governor Yates. The only sad note to the celebration was news of the death of Stephen Douglas, following a speech in Chicago asking support for Lincoln, on the morning of June third.[41] Throughout April, May, and June, the volunteering went on. Officers were elected. The first contingent left for Springfield marching, more likely walking, to the railroad junction. They were led by the Brass Band and were followed by a large procession of citizens. The departure, Patterson reflected, was "a sad and heart rending sight."[42]

Richard Yates, Civil War Governor

By early summer the eager soldiers were gone. The community, with amazing swiftness, settled back to life as usual. Indeed, for the first three years of the war, until the return home on furlough of sizable numbers of veterans in 1864 and the outbreaks of vigilantism against pro-southern sympathizers called Copperheads, it was all but life as before.

The war meant prosperity for the county. This is not surprising for the North as a whole "grew fat and sassy during the war."[43] The Union government was generous in its contracts and extravagant in its expenditures. The drain of men to combat meant higher wages and, often, improved production with labor saving devices, invented before the war, applied by factory owners. For example, the sewing machine eliminated the seamstresses. The Gorden McKay machine mechanized shoe production. Petroleum, a crude Indian cure-all before the war, replaced kerosene and whale oil. The troops ever-expanding food demands led to new packing techniques at Chicago by the houses of Armour and Morris. The mechanical reaper came into general use, increasing harvest capacity five times over the old scythe and cradle. Foreign countries augmented the demand for grains. England, for instance, imported fifty times as much flour and wheat in 1862 as she had in 1859.

Henderson County agricultural output increased at impressive rates. Even before the war the number of agricultural acres had, like the population itself, doubled between 1850 and 1860.[44] During the war production grew for all its farm crops—wheat, rye, corn and oats. More hogs were raised than ever before. A boom mentality reminiscent of the 1840s revived at Oquawka. L.B. Parsons posted a "great sale of lots" in the town. Touted as "many of the most valuable lots in town" which "have long been kept out of market by non-resident owners" were now offered.[45] Terms were lenient enough: only 5 percent down and the balance due within four years. The Warsaw and Rockford Railroad project was revived. Its president, Col. H.W. Thorton came to town to drum up popular support. He gave specifics. What needed to be done was to raise only enough money to complete a roadbed along the line between Warsaw and Port Byron. Only twenty-seven miles, he said, was then being used. Just raise a subscription of $10,000 to push it to Oquawka Junction, he said. To complete the tracks to there, however, would require another $33,000 and still another $1,000 to run it up to Bald Bluff. Patterson was a booster. "Now we have an opportunity to aid a great work," he wrote.[46] Entrepreneurs re-opened the steamboat ferry across the Mississippi to compete with the CB&Q line going to Burlington. They stressed in their promotional blurbs that travelers west should recognize that the most direct line from Galesburg to Mt. Pleasant, Iowa was across the Mississippi on the ferry at Oquawka. The railroad, on the other hand, detoured over eighteen miles south out of the way. The ferry, moreover, was "in good repair and well manned."[47]

Retail business during the war prospered, especially at Oquawka, Gladstone, and Biggsville. The *Spectator* regularly featured pages of advertisements from merchants of all types. Physicians and druggists increased in number. Hotels did a thriving business. The best of the hostelries was the Eagle Hotel run by J.K. Barnes. It boasted a large, well-conducted reception and dining hall. It advertised for travelers the finest first class service, the choicest viands at its tables, and a secure stable and yard. Each morning and evening, as a regular courtesy to its customers, the Eagle House ran a hack, free of charge, to and from the railroad and boat dock for both travelers and baggage.[48] In late summer of 1861 E.M. Patterson bought out Sumner Phelps' entire business. He continued the Phelps' multi-service establishment of being a retailer, a banker and dealer in foreign exchanges, an agent of stock exchanges in New York, Boston, St. Louis and Chicago, and a travel agent who furnished passenger tickets for all American destinations as well as for embarkation to Liverpool, Antwerp, and LeHavre.[49]

Riverview, Oquawka

Social life flourished at home just as before. There was a large Odd Fellows lodge, established as Tranquil Lodge No. 193 at Oquawka in 1855, and a large Masonic Lodge No. 123 A.F.A.M. created in 1851. The county agricultural society, started in 1855 at Oquawka, sponsored its annual county fair at a site just southeast of town until 1867 when it was relocated more centrally to Biggsville. There, over the fourth of July during the war, farmers came to exhibit livestock and produce, and women showed their quilts and wares. An orchestra, made up mostly of German immigrants, provided on-going music. In 1862, the *Spectator* reported that several hundred people daily attended the fair. That year the crowd was addressed in German by Robert Stemple. He was "well received" by "fellow citizens native and foreign-born." Semple was followed by General Rose who elaborated on the duties of all citizens in the "present crisis." The third and final speaker that year was "a Catholic speaker from Macomb." After the ceremonies there was dancing, "waltzing," and "cheers for the Union." Refreshments were ice cream and the "Teutonic Beverage," nine kegs of beer. Patterson did note, though, that there was "not a drop of ardent spirits on the ground."[50]

The ethnic make up of the county fair was an indication of a new social development, the large increase of foreigners in the county. All townships in the census of 1860 registered at least 10 percent of its population as foreign born (Terre Houte was the sole exception with a figure of only 4 percent). In some places the concentration was significantly higher. In the town of Biggsville 31 percent were foreign born, with 28.6 percent from Ireland. In the township the figure was still high, 18 percent. In Gladstone Township 25 percent were foreigners, 18 percent from Ireland. And the village of Oquawka Junction (Gladstone) listed 50 percent foreigners with 33 percent Germans living there.[51] In Lomax Township 40 percent were

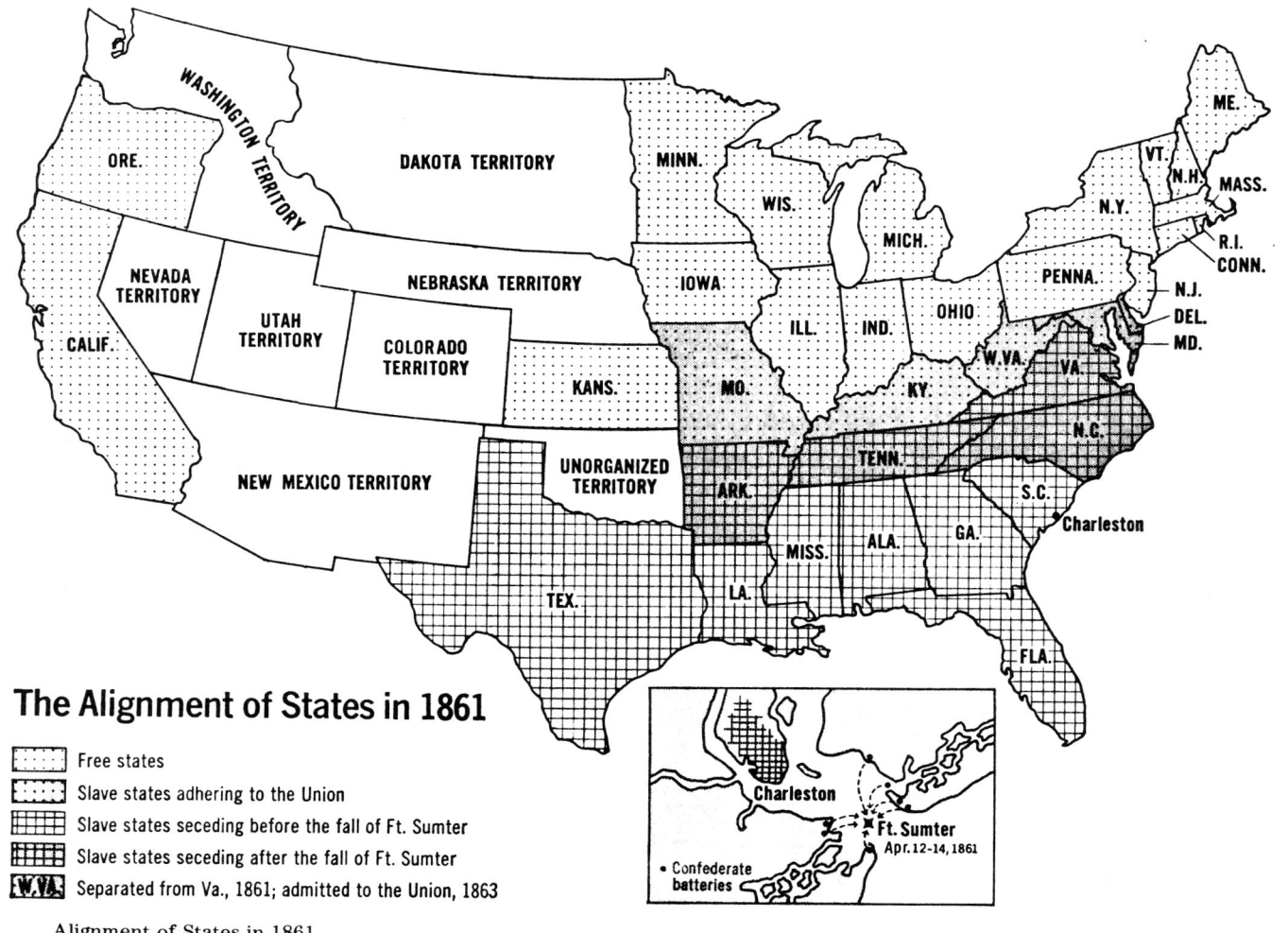

The Alignment of States in 1861

- Free states
- Slave states adhering to the Union
- Slave states seceding before the fall of Ft. Sumter
- Slave states seceding after the fall of Ft. Sumter
- W.VA. Separated from Va., 1861; admitted to the Union, 1863

Alignment of States in 1861

foreigners, 10 percent from Ireland. The town of Oquawka had 35 percent foreign born, with Germans outnumbering every other group at 8 percent. Indeed, the German presence in the Oquawka area translated itself into the building of a new school house there by "German citizens" whose purpose was to "be used for a German and English school." The Oquawka Germans, by the summer of 1860, had raised all but $75.00 needed by subscription among themselves to construct the new brick building.[52]

The large ethnic groups, surprisingly, had no impact on political life: most of the foreign born were unnaturalized and during the war were still unable to vote. The political questions, therefore, were cast entirely within the framework of the two major parties and focused on the conduct of and causes of the war itself. Most voters supported Lincoln in the 1860 election and that fact, coupled with the surge of emotional support for the President's stand on the secession crisis, meant little Democratic opposition within the county, at first. Almost all adult males, in other words the voters, were eager to back Lincoln in his goal of restoring the Union. Democratic Party activity was muffled and, if anything, deliberately unpartisan. For example, the party in September, 1861 quietly announced its convention at Monmouth to select nominees for county offices and to choose delegates to the party's state convention. There was talk among some Democrats of setting aside such routine party activities and to meet instead with Republicans in so-called "Union Conventions."[53] Nothing came of this novel idea, however.

Bipartisanship was short-lived in Henderson County. After the initial war enthusiasm disappeared in the aftermath of the crushing Union Army defeats at Bull Run in July, 1861, a strong anti-Lincoln movement began to shape up within the Democratic Party. It was known by a couple of labels, either the Knights of the Golden Circle, as they called themselves, or as Copperheads, as the Republicans branded them. By either label their aim from the start was to stop the war. In September, 1861, they announced their first county meeting. On the fifteenth they gathered at the home of Colonel Samuel Creswell to deliberate on the "distracted state of the country." They stated that the only hope for peace, and reconstruction of the Union, lay in what they called "democratic principles."[54] At the time this was a vague phrase but given subsequent activities, and rhetoric, of the Copperheads it was plain from the start that the phrase "democratic principles" meant voting Lincoln and his Republicans out of office.

Hardly had Lincoln's administration gotten started when, at the September gathering, men like John B. Junkin condemned "the efficiency of the present administration." They accused Lincoln of unconstitutional acts and condemned "the violation of the constitution no matter what the pretense for its violation might be."[55] They pointed out Lincoln's illegal conduct of the war when, on his own authority, he had called for enlistments not approved by Congress and when in Maryland he had suspended the writ of habeas corpus. More alarming still, that summer, military officers acting on presidential orders through the War Department, started to arrest civilians even suspected of disloyalty to the Union cause. Then the hapless men were incarcerated indefinitely in military prisons without trial. Lincoln tried to rationalize his acts by putting it this way in his July 4, 1861 Message to Congress: "Are all the laws but one to go unexecuted, and the government itself go to pieces, lest that one be violated?"[56]

Simply put, to Lincoln the end justified the means. He had no qualms in dealing harshly with what he called "the enemy in the rear." He labeled them the "most efficient corps of spies, informers, suppliers, and aiders and abettors" who took advantage of the First Amendment of the Bill of Rights to disrupt the war effort. Lincoln advised restraint. But his subordinates, especially Secretary of State Seward and Secretary of War Stanton, grossly abused their powers. The prize-winning biographer of Lincoln, Steven B. Oats, has observed on Seward that he was "convinced that treason lurked everywhere, in every bureau, post office, customs house, regiment, and ship of war." Seward, therefore, took "extraordinary steps to root out subversives." "He not only censored the telegraphs and the mails," Oates concluded, "but utilized government agents, United States marshals, Pinkerton's detectives, city police, and private informers to maintain surveillance of suspicious persons and to help arrest them."[57]

Signs of Copperhead activity increased. In January, 1862 the *Spectator* reported the growth of Confederate support in the southern part of the state where they were daring to "utter secession sentiments."[58] By that summer, some felt compelled to deny that there were in fact Copperheads in Henderson County. The *Spectator* rejected any assertion of "widespread Rebel support" and called such allegations merely "an assumed fact." "We believe," Patterson wrote on September 4, "the masses are loyal, that the party, if there be one, which will rejoice over the success of rebellion is small and utterly insignificant." There *were*

Abraham Lincoln

Copperheads in the county, however, and they saw themselves as standing alone against Lincoln's unconstitutional acts. And, throughout the war, Henderson County Copperheads were fighting at home for the Bill of Rights against the abuse of Presidential power. Others saw them as nothing more than Southern sympathizers and traitors.

The rise of Copperhead feeling in Henderson County coincided with a revived Democratic Party, but not revived enough to carry the general election in 1862. For the Fourth Congressional District, the Republican Charles M. Harris defeated Democrat H. Laurence by 170 to 137 votes and the Republican candidate for Congress at large, Allen, won the county by 156 to 154 votes. The sheriff's contest reflected an almost even balance with Republicans winning that office by only 159 to 154 votes. The vote breakdown by township returns, however, showed four precincts with overwhelming Democratic strength. In Biggsville, Gladstone (South Henderson), Rozetta (Greenville), and Walnut Grove (Media) not one Republican vote was cast for Charles M. Harris.[60]

By the following spring the Copperheads came out in the open, largely because of the Democratic revival in the previous fall elections. On March 14, 1863 there was a "Peace Meeting" at Bald Bluff where a few mild resolutions were adopted critical of the President. First, though they chose a leader, Captain William Morris, a veteran of the Mexican War, and agreed to meet again soon.[61] So, on March 28, at Bald Bluff, they reconvened, elected Percy Cooper chairman, and S.W. Lawrence secretary. They adopted another set of four resolutions. They resolved to support the government in all its *constitutional* efforts to suppress rebellion and take "uncompromising opposition to treason." The second resolution approved generally the "course of the present administration," whatever that meant. The third position cited Stephen Douglas' last speech at Chicago where he said that once war was declared there "should be only Patriots and Traitors." The fourth resolution was a lame gesture at reconciliation, an expression of their willingness to ignore all past party differences between Democrats and Republicans and "unite cordially with all men who are willing to unite in suppression of the unholy rebellion."[62]

Then the Copperheads became bolder. They reiterated their earlier opposition to the suspension of habeas corpus. Then for the first time, but not the last, they made the ugly charge of negrophilia. The Democrats, in April, 1863, labeled the Republicans, because of the Emancipation Proclamation, "abolitionists." They charged them with a secret plan to free the slaves and to pollute the white race. The Republicans were racial fanatics. Lincoln and his men, they said, endorsed "dogmas" of the "radical abolition party" that would "allow our state to be overrun with Americans of African descent in violation of our state constitution and state laws." Lincoln's Republicans did not really want to restore the Union as it was. "They must have slavery abolished first."[63] Lincoln was, simply, a liar in his statement that all he wanted was to restore the Union. The war, they said, was going to drag on with no end in sight. Why? Because "they want more of the lives of the people sacrificed on the altar of fanaticism, they want more war, more devastation and more bloodshed." Copperheads said that they were not traitors but, on the contrary, they were the true patriots who wanted reunion, reunion as it was—with slavery.[64]

Republicans hit out at the Copperheads as dangerous "secret societies." On April 23, 1863 an article was printed in the *Spectator* that called them a "secret cabal," an "oath-bound political society," and a "public danger." The danger lay in their influence on elections where "good men may be tabooed." The Copperheads retaliated. On May 14, Patterson, in a bitter article against the strongly biased Republican editor of the *Burlington Hawkeye*, came very close to embracing the most virulent Copperhead attacks. He denounced the Burlington paper for its "mawkish sensibility and morbid affection for the African race" and sarcastically blasted its concern for its "dearly beloved brethren of color." Then Patterson focused on the heart of the problem, Lincoln. "The war was entered into for the purpose of restoring the supremacy of the Government," he said. "Congress," Patterson believed, "declared this to be the sole object of the war" and that is why "loyal citizens" volunteered for Lincoln's army last spring. We were fighting, so he thought, for restoration of the Union and were not conducting "a raid upon the established institutions of any state," in other words to free the slaves in the South. He was more explicit in his feelings about slavery. "We care nothing for it per se if it stands in the way of the restoration of the Union." If it perished as "an incident of the war," fine. But freeing the slaves cannot be a war aim, he said. It cannot be "a condition of his support of the government that slavery be abolished in every state." Patterson concluded that he was "for the Union, for the war for its restoration, and was willing to let slavery take its chances."

By January, 1864 Patterson abandoned all pretext to political neutrality. He slapped on the masthead of the *Spectator* his new slogan: "The Union, the Constitution, and the Enforcement of the Laws." His goal, now, was to make common cause in the county for men dedicated to "the preservation of the Union and the integrity of the Constitution." He condemned the "Radical Party," the Republicans. He believed the ultimate preservation of the Union rested on the conservative principles of the Democratic Party in general and in particular in the victory of General George McClellan over Abraham Lincoln in the upcoming presidential election. If Lincoln won, he predicted, the war would be prolonged unnecessarily. The President had promised that he would not free the slaves, but he did. The Emancipation Proclamation had only served "to prolong the war by threatening to free the slaves and make the South dig in to the last man."

Besides, what would freeing the slaves really mean? Patterson felt it meant "freedom to die of loathsome diseases, to suffer or starve in contraband camps."[67]

Soon afterwards the rhetoric spilled over into action in a series of physical assaults. On February 4, 1864 an episode was reported in the *Spectator*. According to Patterson, returning veterans forced "several gentlemen from the country" to take a loyalty oath to the Union. Threatening letters had been sent from Oquawka "to certain citizens of town and country." One Copperhead was dragged into a store in Oquawka and almost beaten before he, too, swore loyalty. Patterson was appalled at the outrage.[68] In the days that followed as news of the assault spread, events turned ugly. One Sunday morning a mob of Copperheads converged on the town, unarmed. Fortunately, cooler heads prevailed. The "country people" selected a committee to meet with townsmen. A conference was held at the courthouse and a statement was accepted by "Democrats and Republicans." The resolution read that "while we are ready...to swear allegiance to the government of the United States, we oppose any attempt of individuals without authority to force any citizen to take the oath of allegiance...we discountenance any attempt on the part of soldiers ...to interfere with the liberty of any citizen of Henderson County...and will unite in arresting any or all persons."[69]

It did not work. The next day, some drunken Copperheads stopped a Lt. McKinney, home on furlough, on the road just south of of Warren. Initially they threatened to kill him. After about an hour, though, they let him go on the promise he would keep his mouth shut.[70] On March 15, 1864 at Young America (Kirkwood), just across the county line, soldiers ransacked the hotel kept by a local Democratic politician W.W. Gilmore. They found Gilmore himself hiding out in the kitchen and forced the petrified proprietor to give three cheers for Lincoln and the administration. Gilmore, after the soldiers left, reported what had happened to the local Justice of the Peace, a Mr. Vosburg, who replied that there was nothing to be done. "There was no law that could take hold of them," Gilmore was told, so "we would be obliged to let the soldiers do as they pleased." The end result was at least halfway satisfactory since Gilmore got the Lieutenant in charge of the soldiers to pay him for damages to his hotel.[71]

Two weeks later another group of soldiers attacked a Henderson County farmer from Ellison Creek. Samuel Wilcox had brought his load of grain into Young America and started home to his Media Township farm when three soldiers jumped him and beat him with a stone while onlookers shouted "kill him!" "shoot him!" One soldier pulled his revolver and shot at Wilcox, but the gun misfired. At that point three friends of poor Wilcox, who was almost unconscious, dragged him away and bandaged his head and face. Fortunately, too, a couple of Republicans were able to wrestle the pistol away from the soldier before he could get off another round. The Justice of the Peace, just as before, refused to do anything saying he "did not feel safe in doing so."[72]

At about the same time another gang of Union soldiers went on a rampage. Col. Samuel Hutchinson was attacked while attending, with his family, a funeral of a neighbor, Mr. McDougal. They surrounded the startled Hutchinson with drawn Bowie Knives and cursed him as a "damned Copperhead." They demanded the loyalty oath. He refused. One soldier yelled: "Make him take the oath or I'll blow his brains out!" Hutchinson took the oath.[73] Two other incidents were reported that spring. In late April, two soldiers went to a farm near Carman and forced Denver Johnson to swear loyalty to the Union. In early May the barn of another Democrat, Charles Short, was destroyed by arson.[74]

The tone of the rhetoric kept pace with the spread of violence throughout the winter, spring, and summer of 1864. At a Republican party meeting in February a crowd, cheering for President Lincoln, resolved to suppress the Copperheads or the "country people" as they were called.[75] The Copperheads, countered. The way things were going, they lamented, the time will soon come when the Dred Scott decision will be reversed and the whites will have to contend for equal treatment by the blacks. Then, "a white men, if he behaves himself is as good almost as an American citizen of African descent."[76] The country, they said, needed a President who would run the affairs of the nation "on a white basis." The Republicans were blind on the Negro question and were drifting to a policy "where the blood of the races shall mingle together and be balanced through the social alchemy of the higher civilization induced by Abolitionism." "They do not appear to recognize the stubborn and repulsive fact which it implies, a leveling down of the white race to the capacity of Negroes by conferring upon the latter social and political equality with the former."[77] Democrats must act immediately to avoid this disaster; they must organize precinct clubs and get ready to launch their county campaign to overthrow Republicans who plan "a revolution in our social ethics which shall admit the Negro to equal political rights and social privileges with the white man." "Let Democrats organize and fight these heresies...." Let the rallying cry be: "The Union, the Constitution, and the Enforcement of the Laws!"[78]

By the summer of 1864 the *Spectator* was shrill. "The Issue Is Made Up" it announced. Lincoln represented "the shoddism, the corruption, the official thieves and contractors, national humiliation...and a gross usurpation of power." The Republican Radicals were "rotten on the Negro question." The Democrats stood for "Union, the Constitution, and the Laws," and were "firm, dignified, and independent." They were made up of "the conservative masses, the sturdy yeomanry of the land...."[79] Republicans tried a new line of argument by late summer. Lincoln must be kept in office, they reasoned, until the war was over, until he could be really the President of the United States. Democrats rebutted that one cannot equate Lincoln with the government. Prophetically, it posed the question: "Suppose that Mr. Lincoln should be re-elected and then die within a month after his inauguration leaving the war still in progress?" Then what? Then it would be "even worse" since the (Vice President) Hamlin is out and a former secessionist (Andrew Johnson) is in his place."[80]

The campaign came down to the last few weeks. By late September, Democrats counted over 2,000 people at their rally at Reed Church on the Monmouth road. At Oquawka a McClellan Club was in full operation, holding another rally on October 17 at the Courthouse where Patterson spoke for McClellan's qualifications to bring the "rebellious states back into the Union one by one." The choice, he said, was between McClellan and peace and Lincoln and "war, war, war and yet no Union."[81]

The Republicans won the county. Lincoln received 2,110 to McClellan's 377 votes. This time, only Raritan Township (by 107 to eighty) and Stronghurst Township (seventy to sixty) supported McClellan. Democrat candidate for Congress, Charles M. Harris also carried Raritan and

Stronghurst (seventy-six to fifty-eight) as well as Lomax (seventy-seven to seventy-four) over his Republican opponent Albert C. Harding who received a county-wide majority. The Democrats, though, protested that Harris would have won the county had not "about 2,000 soldiers [been] sent home to vote against him while the Democratic soldiers were left in the field...."[82] In the Senatorial race, the Democrat Henry K. Pfler won Raritan (107 to eighty), Stronghurst (seventy-four to sixty), and Lomax (seventy-six to seventy-five). The Republican, though, James Strain, carried the county by 1,209 to 819. On November 17 Patterson conceded defeat. "We cannot look upon this result in any other light than a disaster."[83]

Whether or not the Henderson County adult males gave their full support to Lincoln and the war the young men who volunteered and then reenlisted, or "reteraned" as it was called, bore their share of the fighting.[84] A total of nine military units were sent from the county, eight of them infantry regiments. The Tenth was made up in Oquawka in April, 1861 of some thirty-eight men. They went first to Camp Butler at Springfield but really did not fully organize until they became part of General Prentis' brigade at Quincy that summer. Then they shipped on to Cairo. After a short time of routine patrol and guard duty they reorganized for a three-year enlistment in August, 1861 and they were joined at Cairo by more Henderson Volunteers raised by Charles S. Cowan that summer.[85] The Sixteenth was put together in August, 1861 after the Union fiasco at Bull Run when Governor Yates was asked to provide Lincoln with thirteen more Illinois regiments for what was recognized by then as a long, bloody struggle.

Company F of the Sixteenth was raised spontaneously in the early fall of 1861 without any individual recruitment efforts and went to Quincy by rail from Galesburg. After some encounters in Missouri in the spring of 1862 the Sixteenth joined with the Tenth in major Union movements into Kentucky and Tennessee. They first saw action in April, 1862 under General Pope at New Madrid. Then they fought together in the siege of the Confederate stronghold at Corinth, Mississippi, in May. In July they engaged the Confederates farther south at Booneville enroute to the major battles at Nashville and Chattanooga. In 1864 they marched with Sherman through Georgia.

The summer of 1861 saw the Blackhawk Cavalry organized in part at Oquawka by merchant T.W. Kinsloe aided by John Pence and William Morris. Sixty-nine men joined this Seventh Missouri Cavalry. They experienced combat in the West, at Macon, Missouri in February, 1862 then went on to Independence where they fought a bloody skirmish with over 800 of Quantrell's Raiders. That fall the Blackhawk Cavalry rode into Arkansas and took the capital of Little Rock, finally, in August, 1863. The next fall, at St. Louis, the cavalry was mustered out.

Another Henderson County group of volunteers, the Fifty-ninth was for a time integrated into a Missouri unit. Containing twenty men from the county it was sent in 1861 to St. Louis as a part of that state's Ninth Infantry Regiment. There it performed guard duty in the city and in the Cape Girardeau area. Action came, though, in early 1862 when they were transferred into the regular United States Army and, like other county regiments, were tested under General Sherman in the vicious confrontations at Murfreesboro, Chattanooga, and Atlanta.

In the summer and fall of 1862 a second batch of volunteers was put together in the county. Four regiments were raised in August — the Twenty-eighth, Eighty-third, Eighty-fourth, and 118th—and one more in September, the Ninety-first. The Twenty-eighth included thirty men from Henderson County and, compared to other units, saw little fighting during the war. It was shipped downriver from Cairo to New Orleans and participated in the taking of Mobile. The Eighty-third was pulled together at Monmouth in August and went to St. Louis. Between the fall of 1862 and August, 1863 it was stationed on the Cumberland and Tennessee Rivers where, in February, it took part in the first major Union victory of the war, the siege of Ft. Donalson under Grant. From then on it was assigned to patrol and guard duty along the tenuous Union line of communication stretching southward into Tennessee from Paducah, Kentucky.

The Eighty-fourth had more men in it from Henderson County than any other regiment.[86] Volunteers were initially sent to Camp Butler in late August, 1862 but soon, like other regiments, it was fully organized at Quincy. Two towns, Oquawka and Biggsville, competed in signing up its new recruits. Company G mustered in at the Courthouse on July 28 and marched out, in a burst of fanfare, to board the troop train for Quincy at Gladstone. Company K of 100 men was signed up at Biggsville. They, too, went by rail to Quincy at about the same time. Both companies were drilling there by August 12, 1862. In September, they moved into Kentucky where, under General Buell they doggedly pursued Confederate General Bragg, in grueling forced marches, throughout the winter. In sleet, cold rain, without shelter or clothing, they walked with bloody feet in the snow.[87] By the summer of 1863 they had moved into Nashville under living conditions so severe that by then only 400 of the 851 men who had left Quincy were still combat ready, hardly prepared for the bloody encounter at the Battle of Murfreesboro in December of that year.

Civil War Monument, Oquawka

The last regiment organized in the summer of 1862 was the 118th. Made up entirely of ninety eight men from Terre Haute Township, it represented the most important contribution of the southern part of the county to that recruitment drive. It went from Quincy to Memphis and by November was with General Sherman at the siege of Vicksburg (between January and April, 1863.) It too, like the Eighty-fourth, was decimated by disease. The last year of the war saw the 118th in the lower Mississippi, in engagements at Baton Rouge and then in the occupation, under General "Beast" Ben Butler, of New Orleans.

The last regiment from Henderson County was put together in September 1862. The Ninety-first, with thirty-six men from the southern townships, mainly Raritan, mustered at Oquawka and, like the others, moved out right away to Quincy. There they were shipped to St. Louis and by October were at Louisville. In 1863 they joined the 118th, the "Terre Haute Boys," at New Orleans but, unlike them, the Ninety-fourth was sent on to further combat at Brownsville, Texas, and Brazos Santiago. They were discharged at Mobile in July, 1865.

Although Henderson County volunteers fought at most battles in the western theater, many of them saw combat in the three decisive campaigns into the southern heartland, namely at the Murfreesboro, Chattanooga, and Atlanta. Four of the nine regiments from the county fought at these major engagements under General Sherman from December, 1862 through the fall of 1864. They were the Tenth, Sixteenth, Fifty-ninth, and Eighty-fourth.

Powder Flasks

The Battle of Murfreesboro (also called the Battle of Stones River) started on December 20, 1862 when the Union army under General Rosecrans moved south on the turnpike from Nashville. Rosecrans knew little about the terrain or exactly where he was headed, except to Chattanooga. During the first day's march intelligence reached Rosecrans, still in Nashville, about a concentration of Confederate troops on the road some thirty miles south of town. There, information further showed, the Confederate commander, General Bragg, had dug in along Stones River to stop the Union advance before it became better organized. Bragg wanted to break Rosecrans' line of communication with Nashville and pin him up against the river. Rosecrans decided on the same plan in reverse, namely to pin the Confederate force against Stones River, if he could.

Because of Rosecrans' delay in mounting an attack Bragg struck first on December 31. At dawn he hit the Union position on its right flank where the Henderson County regiments were deployed. By mid-day Confederate cavalry, under General Hardee, had moved around the Union position and had started to roll them back. The left flank of the Union army, which had pushed off to attack Major General Breckinridge's Confederate units north of Stones River, was also pulled back. Fortunately, the Union center lines held tightly against General Polk's frontal assaults. On their right, though, stragglers, some running in panic from General Hardee's pounding, fled across the Nashville Turnpike. The Union line finally drew up behind Maj. General Crittenden on the north side of the turnpike.

That night, Rosecrans consulted with his officers. Some advised immediate retreat to Nashville. Most of his staff, though, vetoed the idea. On January 1, 1863 nothing happened. On January 2, the Confederates attacked on the right again but a massed Union battery shattered their assault lines. The next day Bragg withdrew. The battle was, in the opinion of military historians, a draw; but Bragg's unexplainable reluctance to continue the fight after just one artillery rebuff gave the Union army the road to Chattanooga.[88] The effect on the Federal troops, however, was severe. They were so badly wounded that Rosecrans would not order another advance for six months. Yet, as one authority has put it, "more than most other battles of the war, Stones River was a conflict between the wills of the opposing army leaders." "Rosecrans," it is agreed, "would not admit himself beaten and in the end won a victory of sorts."[89]

By July, 1863, though, the Union army continued its advance on Chattanooga out of Murfreesboro. Chattanooga was one of the most vital transportation centers of the entire South, the hub of a rail network linking Richmond, the Confederate Capitol in Virginia, with Memphis, on the Mississippi River. Also at Chattanooga, the Tennessee River cut through the Smokey Mountains and made the only natural water link between Tennessee and Kentucky and the Cotton States to the South. Chattanooga, from a strategic consideration, was critical to the Confederacy's survival. If the Union troops held the town they, from there, could go on to attack Atlanta and Savannah or hit at the Carolinas to the north and, ultimately, Richmond itself. Lincoln told Rosecrans that spring that if he could get and hold Chattanooga it would kill the rebellion.

By September 18, 1863 Bragg had drawn up his Confederate defenses east of Chickamauga Creek (meaning, in Cherokee, River of Death) some five miles south of Chattanooga on the road from that town leading to LaFayette. Rosecrans then ordered an immediate concentration of all federal toops along the ridge of the Cumberland Mountains, overlooking

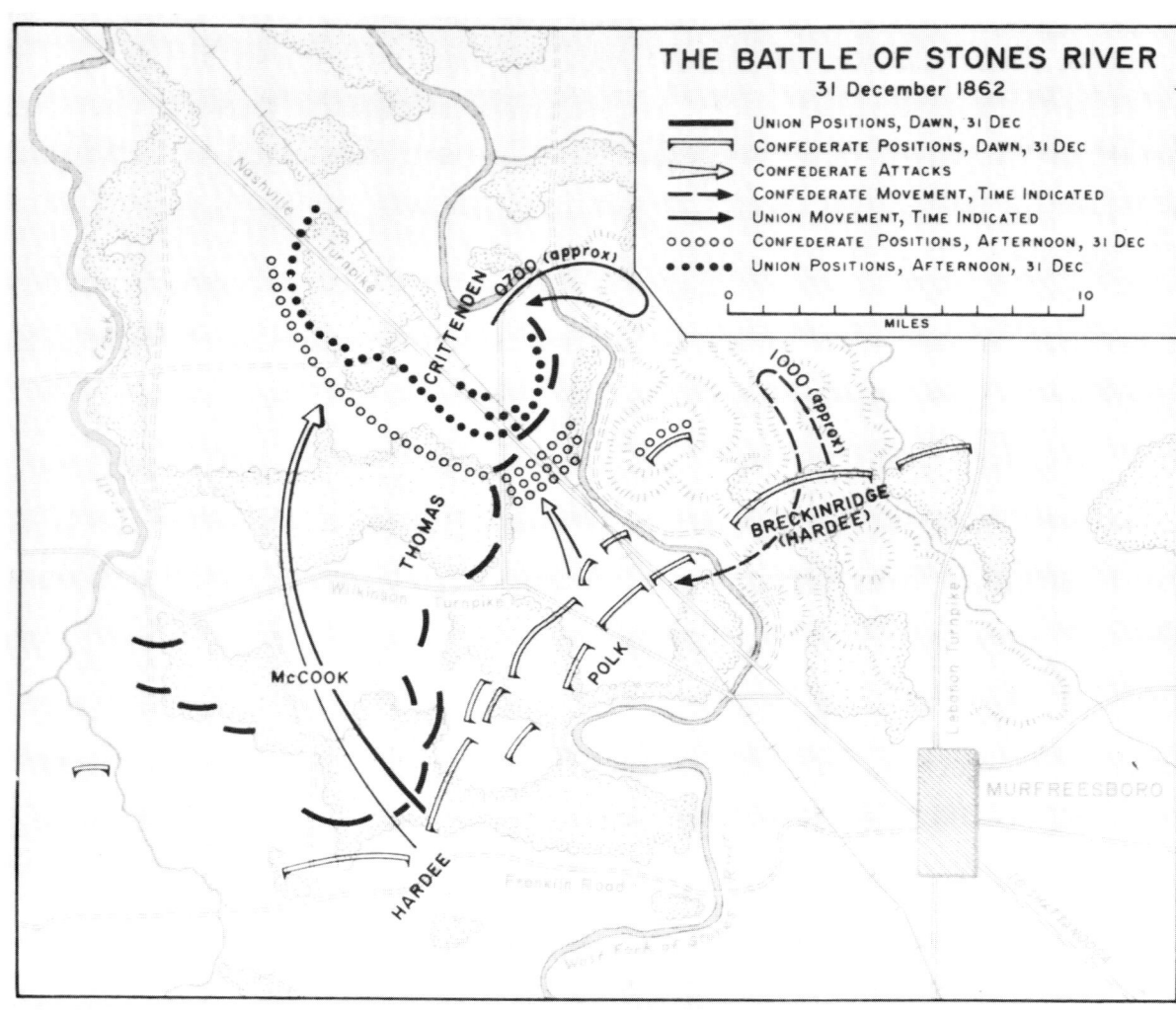

The Battle of Stones River

the town and the Tennessee River, in three columns. First contacts were made east of the Chickamauga on September 19 and the next morning at nine o'clock Rosecrans ordered a full assault against Bragg's line. Confused field communications among Union officers caused a serious break in the Union center line and the Confederate field commander, General Longstreet, drove through it. Rosecrans sounded retreat north into Chattanooga itself.

Rosecrans lost one third of his army that day at Chickamauga, some 15,851 troops, and an indefinite number of arms and ammunition. Bragg's generals wanted to pursue Rosecrans and capture Chattanooga but he refused. Nevertheless, by late September, after Rosecrans' retreat, the Confederates had the Union army bottled up in a trap inside the city supported only by one thin line of communication, a single railroad, to their supply base at Nashville. Bragg deployed his troops, looking straight down on the Union forces, atop Lookout Mountain and Missionary Ridge.

The Union army at Chattanooga was in a mess. On one side was the Tennessee River. On the other side were Braggs troops peering down from 3,000 feet along the mountains. Rosecrans' line of communication north was by then cut off. By October rations ran out. Men went hungry. Horses and mules starved to death.

Finally, Lincoln woke up to the dreadful situation and ordered 20,000 men under General Hooker from the Army of the Potomac, then some 1,500 miles away by railroad, to help out. Next, Lincoln replaced Rosecrans (whom he said after Chickamauga acted "like a duck hit on the head") with Grant, sitting at Louisville, as commander of the Military Division of the Mississippi. For some unknown reason, at this critical juncture, Bragg reduced his forces by over 40,000 men and he sent them off under Longstreet to take a stand against a Union corp under General Burnside at Knoxville. By this time Confederate commanders on the mountain ridges overlooking Chattanooga had become lackadaisical. Most officers just assumed that the Federal troops were already their prisoners.

Grant arrived.[90] He estimated his command at over 60,000 troops and took the offensive with his entire army. Union troops hit both ends of the Confederate line simultaneously, one at Lookout Moutain on the south, the other at Missionary Ridge on the east. Grant's troops, under Hooker, rushed up Lookout Mountain on November 24 and the Confederate positions disintegrated. Missionary Ridge fell. Bragg, surprised and bewildered, retreated into Georgia. The Battle of Chattanooga, unlike Murfreesboro, was an unequivocal Union victory. Bragg's defeat was complete. The Confederacy in one battle had lost both Kentucky and Tennessee and the North now controlled the railroad center at Chattanooga. Now all the Lower South, for the first time, was open to Federal troops.

Ulysses S. Grant

Grant, after his victory, wrote to Lincoln telling him what should be done next. The General asked for an assault on the Confederate port at Mobile and, at the same time, right away in fact, a spring offensive through Georgia. Although Lincoln did not buy all the details of Grant's plan he was impressed with his intelligence, ability, and most of all, his eagerness to fight. On March 9, 1864 he ordered Grant to Washington and promoted him to Lieutenant General in full command of the Western Union Army, reporting directly to the President himself, not to the Secretary of War. By mid-April, Grant issued detailed orders to his successor at Chattanooga, William T. Sherman. He told Sherman to take 100,000 men and march to Atlanta. Grant ordered Sherman to annihilate any Confederate military opposition and if necessary to devastate the natural resources of the state of Georgia. So, on May 4, 1864 Sherman began his "great wheel to the East." Men from Henderson county, still able, marched with him to the sea.[91]

By the time General Joseph E. Johnston took over the Confederate command from Bragg in the spring of 1864 he knew he was outnumbered. The only strategy, in Johnston's mind, was to delay so that he could hold Atlanta until after the fall presidential election. The hope was the North, by then, would have grown so weary of the fight, and so fed up with Lincoln, that the Democratic candidate, McClellan, would be elected and sue for peace with the Confederacy. So, as Sherman marched south there were continuous skirmishes and firefights. From May to July they fought. First contacts were at Dalton, Georgia, on May 14; then at Resaca, Cassville, Cartersville, and Kenesaw.

By July 4 though Sherman was within five miles of Atlanta. Throughout the month he established a curve of fortifications around the city, completing the circle by the first of September. By that time, Confederate

General John B. Hood, who had replaced Johnston in July, quit. Hood pulled out of Atlanta to northwest Alabama. Defenseless, Atlanta surrendered the next day. The timely fall of Atlanta, most historians agree, changed the course of the war. Victory here gave Lincoln his victory in the November elections and this, along with Admiral Farragut's capture of Mobile Bay in August, provided the North with the determination to continue the war to the ultimate defeat of the South.

Atlanta, however, was only a half-way point in Sherman's strategy of ending the war. He telegraphed his plan to Grant in early September. Sherman wanted first to send troops back north under General Thomas to secure Nashville as a supply depot in case Hood moved out of Alabama. Sherman himself would take 62,000 men and march to the sea, cutting a sixty-mile wide path of scorched earth destruction on the way. Grant approved the strategy. Before Sherman left Atlanta, he burned it. The Henderson County regiments which, thus far, had fought together from Nashville to Atlanta were split. Two regiments, the Fifty-ninth and Eighty-fourth, went with Thomas to Nashville. The other two, the Tenth and Sixteenth, marched with Sherman.

Sherman evacuated what was left of Atlanta on October 17, 1864. On November 12 he broke off all telegraph contact with Grant. He had only twenty days emergency rations for his entire army. Sherman's men would live off of the land. They took what they needed and burned what they did not. "It was the sort of war soldiers love," wrote Harvard historian Samuel Eliot Morison. It was a combination of looting, destruction, no discipline, and almost no fighting. The weather was great, the food excellent. The song on the campaign went:

"Hurrah! Hurrah! we bring the jubilee!
Hurrah! Hurrah! the flag that makes you free!
So we sang the chorus from Atlanta to the sea,
While we were marching through Georiga."[92]

On December 10, 1864 Sherman's army reappeared at the edge of Savannah. On December 21, all Confederate forces evacuated the port by sea. Sherman gave the city to President Lincoln as a Christmas present. Then he himself left by boat to join Grant on the final campaign against Lee at Richmond.

In the meantime, while Sherman was out of sight somewhere in Georgia, the only news was that of Thomas' defense of Nashville. As feared, General Hood moved northward but at a bloody fight at Franklin, Tennessee, Union troops, under Major General Schofield, stopped their advance. Hood, after the Battle of Franklin, was in no condition to take on Thomas, by then behind his defenses at Nashville. Thomas, on the other hand, fully aware of Hood's weakened army, planned to wipe him out. On December 18, 1864 Thomas started a flawless sledgehammer attack that, with both cavalry and artillery, drove Hood into a rout. Broken, shattered, and confused Confederate infantrymen ran southward and were pursued by Union cavalry. What was left of Hood's troops dragged themselves into Tupelo, Mississippi in early January, 1865. "It no longer existed as an effective fighting force," Maurice Matloff observed, "Hood was relieved of command...the decisive battle of Nashville had eliminated one of the two great armies of the Confederacy...."[93]

Behind the lines, between the battles, the Henderson volunteers were, after the terrible first winter of exposure in Kentucky, reasonably well-equipped and fed. They were provided muzzle-loading, smooth-bore rifles, adequate ammunition, and appropriate food and clothing. Morale in the beginning was high. A full send-off at Oquawka included in addition to the Brass Band and a parade march to the Junction, a bonus of $100, $25 of which was paid when the regiments organized at Quincy.[94] The troops elected their own officers.[95] Camp life, judged by letters received back home, was comfortable. One soldier, T.O. Memphis, wrote from Mound City in October, 1861 that he was living cozily in an immense brick building. The food was in "over supply," so much so that he could exchange his rations for better fare with farmers nearby. A typical supper consisted of "fine-flour bread, fresh beef, rice, sweet potatoes, butter, honey, coffee & tea," with an occasional "home cake or a jelly."[96] They complained of boredom. One soldier wrote of "plenty to eat and nothing to do but play soldier."[97] They grumbled about "long, excruciatingly muddy" marches into Kentucky, and about being "hungry, thirsty, disagreeable" in January of 1862. We "began to think that the dull routine of camp had passed," but it had not.[98]

A serious problem, however, was sickness. It took an appalling toll. The average soldier came down with some illness about every four months and death from disease during the war was two times greater than from combat. Multiple problems created perpetual sickness. Always somebody was incapacitated. There was poor or no sanitation and bad water. No baths or even washing of hands and face — sheer dirtyness — led to epidemics of dysentery, malaria, typhoid, and the "ague" (most likely the flu). Nursing was non-existent where the Henderson County men were and, of course, there were no hospitals except crude field shelters where the sick and wounded were cared for by military physicians.

"The Walking Wounded", by Winslow Homer *Harper's Weekly*, 1861

God alone helped the wounded, though. Most were left for days lying on the battlefield before anyone picked them up. Anesthetics were known but often not available. Antisepsis was unheard of. Under such conditions most wounds meant death from blood loss, shock, and infection. There are no figures from the three Tennessee - Georgia campaigns but the ones from the Army of the Potomac are reliable indicators of the state of medical care. There, in 1862, half of the amputatees died. Outside observers left appalling accounts. One Union hospital transport had "men in every condition of horror, shattered, and shrieking ... dumped anywhere ... walked over without compassion ... shoveled into top berths without thought of mercy ... without food for three days ... nothing (done) for them."[99]

Reaction back in Oquawka to the progress of the fighting, or the lack of progress, was surprisingly compliant. Casualty lists were not reported in any regularity. They were just a few lines on page two of the *Spectator* among items of routine local interest — equivalent to being stuck in the classified ad section of today's newspaper. The exact location and cause of the casualty was entirely missing or oblique. Such lines as "we are sorry to learn from ... that so-and-so was killed in making a charge upon the enemy works at Atlanta." Or the notice read just "killed" followed by names. None of the information was official, only news gleaned from whatever letters made their way back to the county.

As the war dragged on parents and friends became stoical. Perhaps, in part, this attitude was a reflection of not being fully aware of the casualties or the deplorable conditions under which the wounded and the sick had to live. It also was a result of a tunnel vision of the war itself. Readers of the *Spectator* were concerned only with those campaigns in which their relatives served. There was, for example, just the barest account of McClellan's frustratingly indecisive Peninsula Campaign of 1862. There was no news of the awful Union losses at Fredricksburg, Antietam, or Gettysburg. Even those battles in which Henderson County regiments took part were described laconically. After Murfreesboro, Patterson wrote that the "losses in our companies" were "light," though he mourned the "loss of Samuel Plummer and the others who have fallen."[100] On Sherman's march from Atlanta, Patterson said that he hoped that Sherman "will certainly do whatever is in his power to cripple the rebellion." He expressed the trust that a policy of "desolation" of "burning houses and towns" was not "any part of Sherman's program."[101]

When Grant launched his drive to Richmond on May 4, 1864 the *Spectator* lamented that the "red arm of war again has been bared" in the "terrible fighting, dreadful slaughter" in the Wilderness of Virginia. But this time, Patterson felt, the end was near. He believed it "impossible that Grant should be unsuccessful." The "capture of Lee's Army," he predicted, was "inevitable."[102] It dragged on another year, however. Finally, on April 6, 1865 the *Spectator* announced: "RICHMOND IS OURS!"[103] "The war is virtually at an end," Patterson wrote. Seven days later came the news of Lee's surrender at Appomattox Court House. But, on April 8, a Union officer had written to the mother of Alanzo Curry at Raritan that your "son was killed by a rifle bullet on the skirmish line." "A ball fired by a rebel sharpshooter struck him in the forehead just above the eye...passed through the head and brain." Faithful to gruesome detail, the letter went on to tell Mrs. Curry that "the ball did not kill him instantly as one would naturally suppose for he lived until dark, nearly seven hours after he was struck." "He was washed and neatly dressed and buried today," wrote the officer, and "a board properly marked designates the place where lies his remains."[104]

On April 20, 1865 the *Spectator* announced "Abraham Lincoln is Dead." Patterson wrote that his "death has deprived the nation of its chosen chief magistrate at a time when all men should have earnestly desired his life to be spared." He deplored the "horrid crime" of assassination. Lincoln's death "at this juncture", he said, "will prove a national calamity." Patterson concluded: "The war is over."[105]

END NOTES FOR CHAPTER THREE

[1] For a readable and accurate modern appraisal of the coming of the Civil War and Lincoln's role in the crisis see Stephen B. Oates, *With Malice Toward None the Life of Abraham Lincoln* (New York, 1977).
[2] Roy P. Basler, ed., *The Collected Works of Abraham Lincoln* (New Brunswick, N.J., 1953) Vol. 2, pp 461-69. See also Oates, *Lincoln*, p. 292.
[3] Howard, *Illinois* p. 292.
[4] Oates, *Lincoln*, pp 138-39, 144, 151, 177-79.
[5] Oquawka *Spectator*, October 4, 1858. See also an account of the visits in "Lost History of Oquawka" Henderson County *Quill*, January 29, February 5, 1975.
[6] Ibid., October 11, 1858.
[7] Ibid., 1858-1860, passim.
[8] Ibid., May 17, 1860.
[9] Ibid.

[10] Ibid., July 4, 1860.
[11] Ibid.
[12] Ibid.
[13] Ibid.
[14] Ibid., July 26, 1860.
[15] Ibid., August 11, 1860.
[16] Ibid., August 30, 1860.
[17] Ibid., September 27, 1860.
[18] Ibid., November 1, 1860.
[19] Ibid., November 8, 1860.
[20] Ibid.
[21] Ibid.
[22] Ibid.
[23] Ibid., December 7, 1860.
[24] Ibid., December 20, 1860.
[25] Ibid., December 27, 1860.
[26] Ibid., January 10, 1861.
[27] Ibid., February 14, 1861. See also *Works*, IV, pp 190-249.
[28] *Works*, IV, pp 194-196, 199.
[29] Ibid.
[30] *Spectator*, March 4, 1861.
[31] *Works*, IV, pp 265-66.
[32] Ibid.
[33] Ibid., p 271.
[34] *Spectator*, March 14, 1864.
[35] Ibid.
[36] Ibid., April 11, 1861.
[37] Ibid.
[38] *Works*, IV, pp 33-32
[39] *Spectator*, April 18, 1861.
[40] Ibid., April 25, 1861.
[41] Ibid., May 2, June 3, 1861.
[42] Ibid., April 25, 1861.
[43] Samuel Eliot Morison, Henry Steele Commager and William B. Leuchtenburg. *The Growth of the American Republic* (New York, 1969) Vol. I, p 676.
[44] *Spectator*, August 30, 1860 contains population and agricultural census data for the county for 1850 and 1860.
[45] *Spectator*, April 19, 1860.
[46] *Spectator*, February 14, 1861. See also *Spectator* January 28, 1864 on subsequent activities of the railroad during wartime.
[47] Ibid., March 22, 1860.
[48] See regular advertisements for the Eagle in the *Spectator*, summer 1861, passim.
[49] Ibid., August 29, 1861.
[50] Ibid., July 3, 1862.
[51] United States Census, Population Schedules, Henderson County, 1860.
[52] *Spectator*, August 11, 1860.
[53] Ibid., September 2, 1861.
[54] Ibid., and September 15, 1861.
[55] Ibid.
[56] *Works* Vol. 4, pp 421-41.
[57] Oates, *Lincoln*, p. 254.
[58] *Spectator*, January 20, 1862.
[59] Ibid., September 4, 1862.
[60] Ibid., October 2, 1862.
[61] Ibid., March 19, 1863.

62 Ibid., April 2, 1863.
63 Ibid.
64 Ibid.
65 Ibid., April 23, 1863.
66 Ibid., May 14, 1863.
67 Ibid., January 7, 21, 1864.
68 Ibid., February 4, 1864.
69 Ibid.
70 Ibid.
71 Ibid., March 31, 1864.
72 Ibid.
73 Ibid.
74 Ibid., May 14, 1864.
75 Ibid., February 11, 1864.
76 Ibid., February 18, 1864.
77 Ibid., February 25, 1864.
78 Ibid.
79 Ibid., June 9, 1864.
80 Ibid., September 1, 1864.
81 Ibid., October 21, 1864.
82 Ibid., November 17, 1864.
83 Ibid.
84 Details of military records of Henderson County units are found both in Shepard & Johnson's *History of Henderson County*, scattered throughout their township sketches, and in Gordon's *History*, volumne II of *Historical Encyclopedia of Illinois*, chapter eleven.
85 For accounts of recruiting in the county see *Spectator,* April 25; May 2, 16, 23; June 6, 1861.
86 See the history of Company K of the Eighty-fourth Infantry in *Henderson County Graphic Reporter,* May 28, April 10, 1969.
87 *Spectator,* October 19, 1861; January 31, February 18, May 26, 1862.
88 Ibid., January 15, 22, 1863. See also "Battle of Stone's River." *Henderson County Graphic Reporter* March 21, 1968.
89 Maurice Matlott, ed., *American Military History* (Washington, D.C., 1969) p 219. See also Gordon, *History,* pp 671-76 for further details of the battle.
90 The reinforcement of Rosecrans, by 17,000 Federal troops sent up the Tennessee River under General Sherman, began in late September. By October 26, 1863 General Hooker, on orders from Grant, fought his way into the city across the Tennessee at Bridgeport and reopened the supply line to Grant. For details of the relief of Rosecrans Army of the Cumberland see Matlott, *American Military History,* pp 258-60.
91 Gordon, *History,* pp 677-79.
92 Morison & Comager, Leuchtenburg, *American Republic* V.I., p 703.
93 Matlott, *American Military History,* p 275.
94 *Spectator,* April 25, May 6, 1861.
95 Ibid., May 2, 1861.
96 Ibid., October 19, 1861.
97 Ibid., May 23, 1861.
98 Ibid., April 13, 1862.
99 Morison & Commager, Leuchtenburg, *American Republic* V.I., p 636.
100 *Spectator,* January 15, 1863.
101 Ibid., November 12, 1864.
102 Ibid., May 12, 1864.
103 Ibid., April 6, 1865.
104 Ibid., May 18, 1865.
105 Ibid., April 20, 1865.

CHAPTER FOUR
GOLDEN YEARS, 1865-1900

The decades after the Civil War were the golden years of Henderson County. These were the times when the dreams of the early settlers became a way of life for the farmers and merchants of the post war era. Between 1860 and 1865, except for the labor drain of young volunteers for the army, the county experienced continued economic growth. Politically, the war did cause some disruption. No doubt the isolated acts of furloughed veterans on the Copperheads and the heated comments of the *Spectator* were dramatic. But during the last three decades of the nineteenth century life settled in — it stabilized. The changes that were then at work in the nation--the building of great urban centers, the growing demands of new heavy industry, the modernization of agriculture, the Republicanization of American politics--all were seen in and had beneficial effects on the county. So, between 1865 and 1900, Henderson County was in many ways a flourishing microcosm of the nation itself. The life processes of the entire body politic, as usual, were the same as those of its component cells, and vice versa.

Anyone surveying the history of the United States in the last half of the nineteenth century is impressed with its enormous growth. By 1890, the population had increased two and a half times. Railroads expanded and railroad corporations, with land donated by Federal and state governments, built towns. The towns, in turn, became marketing lines to burgeoning cities. Other new enterprises, located in the major cities, transformed the national economy from agrarian to industrial and at the same time started to monopolize the production of basic goods. By 1900, huge monopolies, called trusts, determined what the average American paid for his fuel, clothing, glass, sugar, and tobacco.

Farm machinery from the urban factories replaced human labor. By the 1890s machines could harvest eighteen times as much wheat, for example, as a farmer with hand tools could gather up in 1840.[1] The small farmer who produced only for himself and the local towns disappeared and farmers grew crops which were sold for cash in distant urban markets. Put simply, agriculture became a business. Editors of rural magazines advised: "Watch and study the markets and the ways of marketmen...learn the art of selling well." Others cautioned that "the work of farming is only half done when the crop is out of the ground."[2] By 1900 the change had brought with it a price, literally. Farm machinery was expensive and most men had to borrow to purchase it and borrow to repair it. So, after 1880 farm mortgage indebtness increased two and one-half times faster than farm wealth.

Growth and change in Henderson County was reflected in its census figures.[3] Extant manuscripts on townships and towns for the years 1860 and 1870 reveal steady population growth. The total number of people in the county in 1860 was 9,501; by 1870 it was 12,582. The adult males outnumbered females three to two in 1860. By 1870 the ratio had changed little although the total number of adults in the county had gone up from 4,624 to 5,368. The most interesting demographic change was the movement from the farms into the towns, and added to this trend were the appearance of the railroad towns of Stronghurst, Media, and Lomax. In 1860, there were 782 adult males and 498 adult women living in five

Opposite: Lynch Barn, north of Raritan

Gaelic Greeting: One Hundred Thousand Welcomes

county towns, or a 1,280 total. Of that number 88.5 percent lived in Oquawka; 680 of the 782 adult males and 452 of the 498 women. By 1870, the number of towns had doubled. And their adult population had grown 13 percent to 1,464. Only Oquawka showed a collapse. Its adult population went from 88.5 percent to only 40 percent of the county's population in just ten years. Even more precipitous was the disappearance of that town's adult labor force. If fell from 680 to 309. In ratio terms, in 1860 Oquawka had 87 percent of the county's town labor force. By 1870, it had just 37 percent of the same labor market. The remaining 520 adult males lived scattered in towns other than the county seat.

The Civil War should have effected the sex ratio in the county in favor of men, especially in the most marriageable age group of twenty to forty. Such was not the case. In 1860, there were a total of 3,325 adults in this age group. They were in a ratio of five males to four females. In 1870, there were still only 3,102 adults in this age category but now the males outnumbered females by 1,989 to 1,113. Or, to put it another way, despite the war the total number of men in the marriageable age group went up from 1,909 to 1,989 but the supply of women went down dramatically.

The occupational profile of the county in 1860 showed that most people were farmers. Eighty percent between twenty-one and sixty years of age were listed as farmers or field hands. Twelve percent were in the skilled crafts or commerce, 4 percent in the professions, and another 9 percent were day-laborers in jobs other than farm work. The farm towns, other than Oquawka, registered about the same occupational ratio as did the townships. Oquawka, though, in 1860 had 218 of the 297 (or 73 percent) of the county's skilled craftsman and merchants and seventy of the

George Reed operating road grader-rural Raritan

ninety-eight (or 71 percent) of its professional people. As expected, most of the non-farm, unskilled workers also lived in Oquawka — 94 percent of them. After the Civil War this profile shifted. The men engaged in agriculture declined from 80 to 73 percent. But within this figure there was another significant change.

Agricultural Productivity, 1800–1900

CROP AND PRODUCTIVITY INDICATOR	1800	1840	1880	1900
Wheat				
Worker-hours/acre	56	35	20	15
Yield/acre (bushels)	15	15	13	14
Worker-hours/100 bushels	373	233	152	108
Corn				
Worker-hours/acre	86	69	46	38
Yield/acre (bushels)	25	25	26	26
Worker-hours/100 bushels	344	276	180	147
Cotton				
Worker-hours/acre	185	135	119	112
Yield/acre (pounds of lint)	147	147	179	191
Worker-hours/bale	601	439	318	280

Agricultural Productivity Chart

In 1860, most people on the farm owned their farms. Then only 267 of the 1,909 men were field hands, or 14 percent. In 1870, though, there were 1,565 field hands out of a farm occupation total of 2,894 men over fifteen years of age. The decade of the war produced not only a ten-fold increase in fieldhands but a proportional increase of those engaged in farming by daywork from 14 to 54 percent. Or, to look at it from another perspective, there was a decline of the family farm of some 30 percent in ten years as indicated by the census data. Lastly, 86 percent of the work force could be considered in 1860 as either being a farmer or being an able-bodied male member of the farm family. By 1870, only 56 percent were in that category.

The data also shows some important shifts occurring in the non-agricultural classifications. Professionals in the county grew in number from ninety eight to 148 with each of the towns in 1870 having its own physician. Oquawka, though, no longer monopolized the professions. In 1860, for instance, seventy of the ninety-eight county professionals lived here. In 1870, only thirty-five of the 148 professionals were in Oquawka, a shift in percentage from 71 to 24 percent over the decade. Those in the skilled crafts and commerce more than doubled in number, growing from 197 in 1860 to 604 ten years later. Again, Oquawka's earlier domination was eclipsed by the other towns. In 1860, 73 percent of the county's skilled workers and merchants lived in Oquawka. By 1870, just 261 of the 445 men were in the town, or 59 percent. A fourth census occupational category was "day laborers not in agriculture." In 1860, there were only eighty-two such men in the county, seventy-seven of them in Oquawka. Ten years later, the number had surged to 316 with 128 (or 41 percent) earning their living by wages for manual labor. The census marshall was careful to make note, though, that of the "laborers" living in Gulfport, sixteen were prostitutes.

Thus the population profile of the county after the Civil War had altered considerably from its first thirty years. Farm homesteads declined and

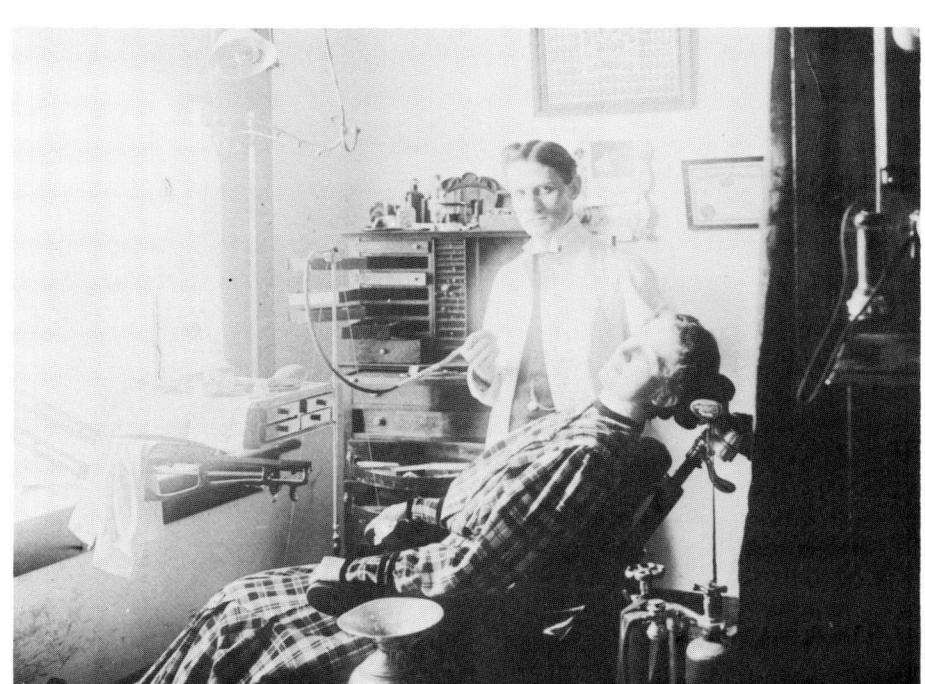

Dr. R.I. Findley and Wife
Stronghurst, c. 1900

this decline created a new class in the work force, the field hand. Almost unnoticed before 1860, he was commonplace afterwards. The percentages of craftsman and merchants remained largely unchanged. But within that percentage the data showed a marked exodus from Oquawka. The town began a permanent decline in population and those "in the know" recognized, apparently, that the moon had set. Opportunity for the man with education, with a skilled craft, or the entrepreneur spirit lay now away from the river town, inland, along the main route of commerce, the railroad. Like the emerging class of field hands, the county saw an unprecedented growth of common laborers--almost a four-fold increase in a decade. There must have been a torrent of men, without skills or education, looking for jobs just after the war. The census marshall, unfortunately, does not say whether or not men calling themselves laborers, (or indicated as such by occupations such as railroad workers, ditch digger, or riverboat hand) actually were able to find jobs either full or half time.

Using the figures on occupation one can arrive at an employment profile analysis for the county. The data for 1860 and 1870 showed that there were more men than jobs before the war and the reverse situation afterwards. For example, in 1860 there were a total of 3,002 men in the workforce, that is, between the ages of sixteen and sixty. There were 2,386 men in that category who said they had jobs in one of the five areas--farming, skilled crafts, commerce, professional, and day laborer. That gives an unemployment figure of about twenty-one percent, rather high in a growing economy such as Henderson County had then. After the Civil War, though, there were more able-bodied men with jobs than there were in the older workforce of men between sixteen and sixty. The conclusion is that boys under fifteen were finding employment--most likely in the growing number of farm field hands or day laborers. Thus there were important shifts in the employment profile as compared to before the war; mainly, increasing opportunities in agriculture and the rise in number of the professions and crafts. Horizontal mobility also was on the increase throughout the county. People were coming in and boosting its aggregate population. Henderson County folks were moving horizontally, too, set-

Stronghurst Painting Crew, c. 1910
Ralph Butler, Harley Hurd, Joe Long, E.E. Bowen, Roy Shook

tling in greater number in the townships along the eastern border and simultaneously filling up older towns and building new ones.

Beyond an economic profile, the county census manuscripts indicate changes in family structure. Birth patterns of the earlier years disappeared. No longer was the percentage of male infants as overwhelmingly high as it had been before the war. For example, the antebellum birthrate was still discernable in Lomax Township in 1860. But in 1870 girl infants outnumbered the males. In the town of Raritan in 1870 there were seventy-four girls to sixty-one boys under five years of age and Stronghurst that same year counted seventy-four girl toddlers compared to only fifty-seven boys. The overall sex ratio became balanced. In 1870, there were 52.9 percent of children under five listed as males and 47.1 percent as females. Family size, compared to an average of 2.45 children in 1840 and 2.88 in 1850, had gone down to 1.9 children in 1860. But ten years later the figure was back up to about 2.87 children per household. So the pattern of family size, like sex ratio, also stabilized in the 1870s. Immigration patterns changed. In 1860 most Henderson county adults were born outside of Illinois and were distributed in terms of region of birth about the same as they had been since 1830, from the Upper South and the Middle Atlantic states. In 1870, though, there were more adults listed as having been born in Illinois, about 20 percent of all people over eighteen were so designated. In 1880 the figure was up to 30 percent. There still were immigrants who were born in Tennessee, Kentucky, New Jersey, New York, Pennsylvania, Ohio, and Indiana. But their children, those under eighteen years of age by 1880, were almost all natives of the Prairie State, the average being about 90 percent. After Illinois, Indiana claimed somewhere around 13 percent of the county's children. The percentage of children born in other states, even in those regions from which their parents came, was insignificant. Although children were listed from most states east of the Mississippi, except for the lower South, their figures were all less than one percent. The older regional diversity, seen in language accents for instance, among the people of the county was softened. Henderson County children, as they matured in the 1880s

W.E. Hurd Homestead, Hopper, c. 1880

and 1890s, unlike their parents, now grew to adulthood with their childhood friends, and often remained as their neighbors throughout life.

Immigration from European countries continued in some areas for a while at pre-Civil War rates due in part to the expanding opportunites for work in the growing towns and on the new railroad lines spanning the county. The 1860 figures showed Irish families on the increase in Biggsville and Gladstone and more German families were living in Oquawka. A decade later the towns of Gladstone and Carman had the county's largest German population with 15 percent and 7 percent respectively. Biggsville claimed 30 percent of its foreign-born from Ireland as did Gladstone with 8 percent. In 1880, Gladstone had Swedish, German, and Irish mixture constituting ninety-five people or 18 percent of its citizens. Germans, Carman's foreign population, on the other hand, had dwindled to only ten people, five of whom were from Germany. Other towns in 1880 had an insignificant percentage of foreigners (under 6 percent) -- like Raritan, Olena, and Shokokon. The rest had almost none, as in Dallas City, Warren, and Terre Haute.[4]

Joseph Dixson

The number of Oquawka's foreign-born adult citizens evened out. In 1860 they numbered 416 out of a total adult population of 1,299, or 32 percent. A decade later this figure changed little. Foreign adults then numbered 217 out of 711, or 30.5 percent. As before, the German element was predominant. Germans counted 140 of the 416 foreigners, or 36.5 percent in 1860. In 1870, they numbered 92 out of 217 or 42 percent, still clearly the dominant ethnic influence there. In 1880, out of a foreign community now of only eighty-one people more than half, forty-seven, were German followed by ten Irish adults. Unlike any other place in Henderson County, though, Oquawka attracted Swedish immigrants. In 1860, there were twenty-four Swedish adults residing there and in 1870 they had doubled to forty-nine adults. But by 1880 they, like other foreign-born people in the town, had diminished to only five adults, or one percent of the town's total 481 adult population. In 1880 there were no foreign-born children at all in the county, not even in Oquawka. With a decline of the European influence on Henderson County's population an ethnic homogenization of the community had taken place. Forty years after it was created, the people in the county looked pretty much alike, thought alike, lived in towns or farms very similar in appearance and, with slight differences in inflection, talked alike.

Two of the greatest changes seen on the landscape by 1880, compared to 1840, were the railroads and their towns.[5] Railroad building had, of course, started before the Civil War with the construction of CB&Q and the promotion of the abortive Warsaw and Rock Island line. But after the Civil War railroads saw their heyday. Just after Lee's surrender, in the summer of 1865, Illinois lawmakers created the Rockford, Rock Island, and St. Louis Railroad Company. The project was ambitious. It proposed a railroad to run north out of St. Louis along the Mississippi River, through Oquawka, to Rock Island. From here it would swing along the Rock River to Sterling and terminate at Rockford. The portion of the road in Henderson County was built in 1868. It went from Keithsburg to Oquawka to Gladstone. But the following year the directors relocated the roadbed southeast out of Rock Island through Viola in Mercer County to a Monmouth terminal. From that point it joined the main line of the CB&Q to St. Louis. Shortly thereafter the expanded CB&Q bought out the Rockford, Rock Island, and St. Louis Company and, for a while, monopolized railroad linkage in western Illinois. The piece of the Rockford line built north out of Oquawka was eventually extended to New Boston where it, too, was connected to the CB&Q. In the southwestern tip of the county a spur of the Toledo, Peoria, and Warsaw line in 1880 called the Toledo, Peoria, and Western Railroad ran northward into Lomax Township to the town of Lomax where it joined the CB&Q about half way between the town and Carman at a point then known as Iowa Station.

Santa Fe Trestle, Media

The only real competitor to the growing CB&Q was the Atchinson, Topeka, and Santa Fe.[6] In 1887, the company, at first labeled the Chicago, Santa Fe, and California Railway Company, laid its plans for a line parallel to the CB&Q. In Henderson County the road was to enter in the southeast corner of Media Township and run twenty-seven miles through open farm land in an uninterrupted southwest direction to a Mississippi terminal at Dallas City. At the time there were no towns along the proposed route, except the tiny village of Lomax.

Three towns sprang from nowhere in the 1880s because of the Santa Fe line. Stronghurst and Media became viable market centers for the southern half of the county and a third railroad village, Decorra, was platted in 1888, and served essentially as a stock-loading stopover. Stronghurst's origins stem from a survey of the Santa Fe line in 1887. In the fall of that year, the company hired Joseph Dixon, then twenty-six years old, as its agent to build a "town company" along the line. Young Dixon was born in Indiana but moved to a farm next to the future site of Stronghurst with his parents in 1850. He saw clearly the advantage of having a railroad town next door to the family homestead. So he surveyed the town, sold lots, and attracted businessmen to locate here. He started the town's first bank and began a stock raising and shipping business. He served as a school director in the township. He personally surveyed and added onto the original plat of Stronghurst; first an eighty acre parcel, then one of eleven acres, then one of five acres, collectively called Dixon's Additions. On New Year's Day, 1893, Dixon and a friend were run over by the Santa Fe express in mid-afternoon in broad day light. Media was the second village created by Santa Fe. In the summer of 1887, a farmer, Nathan Wever, platted a market town on his land. Small wonder, because on November 6, 1887 an elaborate ceremony took place here as the place where the two halves of the Santa Fe, one from Kansas City, the

Stronghurst Depot, J. Dixson, first agent

Gladstone Depot, built 1880

other from Chicago, were linked together at the highest point (some 675 feet above sea level) between the Mississippi and Lake Michigan. The new town was then called Media, or half-way point, instead of "Wever." The first building in the town was the railroad station followed in 1888 by a store run by John Dalton, another farmer who left his homestead to go into business when the railroad came. Over the next decade Media attracted four more stores, a druggist, two hotels, farm stables, a printshop, brickyard, two blacksmiths, two churches, a postoffice, a bank, and two schools. In the 1890s Alex Rankin discovered oil nearby and it was predicted that Media would soon become a metropolis with paved streets and factories. It never happend. Media became, at best, an optimistic, forward-looking town, the sponsor of the earliest effort at higher education in the county, Wever Academy, and the home of Francis Davidson, the inventor of the monarch-engine tractor.

Two other towns already in place, Shokokon and Gladstone, were changed by the main railroad lines. Shokokon had originally been settled as a potential riverport but plans never materialized even though it was, in 1840, the western-most stopping point on a stage line from Macomb to the Mississippi. For a time, in 1843, the Mormons under Joseph Smith planned the building of another community there, a "Stake in Zion" they called it. In the winter of that year Smith himself came to Shokokon on the invitation of John Cowan, a local farmer, and stayed overnight at Robert McQueen's mill nearby. At Shokokon, Smith preached his Mormon revelations to an interested and attentive crowd.[7] Apparently, McQueen and two friends, Jeremiah Rose and Michael Crane, hoped to convince Smith to do for Shokokon (where they held land) what he had just done for Commerce, turn it into a river metropolis like Nauvoo. Smith was taken in with the scheme and visited Shokokon again in May. But soon Smith became preoccuppied with his own troubles with the law and the whole scheme was abandoned. Shokokon became a wasteland.

After the Civil War Shokokon was, literally, relocated on a railroad. In 1869, with the 1867 construction of the Carthage and Burlington

Dr. William Cavins, on right, with wife and son, George, in front of his office, Raritan

Railroad, houses were carted three miles southeast and stuck on the railroad line at a point about half-way between Gulfport and Lomax. It was surveyed as a village in 1870 and, at the demand of the farmer who surveyed the land on which the railroad town was established, Joseph Carman, it was called "Carman." Two brothers from Shokokon, Zeille and Enoch Cisna, started the town's first store in 1871, later known as Babcock Brothers. Richard Hassel opened a business shop there in 1877 and a second general merchandise store was started in 1875 by William C. Walter, who included a drug counter in the shop. In 1878, the town got its physician, Dr. Isaac F. Harter, a graduate of the College of Physicians at Keokuk.

The existing town most dramatically affected by the railroads was Gladstone. Gladstone (called earlier either Sage Town, Lynn, or Oquawka Junction) became Gladstone officially in 1881 after twenty years of steady growth as the replacement of Oquawka as the county's commercial center. The boom began in 1860 when, to an existing population of only sixty-seven people, new arrivals came to the village. By 1870, the town had 249 residents and in 1880, 524 people.[8] Its advantages seemed obvious. It was centrally located, had a fine water supply, and boasted excellent stone quarries nearby. First plotted in 1856, and named then after the farmer, Gideon Sage, who owned the land, its growth was completely tied to the expansion of the CB&Q line from Chicago. Gladstone served from the start as the junction of its spur north to Oquawka. Soon after the war a stone quarry was started by a CB&Q contractor named Wallbaum about one-half mile north of the town. Then, in 1876, he opened a second quarry east of Gladstone along South Henderson creek. Together the quarries employed from fifty to eighty workers, some of them skilled stonecutters. In 1878, the Gladstone Refinery was incorporated with a capital investment, enormous for the time, of $126,000. Its headquarters, a stone building originally 40 x 70 feet, was expanded in the 1880s as was the refinery's operations. At its height it manufactured sorghum, grape sugar, and glucose and hired over forty individuals on a regular basis. By 1880, the town had two schools, two blacksmiths, and a meat market. It also claimed a post office, two saloons, one feed mill, and a physician, a Dr. Bulsford. Gladstone, by then, was the "working man's town" in the county. The 1882 *History of Henderson County* commented that citizens of the town "are of small means, honest, industrious, law-abiding,...their occupations are principally railroad laborers, quarry hands and stone cutters."[9]

One of the older villages least effected by the new railroads was Lomax. By 1889 it had the distinction of having three lines touching it, more than any other town in the county--the CB&Q, the Sante Fe, and the Carthage & Burlington coming north out of Hancock County. But Lomax remained what it had been, a backward settlement of Pennsylvania and Upper South families who had wandered into the area around the fork of Honey and Dugout creeks before the Civil War. The village's namesake, Robert Lomax, was born in Clinton County, Ohio and came to Henderson County as a child in 1853. In 1871, after farming at his father's homestead on section twenty-two he opened a farm machinery shop just across the adjacent section line (section thirteen) and named the location after his father, a county judge. Although the village eventually saw a community of thirteen houses with a blacksmith, preacher, musician, and druggist it never developed as a market town on the railroad lines because traffic bypassed it to end at the river port of Dallas City.

Joseph Smith

House at Sycamore and Liberty, Gladstone
Turn of the Century

Main St., Raritan, 1920's

There were two towns, other than Oquawka, which atrophied because of a lack of a railroad line, Raritan and Terre Haute. Raritan, established in 1856, contained 300 inhabitants in 1880, fifty dwellings, ten businesses, three churches, a postoffice, a physician, and a print shop. In other words, it was clearly at the same stage of early diversified economic development as Gladstone. It even had a hotel then, built in 1858. Terre Haute, laid out in 1854 by the county deputy surveyor William Rice on the location of a Sauk Fox village also, in 1880, claimed merchandise and grocery stores, a blacksmith, two physicians, and a restaurant. Both towns were on the route originally projected by the Atchison, Topeka, and Santa Fe promotors. Indeed, a party of railroad surveyors came to Terre Haute and set the stakes for the new line just north of the town. But for an unexplained reason, most likely a physical inspection of the timbered, rolling countryside on the proposed route, company officials dropped the idea. They switched the roadbed instead some four miles north of Terre Haute, and about six miles away from Raritan, across farmland on which the three villages of Media, Stronghurst, and Decorra were created.[17]

Along with railroads and growing towns, old and new, Henderson County developed aspects of community life that had not been seen before the war, town newspapers. In the 1850s only one major newspaper served the county, the *Spectator,* run by Edwin (E.H.N.) Patterson. This paper continued for a while to be the dominant news source, but not for long. Edwin Patterson stayed in charge until 1875 when he left to live near Denver where he published the *Georgetown Miner.* He died there on April 21, 1880. His son, Harry N. Patterson, then took over the Oquawka paper and with his wife, Florence, continued its Democratic bias. In the summer of 1886, though, Harry announced that he was leaving the Democrats over the temperance issue and that henceforth his newspaper would support the Prohibitionist Party! The decision was a disaster for the paper. His subscribers, one after the other, cancelled. Harry persisted, nevertheless in what, to him, was his Christian duty to wage a holy war on the liquor interests. He went broke. For a time the *Spectator* was sustained by Harry's printing of library index cards and botanical labels for Illinois flora. But on January 22, 1908 the paper folded.

Main Street, Raritan, c. 1900
E.O. Barnes General Store, *Raritan Reporter*, Office

A second county newspaper, the *Oquawka Plaindealer*, had appeared in 1853 as a Whig party organ but it had little circulation even in 1856 when it supported the newly created Republican party and its candidate John C. Fremont. A succession of ineffective owners began in 1857 and finally, ten years later, M.N. Jamison moved it to Biggsville. There he changed the name to the *Henderson Plaindealer*. In 1868 the *Plaindealer* was purchased by Judson Graves. After less than a year of trying to turn a profit Graves gave up and left the county. Biggsville, in 1874, succeeded in launching a newspaper. Mercellies M. Romley printed the first issue of the *Biggsville Clipper* and replaced the defunct *Plaindealer* as the county's second Republican newspaper. Romley operated the paper until 1903 when his son, Samuel, took over. Oquawka had two other papers after the war. In 1883 Fred A. Simpson, a merchant, began the *Henderson County Democrat*. It was published in the town until 1905 when it was relocated in Monmouth. The *Henderson County Journal* was started in 1872 as a Republican paper by Eugene A. Hail. For a while Hail tried unsuccessfully to relocate his paper in Macomb but gave up the idea in 1878 and returned permanently to Oquawka.

Raritan sponsored its newspaper in 1875. That year the *Raritan Bulletin* was started by Robert Barnes and George H. Butler. It was a weekly 5″ x 7″ two-column sheet expanded to four pages two years later. Then it folded. Between 1876 and 1880 another little newsletter called the *Home News* was printed in the village by Joseph S. Nevius. Edward O. Barnes, who had moved to Raritan in 1874 from La Harpe, started in 1884 the longest continuous running county newspaper, the *Raritan Reporter*. In October of that year he put out the first issue. His policy, announced in column one under the title "Our Bow... What We Intend Doing," would be to "issue a small sheet in which we will give the local general news of interest in condensed form." He asked those interested in subscribing to contact him at his "office" over the hardware store. He ran the *Reporter* until his death on October 24, 1934.

Media started a newspaper known as the *Media Record* in 1892. Herman Herbertz was its editor and, with his brother William, attempted to maintain an "independent" editorial policy. It continued in business, with a

First Publication, October 29, 1884

few switches in owners and a brief suspension of publication in 1910, until World War I. The strongest competitor to the Oquawka papers by the end of the century was the *Stronghurst Graphic.* Boasting the most modern printing equipment of the day, it appeared in September, 1888. The paper was run by John F. Mains, who, before becoming a newspaper owner, had taught in the county schools. For twenty-one years he and his wife ran the paper, enlarged to a six-column, four-page issue in 1896, as an ardent and conservative Republican advocate. In December, 1910 he became partners with the forty-one year old Andrew Kershaw, then Postmaster at Stronghurst. Kershaw ran the newspaper until his death in 1926. Just before he died, Kershaw sold the *Graphic* to his foreman Charles M. Bell. Bell, a Biggsville native, took over at the age of forty-four and he, in turn, formed a partnership with his eighteen-year old son Paul G. Bell, naming him co-editor and publisher.

The expansion of information after the Civil War through the various journalistic ventures was only one indication of the increasing complexity and variety of community life. These years also saw a significant expansion of schools, churches, and two new social phenomena - the fraternal lodge and organized amusements.

Public schools, authorized by the Constitution of 1848, had been built in each township before the war.[10] They were small, one-room structures within easy walking distance of farm families. Teacher requirements were minimal: literacy plus a knowledge of arithmetic. After the war the towns lead a revived interest in schools and education. As early as 1868, for example, Biggsville citizens, led by B.H. Martin, backed the idea of a new school house on lot seventeen in the town and one year later "a fine large schoolhouse" in the words of James Gordon, was finished there. The same town led the first fight for creating educational opportunities beyond grammar school. In the early 1890s some of its citizens decided that Biggsville should build a "Township High School." After some considerable debate over the cost of the idea the question was submitted on April 18, 1895 to a township referendum. The vote showed a strong division of town versus farm. The town strongly favored the expense of what was for the day an important education advancement. Farmers in the

Main Street, Biggsville, early 1900's

Biggsville High School
Built 1903, Burned 1906

township complained at the cost, saying it was completely unnecessary. The referendum supported the High School by 154 to 118. The farmers refused to accept the vote and took it to the courts. There they claimed illegal procedure since the secret ballot had not been employed. The judge of the Circuit Court denied the plea. The farmers then appealed the decision to the state Supreme Court. This highest tribunal, in April, 1896, upheld the decision of the lower court.

With the legal questions out of the way Biggsville proceeded to build its High School. An election was held to choose a Board of Education. On May 18, 1895 they elected five members who immediately, after the Supreme Court ruling, contracted the necessary jobs for putting up a frame structure at a cost of $8,000. Ten years later the school, "the pride of the community" in the words of the *Biggsville Clipper,* burned to the ground. The next morning the Board of Education met to start rebuilding. This time there was no opposition from the countryside. They decided, learning a lesson from the fire, on a brick building this time. It was finished within a year as a two story pitched-roof structure with ample room for four high school classes. By the second decade of the century Gordon could boast that the "Township High School," with its title carved in stone over the door entrance, was "one of which the entire county could be proud." "In educational attainment and in athletics," he wrote, "it ranks among the first in the state."[11]

Media Township rivaled Biggsville in the pursuit for high school education. Its citizens, more of whom came from the Northeast, proportionally, than any other township demanded that the educational opportunities they had known as children be available in Illinois for their offspring. There at Media, Nathan Wever, the town founder, gave a tract of his estate to a Board of Trustees in order to construct a first rate High School for those students seriously wanting to go on for a college education. A "preparatory school" Wever called it. His plan was to have the school built and operated by trustees who would raise the tuition from attending students' parents. This fund, in turn, would pay operating costs and upkeep and provide the teachers' salaries. The Academy was put up in 1895 and the teachers were hired. In 1909, however, the Academy closed.

Wever Academy, Media

Township High School, Oquawka

Its failure was due mainly to the competition for students. Most teenagers chose the High School at Biggsville for a variety of reason. It was closer. One's friends went to the Biggsville school. But most students just did not want to make a commitment to attend college. Moreover, the curriculum at the two schools, despite the pretensions of Wever Academy, were identical: it really had nothing more to offer than a greater expense to the parents.

Oquawka, compared to Biggsville and Media, started only a modest effort toward improving education beyond pre-Civil War standards. It had, in 1850, built the first brick grammar school in the county and in 1873 the school was enlarged, about doubled in size, for a cost of about $3,000. In 1880, the rooms were refurnished for another $625. In 1900, the township approved the addition of a two-year high school curriculum and expansion of the teaching staff to four teachers. But it was a weak second to the modern-thinking High School and preparatory school planning in the eastern part of the county.

In Stronghurst Township, at the town of Stronghurst, another spurt of activity on behalf of education was seen toward the end of the era. At the townsite, in 1890, a brick school was put up and almost at once its township Board of Education started to plan an addition. In 1896, a large wing was built on the north side of the original building. But in 1908 it was also leveled by a fire while school was in session, narrowly avoiding a catastrophe. The children and teachers escaped within minutes before the entire structure was enveloped in lethal smoke. The next year, just as in Biggsville, Stronghurst citizens, refusing to be discouraged by the calamity, rose to the occasion. They chose another site in town, raised the money, and, again in the words of an eyewitness, "the finest school building in Henderson County, as well as the most expensive, was there erected, in which under an efficient corps of teachers, the educational interests of the community are being well looked after."[12]

Stronghurst School, early 1900's
W.C. Ivins, principal

Methodist Episcopal Church, Stronghurst

The church history of the county between the Civil War and the turn of the century saw an expansion of the major denominations (Presbyterian, Baptists, Methodist, Reformed, Dutch Reformed), the rise of new evangelical sects, and the demise and relocation of churches themselves in response to the appearance of the CB&Q and the Santa Fe railroad lines.[13] The Methodists of Oquawka, always small in number (about fifty), continued as before to meet at the Courthouse until they built their first church there in 1856. Fifteen years later, though, when the congregation had expanded steadily to about 180 people under the Rev. J.S. Cummings, the building was demolished in a tornado. The church was rebuilt, however, at a cost of $1,200 and the congregation continued to hold about 200 supporters. At Stronghurst a Methodist church was started in the fall of 1888 in the opera house there. The town trustees donated lots for a permanent church. A large, comfortable dwelling paid for by 140 local subscriptions, was completed in 1896. Nearby, at Olena, the Methodists put up a walnut and pine frame structure which Gordon described in 1910 as "romantic now." This church was the Circuit headquarters for Henderson County largely due to its location as the center of the county's Methodist population. There, too, Methodist camp revivals were held. Biggsville, in 1860, started its Methodist church based on just seven families. At first, they used the town schoolhouse near the railroad depot or, in summer, worshiped in a walnut grove just outside of town. From its start it held a Sunday School for the children to which they attracted all the youngsters of the village, regardless of their parent's denomination. In 1867, the congregation purchased a lot in town for $100 and the next year raised money to start construction of their church. It was finished at a total cost of about $4,000 and dedicated by Doctor T.M. Eddy, Bishop of Chicago, on December 30 of that year. Far to the north, county Methodists started the Bald Bluff church in 1878 and at the opposite end, in Lomax Township, they started another in June, 1878. At Lomax they elected a committee to build a church. Then they raised a subscription of about $2,000 for a 32 X 48 frame building. It was completed in 1872. The Methodist church of Gladstone was put up in 1867 with the help of the

Methodist Episcopal Church, Gladstone

Gladstone United Presbyterian Church

Biggsville United Presbyterian Church

Cumberland Presbyterians. It cost over $2,000. Later, the Methodists reimbursed the Presbyterians for their contribution and continued without any further connection with their Calvinist cohorts. The only other new Methodist effort in the county was at Terre Haute. There they first established a mission of the LaHarpe Methodist Church and then, in 1866, began to operate on their own. They built a sturdy 40 X 50 brick church in 1870. Little else is known of their subsequent activities.

The largest groups of Baptists were at Raritan and Oquawka. At Raritan, in 1858, they formally organized under the direction of a Roseville preacher, Henry Johnson, by adopting a declaration of faith to the convention of the American Baptist Publication Society. Seven families affixed their signatures to the declaration. Their first official meeting was held in February, 1859. Under H.B. Johnson's revivals, additional new converts were added. In 1868, they built their church and dedicated it in the summer of the following year. At Oquawka, the Baptists met from home to home until, in 1862, they rented a public hall, called Allen's Hall, as a temporary meeting place for their fifty-seven members. Meanwhile, they raised money for their church and completed it in 1870 for $5,500, the most expensive structure like it in the county seat. It featured the largest bell around and uniquely stained glass windows for atmosphere. The congregation had, unfortunately, like the town overstepped itself. With Oquawka's economic demise many members moved away, some died, and some quit. By 1880, there were only twenty-eight people in the huge, empty building.

Presbyterians, as before, continued to be the most active and the most numerous denomination in the county. At Oquawka, Hezekiah Hanson, a graduate of Marshall College (Pennsylvania) carried on one of the longest pastorates in the state, over twenty-five years of service. Hanson was able, somehow, to overcome the intra-denominational squabbles of the Associate Reformed, Cumberland, and Old School Presbyterians in his congregation and, at the anniversary of his twenty-fifth year, could look back on only "but four cases of discipline, as well as 5,644 sermons, 346 funerals, 256 marriages, and 213 baptisms." Biggsville's United Presbyterians got moving about the same time as the Methodists. In the late summer of 1859 they started holding services in a wooded spot just south of the CB&Q tracks under the Rev. J.B.P. McGraw who came over regularly from the South Henderson Church located about two miles northwest of town. Right after the war the church became independent of its reliance on the South Henderson, raised some $6,000, and put up their own church, a large 65 X 36 structure with a belltower, in the summer of 1869. In 1882 they added a Sunday School room for another $1,000.

Just about the year that the United Presbyterians were pulling together at Biggsville a small group of Cumberland Presbyterians, some twenty-nine of them, organized. They began meeting in the late summer of 1868 in a school house four miles north of town, first under the Reverend J.W. Carter, for three years, then the Rev. J.L. Crofford. Crofford, in the 1870s, served not only the Cumberlands at Biggsville but also those of that persuasion at Gladstone and the South Henderson Church. By 1874, the three groups formally requested the Presbytery, convened at Abingdon, to organize them into one congregation. Their request was granted in February, 1875 and they asked Crofford to continue on as pastor. In 1905, it joined with the Presbyterian Church in the United States thereby renouncing its historic connection with the Cumberland denomination.

In Rozetta Township, the Smith Creek Presbyterians, in 1858, gathered families which had earlier claimed to be either Associate or Associate Reformed into a United Presbyterian church under the congenial direction of Rev. Samuel Millen. There, in 1881, they put up a comfortable frame building seating about 200 people for $2,000. In 1905, largely because of its out-of-the-way location, this congregation dissolved and sold its property. The older Media township Ellison Creek Church, which started as early as 1828, continued its steady growth also as a United Presbyterian congregation. By 1860, it had 159 members on its list of names and, despite a small dispute with families from Olena over the location of a permanent church, built their 46 X 70 structure at Walnut Grove during the Civil War at a cost of $3,800. Under a succession of pastors after the war, membership stabilized at about 100 people. In the 1890s most of its families began attending the Presbyterian church at Stronghurst and what was left of the Ellison congregation formally dissolved themselves in November, 1904. On January 16, 1889 the Stronghurst United Presbyterian Church was organized, largely with the hired help of the ministers from the Monmouth Presbytery. For awhile, that Presbytery directed the pastor at the Olena church to act as "Moderator" at Stronghurst until they could erect their own church in the new town. The Stronghurst Presbyterians lost no time. Nine months later they dedicated their building. And in September, 1892 they installed their first pastor, the Rev. J.M. McArthur. The other important railroad town, Gladstone, started its Presbyterian congregation in the 1870s under the Oquawka pastor Hezekiah Hanson. Beginning in October, 1874 he visited the town, irregularly, to preach and minister at the church, a $4,000 building that was put up in 1867. By 1910, Gordon reported that "it is now...a thriving...congregation...." The railroad also brought to Gladstone more Irish and German Catholics. So, in 1880, they built the county's second Catholic chapel (the other being St. Patrick's in Raritan), a 25 X 40 church costing $1,500, on South Elm street. In that year about twenty-five members, mostly Irish, attended mass there.

Biggsville Presbyterian Church

Gladstone Catholic Church

Olena Cornet Band

In addition to expansion of older church groups, signs of a different sort of religious activity appeared in the years after the Civil War. Evangelical sects sprang up. At Oquawka there was for a time a German Evangelical congregation among that town's nationality. They held all services in the German language, at least till the turn of the century. By then, however, a second-generation of German-Americans had matured. With their rise to leadership in the group, the German language was eliminated. English replaced it and by 1910 only a few people bothered to attend services. At Stronghurst, in 1891, there was a Swedish Lutheran Church formed. For awhile they shared the new Methodist Church. By 1909, under Reverend Gustave Henry, though, they were able to raise the impressive sum of $6,000 to buy a lot in the southern section of the town. By 1920, they were numbering at least 100 members but, more important than numbers, was their social standing. They constituted, Gordon observed that year, "the most influential and wealthy Swedish people of the south part of the county."[14]

At Lomax, a Christian Church was started by a woman. In the fall of 1891, Sadie McCoy held a two-week revival in the town and ended up with five converts. The next spring Miss McCoy ran another camp meeting and eight souls were saved. With these thirteen followers she organized her church. Five years later they had a pastor, Rev. Arthur N. Lunsey, (Miss McCoy became Mrs. Crank) and a total membership of 192 parishioners. The church, dedicated that year, cost over $3,600 complete with baptistry, bible room, and a gasoline lighting system. It was one of the last, but for the day the most modern, church built in the county.

Social clubs, called "fraternal organizations," stood side-by-side after the Civil War with the growing variety of religious preferences and expressions.[15] The largest such organization was the Masons. Next came the Odd Fellows, the Modern Woodmen, the Knights of Pythias, and the Grand Army of the Republic. The first Masonic Lodge was created in Oquawka in 1853 but not until 1865 did it find permanent headquarters in rooms above the Graham Building. Over the following years other A.F.&A.M. lodges were created out of the Oquawka group. In Gladstone, in November, 1868, nine officers were elected and the next year a public installation was held in the Presbyterian church when the Honorable Thomas Hart Benton of St. Louis delivered a speech on the ideas and history of Masonry. Gladstone Masons prospered over the next decade, but by the end of the century membership declined and their charter eventually was surrendered. At Raritan Lodge No. 277 and at Carman Lodge No. 732 were organized in 1875. Then, in 1896, another group was chartered at Stronghurst. All five lodges were described by Gordon as either thriving or prosperous or both on the eve of World War I.

Other fraternal orders appeared simultaneously with the Masons, they attracted men who for some reason or another were denied admission to the Masonic Lodge. One of the most popular lodges, socially, was the Odd Fellows. Indeed, it far out-numbered the membership of the more elite Masons. It, too, was organized in Oquawka in the 1850s where in December, 1855 they started to hold weekly Friday meetings. At Warren, in 1874, the second gathering of Odd Fellows elected their Noble Grand, Vice-Grand, Right Supporter, and Treasurer. It moved back and forth on Fridays between Warren and Olena until 1892 when it finally moved to Stronghurst and constructed a sturdy brick building in the heart of town. Raritan Odd Fellows were charted by the State Grand Master on October 11, 1876. The lodge did not take root and three years later it was dissolved. Biggsville, in 1887, started the largest bevy of Odd Fellows in the county. Lodge 591 was formed with ten men and soon expanded to thirty-seven worthy fellows and officers. A "Left Supporter" and "Right" and "Left Scene Supporters" were added as additional officers to help in the burden of running the lodge. Other Odd Fellow encampments popped up at Carman and Terre Haute.

The Modern Woodmen, an early equivalent of the Kiwanis, outnumbered the Odd Fellows by 1910. At Oquawka that year they had 165 "beneficial members." They advertized their officers as including the most prominent men in the community." The titles and functions of their leaders convey a flavor of their lofty purpose. They chose a Counsul, Advisor, Banker, Escort, Secretary, Watchman, Chief Forester, Two Medical Examiners, and two Managers—altogether eleven men elevated to high office each year. Stronghurst followed in 1889 with its Camp and Biggsville in 1893 put together Camp No. 1037. Then other smaller campsites were pitched at Media, Raritan, Gladstone, and Terre Haute. More oblique in purpose were the men devoted to the Greek god Apollo and the panhellenic games celebrated in ancient Greece at the Island of Delph. They assembled at Stronghurst and Biggsville. Another occult group calling itself the Mystic Workers of the World met in Biggsville in November, 1897. What they did, or what became of them, no one knows.

George W. Evans, G.A.R. Post Memorial Day Celebration, 1912

The most politically oriented of the county lodges was the Grand Army of the Republic. It was formed as a nationwide veteran's club—the forerunner of the American Legion or the V.F.W.—in 1866 in Washington, D.C. By the mid-1880s it claimed more than 400,000 members and was by then one of the most powerful pressure groups, later called lobbies, in American politics. It was exclusively Republican. For example, it intimidated Congress in 1887 to pass a Dependent Pension Bill that gave a large annuity to every veteran suffering from any disability related to the Civil War. Democratic President Grover Cleveland vetoed the bill and consequently was defeated in the next election. In 1890, the G.A.R. got Congress to re-enact the bill and a more obliging Republican President, Benjamin Harrison, signed it into law. At the local level they, like their successor organizations, affixed veterans' casualty names to their units. So, at Oquawka, in January, 1883 Civil War veterans organized the "Ellesworth Post" with Myron H. Mills as commander. Then, at Stronghurst, on March 8, 1890 they met as the "George W. Evans Post" with George J. Morgan elected as its Commander.

T.G. Richey

If the G.A.R. represented the most flagrantly political fraternal group there was, at the same time, another more discreet, yet equally partisan, organization flourishing. This was the Henderson County Vigilance Committee. Self-operated law enforcement along the upper Mississippi was not unique in Henderson County. Indeed, the phenomenon appeared along all states and territories that bordered on the river north of St. Louis between 1865 and 1890. Patrick Bates Nolan, in a 1971 doctoral dissertation at the University of Minnesota, has discovered, though, that Henderson County experienced some of the most virulent episodes of vigilantism.[16]

The organization was first called the Union Vigilance Committee and appeared during the Copperhead violence of 1864. In January of that year a German vagrant, when panhandling supper at the farm of a Mr. Frank, behaved suspiciously and was taken by Frank and some of his neighbors to Biggsville to be questioned by the Justice of the Peace. Then the Justice, William M. Dobbins, a member of the Vigilance Committee, called a meeting of the committee at the depot school house. Four other men attended: William Wallace, Thomas G. Ritchey, George D. Sant, and Albert Small. They asked the immigrant for a confession of horse stealing and, when the man (by then giving his name as Henry M. Saxton) refused, they threatened more stringent measures. He confessed. Saxton also admitted stealing a horse the week before near St. Louis and then having sold it for $60. A telegram to the St. Louis police confirmed Saxton's admission. He was brought to Oquawka and turned over to the sheriff. *The Spectator* applauded the action, commenting that the "citizens engaged in the matter are currently entitled to the thanks of the entire community for the consumate skill with which they have managed this affair."[17] No wonder, the Vigilance Committee were all Patterson's friends and community leaders. Dobbins was a Justice of the Peace and a prosperous Biggsville Township farmer. William Wallace and George Sant were known as "honest yeomen." Small served as County Treasurer. And Thomas G. Ritchey, a pioneer settler, was both a Judge of the County Court and a prominent lawyer.

Theft was a major concern of the Henderson County Vigilanties. In March, 1872, the wife of Jack Evans of Oquawka ran to Thomas Ritchey's house in Biggsville (Jack was out of town at the time) crying that a "whole bunch of horses" valued at over $400 had been stolen from the barn. Ritchey, then the president of the Committee, took $100 from Mrs. Evans to cover expenses and set to work. He called out the Committee. They traced the culprits from Oquawka to LaHarpe where they caught two men, McChesney and Edwards, and dragged them back to the county seat for trial. The horses were returned and the men were given a term of six years at Joliet Prison.[18] In June, 1879 two other horse thieves were caught by the Vigilance Committee in Terre Haute. This time they were sent by train to Peoria, the site of their crimes, for trial.[19] In January, 1880 the committee once more rode out after a horse thief. This time W.H. Voorhees was caught in his home town, Raritan, for having taken two mules and selling them in St. Louis. He was given seven years in prison.

In the 1870s the Vigilance Committee appeared in the so-called "gunboat incidents" near Oquawka. Gunboats in those days were really floating saloons and whorehouses which regularly anchored off almost every river town on the Mississippi. They were all but immune from regular law enforcement, a no-man's-land on the river between state and county jurisdictions. The owner could easily up-anchor and move on if he felt threatened. They were more than just an affront to propriety. They were "centers of every sort of vice and crime....their inhabitants often entered town to rob, murder, steal and spread counterfeit money" before floating on downstream.[20]

From the spring of 1870 till late in 1876 a gunboat at one time or another regularly drifted by Oquawka and anchored about five miles downriver at Gulfport. In July, 1870 there was a fight on one of these boats where a Charles Corburn apparently killed a Fred Watson during a drunken brawl. Corburn was arrested by the Henderson County Sheriff and later tried and given fourteen years in the Joliet prison. But on the evening of Coburn's arrest the Vigilance Committee went to work on the gunboat. They forceably "arrested" two prostitutes they found there and burned the boat to the waterline. The two women were turned over to the sheriff and subsequently were sentenced to six months in the county jail. Two years later another gunboat was back in business at the same spot. In October, 1872 the Vigilance Committee, apparently with the help of men from Burlington, raided the boat and arrested nine men and nine women. In December, they hit the boat again and captured the owner, "Chippewa Jack." They arrested him (along with six more whores) and charged Jack with operating a house of prostitution. Then they set the gunboat on fire.

The Vigilance Committee was involved in matters other than horsetheft and prostitution. In the summer of 1875 some prisoners in the county jail dug a hole through the brick wall and escaped. The jail then was more than a mile from Oquawka, in the basement of the county Poor Farm, and so the escape was unnoticed for a couple days and the prisoners were free. The Vigilance Committee led a protest against the deplorable jail arguing that such a place, where anyone could escape, made all their efforts worthless. In the task of "assisting in apprehending and punishing criminals," they said, "we desire that our labor be not in vain...."[21] In April, 1880 Schroeder's Store in Warren was burglarized. About $300 of merchandise was stolen. Almost immediately the Vigilance Committee was on the trail of Frank Potter and two other men, all local boys. The three were caught and brought to the Justice of the Peace at Warren, who, suprisingly, let them off with just a warning. Flabbergasted, the Committee asked for and received a search warrant at Oquawka, entered Potter's home and confiscated the stolen goods. The three were again arrested, tried, and found guilty. *The Spectator* praised the Committee members as being "singularly adapted to detective work."[22]

The activities of the Committee, although secret and without records, by-laws, or publicity, were regular. They seemed to have held more or less routine meetings at Oquawka and Biggsville. From time to time they advertised by a notice in the newspapers. One such notice was printed on August 23, 1877. It called for a meeting in Oquawka that week and was signed, pretentiously, as the "Chief of Police."[23] On March 18, 1880 the Vigilanties came out with the boldest public admission of their goings-on. That issue of the *Spectator* printed a letter signed A.D.P. which refuted a charge that the Committee had been disbanded. Nonsense, he wrote, "we are still vigilant in aiding the officers of the law to perform their duty."[24]

The county sheriff and his one policeman, located in Oquawka, needed help. The significant surge in population, growth of towns, appearance of ethnic diversity, and rise of a new adult day-laborer population, meant that crime, compared to earlier years, was on the increase. Regular criminal activity in the county, as a feature of social life and as a barometer of changing times really began with the Civil War and expanded in frequency and in seriousness into the early twentieth century.²⁵ During the first months of the war a Grand Jury brought a true bill, an indictment, against W.P. Litton for the largest robbery seen until then in the county. Litton was arrested and charged for the January 3, 1861 burglary of the store of S.S. Phelps. He apparently entered the store through the front door with a stolen key and made off with all the money in the safe, a princely sum of about $10,000. On January 17, he was arrested and nearly $8,000 was recovered. Litton then accused William H. Phelps of being in cahoots with him but later retracted the charge. He did, though, name several others involved. But early on January 24, Litton escaped from the poor-house jail and got as far away on foot as Terre Haute township before, at Honey Creek, the Sheriff caught up with him and brought him back to Oquawka. At his trial Litton pleaded guilty and threw himself at the mercy of the court. The Judge considered "the previous good character" of the accused and was lenient. Litton was sentenced to three years in the state penitentiary.

In December, 1864 the Olena Tragedy occurred. William David and some outlaws from eastern Iowa joined together in a burglary scheme on three wealthy Olena citizens, Isiah Brooks, John Bruen, and John Fort. When the crooks got to planning the details, though, David informed Brooks, Bruen, and Fort about what was going on. So they were ready. Brooks' house was the first target. At night the gang descended on the home where, unknown to them, Brooks' neighbors were waiting. The felons, who by then were drunk, knocked on the door and forced their way in. They demanded Brooks turn over all his money. Brooks said he did not have any. The thieves demanded that Brooks lead them upstairs to search the house. On a signal from Brooks his friends opened fire on the burglars. Two were killed outright. A third, also shot, escaped in the snow where he was soon captured. As soon as the man, an Iowan named Barnum, regained his strength and recovered from his wound, he escaped from the county jail.²⁶

William "Billy" W. Lee

The most gruesome crime of the era was the Billy Lee murder.²⁷ The incident involved a 5 foot 10 inch, mustachioed and goateed pimp named William Wesley Lee. Lee, operator of a permanent gunboat at Gulfport in 1875, became so outraged at the drug abuse antics of one of his whores, Jessie McCarty, that on the night of Saturday, November 6, Bill stomped her head in, dragged Jessie to a nearby tree, and "kicked her in the face and jumped on her till...her neck cracked." Then he "got a club and struck her two or three times."²⁸ Finally, he threw her body in the Mississippi. On November 20, one of Lee's buddies, Dan Brazee, confessed the crime to Burlington officials who then telegraphed Henderson County Sheriff George Bell. On Monday afternoon, November 22, Bell arrested Lee and ten other people on the gunboat and took them back to Oquawka. All other prisoners except Lee were set free on $500 bail. Lee was charged with murder and was committed to jail for trial the next spring. He was petrified. Lee was convinced that the Vigilance Committee would get to him before the trial. Instead, they burned the gunboat. In January, 1876 Lee attempted an abortive escape.

Before the trial started in March Jessie's body had washed up on an island near Montrose, Iowa. Thus, with a corpus delecti, the state charged Lee formally on April 24 with killing McCarty by several "mortal bruises." The defense feebly moved for acquittal on technicalities. The jury was selected. Lee was pronounced guilty and asked "that he shall suffer the punishment of death."²⁹ Judge Smith set the hanging for June sixteenth. So, that dreary, rainy day over 3,400 gawkers came to the enclosure built next to the courthouse. Almost everyone had a good view of the scaffold. Reporters from newspapers all over the state, as well as from Chicago and St. Louis were there. They had to wait until after lunch. At about 2:00 in the afternoon, Lee moved shakily to the gallows, blamed his situation on bad women and whiskey, and was hanged. After about an hour of dangling, Lee's body was cut loose and placed in a coffin. He was buried near his home in Jefferson County, Iowa.

Murder or attempted murder became epidemic, although none were as sensational as the Lee-McCarty case. A Dr. Edward Lawrence was arrested in 1863 for a killing at Warren. Apparently the good doctor had had an on-going feud with a Mr. Hunt over the Copperhead issue wherein Hunt threatened to kill Lawrence. In the town hotel the two men faced-off and the doctor shot Hunt dead on the spot. At his trial, though, Lawrence pleaded self-defense and the jury agreed. It was a shoot-out. On June 11, 1867 Jack Galligher gunned down John H. Cooper at the river dock just north of Oquawka. His lawyer at the Oquawka trial convinced Galligher to switch his initial plea of "not guilty," to "guilty," so as to avoid the death penalty. So, Galligher pleaded guilty to the crime and was given twenty years in prison. In July, 1870 an Oquawka goon named Pig Foot Ewing beat up either one or both sons of Thomas Johnson. Then Johnson and his boys went after Pig Foot and killed him. Sheriff Joe Brader and seven deputies arrested the Johnsons after they had barricaded themselves inside their house in fear of being lynched, they later said, by the Vigilance Committee. Whatever the cause, mostly lack of evidence, the jury acquitted all three Johnsons that October.³⁰

Jessie McCarty

Other homicides litter the court records. Charles Stiltz, a German immigrant living in Gladstone, was charged in 1876 with stabbing his wife to death with a butcher knife. He was acquitted. The following year, John Thompson murdered James Higgins. The incident happened at Raritan that winter. Thompson was found guilty and given thirty-three years at Joliet. In 1874, a young woman living in Judge Ritchey's home named Emma J. Watson, disappeared. Two weeks later her body was found floating along the dock at Oquawka. Dennis Welch was arrested and incarcerated for more than a year before being brought to trial. At the trial, however, he was acquitted and the murder remained unsolved. On Independence Day, 1877 at Carman, Jesse Asher shot and killed another young man. He was found guilty of second-degree murder and was given ten years at Joliet. On Independence Day, 1880 Archibald Toup shot and killed Stephen S. Phelps, the son of Sumner Phelps, at the Oquawka railroad station platform. He was convicted and sentenced to ten years at Joliet. In the fall of 1883, William Diver of Lomax took an ax to his widowed sister-in-law for refusing to marry him. Her terrified screams at the sight of her maniacal, ax-wielding relative brought timely help from neighbors and saved her life. Diver then slit his throat and fractured his own skull with the ax. In the dead of winter, 1887, just south of Raritan, Soloman Zink shot John Robinson with a revolver. Apparently, Robinson had been having an affair with Zink's wife, or so Zink thought. The jury found Zink guilty of second-degree murder and he was given fourteen years at Joliet. In December, 1890 Barnum Brown, with his brother William, visited their brother-in-law George W. Holly at Warren. There, at Hopper's Mill, Barnum blew Holly apart with a shotgun. The Barnum brothers, together, were found guilty and both landed in Joliet for thirty years behind bars. In February, 1892 young Robert A. Rankin disappeared without a trace while on the train between Biggsville and Burlington. His body was never found. At Decorra, Swan Swanson, was charged with killing Gustavus Adolfson by hitting him on the back of the head with a club. The jury found Swanson was not guilty. In November, 1899 Grant Gissall of Oquawka was killed by a blow on the head, his arms broken by an iron bar, and his house, with him in it, burned to the ground. No one was ever brought to trial. On the night of February 9, 1899, at Gladstone, Isaac Niece axed his wife Anetta. A neighbor found Anetta the next morning with the ax sticking in her skull and Isaac, sitting, staring at her from the next room. Poor Isaac pleaded insanity but the jury disagreed. He was sentenced to life imprisonment at Joliet.

In contrast to the seamy excitement of crime and violence the political life of the county was civilized. It became regularly Republican. To be sure, there were Democrats around but they were confined, a definite minority, to the southern townships. Only two towns could be thought of as Democratic, Oquawka and Raritan. At the county seat, J. Simpson, the Democratic chairman, held regular party meetings. At Raritan, Edward O. Barnes became one of the most influential Democrats through his newspaper the *Raritan Reporter.*

Absence of closely-fought elections over party loyalty was matched by a dearth of political issues. One of the basic underlying reasons for the banality of county politics was that the period after the Civil War till after the turn of the century was a time of avoidable choices in American politics. Compared to slavery, secession, emancipation, and reconstruction the main political questions of the day were ones which did not intrude on the daily lives or on the futures of the farmers and townsmen of Henderson County. They could be dealt with or not as one was so inclined. Their consequences, one way or the other, might be of interest but they were not of importance. It might be of concern if your neighbor wanted to pass laws to regulate railroad rates, or believed in the workers' right to strike for his eight-hour day—or it might not matter at all. It could be fascinating to watch Congress in the Sherman Act of 1890 or President Teddy Roosevelt later on try to bring the "Robber Barons" of the big business trusts into line, but what did it really matter after all?

The isssue of prohibition, however, did strike a response in the county during the Golden Years. On this question Republicans generally wanted it and Democrats opposed it. Prohibition started as an issue in the 1870s when Illinois Republican governors John M. Palmer (1869-73) and John L. Beveridge (1873-77) supported the idea. The crusade demanded an end to the saloon. It focused on beer-drinking Germans, in particular. A prohibition candidate, Frances E. Willard of Evanston ran for state Superintendent of Public Instruction in 1884. In the county, Harry Patterson, in 1886, walked away from his family's historic link with the Democratic party to throw his newspaper behind prohibition. Every town except Oquawka banned saloons. Only the county seat was a "license town" allowing taverns, although some places like Gulfport operated them anyhow.

Another national issue which caught the attention of county voters, temporarily at least, was Coxey's Army. The Army was a direct response to the Depression of 1893, called "panics" then, which caused both unemployment among workers and a collapse of grain prices. Nationwide there were a number of violent protests: over 1,300 la' ꝏr strikes and uncounted riots. Miners, angered by wage cuts, took over a silver mine in

Coeur d'Alene, Idaho. Farmers in the Midwest faced, in addition to tumbling prices, serious new competitors: Canadian and Russian wheat growers and Argentine cattle ranchers. Some writers and politicians, such as Daniel DeLeon of the Socialist-Labor Party, predicted that capitalism would be soon destroyed, overthrown by an alliance of farmers and factory workers. Their revolt would bring about in America an elimination of class differences and a new social order.

In the spring of 1894, a small quiet businessman from Massillon, Ohio, captured the spirit of frustration and began the first protest march on Washington. Jacob S. Coxey, in 1894, wanted more money and he wanted the national government to give it to him. That was his formula. Congress should print more dollars regardless of whether or not they were backed up by gold in Fort Knox. Coxey also demanded a federal job-relief program with wages paid by some $500 million of the new paper money. Coxey baptized his new-born son that year as "Legal Tender" Coxey. He started out of Ohio in March with some 200 men, marched eastward through Pennsylvania receiving food and shelter from recruits as they went. At the same time another support contingent of marchers left Omaha. The Omaha Industrial Arm, or Kelsey's Army, headed east too. Before Kelsey's Army got very far they heard news of the fate of Coxey's Army in the nation's capitol. There, on April 30, police troops on horses had moved on the rag-tag group of protestors who had surrounded the capitol building and clubbed them, with their women and children, into respectability. Many were arrested.

Kelsey's troops continued, for a while anyhow. Although they never got to the District of Columbia, they did move across Iowa and through Henderson County. Traveling along what became route 34 to Burlington they crossed the CB&Q bridge to Gulfport and then walked south along the tracks to Carman. From Carman, across township roads, they marched to Stronghurst where they put up camp near the schoolhouse west of town. By then they numbered over 100 men. They carried signs which read: "On our way to see Grover" (meaning President Grover Cleveland, then in his second term in the White House) and "Marching On to Washington." Like Coxey's Army, they were peaceful and as they moved across the county received support, food mainly, from local residents. On June 14, after a day in Stronghurst, they went northward again to Biggsville and from there, back on route 34, to Monmouth and out of the county.

The only other national question to touch Henderson County, and then only slightly, was the Spanish American War. Briefly put, this war was the result of Cuban insurrections starting in 1895 against Spanish control of the island and its policy of political oppression there. Newspapers, especially the New York *World*, run by Joseph Pulitizer, and William Hearst's New York *Journal*, competed in sensational stories about Spanish atrocities and the need to save Cuba from further Spanish tyranny. Truth is, the United States was deeply involved in events in Cuba from the beginning and regardless of the "Yellow Journalism" of Pulitzer and Hearst would have become directly involved in events sooner or later. For example, we allowed the Cuba revolutionaries to set up and operate out of New York City. American bankers subsidized them with loans. Politicians from both parties published articles in national magazines urging intervention on behalf of Cubans.

Congress, against President Cleveland's policy of official neutrality, in

1896 passed a resolution demanding that Spain allow Cuban independence. For awhile, since Cleveland did not push the issue, Spain ignored the United States. But later that year William McKinley was elected president on a Republican platform that pledged, among other things, American support for Cuban freedom. Events moved fast following McKinley's election. On February 15, 1898 the U.S. *Maine* blew up in Havana harbor with the loss of 260 American lives. Congress reacted. It appropriated fifty million dollars for national defense without one dissenting vote. On April 11, McKinley, responding to the pressure of war, asked Congress for authority to direct the "forceful intervention" of American troops to establish peace on the island. On April 20, 1898 Congress passed a declaration of war against Spain. McKinley signed it the same day.

Henderson County citizens reacted just like other Americans during these fast-moving events. There was the outbreak of patriotic, that is anti-Spanish, statements in the Oquawka *Spectator*, the *Biggsville Clipper*, and the *Raritan Reporter*. But just ninety-one young men bothered to sign up and only seven saw any active duty. A reserve company, in case it would be needed in a protracted war, was ordered by Governor John R. Tanner and James O. Anderson was commissioned to raise it. But nothing came of the effort beyond a sign-up meeting at the Oquawka Opera House in April.

The war ended so quickly that only the *Raritan Reporter* mentioned it. Commenting on our defeat of the Spanish at Manila under Commodore George Dewey, Barnes wrote a terrible pun: "My, didn't George Dew (ey) it to the Spanish at Manila, though?"[31] He also reprinted the telegram announcing the final American victory at Santiago, Cuba. That was it. Henderson County, and the nation, had won. Spain surrendered on July 30, 1898, a little over three months after the war had officially started. McKinley dictated the terms: Spanish evacuation of Cuba and Puerto Rico; the American occupation of Manila pending the disposition of the Phillipines. It had been, if nothing else, exhilarating. Warsaw native John Hay, Lincoln's private secretary and soon to be Secretary of State under President Theodore Roosevelt, wrote to his friend Teddy; "It has been a splendid little war; begun with the highest motives, carried on with magnificent intelligence and spirit, favored by that fortune which loves the brave."[32]

END NOTES FOR CHAPTER FOUR

[1] Gary B. Nash, et al, *The American People Creating a Nation and A Society* (New York, 1986) v II, p 567.
[2] Ibid.
[3] United States Census. Population Schedules, Henderson County, 1860, 1870, 1880.
[4] U.S. Census. Henderson County, 1860, 1870, 1880.
[5] Both Shepard & Johnson and Gordon's *History of Henderson County* contain firsthand knowledge of the construction of post Civil War railroads and their towns. The newspapers also contain running accounts of railroad promotion and construction. See the *Spectator, Henderson Plaindealer, Biggsville Clipper, The Raritan Bulletin* and *The Reporter, Henderson County Democrat,* and the *Stronghurst Graphic*, extant issues are available on microfilm from the Illinois Historical Library, Springfield.
[6] In addition to materials mentioned above see also Henderson County *Quill*, July 23, 1975 in "Santa Fe Parent Many Towns."

[7] John Lee Allaman, "Joseph Smith's Visits to Henderson County," *Western Illinois Regional Studies* (Spring, 1985) 46-55.
[8] U.S. Census. Population Schedules Henderson County, 1870.
[9] Shepard & Johnson, *Henderson County*, p. 387.
[10] County schools during the post-Civil War era, like railroads and towns, are well documented by the two earlier county histories, both of which, when used by modern historians with descretion are fine primary sources.
[11] Gordon, *Henderson County*, p. 714.
[12] Ibid., p. 716
[13] See Shepard & Johnson and Gordon, *Henderson County*, on denominational growth between 1865 and 1900.
[14] Gordon, *Henderson County*, p. 721.
[15] Like education, town growth, and churches the two earlier county histories contain almost all of the surviving information on county fraternal lodges.
[16] One recent study covers thoroughly the story of vigilanty activities in the county. Patrick B Nolan's "Vigilantes on the Middle Border: A Study of Self-Appointed Law Enforcement in the States of the Upper Mississippi Valley from 1840 to 1880." (PhD dissertation, University of Minnesota, 1971), and John Lee Allaman, "Greenbush Vigilantes, An Organizational Document," *Western Illinois Regional Studies* (Spring, 1987), 32-41.
[17] *Spectator*, January 28, 1864.
[18] Nolan, "Vigilantes," p. 112.
[19] *Spectator*, January 8, 1880.
[20] Nolan, "Vigilantes," p. 109.
[21] *Spectator*, July 8, 1875.
[22] Ibid., July 1, 1880.
[23] Ibid., August 23, 1877.
[24] Ibid.
[25] Lee Shepard & Johnson and Gordon, *Henderson County*, give further details on incidents of criminal activity.
[26] Gordon, *Henderson County*, has a short chapter on the Olena Tragedy, pp. 686-88.
[27] John Lee Allaman, "The Crime, Trial, and Execution of William W. Lee of East Burlington, Illinois" *Western Illinois Regional Studies* (Fall. 1983) 49-66.
[28] Ibid., p. 54.
[29] Ibid., p. 61.
[30] *Spectator*, November 3, 10, 1870.
[31] *Raritan Reporter*, May 3, 1898.
[32] Morison, Commager, Leuchtenburg, *American Republic*, v.II, p. 256.

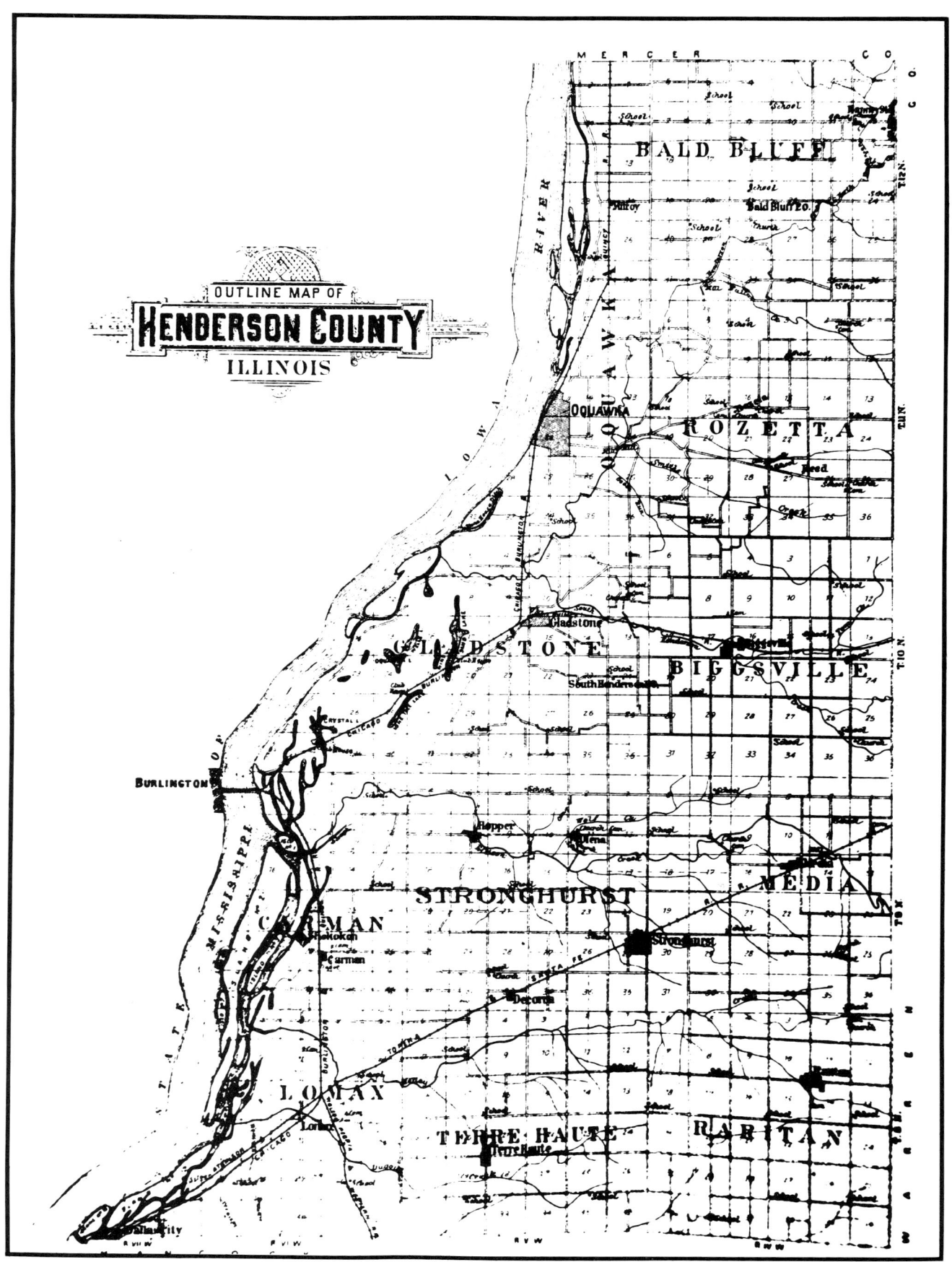

CHAPTER FIVE
COMPLACENCY AND WAR
1900 - 1920

The next war would not be splendid and it would not be little. It would be a world war. But, in the twenty years between the Spanish-American War and World War I, the gentility of rural life in Henderson County ripened and matured. It was, for the county and for the nation, a special time. Those who grew up during these years looked back upon them as an age of innocence, a comfortable time, in the tone of the era if not in its substance. The atmosphere was complacent. Advances in science and medicine extended life expectancy by six years. Aspirin had been introduced in 1894. Foods were processed, preserved, and delivered in new, safe, tin cans at all times of the year. The indoor flush toilet was mass produced after 1900. The sewing machine made garments worth over $1.5 billion by the turn of the century. More and more hours were available for leisure activities. Amusements became organized, for consumption. Political leaders became preachers. President Wilson, in his 1912 Inaugural Address, declared in his deep baritone voice: "We have been refreshed by a new insight into our own life." It was a new age, he said, where "right and opportunity sweep across our heartstrings like some air out of God's own presence, where justice and mercy are reconciled and the judge and the broker are one."[1]

"Equality," "fairness," "reform" were the catchwords of the day. Reform was demanded by both political parties and by both Republican Theodore Roosevelt, in the name of reason, and by Democrat Woodrow Wilson, in the name of God. In Henderson County some of this enthusiasm rubbed off. A cry went up for a more equitable share of county power, physically and politically, and as a symbol of this democratic innovation some people tried to move the county seat out of Oquawka to a new, more central location, say to Gladstone or to Biggsville. The county seat contest was, in fact, a long-standing political, economic, and social issue that went as far back as the Civil War. In December, 1864, for instance, the Oquawka *Spectator* reported that Sagetown (Gladstone) was absorbing much of Oquawka's labor supply.[2] Moreover, Patterson warned that the newer town was seeking to deprive Oquawka its right to be the county seat. He was alarmed that even during that war, when more important matters should have required the attention of county voters, Sagetown had petitioned the state legistrative for a referendum on moving the courthouse. They had been able, he said, to gather the 1,000 signatures of registered voters, a sizable chunk of the electorate at that time. Patterson's views against such a change were couched in economic self interest. This was hardly the time, he said, to burden taxpayers with the exorbitant, and unnecessary, cost of building a new courthouse. The fight continued. In the 1880s, Edward Barnes' *Raritan Reporter* picked it up. He accused the "Oquawkaites" of dragging their feet on the push to modernize county administration by turning it over to a township organization. If that were done, however, then Oquawka "would have to build their own bridges and care for their own paupers."[3] Biggsville joined in. That town allied with Gladstone in 1882 to circulate another petition asking for a change in the county seat. For a time Biggsville and Gladstone competed for the site until a court hearing decided on Biggsville as the more central place. Supporters of the idea raised over $10,000 to help pay for a new courthouse and an election was held. The voters defeated the idea by a majority of 293 ballots.[4]

Main Street, Raritan

Opposite: Henderson County Map, 1910

Henderson County Courthouse
Oquawka, turn of the Century

In 1903 the issue surfaced again. This time Stronghurst led the drive. Another petition was sent around. Another public hearing was held at Oquawka with Robert J. Grier of Monmouth presiding. He threw out the Stronghurst petition on the technicality that insufficient public notice had been given on the hearing. The following year Stronghurst tried once more in the hopes that the newly elected judge, a Stronghurst man, Rufus Robinson, would see the light. But Robinson removed himself from the case on a conflict of interest. Instead, Judge John A. Gray of Canton was called in. The judge had to decide on a procedural question: was the center of Henderson County nearer to Stronghurst than Oquawka? If it were closer to Stronghurst then a simple majority vote could effect removal. If it were nearer to Oquawka then a three-fifths majority would be required. Judge Gray decided in favor of Oquawka.

Folks in Stronghurst were outraged. There was nothing they could do about Gray's decision since there was no precedent to cite against the ruling. So, in November, the election was held. Stronghurst won a strong majority of 1,565 for removal, 1,241 for keeping the county seat where it was. But this number was 121 votes short of the three-fifths required by Judge Gray. Stronghurst tried to reverse Gray by taking his opinion first to the Appellate Court and then to the Supreme Court and lost the appeal at both steps. There the issue rested.[5]

Other local political issues ebbed back and forth on party loyalties, Democrats versus Republicans. The Democratic side was led by Barnes and the *Raritan Reporter*. The Republican establishment was well represented in Eugene A Hail of the Oquawka *Henderson County Journal*, the chairman of the Republican Central Committee. Barnes critized the Republicans of running the county only for the interest of its northern parts. The taxpayers in his township, "the wealthiest in the county," he said, have no say "as to how their money shall be expended."[6] Another problem Barnes saw was the county poorhouse, jail, it was a disgrace. Barnes predictably backed the Democratic candidates for county offices. He pushed Everett L. Werts for judge, Charles A. Brainard for sheriff, and urged every Democrat to "talk and work and vote as they should."[7] He praised Werts endlessly calling him "energetic, and with splendid qualifications" even if he were from Oquawka.

But the Republicans carried almost every office in about every election. In 1910, the year Barnes' hopes were the highest with his man Werts leading the ticket, the Democrats were trounced. Robinson whipped Werts by 1,263 to 777. R.T. McDill, the Republican, overran Brainard by 1,313 to 733. In the 1911 spring elections Republicans captured all of the four Supervisors' positions. So, as usual, the County Board was overwhelmingly Republican, eight to three, a majority which the Republicans held except in 1916 when they kept it to six G.O.P. men against three Democrats (Gladstone, Terra Haute, and Stronghurst), one Progressive (Biggsville), and one Independent (Rozetta).[8] Still undaunted, Barnes backed Werts in 1912, this time as a candidate for the state legislature. Werts won and served two terms in Springfield.

When voting on national issues and candidates Henderson County otherwise stayed with the G.O.P. It backed Taft in 1908. It voted in favor of him again four years later when Wilson won the nation by 6,296,547 to Taft's 3,486,720. In 1916, the Democrats led a much more vocal campaign for Wilson's reelection against Republican Charles Evans Hughes. It was an uphill fight in Henderson County though, Barnes complained in August. Barnes would not pull his punches, however. Republicans he said, were "calamity howlers and flannel-mouthed editors." Wilson should be praised, Barnes wrote, for his heading-off an impending railroad strike, despite a Republican conspiracy to urge on the disaster of a general tie-up of the nation's railroads.[9] On the eve of Wilson's reelection the *Reporter* ran a large advertisement for the President on page three, and under Wilson's photograph was the bold-print caption "He kept us out of War."[10]

E.O. Barnes

Still, Barnes could not help sensing defeat. On November 1, 1916 he wrote that he would like to see the Democrats win but they probably would not. In any event, he was not going "to dress in a sack cloth and ashes" if they lost. He had lived through Republican administrations most of his adult life and had survived. "We can stand another one if necessary," he conceded.[11] Barnes instincts were right. Henderson County by 2,680 to 1,580 went for Hughes, as did Illinois. The state legislature also went Republican by 84 to 17 in the Senate and 84 to 69 in the House. By his election, as the Wilson advertisement plainly showed, a new issue had intruded into national and local politics; an issue, then an event, which would shatter the county's complacent, Republican, rural, life-style. The issue was peace or war. Before then, however, everyday life of the county was comfortable indeed.

Winfield Hixson Threshing Crew, Raritan

Henderson County's economy prospered. Its system of public education expanded. Its routines took on the appearance of steady gentility. The census figures show growth of the family farm. Even as early as 1885, it claimed the cheapest yet best land in the nation.[12] Farm land in the state went up from $46.17 an acre in 1900 to double that in 1910, or to $95.02. County farms increased in value at the same rate during the decade, from $40.74 an acre in 1900 to $91.36 in 1910.[13]. Farms began to change, physically, in appearance. Across the county farmers put up the new cross gable barns. Basically square in design these structures were two-storied with a cupola in the center and shuttered windows on all sides on the second floor. They had considerably more square feet of storage, especially with the addition of the loft. The cost was about $1100. They were put up by teams of carpenters who traveled from farm to farm at wages of one dollar a day plus room and board. There were also new livestock barns erected, most of them about 1910. These structures had a central silo for feeding the animals, almost always cattle. The exterior was extremely weather-tight and sturdy, compared to the more ventilated cross gable structure, mainly for protection of the animals during winter. The carpenters first put up a close-spaced frame made up of elm timbers soaked in linseed oil. The superstructure was then nailed on the frame parallel to the ground. On top of the siding they placed the shingles. Other, more traditional farm buildings still dotted the landscape--the saltbox, the T-type, and the simple gable barns.

Overshot Hay Stacker

Around the farm another change appeared. Woven-wire fences replaced, gradually, the osage-orange hedge fencerows of the last century. Planting and harvesting, though improved, was relatively simple. Usually a Henderson County farmer in 1910 owned a gang plow, a disc, a harrow, and a two-row planter. He would start the planting by stretching a wire across the field. The wire had buttons about every forty inches which the planter would strike and trigger a seed drop. At the end of the wire he pulled it up, moved it over to the next row, inserted the wire in the planter, and began all over. One could cover about twenty-five acres in a day's planting. Husking corn paced about one acre per day. The workers would do everything by a hand grab, pull, twist, and throw. In the fall they never plowed. Farmers just turned the cattle into the stalk fields to graze and to provide the fertilizer in time for next spring's planting. The yield, after all was done, was on the average fifty-five bushels of corn an acre. By then, as the census data shows, much of the farm work was done by the "hired men." These workers were both single and men with families and they lived and ate in the farmer's home while on the job. Many just walked from farm to farm looking for work. They were looked upon as a trustworthy, dependable lot, whose ambition was to save enough money to one day become a farm-owner themselves. They seldom ever achieved their goal.[14]

The Henderson County farm just before World War I was diversified. It had several buildings and a fenced feedlot for livestock. Farmers raised corn, oats, wheat, and barley. They tended cattle, chickens, hogs, and goats.[15] The internal combustion engine, or tractor, was used on some farms but most men still used horses or mules for power since in 1910, almost 27 percent of all harvested land was set aside for workstock feed. Some farmers emphasized certain commodities, but none specialized. Hogs were a mainstay of many farmer's income. Frequently one saw men like Gilbert Voorhees. He owned a farm about three miles south of Raritan and in July of 1910 he delivered to W.H. Penny in Stronghurst sixty hogs averaging in weight at 331 pounds. His total weight was 30,945 pounds for which he received $2,785.05.[16] Others were dairy farmers. Merlin Foresman of Lomax Township recalled, in 1980, his father's dairy farm. In 1910 his family ran a 200 acre operation valued, he thought, at $200 per acre. They sometimes had up to eighty Holsteins fed by hand-cut corn stored in two thirty-foot silos. The Foresman's bedded their cattle in shredded fodder brought to the barn. The feed was grown from their own seed which was hung up to dry every year, until 1918 when the Farm Bureau office at Stronghurst began to sell seed corn that made good germination tests.[17] The Foresman's sold their whole milk to a restaurant in Dallas City for 15¢ a gallon, to a cooperative "creamery" at the same price, or directly, door to door, to customers in the town.[18] Others, like William T. Weir, turned their lands into orchards. On 175 acres in 1910 they were raising the best apples in the state along with raspberries, strawberries, and plums.[19]

Livery, Media, early 1900's

Farm profits zoomed between 1916 and 1920, especially when the United States government started to purchase agricultural products to export in payment of the national debt. During World War I the Allies' demand for Illinois farm products skyrocketed, and so did prices. The state increased wheat production from two to four million acres. Farm values doubled from the 1910 figure of $95.00 an acre to $164.20 in 1920 in the state as a whole and in the county from $91.36 to $166.66.[20]

Farm sales were regularly advertised in the newspapers. In 1910, for example, a 153 acre farm four miles south of Raritan was sold out of the estate of Mrs. Emma Riggs to William H. Van Arsdale for $19,050 or $124.50 an acre. Another farm that year, closer to the town of Raritan, brought $150 an acre.[21] In July 1911, a typed "best buy" advertisement read:

> "400 acre farm for sale. Three miles from town.
> Fine grove, good house, barn granary, and other
> buildings. Well and wind mill. Rich black loam
> soil. $52.50 per acre, $6,000 cash, balance to
> suit buyer."[22]

Or another *Raritan Reporter* advertisement, on September 19, 1917, as prices rose, went:

> "WANT TO BUY A FARM?"
> We have a few choice ones for sale.
> Prices range from $135 to $215 per acre."[23]

Cornelius Brokaw family home

Like the family farm the county school system functioned better than ever. Education changed in some ways, especially after 1917, but still remained geared to a system of small school houses, run at modest cost, which in the opinion of most voters did the job of educating their children. The county itself was divided into fourteen school districts, each of which received an infinitesimally small operating budget. In 1911, for example, only $5,385.69 was signed off to the entire county by Superintendent of Schools A.L. Beall. He gave out the funds as follows: Raritan ($380.40), Media ($491.51), Biggsville ($474.25), Rozetta ($410.21), Bald Bluff ($363.14), Terre Haute ($366.04), Stronghurst ($864.49), Gladstone ($604.33), Oquawka ($468.47), Oquawka Franctional ($70.45), Lomax ($460.34), Carman ($279.13), Gladstone Fractional ($70.46), and Dallas City ($112.46).[24] The county atlas of 1910 located the various school houses operating within these units. Raritan had six structures, Media six, Biggsville nine, Rozetta eight, Bald Bluff eight, Terre Haute five, Stronghurst seven, Gladstone and Gladstone Fractional six, Oquawka and Oquawka Fractional five, Lomax and Dallas City five: a total of sixty-five one-room schools each about two miles from the next one.

Barry School, Media

At these places children were all taught together. Edythe C. Johnson, on March 19, 1980, then aged eighty-five, remembered her grade school experience at the Empire School, as she called it. There, she and seventeen other pupils went through grades one to eight. Each morning they lit the bellied stove before class began at nine o'clock. At four o'clock students were dismissed. The school year went from September to May, ending with a huge community picnic on the closing day. Children's ages ranged from six to fourteen years. Teacher turnover was rapid. She recalled changing teachers almost every year. Small wonder. They were paid only $45 a month in salary.[25]

In June 1917, the state passed a statute which re-organized its system of education. By that law each county was organized into high school and non-high school units or districts. Henderson County was divided into four high school areas: Oquawka, Biggsville, Terre Haute, and Stronghurst. The other sections were left outside the unit but were, on a tuition basis, allowed to send their children to one of the four high school districts. Within each non-high school unit there was to be an elected Board that could tax to pay the tuition of any eighth-grade student wishing to go to high school. The non-high school units in 1918 organized themselves together into District 20 and comprised the townships of Raritan, Lomax, Carman, Gladstone, Media, Rozetta, and Bald Bluff.

Most people accepted this division of the county into what amounted to first class and second class educational units. Edward O. Barnes did not acquiesce. He wanted a high school in his township, right away. "It is a burning shame," he observed, "that the children of Raritan township who desire a high school education should have to go away from home to secure it." His township, he insisted, was "abundantly able to support a high school and should have one."[26] Then, later, he continued hammering away at the same point. It was not fair. "There are a whole lot of young people in Raritan township," Barnes wrote in the fall of 1917, "who could use a high school to good advantage if only we had one." "As it is," he lamented, "several of the more ambitious ones of the community are preparing to go away from home."[27] He lost his campaign to Media Township. The voters of that township agreed on September 28, 1918 to be taxed to establish and support a "Community Township" high school. They then officially removed the township from District 20 and the next year 115 Media students who had been going to high school outside the township returned home for their education.[28]

College education received its first public attention just before the war.

Raritan Grade School

Up until that time the high school had been a fine long-term educational goal. But the need for a college experience was first seen by Barnes in a 1905 editorial. He speculated as to why more of our "farmer boys" do not want to go on to college. After all, there were four close by: Knox, Lombard, Monmouth, and Western Normal. They all offered practical, "up-to-date courses, just such as our young farmers ought to take." He enumerated Zoology, Botany, Chemistry, English, Engineering, and History. These were subjects that one could never "study too much." Besides, he wrote, "a good education brings a substantial return in happiness all of one's days, and helps solve the common problems of life as well."[29] The *Raritan Reporter* ran, after 1916, regular September advertisements for the new Normal School at Macomb, stressing that there one could also receive a high school diploma as well.[30] For the eighth grade graduates the student could select an academic or a vocational curriculum. At the Normal School one prepared for teaching with such courses as music and drawing, library economy, physical education, science, household arts, physics and mathematics, primary education, English, and History.[31]

All teachers who came to Henderson County were expected to attend yearly professional Institutes and take regular teachers' examinations. The Institutes were well advertised in the county newspapers and usually were scheduled for early or mid-June. One held at Oquawka in 1916 was attended by seventy-five or more teachers.[32] Another, the following year, was hosted again at Oquawka. On June 13, 1917, the *Raritan Reporter* noted that "eighty teachers were in attendance at the annual institute in Oquawka."[33] Stronghurst led in the number of teachers sent, followed by Biggsville. In order to qualify to teach each person had to take and pass a state examination. They were scheduled each July at the county seat. The test was, for the times, rigorous. It ran over two days, beginning at about 8:00 each morning.[34] Now and then the examination was given outside of the county, such as the one in 1916 in Monmouth.

Education was just one aspect of the integrated social fabric of the county. There was, overall, a propriety about how one lived. Henderson County people had a strong sense of what should be done and what would not

Telephone Operator, Lomax, 1911

be tolerated. Some of the things which must be done were old-hat (morality, the way one dressed, orderliness, and prices at the store). Still, other things were brand new (the telephone and automobile) and they deserved a strict appraisal. Things forbidden were rather universally agreed upon: wolves, tramps, gypsies, and rowdy youths.

Edward Barnes' frequent sermonizing on social values provided a glimpse into community standards of that era. Granted, Barnes was prudish, even in his own day. He was at times overly didactic but his values were not all that askew from the norm of the friends with whom he lived and worked for over fifty years. Proper conduct, to Barnes, meant obeying the rules, and the rules were clear. "Young man," he advised, "if you desire to be successful in life there are three things which you should shun: liquor drinking, speculation, and endorsing of notes of any kind whatever."[35] Smoking, chewing, and spitting tobacco were an abominable breach of etiquette when ladies were around. A good marriage was the keystone of the community. It was, in turn, based upon courtesy and a businesslike equality. "If more men would treat their wives as business partners, which in reality they are," he mused, "or would show them the courtesy they do a hired girl--pay them $6 to $10 a week for doing the housework...there would be more happy homes and fewer divorce cases in this beloved country of ours."[36] Extra-marital or pre-marital sex was taboo.

Men should dress in business suits when in town or at church and the women must show equal decorum. Never should a woman dress like a man. He was horrified to report that a Raritan woman actually "dawned male attire and rode a horse clothes-pin fashion into Blandinsville one day last week."[37] She should have been arrested, in Barnes' opinion. Farmers, especially, should be more orderly. After the harvest, he ordered, put away the tools. "On nearly every farm are many untidy things that are passed by unnoticed by the owner," he complained, "but are an eyesore to the stranger...and silently brand the occupant of the place as a shiftless individual."[38]

Steady values also meant steady prices. Clothing could be bought at H.S. Calvins in Roseville at a price any man could afford. Gray, blue, or brown serge suits were listed at only $10, $15, and $18 in 1911. Food at Meloans Store in Media in 1917 was within everyone's means: $3 for a sack of flour, coffee at 20¢ a pound, a ten pound bag of sugar only 85¢, a pair of shoes at $1.25, a man's work shirt at 75¢, a yard of woolen cloth 40¢, and a hammer and bucksaw for only 75¢ each. Even doctor's fees were cheap. An office visit cost $1.00, house calls $1.50 during the day and $2.00 at night, although "extra will be charged for a trip over muddy roads."[39]

Some innovations, though, were welcomed by Barnes. In 1900, the telephone came to Raritan complete with switchboard and "all appurtenances." The Illinois Bell Telephone Company operated countywide from its headquarters above the A.M. Thorton grocery store in Oquawka. There, general manager Frank Shorts supervised six day-operators and a night-operator seven days a week. There, one could place long-distance calls by a time clock. Patrons just punched-in when the call was placed and had it stamped when finished. That was the bill.[40] Communication by land, by county roads, was deplorable. People in bad weather could barely travel more than seven miles on the best roads and the appearance of automobiles made their condition unbearable.[41]

Automobile, Rozetta

The earliest cars were reported in 1912 at Dallas City and Oquawka. By 1916 they were seen all over the county, largely as recreational vehicles. In August of that year Barnes observed that "the public highways hereabouts fairly swarmed with automobiles going hither and yon last Saturday."[42] In good weather a person could make it to Macomb from Raritan averaging twenty-five miles an hour at best, although Oren Morris and his family took eight hours to make the same trip in January 1918.[43] Cars were expensive luxuries. A touring car for five people, the Saxon Six, cost $935 f.o.b. Detroit in 1917. The more popularly priced Chevrolet, though, could be bought at J.E. Wells, an "implement dealer" in Raritan, for $730 including taxes and freight charges.[44]

Auto excursions became a regular Sunday event. In 1917, a number of citizens from Raritan banded their cars in a caravan to Burlington and spent the day there in Crapo Park in a picnic which included in its list, a seventy pound pig and a five gallon can of ice cream.[45] Some people, like Barnes, thought that the day of the horse and buggy was gone. Indeed, one Saturday afternoon in June 1917, when the muddy roads kept the automobiles home and folks were forced to go back to the carriage Barnes noted with a touch of nostalgia that "it looked old fashioned to see the tie racks lined with horse-drawn vehicles."[46]

Autos in front of General Store, Rozetta

Road improvements, by that summer, had become a topic of regular conversation. There was speculation that the state legislature was about to launch an ambitious program of paved roads. In fact a "good roads" bill authorizing sixty-million dollars was reported in the Senate in the spring of 1917. Speculation as to the possibility of using asphalt as a new paving technique started as early as 1916. The *Raritan Reporter* noted its earlier success both in Europe and as the surface "used on Pennsylvania Avenue in Washington."[47] In May, 1918 a "Good Roads Meeting" was held in Monmouth to get public support for the bond-issue road bill. "Every person within forty miles of Monmouth, especially automobile owners," Barnes announced, "should attend."[48] Still more money could be raised to help construct the roads through a higher tax on automobile licenses. The program, however, as envisioned in the highway map printed in the *Raritan Reporter* in November 6, 1918, was sparing for Henderson County. The map, entitled "How Illinois Will Look," showed only one road, Route 34, through the county itself. Route 136 ran west out of Macomb and another road went from that county seat northeast to Bushnell, while a north-south road, route 67, connected Macomb and Monmouth.[49]

There were things, as always, to complain about even in that era. Wolves continued to run wild in packs, and the county paid three dollars apiece for their pelts. One man, in 1917, named Nimo Smiddy of Terre Haute township picked up $27 in one trip to Oquawka for nine cub pelts.[50] Joe Norman of Terre Haute was treed by a pack of wolves. He fortunately had his rifle along at the time and killed one of them. The other wolves then "vamoosed" and Joe had a chance to jump down off his perch and head home -- with his three dollar prize.[51]

Adolph Beaty, Rozetta Blacksmith

Two-legged wolves were also a nuisance. Tramps popped up, mainly along the CB&Q and the Santa Fe, every spring. Some were more than vagrants. In June, 1911 five hobos were arrested at Lomax for breaking into a Santa Fe railroad car. They were fined an impossible $25 and, unable to pay, were locked in the county jail. Only their leader was kept behind bars though, since the four others were boys between sixteen and eighteen

Oquawka Button Factory
Warren Street, Near River

Oquawka Button Factory Employees

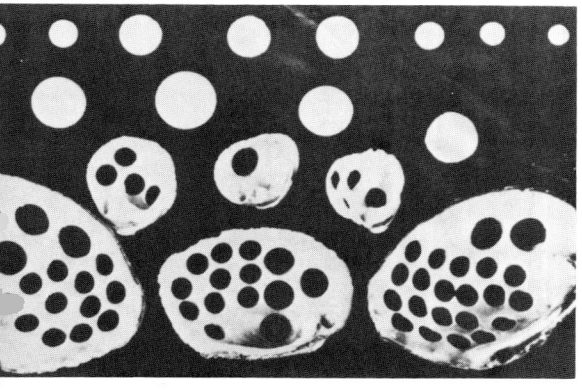

Button Blanks, cut from shells

years of age whose parents claimed them for release on bond.[52] Gypsy caravans wandered through the county every fall. In September, 1916 Barnes described "a band of nomads commonly called gypsies who passed through town last Monday afternoon." "They seemed to be in a hurry to get somewhere," he noted suspiciously, "as they didn't stop to...steal or tallied tell fortunes." He noted that they were traveling in "seven rigs" and about "thirty people" in all.[53]

Next to bums and gypsies Barnes hated the rowdy young men of the local poolhall, a place he labeled a "cesspool of inequity." There, one May Saturday night, they got drunk, or "took on a jug" in Barnes' lexicon, and carried on till all hours of the morning. He could not sleep. The "yells sent up by some of them would outrival the war whoop of a Comanche Indian." Not only that, these fellows "tore up sidewalks, upset buggies and wagons in the street and committed diverse other acts of vandalism."[54] On another Saturday night the same "young men from the county" came to town loaded. They "pranced back and forth through the streets, whooping and yelling...that they were the best lot of men that ever trod on mother earth and (used) the vilest and most obscene language known to the English tongue."

Barnes, this time, had had enough. He got dressed and went out and told them to quiet down. It did not work. "Instead of having the desired effect," Barnes' sermonizing "riled the mob and caused them to hurl vile *epithets* at him." They told the five-foot eight-inch, stocky, bespeckled editor to get lost. A fist-fight started. By then "there were several hundred people upon the streets," along with a constable, who just stood and watched. Barnes did not relate who won the fight. He only groused that "no arrests have been made yet" and if something were not done "our town will become a perfect bedlam...unsafe for decent people to appear upon our streets after night."[55]

Despite such rowdiness, and Barnes' alarm, the level of criminal activity in the county subsided from its early rate. There were two robberies, at Swan Creek and Media, one rape at Stronghurst, and a Biggsville murder episode. On January 31, 1911 Carl Carroll and George Reed stole $3,000 by dynamiting the safe of the Swan Creek Bank. They then took a team and carriage from a local liveryman and made off to Stronghurst. There they planned to hop a Santa Fe car and escape but no train was scheduled until 9:30 the next morning. So, they hired another liveryman to drive them to the CB&Q depot at Gladstone where they were able to get on board. But the train headed east, not west, and back to Monmouth where the sheriff arrested the two men. After their trial they were sentenced to a term in the prison at Joliet.[56] At Media in the spring of 1918 "Dad" Gran's Store was robbed by "local talent."[57] The crooks were tracked by police dogs and within hours the dogs "had a boy so badly frightened that he made a clear breast of it, implicating four other boys of the town with himself." No account survives as to their disposition at court. It seems likely that they were minors who were released to the custody of their parents. There was quite a sensation created at Stronghurst in March, 1911 when a Grand Jury indicted the town dentist, Dr. Hurdle, for raping Lucy McFadden in his office chair. Nothing further was reported on the case.[58]

Biggsville, circa 1900

Then on September 20, 1916 there was an account of a woman's corpse being found one mile east of Biggsville along the tracks of the CB&Q. She was identified as Mrs. Emma Larkins. Emma, while at the Aledo Fair earlier in the week, took some time off in a barn with Bert Sapp. Sapp, one witness said, or someone, killed Emma and then stuffed her into a trunk in a CB&Q boxcar. Later, near Biggsville, the trunk and Emma were thrown off the train. Sapp was held in the Mercer County jail at Aledo to await trial. He was subsequently found guilty of murdering Emma in a bunk stall at the Fairgrounds and sentenced to twenty-two years at Joliet.[59] So, there were felonies within the county but overall the pace of criminal activity had subsided. Typical was the docket of the fall, 1916 term of the Circuit Court. It listed a total of sixty-four cases. Of these, thirty-one were at common law, thirty-one in chancery, three were applications for divorce, and only two were alleged violations of criminal law.[60]

Gideon Dixon Harness Shop, Biggsville

Reports of local crimes in the newspapers ceased to provide a lurid form of recreational reading. Instead, for entertainment, a few Henderson County residents went for a ride in their new motor car. But most families could not hope to own an automobile so other, more organized amusements started to take up a regular part of daily life during the first years of the Twentieth Century. First on the list of "things to do" were the county fairs held every August in Henderson, Hancock, McDonough, Warren, and Mercer counties. Other outings were sponsored by associations, usually a farmer's group such as the "Farmers' Picnic Association." Most of the events were free. A typical advertisement was for the 1910 LaHarpe Fair. It was to run for four days in early September. There were "exciting races every day," two bands playing in concert, $5,000 in prizes, and "great free attractions to boot!"[61] The Farmers' Institute of Henderson County put on less ambitious projects, usually once a year in winter. Most often they were held in December and featured invited speakers sent by the Illinois Farmers Institute. H.W. Mumford, of Springfield, for example, spoke at the Stronghurst Institute Meeting on December 9, 1911 on "Live Stocks." At the "shows" or exhibits held inside Harter's Hall the following prizes were awarded: the best white corn, $10, the best yellow corn, $10, the best pop corn, $3, the best three-pound roll of butter, $5.[62] At the exhibit in Raritan in 1912, twenty-four lads competed for prizes in the corn shown.

One Horse Saloon, Oquawka, c. 1915

Lomax Fish Fry

Fraternal organizations and schools pitched in too. Typical was the advertisement ran in July, 1910 by the Odd Fellows. They touted the "Big Event of the Year" coming up at Stronghurst in July 28 and 29: their Sixth Annual Picnic in the city park. Free demonstrations from 9:30 in the morning until 11:30 at night were promised. There was Homer Hazard the Aeronaut who would make his "great cannon shot ascension." Also on tap were "The Original Vernards," (America's Fearless Equilibrists). The Rozards (swinging, whirling, and walking the wire suspended by their teeth). There was a trick-house called the "Katzenjammer Castle." The Galesburg Military Band would play an open air concert. There was a merry-go-round, an Electric Theater, Vaudeville acts, a side-splitting comedy act, acrobats, heat balancers, barrel jumpers, a funny lady-clown, and "orations by the Best of Orators."[63] Every school, almost, had their annual picnics in May. In 1917, the Union School at Raritan, like the others, advertised its Seventh Annual event where four other schools -- Center, Muddy Lane, Lombard, and Pleasant Gale -- would participate. There were bands from Blandinsville and Western Illinois State Normal School to "help entertain the crowd." "If you go," the caption read, "be sure and take a basket of grub along."[64]

The most interesting recreational innovation in Henderson County was the Opera House. This institution, predecessor of the motion picture house, was the first clear example of the stretching cultural impact of the city on rural life. It was the social and artistic expression of the economic extension of the city to the farms via the railroad in the preceding generation. Opera Houses appeared about 1900 and took root for a generation in Oquawka, Stronghurst, and Raritan. John M. Foster, in the spring of 1980, remembered the Oquawka house. Regularly, weekly in its heyday just before World War I, it put on "hometown" plays with some of the greatest sound effects Foster ever heard. An air compressor, for instance, imitated a steamboat or railroad whistle.[65] The Stronghurst Opera House featured in 1911 the "Musical Event of the Year," William C. Cushman in the "semi-operatic," "The Toymakers Dream." Prices ran 50¢, 35¢, and 25¢. By 1917, the place had changed its name to the more pretentious "Lyric Theater of Stronghurst." Then, on a Saturday evening in December, a man could take his lady friend to see "Broadway After Dark," hyped as "the story of a little country lass who was wrecked upon the shoals of life, who became a derelict and finally drifted like THE PORT OF MISSING GIRLS!."[66] It had "orchestra music." A gentleman could purchase his reserved seats for 50¢ at Beardsley's Store in town during the day. Even more elaborate was the 1918 Lyric Theater production of "The Girl and the Tramp" with the Maytime Gardner Players. This show ran for two consecutive nights in January, 1918 and featured a complete scenic production, five big song hits, three special vaudeville acts and a superior cast of players."[67]

Raritan Opera House, 1902

The Raritan Opera House was built in 1902. It was a multi-purpose structure where the "opera chairs" could be taken out to use the floor for dances or, at election time, a polling place.[68] Most of the events here were one-night stands. The advantage was that it had shows throughout the week, not just on Friday and Saturday nights. On Tuesday, February 15, 1910, for example, "Lowery & Morgan's Mighty Minstrels" the "Best Band Traveling," played there.[69] On Wednesday, October 5, that year you could go to see "Damon's Colored Musical Comedy Company."[70] Seats were on sale at the Raritan Union Bank for 50¢, 35¢, and 25¢. In 1916, there were other one-nighters such as "Ikey and Abey, Three Acts of Glorious Comedy" who gave patrons "a laugh in every line — and the lines are close together" or, later in the summer, the play "Winning Bells."[71] Local talent got its chance on stage. Raritan school children, fifty of them, put on at Christmas, 1911 "Santa's Success" with Santa Claus, the Moon Man, the Fairy Queen and Fairies, Venus and the Stars, and the Goblings. It cost only 25¢ for adults and a dime for children to get in. The Biggsville Dramatic Company came down that same year to put on "A Modern Woodman," a six-act comedy drama. The Media orchestra presented a concert of "orchestra selections, solos, trios, and quartets both vocal and instrumental on November 7, 1917.[72]

As one might expect with two interstate railroad lines bisecting the county, tent circuses were a regular attraction. In 1911, one set up at Dallas City. Everyone who came during the three September days was guaranteed a flight in a Curtis Bi-plane and one chance to "see a Birdman." On August 31, the West Brothers raised a tent east of Raritan. Their center-ring attraction was the "Cowboy, the Indian, and the Lady." The advertisement pushed the "Cowboys, Soldiers, Indians, Mexicans, and Cowboy Girls." "Watch for the Cowboy Band," it said.[73] In July 1917, the biggest act of all, Ringling Brothers Circus, came to Monmouth. Henderson county folks were encouraged to come over by train or road. There would be just one afternoon performance. The *Raritan Reporter* cautioned, but it would be well worth the effort to get there. Over 1,000 persons will take part in the circus," it said, and "300 dancing girls are expected." Four hundred "aerobic artists" will appear in the main tent. The menagerie was unbelievable: 1,009 wild animals (800 horses and 41 elephants)! There were sixty clowns and, on the morning before the circus opened, there was scheduled "a big, free, three-mile street parade."[74] The parade never started. The reason, said Barnes, was because "the Ringlings were so incensed over the treatment received from the mayor that, "without any parade, they gave only one performance, that was in the afternoon, and then pulled up stakes vowing never to return."[75]

Interior Raritan Opera House, c. 1924

Other kinds of entertainment were less spectacular. Like many rural communities the traveling Chautauqua visited the county every year, usually in August. Most of the time it operated off the Santa Fe depot at Stronghurst. Under a huge tent they promised a "most interesting affair" with five attractions, "both entertaining and educational," running all week long starting, in 1917, on August 14. A full ticket cost $5 for adults and $2 for children.[76] Each town had its summer-band concerts. One such

117

Beach at Oquawka

Mart Walter with horn

"Coronet Band" played at a fried chicken festival given by St. Patricks Church in Raritan on August 16, 1911. The church cleared $81 at the event.[77] At Oquawka, another Coronet Band dating back to Civil War, put on weekly concerts until the summer of 1917. That June the citizens of Oquawka regretted to announce the end of the concerts because of the war. "The enlistment into the armed services of four of the members....has put the village band out of business."[78] Baseball teams were sponsored by local business and by the two railroad companies. They played in pastures rather than in anything resembling a baseball field. The crowds at these games were large, though, about 200 or so, such as the one which came to watch the Santa Fe Club of Stronghurst lose to the Lombards of Poverty Flat, twelve to thirteen, at Jim Huston's farm on July 19, 1911.[79] The Mississippi River provided opportunity for bathing and for excursions. Just north of Oquawka families went to swim on a large sand beach in 1910 just before the construction of the lock and dam on the river flooded the site.[80] At Dallas City, J. Waymack and Dr. Cleveland took their families on a paddleboat excursion down river. They went south to Nauvoo and, in 1916, inspected the new hydroelectric dam being built at Keokuk.[81]

Motion pictures, or movies, made their appearance in the county about 1916 on a fill-in basis. At the Opera House in Raritan, for example, merchants began to hire, not regularly, Hedgar Churchill of Monmouth to show his "movies" on those Saturday nights when no live shows were scheduled.[82] By 1918, the Lyric Theater in Stronghurst was advertising a "five-reel motion picture" every Thursday night. During the week the Raritan Opera House started to run "movie reels."[83] These films were, of course, erratic entertainment compared to the fairs, musicals, shows, circuses, concerts, baseball games, and excursions. But the movies did bring to Henderson County, in their brief news clips, a glimpse of events which, till then, had passed-by the farmers and merchants of western Illinois. Here, in the darkened opera houses, people first saw the ominous happenings in Europe. Like America as a whole, they had their first real insight into the carnage of war.

World War I, to Americans, was a war nobody wanted, nobody expected would happen, and nobody ever thought would touch the United States. Americans were wrong on all three counts. The war in Europe began in the summer of 1914 when an heir to the Austrian throne was assassinated in the little Balkan country of Bosnia. In July, Austria and Germany declared war on the tiny nation and almost immediately, in her defense, Russia mobilized her army. Germany responded to the approach troops on her eastern border by declaring war on the Czar and, unavoidably, on Russia's ally France. When the German army went through neutral Belgium to strike at France in August, England, fearing German domination of the lowlands and German control of the English Channel, declared war on the Kaizer.

By August 4, Europe was at total war. Most Americans felt that Europeans had gone mad. The *New York Times* stated a common view: They "have reverted to the condition of savage tribes roaming the forests and falling upon each other in a fury of bloodshed."[84] This sense of revulsion was immediately followed by relief. The Atlantic Ocean was a natural barrier to the spread of such butchery to American shores. Besides, the United States had no vital interest in the outcome, or so we thought. President Wilson echoed these emotions by immediately issuing a Proclamation of Neutrality. We would stay out.

Neutrality was easier proclaimed than pulled off. Great Britain refused to accept it and levied a blockade on all American shipping to Germany and Austria. Wilson recognized the reality of British sea power and acquiesed to the blockade. As a consequence, our trade with the Axis powers dropped precipitously, from $169 million in 1914 to only $1 million in 1916. At the same time our economic ties, already strong with England, were strengthened considerably. We not only increased our trade with the Allies from $825 to over $3 billion but also, through private banks like the House of Morgan, gave them over $550 million of unsecured loans. Germany, feeling she had little alternative to American's "unneutral actions" aiding her enemies, retaliated by submarine warfare. This new weapon, called a U-boat after the German word for it, *Unterseeboot,* had no precedent in international law. So, to the United States, it seemed illegal from the start. Moreover, U-Boats either threatened or took American lives. A crisis was reached in the spring of 1915 when the British liner *Lusitania,* with 128 Americans on board, was torpedoed and sank off the Irish coast. American writers cried "Mass murder!" Others demanded an immediate declaration of war against Germany.

Wilson would not be stampeded. Germany, sensing the imminent threat of the United States entering the fighting alongside the Allies, tried to placate American public opinion. The Kaiser promised that his U-Boats would not attack any more ships without warning. Wilson accepted the promise. Some Americans, led by Theodore Roosevelt, were skeptical and urged the nation to prepare for war. They formed the "National Security League," among other such groups, and demanded that Congress appropriate money to enlarge the army and navy. They wanted a conscription law. They wanted propaganda, "patriotic education" they called it, to get the country emotionally ready for the fight. Other Americans feared that such preparations would, in fact, get us directly involved. They formed the "American Union Against Militarism." The President sided with the militants. He asked Congress, in the fall of 1915, to enlarge the army to over 200,000 men and to pull the National Guard into its chain of command.

There the situation stood as 1915 turned into 1916, an election year. Wilson's strategy for reelection was to play for peace even though he had requested war preparations from Congress. His opponent, Charles Evans

Sterling L. Morelock, Rozetta Twp.
Sterling Morelock received the Congressional Medal of Honor Citation for conspicuous gallantry and intrepidity above and beyond the call of duty in action with the enemy near Exermont, France, October 4, 1918. Leading a patrol in advance of his country's front line he cleaned out five machine-gun nests, and then rendered first aid to the injured, using as stretcher bearers the ten German prisoners that had been captured. His company commander was wounded and while dressing the wounds, Private Morelock was severely wounded in the hip, forcing his evacuation. His heroic action and devotion to duty were an inspiration to the entire regiment.

Hughes, a Supreme Court Justice, spoke unequivocably for "adequate preparedness." Wilson claimed that a vote for Hughes was a vote for war. The President was pictured as the man who "kept us out of war." Wilson won an extremely close contest, getting 49.4 percent of the popular vote to Hughes' 46.2. Wilson then interpreted his earlier pledge for peace loosely. After the election he said, "I can't keep the country out of war. They talk of me as though I were a God." Yet, he did go before the Senate to outline his plan for a negotiated end to the conflict. It would have to be "a peace without victory" for either side, he said.

Germany refused such terms, mainly because the Kaizer was convinced by then that his country was winning. So, on January 13, 1917, he announced the resumption of unrestricted submarine warfare on any ships bound for England or France. The country waited. Between March 12 and March 21 German U-Boats sank five American ships in the North Atlantic. Wilson hesitated no longer. He felt his faith in "a peace without victory" had been betrayed by Germany. On April 2, 1917 the President appeared before a joint session of Congress and read these words:

> It is a fearful thing to lead this great peaceful
> people into war, into the most terrible and disasterous
> of all wars, civilization itself seeming to be in the balance.
> But the right is more precious than the peace...God
> helping her, she can do no other.[85]

Early in the morning of Good Friday, April 6, 1917, Congress declared war on the German Empire.

As these events unfolded Henderson county citizens read about them from time to time in their newspaper and then saw them in their Opera House movie clips. At first attention to the war and to America's problems of neutrality focused on the dramatic. The bias was obvious. British aviators were portrayed as performing "daring deeds" and were called "Knights of the Air." Newspapers dramatized the U-Boats attacks. Bold type letters proclaimed in the *Raritan Reporter:* "TWENTY-ONE AMERICANS DIE WHEN DIVER SINKS US STEAMER" or "TORPEDOED WITHOUT WARNING WHILE IN THE SAFETY ZONE." The German army was pictured as losing the fight on the front while at the same time the "Fighting Power of the French Grows Steadily."[86]

Wilson's war message was reported in county newspapers in detail but with no sensational headlines, as though it had been anticipated. On April 4, the Raritan paper simply stated that Congress had voted to support the President in War with Germany. It demanded that all American citizens "either native born or naturalized," in pointed reference to the Germans living in Oquawka, Gladstone, and Biggsville, "do their utmost to help protect the United States."[87] A week later though the text of Wilson's message was printed without comment. The front page of the *Raritan Reporter,* in this issue, was devoted to the war. Columns were headed by such captions as "Aliens Are Warned" or "Seize Internal German Vessels," or "To War on the Kaiser." An interesting perspective on what had happened was the article called "Germans Force Us to Enter Conflict." The central point of it was that Wilson never wanted war and that the Kaiser was the villian who forced it upon America.[88]

The immediate public reaction in the county to war was unrestrained enthusiasm. It was from the start labeled as a "War for Freedom."[89] Citizens backed up the call for volunteers in a projected force of ten million men. The newspapers told of thousands of young men nationwide wishing to register for the draft or to volunteer. The draft law itself, calling up all men between twenty-one and thirty-one at first, was signed by the President on May 23, 1917 and registration started almost immediately, on June 5. Henderson County applauded the prompt action of Governor Frank O. Lowden, himself a Republican, who went before the legislature in Springfield to pledge his support for the war. He asked all county officials to register 646,480 men for conscription. He called the General Assembly into a special session to establish draft machinery such as local exemption boards, medical examinations, and legal advisory groups.[90]

Illinois, overnight, became a training ground. Northern Illinois draft boards sent young men to Camp Grant at Rockford and southern Illinois boys went to "boot camp" at Camp Zachary Taylor at Louisville. Officers were trained at Fort Sheridan outside of Chicago. There, too, the Navy ran its Great Lakes Training Center which had opened in 1904. Two aviation bases were set up, one near Belleville at Scott Field, the other at Rantoul, at Chanute Field. The Prairie State provided 314,504 men to the armed forces, 9,000 of whom were trained as officers. The first draft quotas, put out in July, 1917 were modest--50,000 for the state.[91]
Henderson County's first goal was seventy-four men. Registration places were set up at the courthouse and at banks in Biggsville and Stronghurst. Evert L. Werts was made chairman of the county draft board. By the second week in September, 1917 a contingent of four Henderson County draftees was shipped out with another thirty ready to go within days.[92] To be sure that men legitimately excused from military service by the boards were not ostracized by their friends the county gave out "Exempt Badges." These were small red, white, and blue buttons with the inscription "exempted U.S."[93] On the first round thirty-one men enlisted. Then another thirty-six were reported as having signed up. There the draft had registered ninety more young men making the county's total list of draftees and enlistees by the end of 1918, 1,130. The largest block of men came from Stronghurst township (198), with Gladstone second (147), and Oquawka third (142). The least number of men came from Carman township (40).[94] Within a year after the start of the war married men were no longer exempted. And, by that time, newspapers regularly told of men being sent not only to Camp Grant for basic training but also shipped to Camp McArthur in Waco, Texas, for combat overseas.[95]

Carl Swanson

American troops landed in Europe in June and on July 4, 1917 paraded in Paris. As the reality of their sons and friends fighting in the war itself settled in, more interest was paid to combat news of the front. All of it was, by then, either Allied or United States government propaganda coordinated, or distributed, to Illinoisans by Chicago businessman Samuel Insull, head of the state's Council of Defense. The Council mobilized opinion behind the president and generated patriotism with horrific accounts of German brutality in Europe.[96] The war was ghastly. British cavalry charged the German lines with swords drawn and machine guns cut them in half. Airplanes created terror with their new bombs. Tanks appeared, an apparition out of a nightmare. Poison gas choked and burned. County newspapers told of an "Unwritten Record of Atrocities." German soldiers, the "Huns," went on rampages of rape and murder against helpless civilians. They shot babies. They pillaged cities and towns. They treated their prisoners like animals. Men were kicked and chained together. Americans were starved to death in Austrian camps. German cooks used human bones (American, French and English) for soup.[97] In a classic understatement, Barnes said that the German troops were, consequently, a "disgrace to the Army."[98]

Men leaving for Army from Oquawka

Reports of what "our boys" were doing were a study in contrast. American soldiers were brave, inventive, even exhuberant. "The men are warmly welcomed," the *Raritan Reporter* said in July, 1917.[99] Their letters home were mentioned but were not reprinted. In fact, there was no news of where they were and how they were feeling. Typical was a March 13, 1918 account of a letter received by Frank Voorhees from his son Harry. It only stated that Harry "had arrived safely somewhere in France and was well."[100] His letters were few. The last one Harry wrote was on Thanksgiving, 1917 when he was still in New York City awaiting embarkation. It was as though once in Europe the men were out of sight and out of touch. No one could have pictured where they were or how they looked. The troops from Henderson County, as Irving Berlin wrote, were in a mental no-place, they were "over there," wherever that was.

The first casualty came a year after the first lads left the county. It was the death of Ralph Simonson. He never got to France. In the fall of 1918 at the Great Lakes Naval Training Camp he came down with the "Spanish influenza." His father was at his bedside in sickbay when Ralph died.[101] Late in November news arrived of the death of Leon Melvin. He died of pneumonia "somewhere in France."[102] In early December, Dr. and Mrs. Cleveland received a letter from a hospital nurse in France that their son Emmett had been blinded by mustard gas.[103] Another casualty was the death, from pneumonia, of twenty-two year-old Harry Voorhees, who had been doing so well in France. He died in Base Hospital #54 "somewhere in France" on October 11, 1918. Ironically, news of all casualties reached home after November 11, 1918.[104] Death came after the armistice, after it was, literally, all quiet on the western front.

The boys who lived, and came home, received a hero's welcome. Celebrations were gala. In Raritan, the Red Cross organized the event. There was "a coronet band, vocal music, dancing, speaking, and a general good time."[105] But the tumult of victory could not dissipate the tragedy of war. In November, 1920 the remains of Leon Melvin were brought to his young widow in Blandinsville. From there the cortege moved to the Old Bedford Christian Church seven miles southwest of Raritan. Then his corpse was carried back to Blandinsville and entombed in a family crypt. His wife, whom Leon had married on October 3, 1917, and infant son then went home.[106]

Before the news of death arrived in early 1919 the folks back home had felt little of the impact of war. The first effect on daily life was the effort to gather support for the war effort. In August, 1917 the Henderson County Red Cross organized. In the beginning it hoped to sign up 1,500 members but almost immediately it had over 1,600 people from every township and town. It spent the next year-and-a-half putting together "Comfort Bags" for all soldiers sent overseas.[107] To help finance the war, Liberty Board drives were organized under Insull's Council of Defense.

The first of many county canvasses began in November, 1917 and sold $137,650 worth of bonds. Then the bonds were sold haphazardly by subscription at local banks. But in 1918 the drive was better organized. Each school district was given a quota for both bonds and for distributing War Savings Stamps. Now there was a county War Savings Bond Chairman, R.B. Parsons. The drive of June, 1918 contrasted with the casual affair the previous summer. There were canvass areas and rallys, called

"War Savings Meetings," in every district. There was a "Pledge Week" from May 11 to 18. June 28 was designated as "National War Savings Day" and each "American" was asked to pledge twenty dollars. Chairman Parsons asked the county to raise $195,000.[108]

The war was at worst inconvenient. During the first year county food prices doubled. Henry Wallace, the Food Administrator for Illinois, who reported to the national head of the Food Administration, Herbert Hoover, tried to break the inflation spiral. As early as October, 1917 he set "proper maximum prices" for retailers. These were well published in the newspapers. Sugar, for example, should cost no more than $8.50 a pound and flour $3.18 a pound. Prices went up anyhow. Clothing, though, was another matter. Prices remained fairly stable. Men's clothing at Perrine & Son, Raritan, sold for about the same in 1918 as in 1917. Men's sweaters cost six dollars, caps twenty-five cents, boy's jersey sweaters thirty-eight cents, and men's heavy underwear thirty-eight cents. There were drives to conserve certain kinds of food so as to leave some for export to the American troops. "Meatless Days" and "Porkless Days" were regular, at least twice a week.[109]

Overseas Service Emblem, WWI

But denial soon came from necessity rather than from choice. By the end of 1917 fresh meat was a rarity. Many meat markets had closed and in the southeast townships the only supplier there was a Roseville peddler who came "only when it suits his convenience."[110] By the next summer sugar was gone. What was left was severely restricted by Insull's men. Ordinary consumption was limited to two pounds to the town family and five pounds to the farm household. For a while housewives could get up to twenty-five pounds for preserving purposes but, Barnes warned, "it is feared that it may become necessary to further reduce the allowances and limit the frequency of purchases."[111]

There was an energy crisis: no coal. Insull appointed James W. Gordon, I.F. Forward, and F. Rehling as a Fuel Committee for the county. They were given authority to supervise all sale and delivery of the fuel. They were instructed to pay special attention to those individuals who could afford only small quantities at a time to be sure they did not run out. They were to demand prompt payment, no credit purchases were allowed. Hoarding of coal was a civil offense punishable by a fine. Even so, the coal supply did not last the first winter. By February, schools were closed because of no heat.[112] Gasoline, too, disappeared along with the coal. Sunday "drives," the time for outings in some families before the war, were out. There were only "gasless Sundays." Fewer cars were on the road during the week, too. Secretary of State Emmerson, in August, 1917 announced that no more new automobile licenses would be issued.[113] For awhile, anyhow, it was back to the horse-and-buggy days. By that time some people, like Barnes, were fed up. Apparently he had a short toleration on inconveniences. His rhetoric blamed the "coal barons" and "railway magnates" for the fuel shortages.[114] He threatened retaliation against food shortages. He wrote that "unless there is a let-up before long, the worm will turn and then there will be something doing, compared with which the present war will look tame." "The wrath of a person goaded on by hunger," he pledged, "is something to be feared."[115]

There was, despite the shortness of the war (just over eighteen months

123

from beginning to end), a shrill note of impatience in the county. The war within memory, the Spanish American War, had been short and splendid. No casualties for Henderson County were tallied then and there were no food shortages, no cold winters, no restrictions on travel and recreation. Within a matter of months in 1918, though, folks became disgruntled. Like Barnes, they were intolerant of what became intolerable inconveniences. They became, even more sinister, intolerant of each other.

The county, and the nation itself, in 1917-18, succumbed to a hysterical fear of German conspiracies against, and American subversion of, the war effort. Congress, a mirror of this nativism, passed the Espionage Act in June 1917. The statute fixed a penalty up to $10,000 and twenty years in prison for anyone who interfered with the draft or "encouraged disloyalty," whatever that meant. The Sedition Act of 1918 extended the penalties to anyone who "discouraged recruiting," or would "utter, print, write or publish any disloyal, profane, scurrious or abusive language about the form of government of the United States, or the Constitution, or the flag, or the uniform of the Army or Navy...or advocate any curtailment of production of anything necessary to the prosecution of the war." Late in 1917, Congress had put into law the Trading-with-the-Enemies Act which gave President Wilson the authority to censor foreign language newspapers.[116] There were, nationwide, over 1,500 prosecutions under these laws. One of them was Eugene V. Debs, a man twice candidate for the Presidency of the United States who had received over 9,000,000 votes in 1912. He was convicted, without evidence, of encouraging resistance to the draft and given twenty years in jail for the speech.[117]

Henderson County was not immune to hate and fear. To most, during war, it was "America First Last, and All the Time!"[118] There was no place in the county for foreigners who could not agree 100 per cent with that motto. "Any foreign born citizen who can't cheerfully subscribe," Barnes warned, "should either get out...or be kicked out." "Your 'Uncle Sam' has enough to contend with," he wrote, "without having to watch a lot of perjured traitors who have taken the oath of allegiance with a mental reservation 'to bite the hand that is feeding him' when opportunity offers."[119] Censorship was welcomed. Barnes applauded the requirement of the Postmaster General to have all mail addressed to "Germany, Austria, Luxembourg, Bulgaria, or Turkey" sent to the dead-letter office to be destroyed.[120]

In the summer of 1918, Henderson County residents were required to sign a "Loyalty Card." If they refused, their names were published in the newspapers. For example, on October 9, 1918, a list of nine disloyal men were printed in the *Raritan Reporter*. Among those named were five from Oquawka, three from Stronghurst, and one from Terre Haute.[121] The county gathered around the flag. Barnes gloated that most of the counties in Illinois should "take off their hats to Henderson County in the matter of Loyalty." Out of the 10,000 people "less than a dozen persons have been reported as failing or refusing to sign our Declaration of Loyalty and to make their financial statement." Watch for the list of these traitors, though. "Watch...and learn who it is in your midst who has the mistaken idea that he is bigger or greater than we, and not amenable to the same laws that we cheerfully obey." It was signed "Executive Committee, the Henderson County War Savings League."[122] By 1920, after the casualties had been buried, the men and women of Henderson County had had their fill of war. They wanted to forget about it, quickly.

END NOTES FOR CHAPTER FIVE

[1] Henry S. Commager, *Documents of American History* (New York) p. 84.
[2] *Spectator,* December 22, 1864.
[3] *Raritan Reporter,* April 5, 1888.
[4] Gordon, *Henderson County,* see chapter 17 on "County Seat Contests," pp. 700-702.
[5] Ibid.
[6] *Raritan Reporter,* December 1, 1887.
[7] Ibid., October 26, 1910.
[8] Ibid., April 5, 1911.
[9] Ibid., September 6, 1910.
[10] Ibid., November 1, 1916.
[11] Ibid.
[12] Ibid., October 29, 1885.
[13] Ibid., March 16, September 14, 1910; July 5, 1911.
[14] Flossye T. Andersen, Tape recorded interview by Rita Souther, March 11, 1980. Western Illinois University Archives and Special Collections.
[15] Merlin Foresman. Tape recorded interview by Rita Souther, March 1980. Western Illinois University Archives and Special Collections.
[16] *Raritan Reporter,* July 10, 1910.
[17] Ibid., May 1, 1918.
[18] Merlin Foresman interview.
[19] John M. Foster, tape recorded interview by Rita Souther, March 3 & 4, 1980. Western Illinois University Archives and Special Collections.
[20] *Raritan Reporter,* September 17, November 21, 1917. United States Census 1910, 1920.
[21] Ibid., March 16, September 14.
[22] Ibid., July 5, 1911.
[23] See also Ibid., November 21, 1917.
[24] Ibid., April 3, 1911.
[25] Edythe C. Johnson. Tape recorded interview by Rita Souther, March 19, 1980.
[26] *Raritan Reporter,* August 30, 1916.
[27] Ibid., September 5, 1917.
[28] Ibid., September 28, 1918.
[29] Ibid., August 16, 1905.
[30] Ibid., September 5, 1917.
[31] Ibid., September 5, 1917.
[32] Ibid., June 19, 1916.
[33] Ibid., June 13, 1917.
[34] Ibid., June 27, 1917.
[35] Ibid., December 22, 1887; February 11, 1914.
[36] Ibid., June 28, 1923.
[37] Ibid., May 10, 1888.
[38] Ibid., April 1903.
[39] Ibid., December 11, 1912.
[40] John D. Cochran. Tape recorded interview by Rita Souther, March 7, 1980. Western Illinois University Archives and Special Collections. See Ibid., April 20, 1910.
[41] Ibid., February 22, 1911.
[42] Ibid., August 23, 1916.
[43] Ibid., June 30, 1918.
[44] Ibid., March 20, 1918.
[45] Ibid., August 16, 1917.
[46] Ibid., June 13, 1917.

[47] Ibid., March 29, 1916.
[48] Ibid., May 8, 1918.
[49] Ibid., November 6, 1918.
[50] Ibid., April 18, 1917.
[51] Ibid., March 11, 1911.
[52] Ibid., June 11, 1911.
[53] Ibid., September 20, 1916.
[54] Ibid., May 8, 1890.
[55] Ibid., June 28, 1893.
[56] Ibid., February 1, September 20, 1911.
[57] Ibid., April 10, 1910.
[58] Ibid., March 15, 1911.
[59] Ibid., May 30, 1917.
[60] Ibid., October 4, 1911.
[61] Ibid., August 31, 1910.
[62] Ibid., December 6, 1911.
[63] Ibid., July 20, 1910.
[64] Ibid., May 8, 1917.
[65] Foster Interview.
[66] *Raritan Reporter*, December 22, 1911.
[67] Ibid., January 28, 1918.
[68] James H. Cook. Tape recorded interview by Rita Souther. February 22, 1980. Western Illinois University Archives and Special Collections.
[69] *Raritan Reporter*. February 10, 1910.
[70] Ibid., October 10, 1910.
[71] Ibid., August 30, 1916.
[72] Ibid., November 17, 1917.
[73] Ibid., August 3, 1911.
[74] Ibid., July 11, 1917.
[75] Ibid., July 25, 1917.
[76] Edythe C. Johnson interview. See also Ibid., August 8, 1917.
[77] Ibid., August 16, 1911.
[78] Ibid., June 6, 1917.
[79] Ibid., July 19, 1911. See also Edythe C. Johnson interview on the Lennox Baseball team.
[80] John Noble. Tape recorded interview by Rita Souther, March 6, 1980. Western Illinois University Archives and Special Collections.
[81] *Raritan Reporter*, September 13, 1916.
[82] James H. Cook interview.
[83] *Raritan Reporter*, April 17, 1918.
[84] Quoted in Gary B. Nash, *et.al.*, *The American People Creating a Nation and a Society,* volume two (New York, 1986) p. 627.
[85] Commager, *Documents*, p. 132.
[86] *Raritan Reporter*, March 28, 1917.
[87] Ibid., April 11, 1917.
[88] Ibid., April 11, 1917.
[89] Ibid., June 20, 1917.
[90] Howard, *Illinois*, p. 437.
[91] Ibid., pp 438-40.
[92] *Raritan Reporter*, September 12, 1917.
[93] Ibid., August 1, 1917.
[94] Ibid., September 18, 1918.
[95] Ibid., October 23, 1918.
[96] Howard, *Illinois,* pp. 441-43, 503-04; Jensen, *Illinois,* pp 109-10.
[97] *Raritan Reporter,* August 22, December 26, 1917.
[98] Ibid., August 22, 1917.
[99] Ibid., July 4, 1917.

[100] Ibid., March 13, 1918.
[101] Ibid., October 2, 1918.
[102] Ibid., November 20, 1918.
[103] Ibid., December 3, 1918.
[104] Ibid., December 3, 1918.
[105] Ibid., September 10, 1919. For another account of the reaction to the Armistice see interview of Flossye T. Anderson.
[106] Ibid., November 24, 1920.
[107] Ibid., May 23, August 15, 1917.
[108] Ibid., November 14, 1917; June 28, 1918.
[109] Ibid., October 31, 1917; February 20, 1918.
[110] Ibid., December 12, 1917.
[111] Ibid., June 19, 1918.
[112] Ibid., February 16, 1918.
[113] Ibid., August 6, September 18, 1918. See also Edythe Johnson interview.
[114] Ibid., January 2, 1918.
[115] Ibid., August 8, 1917.
[116] Mary Beth Norton, *A People and A Nation, A History of the United States,* vol. II, second edition, (New York, 1986), pp. 665-67 on "The Attack on Civil Liberties".
[117] Morrison, Commager, and Leuchtenburg, *The Growth of the Republic,* v. II, P. 385.
[118] *Raritan Reporter,* September 19, 1917.
[119] Ibid., September 19, 1917.
[120] Ibid., May 9, 1917.
[121] Ibid., October 9, 1918.
[122] Ibid., September 25, 1918.

The Burg 6-Cylinder 50 H.P. 1912 Model
Manufactured in Dallas City, L Burg Carriage Co.

CHAPTER SIX
THE TWENTIES

In November 1920 Americans elected Warren Gamaliel Harding President of the United States and tried to pretend that World War I had never happened. Henderson county citizens, too, in a span of eighteen months, had had enough of their meatless days, gasless days, and coal shortages. Government had intruded far too much into their lives by agencies such as Insull's Council of Defense and its incessant propaganda for Liberty Bonds. They were fed up, too, with Wallace's Food Administration and its attempt to tell a grocer what he could charge for coffee or sugar. They were relieved, naturally, that some of their boys were home and not dying of influenza or mustard gas in some God-forsaken spot in Europe. Above all else, though, they wanted things the way they used to be—before the war. They were, like everyone else, tired of self-sacrifice and moral slogans, of Woodrow Wilson's sanctimonius appeal "to make the world safe for democracy."

Warren Harding personified the times. He caught the national malaise when he asked for a return "not to heroism, but healing, not nostrums, but normalcy." Harding's campaign played on this mood of weariness. The Democrats in the 1920 election, on the other hand, were at a loss as to how to respond. Their leader, President Wilson, lay incapacitated in the White House, bedridden from a total physical collapse since September, 1919. So they ran a virtual unknown against Harding, Governor James Cox of Ohio, whose only qualification seemed to be that he and Harding were from the same state. As Cox's running mate, as a standup against the Republican vice-presidential candidate, Calvin Coolidge, Democrats put up another unknown, young thirty-eight-year-old Franklin D. Roosevelt of New York, Wilson's Assistant Secretary of the Navy. Republican Hiram Johnson of California remarked in October of the campaign, "If it were a prize-fight, the police would interfere on the grounds of brutality."[1]

The Republicans' strategy was simple. Wrote one party leader early on: "Keep Warren at home, don't let him make any speeches. If he goes out on tour somebody's sure to ask him questions and Warren's just the sort of damned fool that will try to answer them."[2] Harding went along with this sound advice. The Democrats were decimated. Harding won thirty-seven of the forty-eight states and received 61 percent of the popular vote, winning every precinct in New York City and every county on the Pacific coast.

Harding, then fifty-five years old, was totally unfit to be president and historians rank him only equalled by U.S. Grant as our worst Chief Executive. He was morally weak, had no capacity for day-to-day administration, and his "government by cronies" was riddled by scandal. Harding's own father, a judge in an Ohio County Court, years before had seen the fatal flaw in his son's character which, as president, was tragic. "Warren," he once admonished, "it's a good thing you wasn't born a girl. You just can't say No!"[3]

Harding's only justification for being elected President was that he looked like one. After Harding's mysterious death, on a train trip west in the summer of 1923, the White House was presided over for the rest of the Twenties (all but seven months in 1929) by Calvin Coolidge. This man was a perfect remedy for the sordid Harding rule and restored rectitude, at

Opposite: Gerald Dean and Traxel Kirkenslager
With Plane Built at Lomax Factory

129

least, to the presidential office. Coolidge was, though, the "least" president this country ever had in the twentieth century. He was an unfriendly, cold Yankee who never smiled, a man with a pinched face. Alice Roosevelt Longworth, Theodore Roosevelt's daughter, remarked that "He must have been weaned on a pickle."[4]

Harding or Coolidge, despite opposites in character, shared the same philosophy of government. This attitude, put simply, was to let the people, particularly business people, do what they wanted to do. The federal government, they felt, should get out of everyone's lives. It must stop setting standards of conduct, morality, economic goals, or social justice. Americans would have to make whatever adjustment needed to be made after the war without policy or help from Washington. And so, Americans as a whole and Henderson County in particular returned to "normalcy." But they could not return to the way it was. Old things were not quite the same. Even before the war new technologies had already started to transform how they lived and how they looked—electricity, movies, cars.

The Twenties throughout was a time of conflicting contrasts, old and new, of righteousness and lawlessness. These were years when the small town, small church, small school, small farm were extolled but began to lose their attraction, especially to the young. Their parents might want the good old days, but they did not. For the first time Henderson County showed an ominous trend: steady population decline everywhere. The decade began with Harding's "normalcy" and a cry, almost a plea, for the complacent, tolerant America of, say, 1910. Yet this was the time of the Red Scare, of nativism and a vicious hatred of foreigners, and an insistence on "100 percent Americanism." It was the decade of "the noble experiment," prohibition. Yet while alcohol was illegal and condemned, bootlegging, a flagrant violation of the law, steadily grew.

Nativism or bigotry, defined as the attitude of favoring the native inhabitants of a country as against immigrants, appeared as a hysterical anti-German reflex spawned by World War I and intensified during the events of 1919-20. This was the year just after the Communist victory in Russia and of unprecedented labor strikes in the United States. By the spring of 1919 Russia, under Communist rule, had not only withdrawn from the war but had announced its policy of a worldwide revolution. Uprisings came that summer in Bavaria and Hungary. In America, the new Communist Party was organized. At first, influential American writers idealized the Russian Revolution. Some, like John Reed, published best-selling accounts of it. His *Ten Days That Shook the World* predicted a world-wide revolution of equality on the Bolshevik model. There was a series, one after the other, of devastating strikes: about four million workers took part in over 4,000 of them. Some unions just wanted traditional goals of better wages and hours (wages had stayed about the same during the war while consumer prices in some areas had doubled). But other strikes went beyond these objectives to call for the overthrow of the capitalist system and of the government of the United States itself. For example, 35,000 dock-workers struck in Seattle and paralyzed the Pacific Northwest. Federal troops were called in. All of the workers of U.S. Steel, 340,000 of them, went off the job. Steel owners called them Bolsheviks, advertised in newspapers for public support against the "Red Agitator," and used soldiers and police to break picket lines. In Boston, the police themselves went on strike. The newspapers there said that the Communists started it. College students filled in for absent patrolmen and the strike was broken.[5]

Strikes were bad enough but soon the bomb-throwers appeared. In April, 1919 a bomb blew off the hands of the maid of Seattle's mayor when she opened a parcel delivered to the house. That same week another maid, of a former Senator from Georgia, opened a package and lost both of her hands. Two months later a bomb blew off the front porch of U.S. Attorney General Mitchell Palmer's home in Washington, D.C. Palmer, in reaction, authorized a number of raids on several cities, arresting without cause or warrant 250 men. Then 500 suspects were rounded up, many clubbed and beaten, out of their private homes in the middle of the night. Another 800 more men were arrested and shackled in chains in Boston Harbor. One historian, in 1986, labeled the raids "the most massive violation of civil liberties in American history to this date," which found few dangerous radicals, but fanned the flames of fear and intolerance in the country.[6]

Henderson County was no exception. Hatred of foreigners was overt by the end of the war. Barnes called for removal "the minute he commences to stir up a feeling of discontent among his fellow workmen or joined in a strike."[7] He wanted all foreigners to take an oath of allegiance that they would never walk out on a job. "America," Barnes flatly said, was "for loyal Americans only." And that was the "motto" which should hang in every liberty-loving home in the United States."[8] We should waste no time with the Bolsheviks. They infested the country, Barnes believed. "They should be deported first and tried afterwards," according to his standard of American justice.[9]

Barnes had nothing but praise for the Palmer raids. They were led in Chicago, he reported, by the city's best "merchants, bankers and businessmen" who would "rid the city of radical elements."[10] They would serve, he thought, "to make America safe for true Americans." The foreign anarchists abroad in the land numbered at least "several thousand" by then. They all have been "plotting for the overthrow of our government." They must be exterminated. Palmer and his agents, Barnes wrote in January, 1920, were only doing "what should have been done long ago."[11]

Later on that January his bigotry became frantic. "Brand all foreigners," he said, "Send them back where they came from!" "Arrest all strikers, foreigners as well as American citizens!" "Lock up every American-born citizen who violates the laws of this country (against labor pickets)...until he promises to behave." This was, to Barnes, the only way to deal with traitors. Tear up the Bill of Rights. "Such a procedure would...curb anarchy and sedition quicker than anything else we know of."[12] Get them all out, he printed, the more deported the better. In April, 1920 he was glad to note that within two months over 61,000 foreigners had left the United States.

Purging the country, and the county, of foreigners would not really purify America, would not solve the basic problems facing Americans in the 1920s. The challenge was not cultural corruption but how to adapt the older values and ways of doing things with the new ideas and practices, or more simply, how to reconcile the morals, expectations, and lifestyles of the late nineteenth century with the changing demands and requirements of the twentieth.

One of the new demands was for American farmers to change their method of production to different market requirements. For them not to adapt to the changed conditions meant a drop of farm income and, to survive, a dependence on the Federal Government for an annual relief subsidy. During the 1920s, American farmers as a whole, and Henderson County farmers, unfortunately, chose not to adapt. As a consequence, by the 1930s they were, under the agricultural programs of the New Deal, put on the Federal supports. This program enabled them, with the enormous influx of money from Washington to survive another generation, but the inevitable happened. The family farm started to disappear.

The national farm situation, during the war at least, seemed beyond regression. A new prosperity developed on top of almost twenty years of good times, rising prices, and increasing land values. During the conflict Herbert Hoover, as head of the Food Administration, had his assignment from the President: increase farm production while decreasing food consumption so as to supply the troops. Hoover, accordingly, was energetic and ingenious. He fixed grain prices at an all-time high, established Federal grain cooperatives to purchase it, and licensed Federal food distributors to sell it. Within one year the United States Government was exporting about three times the 1917 level of grain, sugar, and meat. Right after the war, with Europe's economy in shambles, demand for American grain skyrocketed and prices took off on their own. During the years between 1917 and 1920, Henderson County farmers and their counterparts everywhere succumbed to the temptation of prosperity. They invested in more land, bought more machinery, and built more barns and out-buildings.[13]

By 1921 the farm economy collapsed. It was the beginning of the end of a rural America as it had been known since the eighteenth century. The price of wheat fell 40 percent. Corn dropped 32 percent. Hogs went down 50 percent. Total farm income went from ten million dollars to four million dollars. Farm acreage decreased; in five years thirteen million acres were abandoned. Farmers, because of the decline in land values, could not make mortgage payments and lost machinery, land, and homesteads and still owed the banks money.

For those farmers who made it through the post-war crunch another problem hit by mid-decade, over-production. In the 1920s chemical fertilizers and new hybrid seeds made farming more efficient and dramatically increased the yield per acre. As tractors and trucks replaced mules and horses, land which before had been set aside for pasture and feed was returned to production. So, the pattern set in. American farmers by the late 1920s had more grain to sell than ever before while the world-wide demand evaporated. We exported in 1929 only one-third of the grain the country had shipped out just ten years before.[14]

What happened? American agriculture had fundamentally changed. By 1930 farmers in Henderson County were separated into two classes. On one hand were those who just could not make it or were barely meeting their bill payments. On the other hand were the few individuals who realized large profits because they were close to railroad centers, such as Clarence Hartquist's Stronghurst Cooperative Shipping Association, with branches also located at Media and Decorra. These entrepreneurs were able to buy and keep up mechanized equipment and abandoned diversified field planting to grow only one cash crop. These farmers became the first generation agribusinessmen. They stayed on the farm, but not the same farms their fathers had known. The rest, small farm-owners and field hands, became farm workers either laboring for wages or leasing as

Plowing Demonstration, Rozetta 1920

tenants. But by the end of the decade this dependent rural class gave up. They started to leave the farm. They moved out of the small marketing towns and villages. They left the county altogether. Yet this was a national phenomenon. In 1900 more than 40 percent of the American labor force was farm workers. By 1930 this group had been cut in half.

For the agribusinessman still making a living on the farm there was less income to share among themselves. In 1919 they got 16 percent of the national income. In 1929 it was 9 percent. They pushed for help politically. They could see the inevitable, that unless somebody would bail them out they, too, would eventually go the way of their neighbors. They would be out of business. So, they demanded that Congress help them. American farmers got Congress to pass the McNary-Haugen Farm Relief Bill in February, 1927. The bill set up Federal price supports (a guaranteed minimum price) for all farm products. It planned to use the United States Department of Agriculture as the farmer's market manager. It would take the responsibility to dump American farm products abroad and at the same time raise the price of farm products in the American grocery store. It would, in a word, protect the American farmer by isolating him from competition. President Coolidge vetoed it. Congress passed the bill, in revised form, in 1928. President Coolidge vetoed it again.[15]

The mad scramble to buy land and machinery began in Henderson County in 1919, according to Barnes. He remembered that because of this "I want more" cry, prices were "kicked out of sight."[16] Land which before the war was thought of as marginal doubled and tripled in price. Everywhere in the county one heard "Buy land now or you will never be able to own a farm." Some splurged, plunked a life's savings into a down-payment and took a huge mortage for the balance with 5¼ percent interest on a twenty-five year loan, depending on the value of the farm. By 1920 the prices and the land boom peaked. A 160-acre farm that summer could bring the "magnificent sum" of $62,625 or a little over $391 an acre.[17] Then the market fell apart.

County corn prices went down to $1.16 a bushel, beef sold at $10.65 per hundred pounds at 290-300 weight. Land prices collapsed. A 320-acre farm with "fair improvements" near a town on a good road brought only twenty-five dollars an acre by the late 1920s.[18] Even the best prices were less than one-half of what they had been in 1920. In 1924, prime land sold for $172 an acre. Sometimes no one showed up at a sale to bid on the property. In the early fall of 1929 a farm south of Olena containing 223 acres was offered at auction by the First State Bank of Stronghurst. The sale was in default of mortgage payments. Twice it was advertised for sale. Twice it "was not sold on account of there being no bidders." Assessed land and personal property values dropped sharply in the County Assessor's office.[19]

Two organizations surfaced to help county farmers cope with these developments. One group was the Farmer's Institute, an organization which before the war flourished mainly as a social outlet in sponsoring fairs and lecture meetings.[20] They still emphasized the social aspect of their gatherings, interspersing the programs with musical events, for example. But in the 1920s they concentrated on new scientific advances in hybrid seed corn and conservation-plowing techniques. Their itinerary expanded. Literally, the "Institutes" peddled ideas all over the county, holding two-day lectures and exhibits at Bald Bluff, Media, Raritan, Gladstone, and Oquawka. Usually they would begin on an afternoon at 1:30 with a special guest lecturer brought in from outside the county. Typical was the Media Farmers' Institute in November, 1924 which featured the Honorable H.C. Kessinger of Aurora on the first afternoon, followed the next morning by the Honorable Henry Rathbone.[21]

The Henderson County Farm Bureau, the local counterpart of Hoover's Food Administration during the war, expanded to an indispensible organization in the 1920s. Its purpose, at the time, was informational. It published regular prices on grains and livestock. It stipulated what could be considered "fair prices to pay for corn husking this year."[22] It located places where farmers could purchase the latest hybrid seed corn, such as at Edgar Lewis seedhouse in Media.[23] It met usually in the Biggsville High School gymnasium where members elected their standing committees and officers. Sometimes the event would feature a chicken dinner for the entire family. But such socializing was rare in the Bureau. Unlike the Institute, its primary concern was the business, the serious business, of survival. It was the first to warn those farmers who were making the postwar transition not to over-produce. As early as 1920, it cautioned that "big crops do not mean big profits." Production was only a part of the county's farm problem. "We must make our farm business efficient and produce what is necessary" it advised soundly. It tried to get farmers to realize that the future posed unprecedented problems. These problems, moreover, were "outside the fences of the farm." "We cannot solve these problems as individuals anymore," the Bureau observed. It will be essential, from then on, to "speak and act together."[24]

Despite these basic alterations in the nature of the farm economy little physical change appeared on the farm at first. During most of the 1920s any visitor to a Henderson County farm would have seen things done the same way as they had been done for generations. Mabelle Sanderson of Stronghurst vividly recounted her early experiences as a bride on the farm during the years from 1923 to 1928. In 1923, she moved to a farm of 200 acres some four miles north of the town. It had a small frame house of

Biggsville Mail Carrier, August Wiegand

three bedrooms, a kitchen, and a living room. There was no running water and no electricity. Milk was kept cool in gallon earthenware crocks stored in underground root cellars or caves. Each morning she would go down to the crock and skim off some top cream for a churn which, "every few days" was worked into butter. It was not until 1928 that the family was able to get an ice box and have ice delivered to them on a regular and dependable basis. Even then, when it rained and the roads were muddy there was no ice and hence a real danger of spoilage. Travel to and from Stronghurst was with horse and buggy or by wagon. Not many people came to visit or even passed by the farm. Life went on day-by-day without contact with outsiders.[25]

Farm routine was hard and humdrum. Kerosene lamps had to be washed every morning and refilled. Coal, in winter, had to be brought in and the ashes carried out. Cleaning was done with a straw broom, in every room. Water was carried either from the well or the cistern to a wash-tub in the kitchen next to the stove, where it was "nice and warm." Their kitchen sink had no water pump. The only convenience was a drain pipe from the sink that extended "to the creek to pour waste water." The device saved a little water-hauling time at least. The family raised corn, beans, and hogs. Children never worked in the fields, at least not until the boys were "of high-school age." [26] Before then, they helped by drawing drinking water, feeding the livestock, or, if young girls, assisted in the cooking and cleaning.[27] Threshing was the big event of the year. Twenty-four "hired men" came and lived at the house. They worked hard for wages and room and board. The hired men, however, owned the threshing machines. Everyone got up at four o'clock. The first order of business was to "fire the thresher" to "steam it up." After a morning in the field the same two-dozen men sat down to dinner, then, later, for supper.[28]

Each Saturday, though, Mabelle went to town. At Stronghurst she "saw all the neighbors." She attended regular band concerts "played out in the street" during summer months. While in town she visited the stores and

Fur Collared Overcoats.

We have made a specialty of fur collared overcoats for several years and each year they grow more popular. We find a lot of fellows who drive open cars find the added warmth mighty attractive. They start in prices at

$16.50 and run up to $25

Fur Lined Dress Coats

Here's the coat that takes the place of a fur coat. A good looking cloth shell, sheep lined, with leather-lined sleeves, and a fur collar. These coats sell at

$22.50 to $35

Get the kind of an overcoat you want, and get it of the

LaHarpe Clothing Co.

LaHarpe, Illinois.   On the Corner, and "On the Square"

Ad from *Raritan Reporter*, 1924

Media State Bank
Directors: C.G. Richey, R.N. Marshall, Gust A. Swanson, W.B. Harbison, Edwin Voorhees, C.R. Pendarvis, Fred Ross, James J. Mathers, Josiah Schenck, J.C. Brooks

bought family food supplies and clothing.[29] Food prices ran a typical gamut of bacon for 22¢ a side, "choice steaks" went for 20¢ each, "Cola" hams were 16¢ a pound while Armour's Star hams cost 25¢ a pound. Clothing cost about the same. As before the war, a man's shirt cost 75¢, ladies' skirts 50¢, and boy's pants 40¢. Men's dress suits, "pure worsted," went for $25 or $35. A man's fine tweed jacket cost $25 and his Stetson hat $8.50 to $10. Ladies' dresses were selling at $9.80, $13.50, or top-of-the-line at $16.75 at Mason Dry Goods Company in LaHarpe. Women's shoe prices were $2.85 for "comfort oxfords," $2.98 for a "dress patent-covered heel," and $3.85 for an "arch support ladies' heel." She could get a "permanent" which included "everything from the preliminary shampoo to the setting and drying of the finished wave" for $4.00.[30]

The towns, like the farms, changed little in physical appearance from what they had looked like twenty years before, at least for most of the 1920s. There were the general stores, blacksmiths, who also drilled wells, physicians (two per town was common), and livery stables. Some towns grew for a while. At Lomax, the Lomax Industrial Corporation in 1925 produced over 300,000 cans of tomatoes and that fall started to can pumpkins. Gipe's Cafe opened in Raritan in 1924. It was advertised as "the best place between Burlington and Macomb to obtain anything from a sandwich to a square meal in short order."[31] It was also a grocery store where one could buy meats, can goods, cigars, confections, and soft drinks. Oquawka, still the largest town, had its button factory with over 100 workers, a cigar factory, fish house, harness shop, pool hall, dry-goods stores, drug store, and a staff of dentists and physicians.[32]

Of all the town businesses, banks expanded the most during the decade. Most had been in business well before World War I, some like those at Oquawka since the last century. All prospered. The turning point in the history of banking was 1920. That year the state legislature put private banks out of business. Every bank from then on had to be licensed by the

State. Many, like the one at Raritan, did not change much. There, only the name was altered to Raritan State Bank while the personnel remained the same. At Oquawka, though, the older "Moir Bank" changed hands. Its stock was purchased by the Farmers and Merchants State Bank and a new Board of Directors, led by Everett L. Werts, was elected.[33] By the mid-twenties there were nine banks in the county and each showed a considerable increase in resources. Figures available for the year just before the war and those for 1924 show the impressive growth of these lending institutions:[34]

BANK	1916	1924
Stronghurst State	$593,620	$727,506
Stronghurst National	227,848	395,944
Raritan	136,029	183,649
Media	342,185	413,676
Biggsville	436,637	547,278
Lomax	133,993	194,294
Gladstone	80,333	204,335
Oquawka State	372,094	386,707
Bank of Oquawka	81,245	302,089

Steam Train at Biggsville

Education changed little on the surface. In some ways public support for education, such as for more high schools and better teachers' salaries, waned from the booster spirit of the early part of the century. Grade school education continued to be offered to all children in the one-room school buildings within walking distance of every child. In most places the older buildings were still in use. In a few other locations new structures appeared. Raritan, for example, put up a solid brick building on the east edge of town in 1924 after fire destroyed the old schoolhouse. The cost was unprecedented: over $10,000 in tax dollars. By mid-decade grade schools had proliferated in number. The county, by the mid 1920s had well beyond the sixty-five schoolhouses of 1910. It appropriated twice the $5,000 annual tax support that had been levied in that pre-war year. Raritan Township was typical of this expansion of the concept of diversified, as compared to consolidated, grammar school education. In 1910 the township had six schools. In 1924 it had nine buildings each with one teacher, each a woman. Enrollment had risen from a low of seven students to a high figure of twenty pupils.[35]

South Prairie School

Marie Swedlund, a teacher, recalled a typical day at one of these schools. She taught at the Cork School, starting in 1922, located about four miles south of Stronghurst in Terre Haute Township. Every morning she rode on horseback from Stronghurst down the township dirt road. The trip took forty-five minutes each way. Her day began with bringing in fresh water from the well and in colder weather building the coal fire in a potbellied stove located in the northeast corner of the one-room building. The stove, though, was inadequate. She remembered vividly how cold those winter mornings were. The stove, called a "furnace," was so weak that she had her thirteen young pupils gather their desks dangerously close to it. Usually, just before lunch, however, the room would be warm enough to conduct the rest of the lessons in a regular seating arrangement. She taught at four class levels each week, in the basic subjects. While one group was being taught the other three would work silently on their assignments. The curriculum covered reading, spelling, writing, arithmetic, history, and geography. At year's end, as always, there was the annual school picnic for parents and friends in the school-yard.[36]

Wever Academy on fire

Teachers like Marie Swedlund were poorly, and unfairly, paid. The average salary in 1920 was only $105 a month, up from a paltry $45 in 1910. Only three other teachers in the entire county, one in Media, Biggsville and Terre Haute, were given the $150 top pay. The annual salaries listed in the spring of 1920 were not only low but were overwhelmingly sexually biased. Money was not the only means of sexual discrimination. Only single women were hired as teachers until a teacher shortage occurred during World War II. Men were usually paid a yearly sum of $1,080 while women averaged just $575.34. This discrimination was typical for all surrounding Illinois counties. Hancock County, for example, gave male teachers a yearly salary of $863.83 and women $521.40. McDonough County, too, thought men were worth $893.74 in the schoolhouse while women should get just $564.20 for the same job.[37]

Each year, just as before, all teachers were invited by County Superintendent A. L. Beall to attend the Teachers' Institute. They were usually scheduled for the High School Auditorium at Biggsville, as the most central location, and held in early August. There they would participate in workshops on new developments in teaching theory or hear guest lecturers often from out-of-state. Regular examinations for teacher certification were held, usually in Oquawka, late in the fall semester. Finally, in addition to the Institutes, each teacher could expect a personal visit, probably three times a year, from the Superintendent to check up on decorum in the classroom.[38]

The county had seven operating high schools in the 1920s. The Biggsville school continued as the county's four-year high school since it first started operation in 1895. Oquawka ran a two-year curriculum until 1922 when it became the second four-year high-school with about forty students and two teachers.[39] Media started the "Media Township" Community High School out of the defunct Wever Academy. It was a hybrid organization whereby the principal of the old Academy administered the school, hired the teachers, and purchased supplies. The school board of the high-school District, formed in 1917, paid the teachers, approved the curriculum, and furnished tax funds. In March, 1929, when the old Academy building burned, this unorthodox arrangement terminated and the entire operation of the high school, which the voters approved to be

First School Bus, 1926
Loren Van Doren, Owner and Driver

rebuilt, was placed under the District board.[40] By 1924, four other towns had started two-year high schools: Stronghurst, Gladstone, Lomax, and Terre Haute. By 1928, though, all so-called high schools, two and four year alike, competed together in a rudimentary system of high school athletics and in the spring participated in a Bi-county Track Meet held at Alexis.[41]

Some townships ignored the need for local highschool education entirely and were quite content to send their children, if they wished, away from home for schooling beyond the eighth grade. In these communities, some individuals still pushed hard for their own high school. Their efforts failed. One such locality was Raritan. There, Edward Barnes carried on his old crusade for a high school. His arguments were formidable. One reason for a "Raritan High School," he said, was financial. Why pay a high school tax, Barnes asked, without reaping any benefits from it? Raritan taxpayers could afford to pay for a high school. Media, next door, had one and "her citizens are not better off financially than are the citizens of Raritan township."[42]

There was, Barnes argued, the extra tuition cost levied, under the 1917 statute, in those townships which exported their children to outside high schools, roughly between $125 and $185 per student each year.[43] In Raritan, the assessment for 1920 was an alarming total of $4,000.[44] That sum alone could go a long way toward building and operating a high school of their own, Barnes reasoned. Moreover, the lack of a high school was just bad for the town and the community as a whole. Without such a school they were "considered a back number and its citizens classed with old fogies." "Remove the stigma!" he exhorted.[45]

Opposition came from an expected quarter: taxpayers with no children to educate.[46] That was enough to defeat the idea. Barnes was outraged. He chastised his neighbors for aligning themselves with the "dead weight of Raritan" against a high school. He hated those who threw such "obstacles in the path of progress." He denounced their stinginess. "Get it out of your system," he wrote in 1929, "that you can't afford to favor anything that you did not inherit from your father-in-law." "Don't argue with inferiors," he concluded, "simply tell them that Raritan needs, and must have, a high school, now, this year."[47] Barnes was ignored.

Stronghurst Mandolin Club, 1903

Some of the recreation and entertainment patterns of pre-World War I days persisted. Picnics and fairs were as popular as ever. Biggsville, in 1920, held its Tenth Annual Picnic in August. That year the first day was "Veterans' Day" where "all war veterans young and old" were given a free dinner. There were also folk dances, a sixty-voice chorus, and concerts day and night by the Orchard City Band. There was the Farmers' Picnic held on August 5, 1920 at Blandinsville where none other than Big Bill Thompson, mayor of Chicago, was the featured speaker. Folks were invited to come to see trained dogs, thrilling trapeze acts, contortionists, clowns, side-shows, and two "aeroplanes" in thrilling exhibition flights.[48] The Farm Bureau held its Annual Picnic on August 25, 1924 at Crapo Park in Burlington.[49] Tri-County "fairs" were held each August at La Harpe. It was advertised in 1924 as "one of the best and cleanest fairs in the State." These were week-long events, featuring races, vaudeville acts, fireworks displays, amusement rides like the ferris wheel, whip and merry-go-round, and a thirty-piece band from Iowa.[50] In 1929 the Fifth Annual Henderson County Country Club Picnic was held at Stronghurst the second week of September. Events started with an afternoon parade on Saturday. Then one could go to a band concert, watch vaudeville acts, or root for the favorite team in a baseball game between Raritan and Gladstone.[51] Families, if they had an automobile or the price of tickets on the CB&Q could travel to Monmouth for the Free Fall Festival of 1924 when for five nights and four days "in the paved streets" of the town there was free admission to "agricultural, industrial, mercantile, educational and home economics exhibits."[52] Or, in 1929, one could go to Burlington to the Rubin & Cherry Carnival topped off with horseraces on Saturday, called "Derby Day." During the week, each night, one could see the "Winter Garden Follies of 1929," labeled as a "beautiful revue."[53]

Raritan Prairieside Cornet Band

The Chautauqua offered more staid entertainment. In 1924, for only 50¢, adults, and 25¢, children, each day's admission, there was at Raritan a Saturday concert by the Missouri Wesleyan Male quartet followed by a lecture by James Hannibal Clancy on "The Law and Its Sorrows." On Sunday there was the religious play "Dust of the Road" in the afternoon and in the evening the Booth Tarkington success "Clarence" with a professional cast. On the third day one was exposed to "readings" and soprano solos by Mary Hollingsworth followed by another lecture, this one by George Emerson Frances, on "The Monarchy of Public Opinion." On the last day there was a "brilliant concert" by the Cleveland Symphonic Quartet and a closing "spectacular" magic show by Ulrich and Company.[54]

Town band concerts continued every summer, such as the ones played in Stronghurst each Wednesday night by the Merchants' Band.[55] Oquawka had two such bands, one called the "Kids' Band," which entertained on warm evenings by the river. On the river itself, excursions still operated. One trip left Burlington in the afternoon and paddled leisurely to Keokuk and back.[56] Or, in 1928, people could watch the Graf Zeplin float above the Mississippi slowly up the Iowa side from Burlington to Rock Island.[57] The Opera Houses continued with their traditional bill of fare for a while. To packed houses they put on the vaudeville acts and plays, such as "That's One on Bill, a Youthful Comedy in Three Acts," which ran at the Raritan building as late as the summer of 1930.

By then, however, Opera House live theater had become passe. It had been made extinct by a new technology, electricity, and a new medium of entertainment, the movies.[58] Electricity first came to Henderson County in any meaningful sense in 1919. That year Oquawka opened its "electric

Oquawka Light Plant

light plant" with direct 220 volt current generated to potential users.[59] That same year signs of the coming impact of electric power appeared in newspaper advertisements for "electric fixtures." Places like the Monmouth Plow Factory boasted that it would "supply all your needs in electric fixtures for the home or electric motors for any type of work." Their stock included vacuum cleaners, motors, electric irons, portable lamps or anything else in the electric line at the best prices we can possibly get."[60] A public bond subscription was raised in Raritan in 1919 for $2,500 to facilitate electric power for the town. Poles and wire for "bringing the juice to Raritan" were ordered and construction work began that summer.[61] By 1924, all over the county electrical contractors were pushing the need to wire homes properly for electricity under terms of a "national electric code." They could, with prices quoted in advance, put in floor, ceiling, and wall lamps. They would at the same time provide "everything from a lug socket to an electric range." Specific items to buy from contractor Coulsen, Brundage and Company, for example, included bulbs, heating pads, toasters, percolators, curling irons, and electric washing machines.[62]

One of the earliest signs of the intrusion of movies into the social life of the county appeared in the electrification of the opera houses. At Raritan, Barnes eagerly anticipated the coming of the movies. When the town got electric current, he wrote, "It will no longer be necessary for the people...to go to neighboring towns to see a moving picture show."[63] By early 1920, electric lights were in use at the house and the first silent movies were shown that spring.[64] John D. Cochran remembered movies being shown in Oquawka once a week. The projector operator would come to town with projector, movie, and portable screen. He showed one reel of a silent film, such as a Tom Mix and William S. Hart western, then turned on the lights and, while he rewound the film, Ruby Essex would play ragtime on the piano.[65] Admission was rather steep at the beginning for these showings, 15¢. However, that was still lower than the going rate for a play which in 1920 was 25¢, 35¢ and 50¢ depending on seat location. The neighborhood theaters that were drawing people away from places like Raritan were the Hatcher's Theatre in La Harpe and the Isis Theater in Roseville. By early spring of 1919 they were running hits like Charlie Chaplin in "Sunnyside" or the epic "Civilization" touted as a stupendous production of 40,000 men, women, and children, "greater than the "Birth of a Nation."[66] Shows at these establishments were at 7:30 and 9:30 on Fridays and Saturdays nights with a matinee at 2:30 on Saturday afternoon.

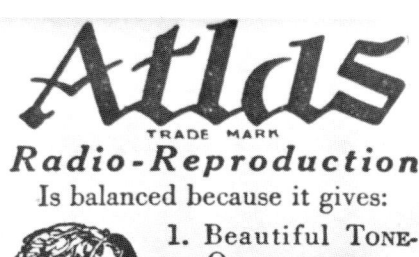

Radio Ad from *Raritan Reporter*

By 1920, movie advertisements were in full swing with whole page newspaper lay-outs bannering:

MOVIES! MOVIES!
Do you want to know where to spend your Friday evenings?
Do you want to keep posted on the world's latest news?
Do you want to know things of educational value?
Do you want to see what other people are doing in the world?

If so, come to the Motion Picture Show in the Media Township High School and Wever Academy Building

Every Friday Evening
Prices Nominal[67]

By mid-decade movies were a way of life and replaced the live performances of the Opera Houses. A typical week's movie run included a Monday night show called "Masters of Men." On Wednesday it changed to "Gimme." Then on Saturday, Edgar Churchill, the manager of the Raritan Opera House, pushed "Skin Deep" as a "wonderful picture that carries a little of everything that goes to make up a first-class show--Educational Comedy. Admission, 10¢ and 30¢." A regular feature then was the "Movie News" and previews of coming attractions. Out-of-county competition still drew away citizens. In Burlington at the huge Rialto Theater one could purchase a one-week admission ticket for just 50¢. For that ticket a person saw, in 1924, "The Covered Wagon," (which claimed 3,000 actors, 1,000 Indians, 500 horses, and 600 oxen) as well as "King of Kings," and "Old Ironsides."[68]

By 1929, Oquawka, Media, Stronghurst, Biggsville, Gladstone, and Raritan were showing movies. Frequently one movie made the rounds to each of these towns. For instance, in the summer of 1929, Helen Foster was top-billed in "The Road to Ruin" at Raritan. The advertisement noted that "this picture will also be shown at Media next Tuesday, July 23, and at Stronghurst next Wednesday, July 24."[69] That year "talkies" arrived. The first theater to feature the phenomenon was the Illinois Theater at Macomb at a grand opening on July 4, 1929. The theater had installed that spring the "Western Electric Sound System" that embraced "both vitaphone and movietone methods of reproducing sound and talking pictures." The cost was over $16,000 and was every bit as good "as at the McVickers and Roosevelt theaters in Chicago."[70] by 1930, most of the silent film equipment at the town Opera Houses also had been replaced by talking pictures.[71]

Along with movies, electricity brought another modern medium, radio. Radios were hustled along with all the other appliances that came with "electrification," the most popular being the Zenith and Crosley brands.[72] Newspapers ran regular columns instructing the reader how to build his own crystal radio like the Three-Tube Reflex Receiver.[73] The increased power output of many broadcasting stations, the *Raritan Reporter* claimed in 1925, made it possible to hear, even with a simple crystal set, over twenty-five miles from a transmitter. At Oquawka, Larry Werts built and operated station WCST and pushed popular songs available on phonograph records for only 15¢ each. Radio station operators in Galesburg, however, shut down the operation in 1929 because Werts' signal reached as far away as Quincy and therefore Werts was operating as a "wildcatter" without a license. By then, though, a decent Zenith radio could pick up broadcasts not only from Galesburg and Burlington but also from WOC in Davenport, and sometimes from as far away as WHO in Des Moines.[74] The ultimate in radio luxury was a visit to Maddock's Cafe in Raritan where patrons could have "music with your meals!" The advertisement claimed that a "traveling man who brought another salesman twenty-four miles to eat at Maddock's Cafe meant it when he said, Now, this is a real meal!"[75]

No assessment of the new modes of amusement could ignore jazz. There were dances before the war but these were family events, mostly, held in conjunction with picnics and fairs. In the Twenties, though, young people went to dances by themselves to hear the new "jazz orchestras."[76] Even the Raritan Opera House, when not showing movies, was converted into a dance hall. Manager Clarence Maddock each Wednesday paid bands like Chaplin's Orchestra to come over from Monmouth to play for "all lovers of the light fantastic."[77] Anderson's Orchestra played there "on one of the smoothest floors in the country." Dance tickets were available at the door for $1.50 a couple. Male "spectators" could get in for 25¢.

Many young men took their dates to Galesburg, Macomb, and Burlington. At Galesburg, in the spring of 1929, they danced at the Anchor Roof Garden "Where the Sky Begins." At Macomb, it was the Eahren Roof Garden. Both places featured Dan Russo's famous "Oriole Orchestra" at Galesburg on Tuesday, Thursday, and Saturday, and at Macomb on Monday, Wednesday, and Friday.[78] Or, they drove to Burlington, to the Spanish Roof Garden, on Wednesday and Saturday nights. There, for only 25¢ admission apiece, they listened to a steady variety of bands. On July 27, 1929 the "Capitol Band" from Hannibal played. On July 31, it was the "Sherman Play Boys" from Minneapolis. On August 3rd, Larry Haggerty and his Band came over from Galesburg.[79]

The Jazz Age was synonymous with prohibition. The crusade against Demon Rum ran deep in American history, back to the early days of the Republic in fact. By mid-nineteenth century, temperance forces had damned liquor in Maine. After the Civil War the liquor business increased seven-fold, with Chicago and St. Louis claiming about one saloon for every 200 inhabitants by the turn of the century. By then it was becoming to many old-stock Protestant middle-class Americans, a plague. Drinking was denounced as a sin. Women condemned it as a home-wrecker. Businessmen blamed it for accidents on the job by employees. Social writers, such as Sinclair Lewis, envisioned a world free from alcohol and so consequently free from crime and poverty.

The temperance movement changed to prohibition under three nationally organized agencies, the Women's Christian Temperance Union, founded in 1874, the Anti-Saloon League, created in 1895 in Ohio, and the Methodist Church. By 1900, their combined pressure on lawmakers dried up five states. By World War I, over two-thirds of the states were arid. By that time the momentum to cleanse the rest of the nation was irresistible. During the war, on the excuse of regulating the economy in the crisis, Congress forbade all manufacture and sale of intoxicants. While this measure was still in effect Congress wrote, and sent out to the states for ratification, the Eighteenth Amendment. It was promptly ratified by more than the required two-thirds majority of states and on January 1, 1920 became a part of our constitutional law, enforceable by Federal courts and their agencies.[80] One educator, a college president, called the Prohibition Amendment, "the longest and most effective step forward in the uplift of the human race ever taken by any civilized nation."[81]

Henderson County supported the temperance-prohibition movement from the start and eagerly embraced its adoption as the law of the land. It voted-in dry delegates to the General Assembly in 1918, Everett L. Werts of Oquawka and Frank E. Abbey of Biggsville. It supported the ratification of the Eighteenth Amendment. Barnes even thought prohibition would have a salutory effect on the distillers. The five large Peoria distilleries, he wrote, which had used 54,000 bushels of corn daily and paid 1,275 men in 1920, after being taken over by the U.S. Food Products Corporation used 60,000 bushels of corn and gave "employment to five times as many men as formerly."[82] Prohibition would get rid of foreigners. Barnes saw 61,000 thirsty aliens leave American between January 1 and March 12, 1920 alone. Why? The answer was obvious, "Inability to buy wine or beer is said to have been the chief cause of the hegira."[83]

Not everyone in the county felt like Barnes. Bootlegging and illegal consumption of liquor was commonplace. Although evidence of such activity

Ford Touring Car Ad, *Raritan Reporter*, July 17, 1924

is hard to come by for historians, given the clandestine nature of the activity, nevertheless extant information indicates widespread violation of the law. Prohibition was in effect for just nine months when Federal officials launched a dragnet probe in Illinois.[84] Allegedly, the source of the traffic at that time was Canada and Chicago, with the Illinois and Mississippi Rivers as the main connections.[85] In November, 1920 the first Henderson County moonshiner was arrested. Nick Alpesch, an Austrian, had set up a still in the cellar of his home, was caught selling the stuff, found guilty, and fined $288. He had, unfortunately, only recently filed naturalization intent papers, even though he had been living in the county for fifteen years, and Barnes pointedly asked for his immediate extradition.[86]

Individuals who lived through the Prohibition Era recounted extensive bootlegging operations in the county. John Noble, whose father had owned a saloon in Oquawka before World War I, remembered the regular Mississippi River liquor traffic coming down from a stop-over at New Boston. The boats anchored just south of Main Street where a nearby distillery operated just off Putney's Landing. Distribution of the moonshine was controlled by an Oquawka store owner, Bob Hostler, and young Noble himself ran deliveries of "Bob's Whiskey" up to about fifteen gallons a day.[87] John Foster also remembered the difficulties the county Sheriff encountered trying to enforce the "bootleg act." One episode resulted in a "big fight" between the Sheriff and the State's Attorney where each accused the other of cooperating with the violators. Both Oquawka and Gulfport were centers of bootlegging activity and Foster recalled that enforcement of the law was "nearly impossible" in these towns. A bootlegger named Jaggers openly peddled whiskey to lumber workers on the river from his home still north of Harvey Martin's place. His still, made out of an old creamer with a copper coil on it, went twenty-four hours a day. Jaggers was arrested but posted bond immediately and was back in business.[88] Others, like Jaggers, were arrested for making and selling "white lightning" and numerous stills were destroyed. Sometimes law enforcement was more vigorous. Now and then raids by the Sheriff, instead of isolated arrests, were conducted. One such raid in the fall of 1924 netted nine defendants who pleaded quilty and paid fines from $100 to $150 plus costs.[89] But the bootlegging went on.

Foster's account of alcohol consumption showed a regular patronage. At Gulfport there was a dance hall, called Turner's Hall, where whiskey was openly served because "people wanted something to drink." High School students drank. A bootlegger called "Squares" supplied them with the white liquid. The usual procedure, according to Foster, was for a fellow to take out his date and order two cokes. He then poured out some of the pop, and poured in the white lightning, put his thumb on the top of the bottle and shook it a little. It was, he said, the "in" thing in those days. Foster remembered that it "made you a wonderful drink." Parents drank. They made a "home brew" which Foster described as "all right" for home consumption. So, on family picnics, Foster observed, there "was nothing to see but whiskey."[90] There were regular sales in Raritan and, as a result, by 1924 there were "persistent violations of the dry law" in the town. And, moreover, everyone seemed to tolerate it. Barnes scolded his neighbors for their sins. It was their "duty" to report the law-breakers, he wrote. "Unless they do so they are at least morally guilty of being an accessory."[91] Apparently Barnes was ignored. Raritan folks kept on being unthirsty "accessories."

Prohibition Era Still, on Oquawka Island

Repeal of such an avoidable law was inevitable. A plank of the Democratic Party, in 1932, called for an end to Prohibition. With their victory in the fall election the era of the bootlegger vanished overnight. First, Congress enacted the Beer-Wine Revenue law which legalized beer and light wines--and put a Federal excise tax on both. On December 5, 1933 the Twenty-first Amendment was ratified, the Eighteenth Amendment repealed, and the "great experiment" in moral betterment ended. The Twenty-first Amendment, however, still permitted local option: states could outlaw liquor within their borders.

Some Henderson County people were furious. Barnes was beside himself with indignation. By 1932, with the Depression beginning, he lamented, "Who needs another weight on the morale of the community?" "The Lord knows times are hard enough now," he preached, "without the extra burden that would be put upon the honest, industrious and frugal temperance people of the country to care for the paupers that unleashed toxicants would make."[92] When Barnes saw the Republican Party endorsing the repeal of prohibition he was convinced that "the morals of the country have reached a low ebb."[93] And, moreover, even his own state refused to hold the law and go for "local option" against the "dripping wet" platform. In March, 1933 the House at Springfield repealed the state prohibition law by 115 to 29 votes. Only two Democrats (Frank McClure of Abingdon and Mary Davidson of Carthage) and one Republican (Clinton Searle of Rock Island) from the area opposed the repeal.[94] Henderson County, though, dug in. It absolutely refused to vote for alcohol. It went 1,420 to 931 against repeal of the Eighteenth Amendment, 1,271 to 766 on the question of whether even to modify the existing prohibition laws, and 1,370 to 861 against the repeal of the Illinois prohibition statute.[95]

Crime and prohibition were linked. And so, during the 1920s, the county, just as the nation, recorded an upswing in felony offenses. Ralph Rothland was found guilty of shooting at Sheriff Gregory and some deputies when the Sheriff raided his still on Big Island in the Mississippi. He was given four months in the state farm at Vandalia.[96] The number of cases of theft in the county shot up. In 1920, Robert Harden drove his new car into Raritan and parked it for a few minutes in front of Stewart's Restaurant. When he returned his overcoat was gone.[97] In December of that year Lee Heller was sentenced for auto theft (Jake Waymack's Ford car) and also for forging Lewis Cavin's name "to a check of good size" to buy a motorcycle in Galesburg.[98] In the summer of 1924, someone broke into Cook's Garage at Raritan and stole I. Perrine's big Buick Six. It was

Auto, Stronghurst

Auto, Raritan

later located, abandoned, at Iowa City by the Sheriff.[99] In 1930, thieves broke into St. Ledger's Garage and got away with a car belonging to Raymond Galbraith. The same crowd also stole a grocery truck from the garage of Perrine's store. No arrests were made in this case.[100] Media was the scene of a burglary in January where Link's Garage was forcibly entered by theives who took a six-cylinder Chevrolet belonging to two young high-school teachers.[101]

The upswing in auto theft reflected an important change in the economy and social life of the county: the coming of the paved roads and easy availability of the automobile at a price almost every middle-class family could afford. Road conditions had been a perennial topic of woe for a generation. Rains and floods made them impassable. A traveler lamented in the 1890s that of Henderson County roads "nothing flattering can be said." A few of them were usable when the weather was clement but the narrowness of even these roads "renders it almost impossible to make them what might be called 'good'." In most places roads were "but narrow lines meandering from farm to farm regardless of lines or direction of route."[102] Early promoters of improved roads were specific. Barnes wanted them graveled and labeled. He insisted that farm homes have numbers, like town homes, for identification. Let townships in the meantime, he said, use horse-drawn graders to keep the dirt roads smooth and rut-free.[103]

Deplorable conditions were also epidemic throughout the state. There was no state system of road repair or building. Everything was handled, if at all, by townships. Only a couple of "experimental" hard-surface highways had been tried. In 1911, a law required the new revenue from automobile licenses to be earmarked for county roads and bridges. In 1912, there was an Illinois Highway Improvement Association organized by William G. Edens at Peoria. In 1913, Governor Edward F. Dunne signed a law which transferred road maintenance from township to county officials and required the Superintendent of Highways to report to a State Highway Committee. The law also gave counties State funds to help in the building and upkeep of their roads. In 1916, Congress got into the act by matching state highway funds with federal dollars.[104]

That year the Illinois Highway Committee started its program to pull the State "out of the mud."[105] It was ambitious. It planned for 4,800 miles of paved highway financed by a sixty-million dollar bond issue. Under Governor Frank O. Lowden, Dunne's successor, work was begun.

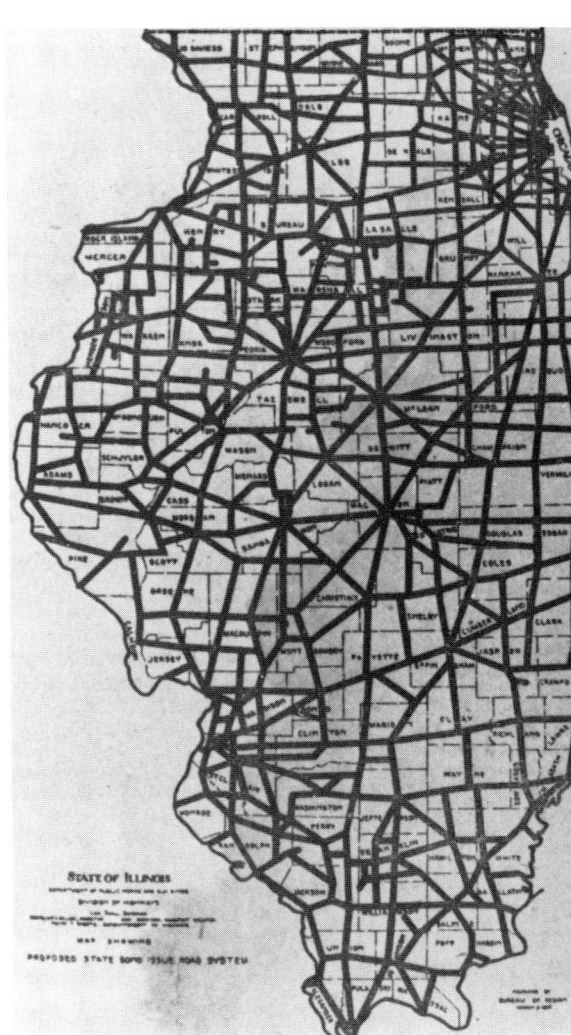

Raritan Reporter, November 6, 1924

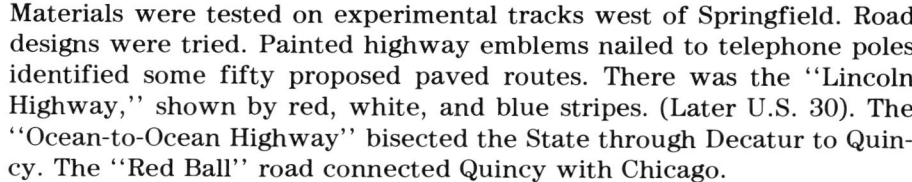
Raritan Hardroad

Materials were tested on experimental tracks west of Springfield. Road designs were tried. Painted highway emblems nailed to telephone poles identified some fifty proposed paved routes. There was the "Lincoln Highway," shown by red, white, and blue stripes. (Later U.S. 30). The "Ocean-to-Ocean Highway" bisected the State through Decatur to Quincy. The "Red Ball" road connected Quincy with Chicago.

Under Governor Len Small (1921-29) work began in earnest. He was firmly convinced that good roads meant prosperity and growth for the state. He doubled the planned mileage to 9,900 miles and got a second bond issue approved in the legislature. The *Illinois Blue Book,* an annual publication of developments in the state, boasted record engineering surveys in all counties. By 1924, Small claimed that every county had at least one paved road. Lewis L. Emmerson, who became governor in 1929, reported that Illinois had built 7,500 miles of paved highways, all of them a comfortable eighteen feet across. Gravel, he said, had been spread on most county roads as well.[106]

Henderson County voters approved all of these measures. They supported the bond revenues. They applauded the anticipated beneficial effect on farms, even expecting a "back to the farm movement" by making them closer to towns and villages. Maps were printed showing the proposed new hard roads and their new route numbers.[107] By 1929, results were seen in the county. Contracts were awarded to Hartmann Clark Brokers Company of Peoria for Route 97A, section 135, and to Cameron, Joyce and Company of Keokuk for section 136 of Route 97.[108] In other areas of the county similar contracts were let out. By 1930, the main highways were opened: 94, 164, 96, 34, and 116.

Governor Small Campaigning in Biggsville in the 1920's

Roads were supported because most people expected to use them. Cars, at the beginning of the decade, were still relatively expensive. The

Motor Vehicle Registration and Sales, 1900–1930		
YEAR	MOTER VECHICLE REGISTRATION	FACTORY SALES
1900	8,000	4,100
1905	78,800	24,200
1910	468,500	181,000
1915	2,490,000	895,900
1920	9,239,100	1,905,500
1925	20,068,500	3,735,100
1930	26,749,800	2,787,400

Motor Vehicle Chart

Paving Route 8, 1924

"Chevrolet 49" sold for $735 in 1920. That year the top-of-the-line Chevrolet "Touring Car" ran $1,285. By 1925, the prices had dropped. Then a Ford "Runabout" sold for only $265 while the most expensive "Ford Sedan" listed at $685 at Mudd Motor Company in Stronghurst. Other models, soon extinct, kept the prices down by competition. For example, a "Whippet" with "finger-tip control" made in Toledo, Ohio ran its four models between $475 and $535.[109]

Moreover, financing became a lure for those who could not come up with the $265. Roy Mudd advertised that "if you do not wish to pay cash for your car, you can arrange for a small payment down and easy terms on the balance." "Or," he wrote, "you can buy in the Ford Weekly Purchase Plan."[110] By the close of the twenties car prices had climbed up to their earlier level but by then, too, wages and salaries were up. In 1929, a Chevrolet cost $525, a Pontiac $745, a Buick $1,195, and a Cadillac $3,295.[111] In that year the used-car business had brought cars to those heretofore excluded from the new auto market. Their advertisements first appeared in the spring of 1929, often on the front page of newspapers. The typical ad would list the names and numbers of used cars in stock, although it never printed the asking price.[112] One can assume that then, as always, they were considerably below the retail listings for the latest models, f.o.b. Detroit.

Highways and county politics were inseparable. Indeed, that issue seemed to be the only matter of discussion at election times. The equation was simple. Governor Small's main program was highway construction. He was a Republican and so were most voters in the county. Therefore, what opposition there was came from county Democrats. But even their opposition was strained in its sincerity and in its consistency. Democrat Barnes, although he wanted improvement of existing roads, printed a strong condemnation of the expense of new ones. In December, 1920 he put paved highways and a proposed state Mounted Police System in the same boat. Both were an extravagant waste of taxpayers' money. The police, he wrote "would be about as beneficial to a majority of the people…as is the

Route 8, Now U.S. 34, Biggsville

sixty million dollar hard roads system."[113] Yet here was a man who had pushed for better county roads since the 1890s and who would praise them later as the salvation of the local farmer.

Barnes, faced with the popularity of the new highways, backed off. By 1924, he acknowledged the viability of the roads but sarcastically wrote that "one could imagine that Len Small was a candidate for state Hard Road Commissioner instead of Governor."[114] Barnes implied that paved roads equalled political corruption. The state, he charged, had acquired miles of new roads but no honest and conscientious government. Elect Democrats instead of Republicans, he advised, then one could have hard roads and at the same time purge the state payroll of "a horde of useless grafters."[115] Such counsel was a waste of time. "Not once during the 1920s," wrote Robert Howard, "did the Democratic party elect a state-wide candidate."[116]

Henderson County was, like the state, overwhelmingly Republican. In the Presidential election of 1920, Harding trounced Cox by a vote of 2,757 to 740. Harding took every precinct and even former Democratic areas turned Republican that year. Oquawka went Harding 407 to eighty, Gladstone by 254 to eighty-seven, Carman ninety-four to thirty-five. Since this was the first national election in which the women voted, a sexual preference was seen in the vote profile. Nationally, women went for

Presidential Elections, 1920-1928

YEAR	CANDIDATES	PARTY	POPULAR VOTE	ELECTORAL VOTE
1920	WARREN G. HARDING	Republican	16,152,200 (61.0%)	404
	James M. Cox	Democratic	9,147,353 (34.6%)	127
	Eugene V. Debs	Socialist	919,799 (3.5%)	0
1924	CALVIN COOLIDGE	Republican	15,725,016 (54.1%)	382
	John W. Davis	Democratic	8,385,586 (28.8%)	136
	Robert M. La Follette	Progressive	4,822,856 (16.6%)	13
1928	HERBERT C. HOOVER	Republican	21,392,190 (58.2%)	444
	Alfred E. Smith	Democratic	15,016,443 (40.8%)	87

Note: Winners' names appear in capital letters.

Christ A. Apt
County Superintendent of Schools

Harding two to one. In the county they voted for him five to one or 1,064 to 221.[117] The County Board of Supervisors remained in Republican control with eleven Republicans and only one Democrat on the panel.[118] Democrats failed to gain anything from a visit in 1924 of the Great Commoner William Jennings Bryan. Bryan, twice the party's candidate for the presidency, spoke at a free Chatauqua in Biggsville that summer. His remarks were carried on radio at the time. But Bryan ignored politics and rambled on about evolution. He denounced teaching the idea in the schools as a contradiction to the biblical story of creation. He said the Bible forbade teaching the scientific theory. John Foster, who saw Bryan at Biggsville, recalled that Bryan was still "one of the best speakers" he had ever heard.[119] But politically Bryan was irrelevant. By 1925, Democrats, as a county party organization, had become all but extinct. That year they ran no party candidates for local offices except for a justice of the peace and a constable in Oquawka.[120] By 1930, they showed some vague signs of revival. Three Democrats ran for, and won, County Board seats from Stronghurst, Lomax, and Carman.[121] Luckily, the previous year, they were fortunate enough to attract an individual of enduring popularity. In 1928, Chris A. Apt won his first of a lifetime series of terms as Superintendent of Schools.

In 1920, the state convened a Constitutional Convention. This was the second time since the Civil War that Illinoisans tried to revamp their fundamental law. Once before, in 1870, eighty-five delegates met at Springfield in a non-political atmosphere (forty-four Republicans to forty-one Democrats) and drafted a lengthy revision of the 1848 law. Basically, it expanded considerably the power of the legislators, set limits to the state debt, designed representation in the House so that the minority party almost always got one of the three seats in that district, extended suffrage to all males over twenty-one, increased the Supreme Court from three to seven men, and reaffirmed the personal property tax. After fifty years the document needed modernization. "Reform and reorganization" was the slogan. For example, reformers had tried since 1890 to amend the constitution so as to allow the use of the "Australian" or secret ballot. They failed. Now they wanted to write it into the body of the law itself. At the same time they hoped to make it easier to amend the constitution. Cook County, which had grown tremendously in population over the preceding half-century, demanded reapportionment. "Reorganize the Legislature," they insisted. Get rid of the old system of representation where downstate counties got more men in the House than they were entitled to have. Mathematically, they showed that Cook County should have forty-eight of the 102 delegates. They had only thirty-eight. Cook County, in the Senate, was also short-changed. They had, according to a reapportionment law passed in 1901, just nineteen of the fifty-one senators.

At the Convention, downstate delegates controlled the proceedings. They were agreeable to the Australian ballot. On other reforms, though, they balked. They would not liberalize the cumbersome 1870 amendment process. They refused to permit municipal corporations like Chicago to acquire public utilities. They were mid-way on fiscal changes. The property tax was retained, although a new state income tax was put in to supplement it as a revenue. On apportionment, after fifteen months of wrangling, they allowed Cook County proportional representation in the lower house but fixed its power at only one-third of the Senate. They also gerrymandered the Supreme Court in favor of downstate judicial districts so as to give Cook County only two of the nine seats on the bench.

It was not until 1922, after two years of debate, recesses, and compromise that the document was sent to the people for ratification. Only three months were set aside for the voters to scrutinize the results. Chicago papers were incensed at what had not been done. They cried unfair, unjust, prejudicial! They asked for its rejection out of hand. Former governors Republicans Frank Lowden and Charles Deneen gave it only their lukewarm endorsement while another former chief executive, Democrat Edward F. Dunne, condemned it. So did the voters of Illinois. It lost by 921, 398 to 185, 298 and Cook County voters threw it out by a nine to one rejection.[122] Barnes, although an ardent Democrat, gloated over the Convention's persistent effort to curb the political power of Cook County. "Curb Chicago is the aim of Con Con," he printed in bold type on page one.[123] Barnes, by a regular front-page column summarizing events at Springfield, kept his readers informed on events, issues, and debates throughout the proceedings. He applauded, overall, the conservative retrenchment. He was glad to see delegates rejecting labor union demands to be able to strike.[124] He was pleased with the exclusion of Cook County justices on the state's highest court. He deplored the rise of municipal corporations. He approved of the Senate apportionment plan, the property tax, and the Australian ballot.

Toward the end of the decade a painful sense of change, of loss, began to cover the county. The apprehensions were, in fact, justified because with the coming of the paved roads and the new technologies of electricity an old order was passing. Henderson County's Golden Age of prosperous small towns whose prosperiety in turn rested on the flourishing family farm was giving way rapidly to another era; and along with this changeover came a fundamental alteration in the attitudes of the people. In a word, the social and economic life built upon railroads and small towns was changing to a new one built upon highways, later interstate ones, and large urban centers. The center of gravity had shifted out of and far away from Oquawka, Biggsville, Gladstone, Stronghurst, and Raritan to St. Louis, Peoria, and Chicago. Henderson County and its citizens were no longer as important in the larger scheme of things as they had once been, and they knew it. They had become tangential. And no one likes to feel left out, unimportant, and second rate.

The first indications of this changeover were editorials in the *Raritan Reporter* in 1928 in which Barnes started to decry the landscape he saw around him. He pictured his neighbors as becoming blase, lackadaisical, nonchalant about their community. They cared more about their new cars and tractors than the education of their children: materialism had been substituted for pride in the priority of values. At times Barnes' sense of the demise of the vitality of life in the small town was acute. In the spring of 1929, for example, he penned an obituary for all of the county's towns. It was a pathetic lamentation about what had happened to the life Barnes had known.

"When a town dies there isn't any funeral, no flowers, not even
a pall-bearer — it just DIES.
When a town dies the trains run on past it, the sidewalks revert back to their native element, and birds build their
nests in the town hall and graze in the public park.
It's a sad and sorry thing when a town dies, for it hasn't
the satisfaction of ever knowing who killed it.
But when a town dies, it just dies and dies and dies...."[125]

There were other signs of the ebb of older life. Country churches closed down in the Twenties. The Coalfax church, for instance, was sold in the fall of 1925 and converted into a town hall. The Methodist Conference of Central Illinois that year ordered all of its country churches sold.[126] Local news items, by 1929, disappeared from the newspapers. There were fewer announcements of picnics, of local merchants' sales. Instead, there were spreads of things going on, and for sale, in Burlington, Monmouth, Galesburg, and Macomb. The town dry-goods merchant or clothing store owner now competed with the department store, with John Boesch and Company's four-story operation at Burlington. Dance bands in Burlington were better, too. Talking movies first were seen in Macomb.

Lynn Hotel, Biggsville

The atmosphere of the Henderson County community, by 1929, was depressing before the Great Depression. The perspective by then was in the past. People might purchase all the modern gadgets but their values, and their commitments, were to the way things had been. Len Small's paved roads might well have gotten Illinois up out of the mud, but

Henderson County, mentally, was stuck there. Barnes was sensitive to this old-fogey attitude around him, and could not understand it. He could not reconcile the contradiction of spending money for the wrong things. Somehow, he said, his neighbors had gone off-track, morally and spiritually. They had been seduced by the outward appearances of the new modern age while underneath the community was terminally ill. It was as bizarre as dressing up an old man in the gaudy clothes of a twenty-year-old boy. Writing a fictionalized editorial in 1929 he proposed to look backward at his friends from the vantage point of 1979. He stated flatly: "Raritan was a backward community" even in the 1920s; it had its values backwards. They had money, they were reasonably prosperous middle-class families then. But they "had no waterworks, or hospital, no adequate fire-fighting apparatus, no public park...." These same residents bought high-powered automobiles, expensive radios, and modern household appliances." "In many cases," he wrote, "they took better care of their cattle than their children."[127] Why? Barnes had no answer.

Their children were leaving. Between 1910 and 1920 the population of Henderson County barely held its own, having a net gain of only forty-six people. That was a portentous sign. Between 1920 and 1930 the figure went down by over 10 percent, by just under 1,000 inhabitants, from 9,770, to 8,775. In 1870, there were 12,582 people living in the county. In 1930, every township but two had lost population. The number of farms in each township declined.[128] The year before, in the fall of 1929, just as the decade itself was ending, the Great Depression began.

END NOTES FOR CHAPTER SIX

[1] William E. Leuchtenburg, *Perils of Prosperity 1914-1932* (Chicago & London, 1958) p. 87.

[2] Ibid., p. 88.

[3] Ibid., p. 90.

[4] Norton, *A people and a Nation*, vol. II, p. 684.

[5] Lee Leuchtenburg, *Perils of Prosperity*, Ch. IV "Red Scare".

[6] Nash, *The American People*, vol. II, p. 758.

[7] *Raritan Reporter,* October 8, 1919.

[8] Ibid., October 8, 1919.

[9] Ibid., November 19, 1919.

[10] Ibid., January 7, 1920.

[11] Ibid., January 7, 1920.

[12] Ibid., January 28, 1920.

[13] John D. Hicks, *Republican Ascendancy*, 1921-1933 (New York, 1960), p. 18.

[14] Ibid., 18-22.

[15] Leuchtenburg, *Perils of Prosperity*, pp. 101-2; Hicks, *Republican Ascendancy*, pp. 198-9.

[16] *Raritan Reporter,* September 5, 1929.

[17] Ibid., August 25, 1920.

[18] Ibid., August 28, 1920.

[19] Ibid., July 25, October 3, 1929.

[20] Originally called the American Farm Bureau Federation, it began with the Smith-Lever Act of May, 1914, when Congress earmarked $5,000,000 for agricultural extension activities. States were required to match the Federal funds. In 1919, the early Farm Bureau agents met in Chicago to form a national lobby group, The Federation. After that date, Hicks observed, the Farm Bureau "no longer restricted itself to the task of increasing agricultural production, but also sought to promote all the wider

interests of agriculture..." See *Republican Ascendancy,* p. 21.

[21] *Raritan Reporter,* November 13, 1924.

[22] Ibid., October 20, 1920.

[23] John M. Foster, tape-recorded interview by Rita Souther, March 3-4, 1980, *W.I.U. Archives of Special Collections.*

[24] *Raritan Reporter,* September 15, 1920.

[25] Mabelle Sanderson, Tape-recorded interview by Rita Souther, February 27, 1980, *W.I.U. Archives & Special Collections.*

[26] Ibid.

[27] James H. Cook interview.

[28] Mabelle Sanderson interview.

[29] Ibid.

[30] *Raritan Reporter,* March 10, 1920, April 1, May 29, 1930.

[31] Ibid., September 18, 1924.

[32] Earl Knox, Tape-recorded interview by John Hallwas, August 20, 1979, *W.I.U. Archives & Special Collections.*

[33] *Raritan Reporter,* July 19, 1919.

[34] Ibid., October 4, 1916; November 6, 1924.

[35] Ibid., September 4, 1924.

[36] Marie Swedlund, Tape-recorded interview by Rita Souther, March 1, 1980, *W.I.U. Archives & Special Collections,* See also James H. Cook interview.

[37] *Raritan Reporter,* May 5, 1920.

[38] Ibid., November 6, 1925, August 7, 1930.

[39] Earl Knox interview.

[40] *Raritan Reporter,* April 10, 1930.

[41] John M. Foster interviews, Earl Knox interview.

[42] *Raritan Reporter,* June 11, 1919.

[43] Ibid., October 16, 1924.

[44] Ibid., October 20, 1920.

[45] Ibid., October 20, 1920.

[46] Ibid., December 23, 1920.

[47] Ibid., April 4, 1929.

[48] Ibid., July 28, 1920.

[49] Ibid., April 21, 1924.

[50] Ibid., July 24, 1924.

[51] Ibid., September 11, 1929.

[52] Ibid., September 18, 1924.

[53] Ibid., July 23, 1929.

[54] Ibid., December 7, 1924.

[55] Ibid., May 29, 1924.

[56] Merlin Foresman, Tape-recorded interview by Rita Souther, March, 1980, *W.I.U. Archives & Special Collections.*

[57] Francis Joseph Haney, Tape-recorded interview by Rita Souther, March 10, 1980, *W.I.U. Archives & Special Collections.*

[58] For a full , contemporary discussion of the early motion picture industry, see Lewis Jacobs, *"The Rise of the American Film; A Critical History* (New York, 1939).

[59] John M. Foster interview.

[60] *Raritan Reporter,* August 13, 1919.

[61] Ibid., July 9, 1919.

[62] Ibid., December 18, 1924.

[63] Ibid., July 9, 1919.

[64] Ibid., May 5, 1920.

[65] John D. Cochran, Tape-recorded interview by Rita Souther, March 7, 1980, *W.I.U. Archives & Special Collections.*

[66] *Raritan Reporter,* March 26, September 3, 1919.

[67] Ibid., May 5, 1920.
[68] Ibid., August 28, 1924.
[69] Ibid., July 18, 1929.
[70] Ibid., June 27, 1929.
[71] Ibid., March 2, 1930.
[72] See Erik Barbouw's study of radio in *A Tower of Babel; A History of Broadcasting in the United States to 1933* (New York, 1966).
[73] *Raritan Reporter,* December 18, 1924.
[74] John D. Cochran, interview.
[75] *Raritan Reporter,* May 29, 1980.
[76] See Leuchtenberg, *Perils of Prosperity,* Ch. 18, the Revolution in Morals."
[77] *Raritan Reporter,* February 18, 1920.
[78] Ibid., May 9, 1929.
[79] Ibid., July 25, 1929.
[80] The most informative histories on the subject of temperance and prohibition are Charles Merz, *The Dry Decade* (New York, 1931) and HerBert Asbury, *The Great Illusion: An Informal History of Prohibition* (Garden City, N.U., 1950).
[81] Quoted in Morrison, Commager, Leuchtenburg, American Republic Vol. II, p. 438.
[82] *Raritan Reporter,* March 17, 1920.
[83] Ibid., April 17, 1920.
[84] See Howard, *Illinois,* Ch. 24, "The Prohibition Era".
[85] *Raritan Reporter,* October 20, 1920.
[86] Ibid., November 24, 1920.
[87] John Noble, tape-recorded interview by Rita Souther, March 6, 1980, *W.I.U. Archives & Special Collections.*
[88] John M. Foster, interviews.
[89] *Raritan Reporter,* November 27, 1924.
[90] John M. Foster, interviews.
[91] *Raritan Reporter,* November 27, 1924.
[92] Ibid., March 17, 1932.
[93] Ibid., June 2, 1932.
[94] Ibid., March 2, 1933.
[95] Ibid., November 6, 1933.
[06] Ibid., April 18, 1929.
[97] Ibid., October 20, 1920.
[98] Ibid., December 1, 1920.
[99] Ibid., July 17, 1924.
[100] Ibid., May 29, 1930.
[101] Ibid., January 30, 1930.
[102] "Tribute to Biggsville," *Monmouth Review Atlas,* March, 1942.
[103] *Raritan Reporter,* May 9, November 7, 1889.
[104] See "The Coming of the Hard Roads, Howard, Illinois, pp. 487-91.
[105] David R. Wrone, "Illinois Pulls Out of the Mud", *Journal of the Illinois State Historical Society* (Spring, 1965) pp. 54-78; Robert P. Sutton, *Prairie State,* v. II, pp. 263-71.
[106] Howard, *Illinois,* p. 491.
[107] *Raritan Reporter,* April 2, November 6, 1924.
[108] Ibid., January 24, 1929.
[109] Ibid., February 18, March 24, May 5, 1920.
[110] Ibid., April 6, 1924.
[111] Ibid., April - May, 1924.
[112] Ibid., May 9, 1929.
[113] Ibid., December 15, 1920.
[114] Ibid., October 19, 1924.

[115] Ibid., October 16, 1924.
[116] Howard, *Illinois*, p. 475.
[117] *Raritan Reporter*, November 17, 1920.
[118] Ibid., May 8, 1924.
[119] John M. Foster interviews.
[120] *Raritan Reporter*, April 10, 1925.
[121] Ibid., April 18, 1929.
[122] Howard, *Illinois*, pp. 469-73.
[123] *Raritan Reporter*, June 23, 1920.
[124] Ibid., April 14, 1920.
[125] *Raritan Reporter*, April 4, 1929.
[126] Ibid., October 15, 1925.
[127] Ibid., April 18, 1929.
[128] *U.S. Census Population Schedules, Henderson County, 1870, 1910, 1920, 1930.*

Airplane Assembly Plant, Lomax, 1928

CHAPTER SEVEN
THE GREAT DEPRESSION AND THE NEW DEAL
1929-1940

The Great Depression changed the way Americans lived. Yet for most people it was unexpected and for everyone it was unwanted. The Twenties were, overall, an era when everyone felt pretty good about themselves. Americans were confident that, despite signs of a fatal weakness in the farm economy the family farm could, as it had for generations, withstand any setback. All around were visable marks of the good life: electricity, radios, modern appliances, movies, paved roads, automobiles, and Republican officeholders. When the end of the Twenties came with dramatic suddenness in October, 1929 only a few observers understood what had happened. The nation, hit by a catastrophy, reacted like a person devastated by a deep personal and unexpected calamity. At first there was disbelief and denial, then came the unavoidable pain. Then there was anger and self pity. Finally, there was acceptance and a long steady readjustment or recovery.[1]

Historians will forever debate when the Great Depression began, but most Americans then alive had no hesitations about fixing the date. It stuck in their minds along with July 4, 1776 or Armistice Day, November 11, 1918. It was October 29, 1929. It was a Tuesday, the day of the stock market crash. The crash, in the words of Harvard scholar Samuel Eliot Morison, "soon confronted the United States with its greatest crisis since the Civil War."[2] This was no hyperole. A spiral of depression expanded like a tornado across the nation, ever increasing in strength and size. People were fired, lost their life's savings, their homes, and their farms. Some families, in a short while, had no place to live and nothing to eat.

The crash in the 1930s was viewed as a crime. It was, to many, the end-result of a mania of buying and selling "with other peoples money" as Roosevelt put it. The trouble was that, by 1929, too many people believed John Raskob's article published in the *Ladies Home Journal* early that year entitled "Everybody Ought To Be Rich." The article showed how anyone who saved $15 a month and with it bought common stock would be worth $80,000 in twenty years.[3] Many wage earners, too many, believed it. With the entrance of unprecedented numbers of small investors into the stock market the price of stock, because of the demand to buy, rose out of sight. By the spring of 1928 the market frenzy began in earnest. For example, R.C.A. on Friday, March 2 closed at $94.50 and by the next Friday it was up to $108. By Tuesday, March 13, it was at $160 and by March 20 was selling at $178 a share.[4] This was not happening just on the New York Stock Exchange, it was taking place all across the nation, in major cities like Chicago, St. Louis, and San Francisco. In countless brokerage offices in small cities and towns across the land the same thing was going on. It continued through the summer and fall of 1928 and lasted for one year.

In the third week of October, 1929, a Wednesday, industrial stocks fell eighteen points across the board. The following day prices broke in all areas. The banking firm of the House of Morgan gallantly tried to stop the

Opposite: Farming in the Thirties
Ed and Bert Olson, Bald Bluff

obvious by offering to purchase any stock anybody wished to sell. This effort stabilized the market for the rest of the week. On Monday, the 28th, panic selling began all over again, led by three industrial blue-chip giants. United States Steel lost $17.50 a share that day. Westinghouse Electric lost $34 and General Electric $47.50. Tuesday October 29th was the disaster. The ticker on Wall Street closed two-and-one-half hours late just recording all the selling. By the time the last sales were registered all industrial stocks had plunged downward another $43 a share. This was only the beginning. The market went in a tailspin. General Electric, despite its initial losses, still sold for $396 in November of 1929, two years later it was worth $34. United States Steel held its own, too, in 1929 at $261 and it, too, went to $21 a share the next year.[5]

No one escaped. Banks locked their doors and millions lost their savings. Construction work stopped, factories cut production or closed down. Workers were fired or dismissed and wages and salaries were slashed. Farm income dropped. Corn went from a terrible 61¢ in 1929 to 32¢ in 1931. Real estate values disappeared, tax revenues declined and local government services and utilities were terminated. Unemployment mounted. Business confidence disappeared. Men brooded over their fate. They were angry, confused, and desperate. Small wonder: by late 1931 one fourth of all bread winners in America were out of work, not just layed-off but fired, forever it seemed.[6]

Reaction at first was suprisingly mild, closer to astonished disbelief in what was happening. President Herbert Hoover led the way in an amazing process of national denial. He announced in December, 1929 through his Secretary of the Treasury, Andrew Mellon: "I see nothing in the present situation that is either menacing or warranting pessimism." In early 1930 the President predicted: "All the evidence indicates that the worst effects of the crash upon unemployment will have been passed during the next sixty days."[7]

These were public statements designed, he later explained, to bolster public confidences and to prevent further panic. Hoover, less dramatically, convened conferences at Washington of labor and business leaders to try to get cooperation between the two to stabilize prices and wages. He asked governors to provide state-level credit relief and to continue public work projects such as highway construction. He asked Congress for $500 million to subsidize farm cooperatives which, in theory, could guarantee farmers a minimum price for their crops. This Federal Farm Board, though, was to be temporary. In the Agricultural Marketing Act of 1929 the Board was created by Congress to loan money to farmers and then to disband when the loans were repaid and the farmer was back on his feet again. The President proposed a tax cut to give consumers more money to spend, thereby creating new demands to revive industrial production.

Nothing worked. Perhaps nothing conceivable at the time could have worked. At any rate, Hoover was just putting a federal finger into the dam which was holding up an enormous backwater of oversupply. At the core, over production was what was wrong with the economy. Simply stated, business and industry during the 1920s had poured more money from profits back into capital expansion than into higher wages so, eventually, the purchasing power of the consumer could not continue to buy all the goods that were being manufactured, or the food that was being grown on the farms. And, because of the economic chaos in Europe after World War I, there was no foreign market on which to dump the surplus of American goods and commodities.

The President's efforts did not help at all. In the face of Secretary Mellon's optimism the dam broke and economy collapsed. Production and wages, despite the meetings in Washington, were cut and people were out of work. Governors tried to help with state relief programs but soon they, too, were flat broke. Voluntary organizations, like church and private charities, pitched in but their resources were likewise soon exhausted. The Farm Board gave out loans but found most farmers could not meet their payments and it had no authority to intervene to stop the sheriff's sale when the farm was auctioned to pay delinquent taxes. Hoover's proposed tax cut to stimulate consumer demand was a joke. Congress cut taxes so little that it was no real stimulus to spending. Besides, what good was a reduction in income tax if one had no income? The President, in a last effort to cope, established the Reconstruction Finance Corporation. This agency was supposed to make loans to local governments, banks, and businesses which, in turn, would lend money to the average citizen. It was modeled on the perculator coffee pot: the money would eventually trickle down to the people at the bottom. The R.F.C. did not perculate.

It was too little, too late anyhow. Hoover continued to intone that "the only thing America needed was confidence" and then everything would be all right. The President dug in. He asserted that his policies were right and he would not change no matter what. "We cannot legislate ourselves out of a world depression," he said, "we can and will work ourselves out." He pushed for more vigorous enforcement of the Eighteenth Amendment. He vetoed further Congressional efforts at providing work relief projects such as a multi-purpose dam for the Tennessee River. He was photographed on the White House lawn feeding his dog. He confided to a friend just before the 1932 election: "No President must ever admit he has been wrong."[8]

By late 1932 many Americans were getting desperate. The mood of the country turned ugly. Unemployment in some places was 60 percent. Local governments were without money. In the cities large lines of hungry men, shoulders hunched against the biting winds, edged along sidewalks for a sandwich from a "soup kitchen." In Chicago, men stood outside of the backdoors of restaurants for leftovers or scoured the market districts for spoiled fruits and vegetables. In the St. Louis dumps, small groups of families dug for rotten food. In empty lots they built crude packing-crate shelters, since they no longer had their homes, and called them "Hoovervilles." In Taylorville, Illinois, an army of 1,500 men stopped the operation at the Christian Company Mines. In Eastern Iowa, Farmers barricaded highways in a vain effort to keep grain and milk from market and force prices up.

In the summer of that year an army of unemployed veterans of World War I, the Bonus Marchers, had walked on the nation's capitol. There, on the mall within sight of the White House, they camped out with their wives and children. Several thousand of them spent steamy weeks in unsanitary shacks demanding a loan from Congress up to 50 percent due them for military service. The bill was passed in the House of Representatives for that purpose but the Senate defeated it. President Hoover refused even to talk with their leaders and called out the Army, under General Douglas MacArthur, to disperse the mob. MacArthur entered the settlement with tanks, tear gas, and bayonets. Two Bonus Marchers were killed and several were injured.

In Illinois, the Depression hit, like the nation, amid bank closings, collapsing farm income, foreclosures, falling prices, and unemployment.[9]

Historians who have studied Illinois during these years all agree that the effect was uneven, most severe in communities built around basic industry or coal mining. Such was true of the agricultural machinery industries of the Quad Cities. In Moline, for example, only 7 percent of those who had a job in 1927 were working in 1932. In Peoria, also a city with a heavy dependency on farm implements, the unemployment rate was up to 53 percent. In Quincy the figure was a devastating 70 percent. The state payrolls by 1932 were almost 30 percent less than they had been in 1927. Factories kept on just about half of their earlier workforce. Railroads saw revenues go down by 50 percent and most companies fired or laid-off the same percentage of employees. People with savings accounts in banks were repaid at the most with 80¢ of the dollar. Half the families in the Prairie State, between 1929 and 1932, were without a paycheck at one time or another.

Unemployment was a threat to family life. Weddings were postponed, new or first babies delayed (the birth rate fell to zero), backyard gardens supplemented food budgets, old clothes were fixed and worn again, cars were repaired. Families moved in with relatives who still had their jobs. Landlords could not collect rent and so they eventually went broke. Drifters and bums rode empty railroad boxcars from town to town asking for handouts or odd jobs. The psychological impact of the disrupted family was devastating. Guilt, humiliation, rejection, inadequacy, bitterness, and resentment replaced self-confidence, hope in the future, compassion and love.

Governor Louis L. Emmerson tried to help. He called the legislature into special session. Together they created an Illinois Emergency Relief Commission and appropriated a $20 million annual budget for its work. The money lasted six months. Illinois voters approved the governor's request for a $25 million bond issue for the state as a whole and Cook County floated a $17 million issue of its own. Emmerson increased expenditures for state construction projects. He reduced property taxes. But nothing seemed to stem the tide of the Depression. Reports of violence appeared in the newspapers. Mines were dynamited in southern Illinois. The National Guard discovered a threat of mob violence in Granite City. In some cities "unemployment councils" were formed to consider what action to take if things became worse. These were, fortunately, only threats of violence, not incidents, except for the mine explosions. The mood in Illinois by 1932 was not revolutionary; it was apathetic. Men were not ready for decisive action, they were innervated by despair.

There was no news in Henderson County about the beginning of the Depression. There were no accounts at all in the newspapers of the stock market crash of 1929 or its immediate aftermath. It was as though the rest of the state and the rest of the country either did not exist or did not matter to these farmers and smalltown people. Not until the end of November, 1929 did the *Raritan Reporter* mention the disaster. It likened "the figuring with which the national banks through the country have been going out of business to the financial condition which existed during the Civil War" when the states took over bank operations.[10] In other words, Barnes' perspective of what was happening, and what would happen, was backwards. The problem, he thought, was the national banks and the solution was state action to save these national institutions.

Unnoticed was the 1929 yearly report on the financial resources of the seven county banks. They were off another $100,000 from their April

Stronghurst Bank

statement. By June, 1930, nine months after the crash, they listed total resources of only $1,909,002.15. The 1924 figure had been $3,355,482.41.[11] In other words they stated a drop of over 43 percent. The Media bank closed its doors in 1931 after thirty-six years of business. The Stronghurst Bank shut down in December 1932. The Houston Bank in Blandinsville, a service to the farmers of southern Henderson County townships, was locked in November 1930. The Bank of Swan Creek, on the county's eastern border, shut down in 1932 "because of diminishing cash resources and gradual withdrawals of depositors."[12] The Raritan bank came within an inch of shutting its doors. The bank's sources went from $183,649 in 1924 to $171,825 in April 1929, to $141,782.76 in January 1932. By September 1932, it had deteriorated to $135,669.79 and by the end of the year it was doing business with only $129,611.91 behind it. Then the Raritan bank had only $17,486.98 in cash-on-hand yet had $108,742.62 out in loans. The bank itself, including furniture, was worth only $2,900. To some individuals these financial disasters and near disasters were too much to bear. Henry S. Meyers, of Raritan, hanged himself in a hay mow. Henry had just lost his life's savings in the defunct Houston Bank of Blandinsville.[13]

Gradually other tangible signs of the Depression were seen. Towns went without street lights in the fall of 1932 because of depleted treasuries. Some were able only to collect on the average, one-fifth of those taxes levied that year.[14] Cars were repossessed and listed in the newspapers for sale at bargain prices. In January, 1932 the Monmouth Motor Sales Company had nine Chevrolets in stock. The Stronghurst Canning Factory in June, 1932 announced that it could not reopen. The factory, a purchaser for scores of farmers and an employer of over 100 people, was abandoned. The reason: the "falling market and the inability to find a market for their goods."[15] Farm foreclosures multiplied. Stock liquidation sales proliferated among town merchants anxious to get rid of their inventory before prices declined further. By the summer of 1932 businesses were competing in sale-wars. Furniture went at cost. Shoes went wholesale. Clothing stores just could not unload their seasonal stock in time. Some, like the Model Clothing Store in Monmouth, went out of business after forty years of merchandising.[16] At the nadir, in the spring of 1933, merchants who had stayed in business were desperate. A typical advertisement read "all the entire stock...at these ridiculous prices. Everything must be sold regardless of price."[17]

Reaction of Henderson County citizens to these events was a combination of denial and anger. Although nothing exists like the investigation of attitudes during the Depression in McDonough County, done by John Cernocky as a Master's thesis at Western Illinois University in 1973, bits and pieces of information reveal a pattern in Henderson.[18] At first the calamity seemed little more than starting the year in the red instead of in the black. "Try to get into the black, pay your debts," and "thus obliterate the depression," Barnes admonished.[19] Above all, do not even think of any expenditures for relief for those without jobs. Such projects could only "relieve the reckless unemployed from distress, and the frugal, employed of their earnings."[20]

"Hooverism" was the orthodoxy in the county and Barnes its pastor designate. You "cannot create prosperity by heaping additional tax burdens on businesses and individuals already struggling....," he wrote. "Robbing Peter to pay Paul is not sound economics." Temporary relief schemes he labeled as "the height of folly."[21] Voters must write their Congressmen and Senators to tell them to kill the idea of relief. Time itself will rectify the situation; things will get better he prophesized. He warned that any relief would in turn cause industrial stagnation where no one would have to work, and severe unemployment "instead of being a temporary evil, becomes a permanent one."[22]

Barnes even saw his friends profiteering from the Depression, and applauded it. Many, he said, have actually made money from the "present liquidation period" using it as a time for "provident buying." He suggested that readers watch out and take advantage of the hard times. Great fortunes were amassed in past depressions, he said. "Opportunities at the present," he wrote in the summer of 1932, "have not been equalled on the Raritan plain since the last Indian drank from Media springs." Sarcastically impervious to the reality of events he observed: "In fact, the only fear that some of us have of the depression is that it won't last long enough for all of our relatives to lay in a supply of winter underwear to last their lifetime."[23]

Opportunities not withstanding, how could one get out of the Depression? Barnes concocted the quick fix. "Buying will increase employment." "Employment will increase buying." Specifically, he told every reader to spend one "mattress dollar" every day for a week. This simple effort would provide an enormous psychological lift. One week of relief from "bad news" will, he assured everyone, "put our feet back on the ground ... will put enough men and dollars to work to break the backbone of the depression."[24] Eight months later he apparently concluded that this scheme would not do. So, he pushed another remedy. On page one, in bold type, he advocated that the Federal government issue fifty "Trade Certificates" to every citizen. Each certificate was to be worth one dollar and have a dated 3¢ stamp attached to it. The receiver then had to purchase something that week or add another dated stamp as a penalty. "No one would lose" with Barnes Plan, he concluded. "Our entire unemployment problem with its attendant demands for charity, would be wiped out." "Our concern for foreign trade would be lost in an endeavor to supply the great American market," he went on. To these "material advan-

WPA poster

tages," he wrote, would be added "the joys of a nation relieved of depression...we would be rid of economic fear."[25]

Franklin D. Roosevelt, the 37th man to serve as President of the United States, had another idea. F.D.R. may have had a solution 180 degress opposed to Barnes but, ironically, both men by 1933, were sensing fundamentally the same thing. In his Inaugural Address, Roosevelt announced: "This is pre-eminently the time to speak the truth, the whole truth, frankly and boldly." "So first of all let me assert my firm belief that the only thing we have to fear is fear itself—nameless, unreasoning, unjustified terror which paralyzes needed efforts to convert our retreat into advance."[26] He promised to ask Congress immediately for the only instrument remaining to fight the crisis—"broad executive power to wage a war against the emergency as great as the power that would be given me if we were in fact invaded by a foreign foe."[27] Congress responded and Roosevelt acted.

In the long run historians grant Roosevelt the label he himself gave to his recovery program, the "New Deal." In the short term his emergency actions constituted what the press called the "One Hundred Days." The

Results of CCC plantings, Big River Forest current photo

Big River State Forest, current photo

most immediate problem facing the President in March, 1933 was fiscal. Banks had closed or soon would close. People were hoarding money. Roosevelt declared a Bank Holiday on all banks, savings and loan establishments, and credit unions. Three days later, Congress passed his Emergency Banking Relief Act and, then, in the next couple of years other laws which made the Federal government the regulator both of banks and the stock market. Roosevelt took the nation off the gold standard and thereby laid the basis for printing more dollars—pump-priming, it was called.

The President next hit at unemployment. He created through Congress the Federal Emergency Relief Association to make $500 million in grants to states and cities. Congress established the Civil Works Administration to put four million people back to work on Federal jobs. Later, this agency was expanded in money and scope under the WPA (Works Projects Administration) and the PWA (Public Works Administration). The President got farm relief legislation in the Agricultural Adjustment Act. Actually, the farm program consisted of a composite of separate acts and bills which basically sought to guarantee parity prices (the average prices between 1909 and 1914 of the major staples of corn, wheat, hogs, milk, tobacco, cotton, and rice). Farmers could participate, and receive a federal check for their products, by agreeing to reduce acreage and embrace conservation practices. To bolster the nation's industries Congress passed the National Industrial Recovery Act to set prices and control production. Under section 7a, unions were given the right to collective bargaining. The CCC, or Civilian Conservation Corp, put young unemployed men between the ages of eighteen and twenty-five to work preserving the nation's natural resources. Roosevelt, picking up on a scheme advanced by Congress in 1930 but rejected out of hand by Hoover, created the huge conservation dam of the Tennessee Valley Authority.

The New Deal had its critics. Conservatives were appalled at the basic assumptions of what they called a national "dole." They charged FDR with deliberately leading the nation to socialism. The Supreme Court struck down both the AAA and the NIRA as unconstitutional. Critics on the political left said Roosevelt was not doing enough to help unemployment. Some, like the writer Upton Sinclair, who ran for governor of California, asked Congress for a pension of $50 a month to every person over sixty-five. Dr. Francis E. Townsend wanted to pay every unemployed American over sixty years of age $200 a month provided they promised to spend the money the month the check arrived in the mail. Senator Huey Long of Louisiana promised to "Share the Wealth" by taxing the rich to build hospitals, schools, and highways.

Illinois put the New Deal into operation under the leadership of Democratic governor Henry Horner. The state was in dire need of assistance: it was financially strapped by the spring of 1933. Horner called the legislature into special session and passed the first sales tax, a two-percent levy on all retailers. He found other sources of revenue in a 3¢ gallon tax on gasoline and a license tax for the upkeep of highways. He placed a tax on all alcoholic beverages. He asked for, and received, direct federal dollars from the FERA and by 1935, started a service of state work projects, Horner, under the act, evne put unemployed historians back to work in the Illinois Historical Records Survey, an inventory of all records then housed, often stored by gravity, in the 102 county courthouses. Under the new Social Security Act of 1935, the state gave federal money (matched by state funds) to needy persons over sixty-five. A new state agency, the Department of Public Welfare, established offices in every county. At its height, in 1939 1,226,686 people in Illinois were receiving federal and state assistance in some way or another. They were on general unemployment relief, old-age pensions, or were receiving government paychecks as a participant in the WPA, PWA, and AAA (repassed in 1937 and subsequently declared constitutional by the Supreme Court).[28]

The New Deal can be said to have started in Henderson County on March 4, 1933. On that morning, a Saturday, a telegram signed by President Roosevelt arrived at every bank in the county from Washington, D.C. It stated that all business would cease henceforth until further notice. Bank clerks just told people they could not come in and could not have their money. By early June most local banks were back in business on a limited basis. These banks included two at Oquawka, and one each at Biggsville, Stronghurst, Raritan, and Lomax. Barnes grumbled that Roosevelt had succeeded in doing in all of the banks of the county "at one fell swoop."[29]

Bank of Oquawka

During the next month county bank presidents convened stockholder's meetings similar to the one held at Raritan on April sixth. The Raritan plan of action was typical. The stockholders agreed to issue all depositors a "deferred certificate" at two percent annual interest for their claim "payable only from future profits" of the bank. The certificates, though, would be worth only one-fourth of the individual's dollar deposits. The Raritan bank would pay only 35 percent of demand accounts and even these would be dealt with in deferred payments. It would, however, agree to the repayment at 4 percent interest. At least, to start with, where cash on hand allowed, the bank would pay 40 percent of existing claims (operating expenses and bills) "as soon as the bank opens." The results were extraordinary. Seventy-eight of the 168 depositors at the Raritan bank signed waivers for a total of $34,542.21. On April 13, two state auditors visited the bank and "found everything in good and regular order and said that there is no reason why the bank cannot open for business on Monday of next week."[30] It did.

The State Bank of Stronghurst, which had closed in December, 1932, before the Holiday, also took stops to reopen. By late April bank representatives met with a state bank examiner in Chicago. There the state

Waldo Erickson, Raritan Banker

Burkett Store, Biggsville

official told them that he "would not at present accept the formula for the rehabilitation" of their bank. If they wanted to reopen they had to raise $62,000 in cash as a starter. Then the depositors, like Raritan, would have to waiver indefinitely a claim on their deposits. The bank stayed closed.[31] The other Stronghurst bank, the First National, was in worse shape in the judgment of the auditors. Its stockholders, only a dozen, had to pay a stock assessment in the sum of $33,100. The men, apparently, tried to evade the payment arguing that they had already paid out a sizable portion of the total amount, but the state officials remained adamant. The stockholders were, in Barnes words, accordingly "mulcted."[32] The stockholders and depositors at the Media Bank were also in bad shape. After paying the receiver's salary and expenses of $2,090, plus the liquidating expenses of $7,470.14, they had just a little over $3,000 left to pay all claims. In other words, the Media people lost everything.[33]

The stories of Stronghurst and Media were not untypical of what happened throughout the state. In May, State Auditor Edward J. Barret announced that he would not allow the "major portion" of the 223 state banks to reopen "on the grounds that it would be a fool-hardy move." Many of the banks, he said, "have no reason for being open" since they "were merely payroll offices or currency exchanges and not economically sound banking organizations."[34] By mid-June, however, five county banks had reopened on a part-time basis: Raritan, Biggsville, Lomax, and the two banks at Oquawka.[35] By that time they all had publicly announced their membership in the new Federal Deposit Insurance Corporation wherein each depositor was insured up to $5,000.

The banks which survived the shock of 1933 recovered steadily throughout the rest of the Depression. By 1936, using the Raritan Bank's published records as an example, the recovery rate seemed encouraging. From its all-time low report of resources in January, 1933, of $129,611.91 and cash-on-hand of just $17,486.00 it was able by July, 1934 to list resources of $248,049.31 and cash-on-hand of $101,667.20. Two years later it listed $417,587.93 in resources and $144,762.86 in cash and by that fall Cashier Waldo M. Erickson signed off to a total of $526,77.12 in resources and $212,989.47 in cash.[36] By the end of the Depression, in October, 1940, the Raritan State Bank had rebounded to resources of $718,344.68. That Christmas it gave a 6 percent dividend to its stockholders.[37]

County farmers, like the nation's farmers, were floundering in 1933. Although not out of work or unemployed in the strict sense of the word, their family income dropped just the same. Corn was under 30¢ by then. Other farm staples in the county hit new lows corresponding to drops on grain and future market prices. Wheat went down from $1.82 to 38¢ a bushel. Farm income was cut 50 percent, prices overall dropped 60 percent—yet production kept up at a loss of only 6 percent. With that formula in operation things were bound to get worse. Ten percent of the nation's farms were foreclosed. In the county, foreclosures multiplied. In the summer of 1932, the *Raritan Reporter* had on page one, bold-type announcement: "Farm Land Prices Ridiculously Low."[38] Prices ranged from $20 to $38 an acre at the auctions. Four such auctions were advertised in that one issue of the newspaper: two in Terre Haute, one eight miles west of Raritan, and a fourth four miles north of LaHarpe. Henderson County farm cash expenditures hit an all-time low in 1934. That year a county farmer averaged just $332 on machinery, $57 on improvements, $100 on "labor expenditures," and, if he were able, he paid about $218 to the treasurer's office.[39]

In the event a farmer needed start-up money in the spring of 1933 he was in real trouble. No banks were able to advance loans. Taking the place of banks were three credit organizations. One was the Monmouth Production Credit Association with its office at Stronghurst. In charge of Clarence A. Hartquist, it offered loans to finance crop production and livestock. Right next door, in the same building, was the Henderson County Farm Loan Association with George Chant in charge. They were exclusively concerned with people wanting farm mortgages. The third organization was the Farm Bureau Cooperative, which made secured loans on collateral with federal funds. Sometimes farmers, at market time, could receive limited credit from the Stronghurst Shippers Association in order to get their livestock to market over the Sante Fe Railroad. And, by the same token, the Stronghurst Grain and Merchandise Company would help out selected farmers.

It was not until the New Deal's AAA was passed that, like bankers, farmers were able to break the downward momentum of the Depression. Before then, farm problems were untouched by the credit-adjustments of the Hoover administration. All the substitute loans would be of no help whatsoever if market prices declined and production levels remained up. That is what the AAA tried to tackle. On May 12, 1933 Congress enacted the legislation. Under the law the Secretary of Agriculture, Henry Wallace, through his county representatives made arrangements with each farmer on a voluntary basis whereby they would cut production and the Secretary would guarantee them a certain income for what they did produce. The uncultivated or unused land would be rented by the federal government and the farmer would get "benefit payments" for it.

So, the direct and immediate benefits of the AAA to farmers were tangible and the alternative unthinkable. The program promised cash income and rising crop prices. The general formula used in Henderson County in 1933-34 was for farmers to sign contracts to reduce their acreage, or livestock production, by about 25 percent. If they happened to produce more than was calculated that year the federal government agreed to put crops, on a federal loan, in storage until prices rose, thereby avoiding any possible market glut. The result, initially, was impressive: the smallest corn crop since 1881 and the highest hog prices in five years.

The place to go in Henderson County to sign up for the AAA was the second floor above the offices of the Farm Bureau at Stronghurst. There farmers talked their situation over with William L. Forgey of Gladstone, chairman of the county committee of AAA or with Clarence P. Gibb of Biggsville, its vice-chairman. During the next three years, until the Supreme Court struck down the first AAA in the winter of 1936, this organization signed up more than $1,363,000 worth of loans on the broad requirement of only "experience, equipment and a reasonable down payment," whatever that meant.[40] The benefit payments for county land set-aside to October 31, 1935 alone amounted to $615,439.05. Corn and hog payments from July 1, 1934 to October 31, 1934 totaled $596,484.94. Emergency loans then came to $2,848.[41] Public opinion, in the beginning, was "square behind the new farm plan." Edna Barnes Simonson, who continued the *Raritan Reporter* after her father's death in 1934, called it an "effective program." She was encouraged about its positive effect on attitudes and saw a "spirit of unity" among farmers.[42]

Others saw the need to stay with the old Farm Bureau and just secure loans without strings attached. They felt more comfortable with what was seen as a farmer-owner and controlled cooperative organization. In

Edna Barnes Simonson and nieces

Oquawka in 1930's

an editorial, "Two Kinds of Farm Relief," Mrs. Simonson noted that the farmer in the co-op "feels, and rightly, that he and his fellows are working toward their own solution and that the future is up to them."[43] Still others just did not want to turn over their affairs to a bunch of Washington bureaucrats. Besides, the Farm Bureau, in focusing on saving farms from foreclosure or in exercising right of redemption to regain lost homesteads, seemed to be more helpful to those really in need and thus gained another psychological advantage over AAA.

Farm Bureau activities appeared more practical and to the point. In the winter of 1936 it held a one-day "machinery repair and maintenance meeting" in Stronghurst under the direction of the University of Illinois. It aimed at the simple cost-saving process of cutting down on machinery replacements. The Bureau continued local informational meetings, just as before. Its advisors explained the pros and cons of the AAA programs while George B. Whitman, the county farm adviser, explained the uncomplicated terms of loans through his office. Over radio station WLS he broadcast the same information into farm homes every Tuesday, Thursday, and Saturday afternoons at a quarter till one. The Farm Bureau kept its down-home touch by sponsoring a baseball team that competed with other Bureau teams from McDonough, Warren, and Hancock counties.[44]

Membership in the Bureau however, declined. By the summer of 1936 it was down to only fifty-one members, about half of its earlier membership. The Bureau organization director H.H. Schweitzer said that the decline happened because farmers in the "past two years" in AAA had profited by that organization.[45] That year, the Farm Bureau activities, and membership, did pick up somewhat after the AAA was struck down by the Supreme Court and it announced a big meeting in Decatur at the end of January.[46] But the Court's decision was only an interlude. In 1938, Congress re-enacted the law and this time the Court allowed it to stand. From then on county support was even stronger for AAA because now the federal government, in addition to offering former benefits, added crop insurance and more efficient administration of marketing quotas and acreage allotments.

The AAA and the Farm Bureau programs together helped county farmers turn the corner. Farm income increased from an average of $3,171 in 1934 to $4,531 by the middle of 1935. Farm outlays doubled on machinery and cash expenditures. Money spent on improvemens increased three times.[47] By mid-1936 Henderson County had 1,060 farms valued at $12,871,024. The average farm size was just under 200 acres. That year the AAA reported that 80 percent of the county farmers had signed up for their program. It had sent out final checks to corn and hog farmers for $21,199.66 or 20¢ for every acre of corn land out of cultivation and $7.50 for each hog up to 10 percent of hog price.[49] Soil conservation efforts were a success. The county farmer averaged $14.10 an acre for diverting soil-depleting acreage under the new program.[50] By 1936 AAA gave $2,840 in crop and feed loans. It recorded benefit payments of $755,686 by the time of its temporary demise late that year. It had made loans to 886 farmers of $1,158,186.00.[51]

St. Ledger Brothers Garage, Raritan
Tom St. Ledger, Pat McCleary, Joe McCleary, Tony McCleary and Tony St. Ledger

When AAA was declared unconstitutional Henderson County farmers responded in anger. They showed a "militant spirit of determination to continue to fight for equal privileges and price parity."[52] Farm Bureau officers even protested. Their answer was a telegram to Washington promising "100 new fighting members within ten days." They joined a regional meeting of six counties at Monmouth that adopted a resolution pledging continued support to secure "a fair share of the nation's income for agriculture with government assistance comparable to that legislated to other important groups."[53]

While the county came to embrace the fiscal and agricultural programs of Roosevelt's New Deal, it had little sympathy with the rest of it. The President's plan for recovery of industrial America and relief for the unemployed worker found little support in this rural community. Relief money spent by Illinois was quoted at a shocking $170,000,000 by November of 1934.[54] County relief costs, proportionally, were up to $6,300 a month by the spring of 1936 with between 275 and 375 families on the rolls.[55] The problem was aggravated by Roosevelt's NIRA minimum wage of fifty cents an hour. This policy, most people felt, just served to create more unemployment. Farmers could not afford such wages for their hired help and the effect was painfully obvious. Many men who would have been willing to work for as little as twenty cents or thirty cents an hour just left the fields, registered with the county "re-employment bureau" as it was called, and "are laying around awaiting for state and government jobs."[56]

NIRA codes meant higher grain elevator prices in the midst of the Depression! In the fall of 1933 the Blandinsville Farmer's Elevator Company displayed the NIRA Eagle with its motto "We Do Our Part" yet it announced that because of its support of NIRA "we find it necessary to raise our prices on merchandise and service enough to take care of the added expense of conforming to their agreement."[57] By 1936, 11.2 percent of the county's population was on relief and was receiving public aid.[58] To handle such county relief problems across the state a gargantuan bureaucracy of 10,082 men and women were employed by the Illinois Emergency Relief Commission at an administrative cost of $1,067,531 a year.[59]

Stop the waste, Barnes yelled. The people had been through depressions before. They would come out of this one without the boondoggle of New Deal relief. Leave folks to "run their own business." "That would bring back prosperity a lot quicker" he said, "than a lot of white-collared,

Lock and Dam 18, Gladstone

swiveled-chaired dreamers located many miles from the seat of action." "As things stand now," he wrote, "many people are afraid to launch out independently for fear of incurring the displeasure of some government dictator."[60] Federal old-age pensions and, after 1938, Social Security were other dangerous wastes of money. His daughter noted with alarm in 1936 that there were more than 16,000 applications approved in the state. In the county there were 302 applications and 217 were approved for the $15 a month allotment.[61] With pleasure Mrs. Simonson reported a cutback in relief programs in the spring of that year. Payments will be stopped "for every family in Henderson County in which there is an employable person."[62] She was contradictory. She condemned one part of the New Deal, its expenditure of federal money for unemployed workers and minimum wages, but at the same time she embraced the AAA with its federal minimum wage, or parity, for farmers. She was not alone in the county. Nor were Mrs. Simonson and her neighbors consistent. They condemned most parts of the relief measures while selecting out a few things which directly benefitted them and which they, understandably, liked.

New Deal construction work was all right even though it siphoned off as many federal dollars as the NIRA or Social Security. Road building with WPA money and PWA work on a dam on the Mississippi between Burlington and Oquawka both were applauded. In fact, in addition to the lock and dam there were four major road construction projects going on simultaneously in the county by the winter of 1934 alone. Barnes at the time happily described the county as a "busy baliwick the coming spring and summer." He confidently, and wrongly, predicted that "when the several projects get underway unemployment ought to be an unknown quantity thereon."[63]

When the voters of the county, in the fall of 1936, approved a bond issue for further improvement of county highways it was noted with approbation that the PWA was up front with 4.5 percent of the share, or $133,533.44 sent to the County Board. The improvements involved road widening and grading as well as graveling all remaining dirt roads.[64] Men employed on these WPA projects averaged about $40 a month.[65] PWA money was sent from Washington to Oquawka for the county jail, $6,600 in the first allotment in July, 1936. Terre Haute received a $13,909 allowance for its streets. WPA projects were begun in Rozetta (road construction), Biggsville (improvement of its public water system), and Oquawka (survey of local finance and taxation system).[66]

There was no objection to the fact that 217 elderly were receiving "Old Age Assistance" that summer from the federal government. A.S. McElhinney of Stronghurst, the county agent for the Department of Public Welfare, announced in August that 72 percent of those who had applied for relief had been approved thus far and were regularly receiving their $15 in the mail.[67] The Civilian Conservation Corp was active in the county from the start. They began with regular monthly enrollment meetings in 1934 to which all the young men were invited, whether or not they had a job at the time. Those who were out of work, or feared that they soon might be fired, were urged to get their application filled out immediately and to give it to the County Illinois Emergency Relief Commission Office. Eligibility was open-ended. One only had to be "physically and mentally able to do outdoor work." Specifically, the application asked whether you were a citizen between the age of 17 and 23 and one-half years, unmarried, not in school, of good character, and out of a job. So, the New Deal to Henderson County, was the same as the New Deal

Thompson Grocery, Oquawka, 1927

throughout the land, a potpourri. A person took what was needed and, if so inclined, condemned the rest.

Daily life during the Depression was the same mixed combination of the good and the bad. A new part of everyday routine was the new jobs created by WPA, PWA, and CCC. Masons and carpenters turned the blacksmith shop of Tony and June Stencil at Oquawka into a new county jail that housed prisoners who, since the destruction of the County Poor Farm-Jail by fire in 1929, had been locked up at Monmouth. By the fall of 1934 important gaps in Len Small's paved road program for the county had been filled in with WPA workers. Route 164 between Oquawka and Gladstone finished county main-line highway construction from Monmouth to the Mississippi River. The telephone system was improved in the late Thirties. Each township had a switchboard that operated six days every week. On Sunday it served emergencies only. All lines were shared or "party" lines.[68] Towns like Raritan got their first public library. It was opened in the fall of 1936 at the Opera House with the state supplying the books supplemented with volumes donated by the town's Community Club. Books were loaned for two weeks without charge from the library whose hours ran from two till six daily and during the evenings on Wednesday and Saturday.[69] The Farm Bureau held regular cooking schools for the women under the auspices of its Home Bureau.

Henderson County teachers, unlike others in the state, stayed on their jobs. They were still underpaid, however. Over half of them in the 1930s received under $100 per month compared to only 27 percent so compensated across the state outside of Chicago.[70] Children, with PWA money, started to ride the new school-buses in 1938 paying ten cents a ride as a subsidy.[71] The landscape of education changed little from the previous decades. The same high schools and scattered one-room grammar school buildings remained with the same unmarried female teachers reconvening classes year after year.

Only one note of future change in county education was sounded. Early in January, 1933 when faced with the expense of paying teachers and providing the upkeep of so many buildings, some taxpayers talked about consolidation. Later a meeting of the state Teacher's Association in Springfield that winter approved a consolidation plan that saved between $800 and $1000 in each school district within the counties. The scheme was to shut down the rural schoolhouses, 10,000 of them in the state then, reduce overhead expenses, and create a County Board of Education of five members who would serve without pay and abolish all district officers.[72] The necessity of hard times, as far as public education went, proved to be the mother of invention.

Another by-product of the Depression was rural electrification. Electricity first came to the county in the 1920s in part as a result of the hydroelectric project completed during World War I at Keokuk. But this phenomena was largely town-centered or at best went to rural areas adjacent to trunk lines. In the Thirties, however, with New Deal money, the farm electric generators were thrown away.[73] Working through both the Farm Bureau and AAA offices at Stronghurst, electric lines were strung to family farms, beginning in 1936. At first the expansion of service was slow because it was voluntary. Farmers were hesitant to commit themselves for the high cost of wiring and equipment, about $500 in the summer of that year. Then, too, there was the five dollar monthly fixed charge for electricity to consider.[74] Farm advisor Whitman urged that rural electrification be considered not as a matter of individual choice or convenience but rather as a community problem, like paved roads.[75]

Surprisingly, the cost of living in the county did not remain down in the Depression years. True, in 1934, consumer prices for clothing, for example, fell. A man's suit went for between $10 and $25 at the Model Clothing Company in Monmouth. Dress shirts were only a dollar and a pair of slacks, at Simon and Phillburg, cost just $1.50.[76] Haircuts were just 25¢ and shaves 15¢. A dentist would extract a tooth for 50¢ with all work guaranteed.[77] Gasoline ran 11¢ a gallon. But by 1936, inflation began to rectify the bargains. Model Clothing Company suits were up to $25 to $35. Mens' dress shirts were tagged at $1.95 and ties were two for a dollar. And, four years later, the same suit at the same place cost $25 to $40 and a Dobbs Hat was $5 to $7.50.[78] By the end of the Depression decade used cars were selling for as much as the new models had brought back in 1932. By then, a 1939 Dodge Deluxe listed at $545 and a Dodge two-door with heater at $595. A three-year old Dodge Sedan ran $385.00.[79]

Business Section, Media

Another interesting, and unexpected, phenomena of the Depression was the absence of serious crime. Although faced with the hard times of the Depression few individuals acted-out their frustration. Indeed the county reacted much as the nation did to the worst years of the calamity, with more of a numb apathy than with violence. There was a spurt of petty robberies in the darkest years, 1933 to 1934, but after that property crime all but disappeared. In the spring of 1933, Shoemaker's Store at Media was robbed of groceries and canned goods. The estimated loss was only $25 or $30. Fagan's Oil Station on the paved road south of Biggsville was broken into and inner tubes, gasoline, cylinder oil, and a car radio were taken.[80] In June of that same year seventy-six-year-old Clorissa Cummp of Gladstone was bound, gagged, and robbed one Saturday night of $300 in cash and some certificates of deposit.[81]

In 1934, there was a much-touted case of attempted extortion of William Weir of the Oak Grove Fruit Farm near Gladstone. According to the *Raritan Reporter* a twenty-year old neighbor sent Weir a letter directing him to put $2,000 in small bills in two packages in the mailbox in front of his home. "Dire disaster" was threatened, if the instructions were ignored. Weir immediately notified both the Sheriff and the State's Attorney. They told him to place two packages in the box and they would hide nearby to catch the culprit at the pickup. Weir did as instructed and about ten o'clock that night the pickup was attempted. The sheriff hollered at the culprit to stop, that he was under arrest. The lad broke into a run, but was tackled by the two men, handcuffed, and taken to the Warren County jail at Monmouth.[82]

Bad times or not, the 1930s had a tone of irony to it. It was a decade of anxiety, malaise, and uncertainty. It was also a time of escape. It was a great decade of the silver screen and radio's finest hour. The movies in those years became a family institution. Over the paved roads and in their cars people took children, friends, and dates to see Joan Crawford, Jean Harlow, Mae West, Clark Gable, Cary Grant, or Mickey Mouse. Distances seemed irrelevant anymore. "Before the day of the hard roads and automobiles," Mrs. Simonson observed, "the idea of going all the way" from Raritan to Oquawka to see a movie, a one-hour drive, "would have been unheard of."[83] As one historian has concluded, "for many families, even in the depth of the Depression, movie money was just as important as food money."[84] Indeed, if you had the money, you could see four different movies every week.

Radio sets played in every home, village, and farm. They became a piece of the living-room furniture, a replacement for the traditional mantel where family photos and trophies were displayed. Every night of the week featured a main show starting at about seven o'clock. "Dragnet," "The Shadow," "The FBI in Peace and War," "Lux Radio Theater," "Edgar Bergen and Charlie McCarthy," "Jack Benny," "Mr. and Mrs. North," and the "Lone Ranger" were standards. During the afternoon the soap operas addicted housewives. Not an afternoon went by, for many women, without hearing the latest episode of "Stella Dallas" or "The Young Widder Brown." Saturday morning was the kid's time to listen to "Tom Mix," "Buster Brown," and "Superman."

Radio Ad from *Raritan Reporter*

The Thirties were also the heyday of the "big bands". Financed by WPA funds, professional musicians swelled the orchastras of Benny Goodman and Glenn Miller or the lesser-knowns. Bud Haney vividly recalled the dances at "Queen Paradise" at Oquawka where every weekend the bands "packed them in."[85] Two big bands a week played here. On one Saturday in October, 1933 there was "Jack Straws and his Orchestra." Then, after he left on Tuesday, Jack Everett played from Wednesday till Friday. Then the following Saturday night, October 11, "Dale Larson and his Silver Band" were in town. Admission was just 25¢. Or one traveled across the bridge to Burlington to the popular Roof Garden over Pennys' store. There you danced for a higher-price (65¢ for "gentlemen" and 35¢ for "ladies") to "Coon Saunders and his Famous Orchestra."[86]

More traditional amusements also flourished. Again, WPA funds helped out. In 1936, for example, 150 professional entertainers, musicians, and artists performed at the Henderson County Fair in early September. The fair sponsors were explicit about their indebtedness to the New Deal. "The Fair Board feels particularly fortunate to be able to present such entertainment this year," it wrote in August when advertising the event, "and could not financially do so if it were not because of the WPA program of employing entertainers and musicians...."[87] John Foster remembered the county fairs at Stronghurst in the Depression years. There he, along with Eddie Sherer and Page Randall, saw the horse races, both sulky and bareback, on Thursday, Friday and Saturday nights. There, too, was the Big Tent with its 4-H exhibits, its displays of household appliances, and an Indian relic collection. The Stronghurst

Band played afternoon concerts. Judges awarded prizes from the Farm Bureau for the best beef cattle, hogs, lambs, and corn.[88] In 1935, the second year of the county fair, six towns and forty-five schools had entries in the contests. In 1933, the Henderson County Music and Drama Society organized. It held its first meeting at Stronghurst in the Farm Bureau building. Then, each year thereafter, it sponsored tryouts and then plays. It sent county "drama entries" to compete in state contests at Urbana each January in connection with Farm and Home Week.

Amusements and entertainments might well have provided a psychological safety-valve for the pressure of dealing with the unwanted, the unexpected, and the unpredictable. But one aspect of life in the county, politics, could not sidestep the incessant realities of those years. Politics and depression, in the form of FDR and his programs, forced choices. The New Deal cut across the grain of life in Henderson County. Unlike the earlier days there were no more avoidable political questions in the Thirties. One just could not ignore Franklin D. Roosevelt and his Democratic Party. Voters could not sidestep the fundamental intrusions of the federal government into their daily routines.

YEAR	CANDIDATES	PARTY	POPULAR VOTE	ELECTORAL VOTE
1932	FRANKLIN D. ROOSEVELT	Democratic	22,809,638 (57.3%)	472
	Herbert C. Hoover	Republican	15,758,901 (39.6%)	59
	Norman Thomas	Socialist	881,951 (2.2%)	0
1936	FRANKLIN D. ROOSEVELT	Democratic	27,751,612 (60.7%)	523
	Alfred M. Landon	Republican	16,681,913 (36.4%)	8
	William Lemke	Union	891,858 (1.9%)	0
1940	FRANKLIN D. ROOSEVELT	Democratic	27,243,466 (54.7%)	449
	Wendell L. Willkie	Republican	22,304,755 (44.8%)	82
1944	FRANKLIN D. ROOSEVELT	Democratic	25,602,505 (52.8%)	432
	Thomas E. Dewey	Republican	22,006,278 (44.5%)	99

FDR's Presidential Campaigns, 1932-1944

In the election which brought Roosevelt to power a life-long county Democrat bolted his party and backed Republicans for state office. Edward Barnes, on the eve of the election, asked readers to vote for governor Len Small. The reason was the paved roads program. "The people of Henderson County without regard to political affiliation," he wrote, "owe a debt of gratitude to Gov. Small which they can partially repay on Tuesday...by voting for him."[89] Barnes reluctantly endorsed Roosevelt over Hoover, however, confessing "a change is worth trying for." Echoing the frustration of many Americans by that time he stated that "things can't be much worse, and here is a possibility that it would prove beneficial," "Let's try it and see," he concluded.[90] For the first time his neighbors agreed. Raritan township voted 228 for Roosevelt and 130 for Hoover. The state, however, went for Hoover by 566,000.[91]

After 1932 political attention inevitably focused on the New Deal programs in banking and finance, agriculture, and unemployment relief. The programs at first were accepted or condemned more on philosophical grounds dealing with the "proper role" of government, and for a while a purely local issue did not flare up. The decision of the County Board in

1934 to build a $25,000 jail in Oquawka fanned old sentiments of resentment against the county seat. Some, in Stronghurst and Raritan, tried to revive the plan, defeated thirty years before, of moving the courthouse to another town. There was some talk of securing a court order against the building of a new jail until the question of relocation of the county seat could be decided by the voters. Nothing came of the fight.[92] But in Congressional elections of 1934 a political revolution took place. Democratic candidates won in most precincts. The only Republican to win that year, and he ran without opposition, was Judge James W. Gorden. Democrat Alfred L. Shallenberger, a popular Stronghurst man, won the office of County Clerk by a majority of 300 votes. George Voorhees was elected Sheriff. Chris S. Apt, "by common consent," was returned as the Superintendent of Schools. Democrat candidates for Congressmen-at-large, Michael L. Igoe and Martin A. Brennen were elected. The incumbant Democratic Congressman Chester Thompson was re-elected by an unheard of majority of 6,000 votes in the district. At the state level the same thing happened. Democrat Robert M. Harper defeated Republican William Schroeder by over 3,000 votes, and Democrat Thomas P. Sinnett over one of the three seats in the General Assembly along with two Republicans, Clinton Searle and Harry McCasklin.[93]

Charles W. Cooper, center, turned the first shovel of dirt for the building of the present-day Henderson County Jail. Standing on the far right is Judge Earl Knox.

Ground breaking for new county jail

The Democratic ascendancy was an unnatural act for Henderson County voters. By 1936, the Republican reflexes of the county, so deep historically, began to revive. The campaign that year was clearly pitched as a referendum on the New Deal, not only in Henderson County but throughout the nation. To head the Republican ticket the party nominated Kansas governor Alfred Landon, a moderate and a farmer, a backer of Theodore Roosevelt against Taft in 1912. He attacked the New Deal at every level. He condemned the outrageous spending. He was against prohibition repeal. He fretted that Roosevelt had created a dangerous, permanent bureaucrary but he never said what he, if President, would do differently. FDR was backed by organized labor and supported by farmers, nationally. He campaigned on the success of the economic recovery. Roosevelt carried every state except Maine and Vermont and won over ten million popular votes. In Illinois, Governor Horner won hands-down over Republican challenger "Curley Brooks."

Landon visited Henderson County by train in September. He stopped at Stronghurst and Oquawka where he spoke "a few words of greeting." A number of local Republicans went to Galesburg for the privilege of riding with their nominee.[94] Most of the local attention, however, was on Horner. Democrats praised him for his wise handling of the recent crisis saying that no one could have managed better under the stress than he did. They especially liked his stand against Chicago Democrats, led by Mayor Kelly, in their attempt to dominate the state ticket and portrayed Horner as something of a hero for downstate interests. The Governor came to the area twice that year to speak. In March, "thirty carloads of people from the county drove to hear him speak at Galesburg."[95] In early October, a large crowd again heard the bald and pugnacious Democrat speak about the "forgotten man" and how his party had been their only salvation.

The county election results disappointed Democrats who anticipated a further growth of party support. Instead, voters showed a Republican resurgency in the face of the Roosevelt juggernaut. Republicans won the Congressman-at-large contest. Henderson voters chose Republicans for Attorney General, State Treasurer, State Auditor, and Secretary of State.

177

Even FDR lost the Henderson County vote by 2,496 to Landon's 2,663. His support stayed on top only in Bald Bluff, Oquawka, Gladstone, Terre Haute, and Carman. Horner went down to Brooks by 2,493 to 2,614, and took just Bald Bluff, Oquawka, Gladstone, and Lomax. In some townships though, the vote was more lopsided than the aggregate figures indicate. For example, Landon trounced Roosevelt in Stronghurst by 488 to 262 while FDR swamped Landon by almost the same ratio, 427 to 21, in Gladstone township. The same block-voting appeared in the gubernatorial race. Brooks defeated Horner in Stronghurst by 457 to 289 and Horner won over Brooks in Gladstone by 413 to 218.[96] Simonson felt the results showed that the people of the county were sound, politically, and could not be seduced to follow any national bandwagon. They could not, in her words, be stampeded. In spite of exaggerations, wild propaganda, and distortion of facts on both sides, she concluded "the people still voted as they deemed was for their best interests."[97]

Still, Mrs. Simonson could not help but see the national election results as "a mandate" for the New Deal. But that was not to be. "Everything went wrong for Roosevelt in his second term" historian Richard Jensen has declared correctly.[98] He tried to put liberals on the conservative Supreme Court and his own party in the Senate went against him. The *Chicago Tribune* cried "dictatorship." Excesses of labor union leaders like John L. Lewis undermined the reputation of that part of the Roosevelt political coalition. The state Democratic Party never got over the downstate-Chicago split of the 1936 campaign. Horner himself suffered a stroke. The economy, apparently revived in 1936, had a relapse and by 1938 was in serious decline. Republicans found vigorous and articulate young leaders in Congressmen Everett Dirksen and Dwight Green. Then, too, the GOP by 1937 had gotten hold of a program which finally could be offered as an alternative to the New Deal. Instead of merely opposing the New Deal, Republicans stressed middle-class values: efficiency, clean government, and opportunity through private enterprise rather than federal relief or union protectionism. They appealed directly to white collar employees, businessmen, farm owners, and professionals who by then resented higher taxes, welfare payments, and angry union bosses.

The New Deal did work, however, both in Illinois and in Henderson County. It broke the spiral of the Depression. Relief rolls reached a peak in 1936 and receded steadily thereafter. After 1935, federal aid was shifted from the earlier direct grants to grants to the state on the basis of demonstrated need. WPA and PWA rolls went down from their all-time high of over 160,000 in 1936. By 1939, too, there was an economic upswing because of American aid to England following the outbreak of war in Europe. America's own rearmament helped the recovery. People in Illinois still on public assistance went down. Employment figures shot up to over four million in 1940, greater than any other time in history. Family income rose accordingly to almost equal the 1929 figure. In 1941, the CCC programs in Henderson County ended, then the WPA projects were terminated. The Illinois Emergency Relief Commission was reorganized into a much more modest Illinois Public Aid Commission with a focus in dependent children and aid to the blind. Newspaper writers like Hugh Moffet of the Monmouth *Review Atlas* wrote in featured local stories called "Salutes" about the new vigor seen in the Henderson County farmer who, he said, "has gone a long way from his condition in 1932 when corn was considered for fuel and there was no profit in raising livestock." By 1940 "a secure future lay in store" for the merchants of the towns and villages of the county. By that year AAA abandoned the controls and restraints in production which had been the hallmark of its operation since 1933.[99] Reports in the 1940 Bureau of Census showed the uncontested return of prosperity.

The essential character of the Depression and the New Deal was ambivalence. The county was receptive to emergency federal legislation on the banks, the farms, unemployment relief, and Social Security. But behind the acceptance was a lurking fear that it was somehow wrong and un-American. The initial response to the Crash of 1929 was an unabashed flaunting of the American capacity to overcome all obstacles. If let alone, Hoover had said, we would get over it. Henderson County citizens believed him because they wanted to believe in the essential soundness of American character and in the capitalist system. When, under crushing evidence from all around it was necessary to discard this faith a primitive fear of survival surfaced and substitutes were tried and tested. Henderson County bankers, farmers, businessmen, and young people proved adaptable. Yet, almost as soon as the panic anxiety of 1933 began to recede the voters registered a reflexive return to their traditional faith. They took what they needed from FDR and his New Deal, but that was all they took. And that gesture, really, was only a temporary one.

But the Depression and the New Deal did change Henderson County people. It strengthened, for better or for worse, the impact of the President upon their lives and plans. It established the principle that the federal government, not just Springfield or the Courthouse, had a responsibility for their welfare when no other agency, state or local, could meet it. It created new and permanent expectations: when one was old there was a likelihood of a pension, when one was out of work there would be some help to find a job and a modest income to tide you over until you did. Some of the New Deal was transitory if not frivolous. The big bands, with their WPA subsidies, passed away with the era. The compulsive movie-going disappeared never to return in the same way.

In the last analysis the New Deal did for the county what it did for the nation. It preserved its way of life in the face of the greatest economic calamity ever experienced. On March 5, 1933 when the new President sent that Saturday morning telegram shutting down the banks, the capitalist system had ceased functioning. It had halted, period. There was no buying or selling, no exchange of goods and services, no more investments, no more profits. The nation's heart had stopped. FDR with his New Deal performed an emergency cardiovascular resuscitation, and it worked. The economic system started up once more, feeble, but it never again threatened to quit.

Perhaps that single achievement, survival, is FDR's legacy, especially when seen in the broadest historical perspective. For in the 1930s the United States *extended* the democratic system of popular participation at a time when the world itself was swept away by confusion and then dictatorships. Roosevelt, sensing America's "rendezvous with destiny," as he called it, put it this way. "The only sure bulwark of continuing liberty," he said, "is a government strong enough to protect the interests of the people, and a people strong enough and well enough informed to maintain its sovereign control over its government." Historian Samuel Eliot Morrison later wrote that for "such a people to flourish was of fateful significance, and it helped restore the United States to its traditional position as the 'hope of the human race'." "For in the 'thirties'," he observed, "it became doubtful whether liberty or democracy could

Barn east of Biggsville

survive in the modern world, and when at the end of that decade totalitarian states felt strong enough to challenge it...it was of utmost importance to the peoples of the world that the American democracy had withstood the buffetings of depression...and emerged strong and courageous...."[100]

END NOTES FOR CHAPTER SEVEN

[1] The two best comprehensive treatments for the general reader to the Depression with a focus on its impact on American expectations of the Twenties are chapter eight, "Smashup," of Leuchtenburg's *Perils of Prosperity* and chapters ten and twelve "Hoover Takes Over" and "The Years of the Locust" of Hicks' *Republican Asendancy.*

[2] Morison, Commager, Leuchtenburg, *American Republic,* v II, p 471.

[3] Cited in Leuchtenburg, *Perils of Prosperity.* p. 242.

[4] Ibid., p. 243.

[5] Ibid., p. 243.

[6] See William E. Leuchtenburg, *Franklin D. Roosevelt and the New Deal 1932-1940* (New York, 1963), chapter one, "The Politics of Hard Times."

[7] Nash, *The American People,* v II, p. 789.

[8] Norton, *A People and a Nation,* v. II, pp 726, 729.

[9] David J. Mauere, "Unemployment in Illinois During the Civil War," *Essays in Honor of Glenn Huron Seymour,* Donlad F. Tingley ed., (Carbondale, Il. 1968) pp. 120-32 See also the original narratives contained in Sutton, *Prairie State,* vol II. pp 302-332. Robert Howard's chapter contains the factual story of the depression; see *Illinois,* ch 26, "The Great Depression," pp. 499-520. For an interpretative essay see Jensen's "Depression and War: Traditionalism Resurgent," ch. 5 of *Illinois,* pp. 121-52.

[10] *Raritan Reporter,* November 21, 1929.

[11] Ibid., July 17, 1930.

[12] Ibid., March 2, 1933.

[13] Ibid., October 27, 1932.

[14] Ibid., October 13, 1932.

[15] Ibid., June 7, 1932.

[16] Ibid., October 27, 1932.

[17] Ibid., June 18, 1933.

[18] John Cernacky, "A Oral History Approach to the Effects of the Depression, 1929-1941, in McDonough County, Illinois" (Master of Arts thesis, Western Illinois University, 1973).

[19] *Raritan Reporter,* January 14, 1932.

[20] Ibid., January 21, 1932.

[21] Ibid., February 4, 1932.

[22] Ibid., February 4, 1932.

[23] Ibid., June 16, 1932.

[24] Ibid., June 23, 1932.

[25] Ibid., February 1, 1933.

[26] Commager, *Documents,* p. 240.

[27] Ibid., p. 242.

[28] Theodore Calvin Pease, *The Story of Illinois,* third edition, revised (Chicago, 1965), p. 247.

[29] *Raritan Reporter,* March 16, 1933.

[30] Ibid., April 13, 1933.

[31] Ibid., April 20, 1933.

[32] Ibid., July 6, 1933.

[33] Ibid., April 27, August 3, 1933.
[34] Ibid., May 4, 1933.
[35] Ibid., June 10, 1933.
[36] Ibid., July 5, 1934; January 16, March 19, October 15, 1936.
[37] Ibid., October 10, 1940; January 2, 1941.
[38] Ibid., July 21, 1933.
[39] Ibid., June 6, 1936. Edward O. Barnes died suddenly in Chicago on October 8, 1934 and editorship of the *Raritan Reporter*, was taken over by his daughter, Edna, who ran the paper as "Edna Barnes Simonson, Editor and Publisher."
[40] Ibid., September 24, 1936.
[41] Ibid., February 6, 1936.
[42] Ibid., February 20, 1936.
[43] Ibid., December 13, 1934.
[44] Ibid., May 14, 1936.
[45] Ibid., July 30, 1936.
[46] Ibid., January 23, 1936.
[47] Ibid., June 4, 1936.
[48] Ibid., July 23, 1936.
[49] Ibid., April 30, 1936.
[50] Ibid., July 16, 1936.
[51] Ibid., October 29, 1936.
[52] Ibid., January 23, 1936.
[53] Ibid.
[54] Ibid., November 18, 1934.
[55] Ibid., August 9, 1936.
[56] Ibid., December 14, 1933.
[57] Ibid., September 7, 1933.
[58] Ibid., June 11, 1936.
[59] Ibid., August 13, 1936.
[60] Ibid., March 8, 1934.
[61] Ibid., May 13, 1936.
[62] Ibid., May 7, 1936.
[63] Ibid., March 8, 1934.
[64] Ibid., September 10, 1936.
[65] Lillie Hall. Tape recording of an interview by Rita Souther, March 26, 1980 Western Illinois University Archives & Special Collections.
[66] *Raritan Reporter*, July 16, 1936.
[67] Ibid., August 13, 1936.
[68] James H. Cook interview.
[69] *Raritan Reporter*, November 19, 1936.
[70] Ibid., March 13, 1941.
[71] Mabelle Sanderson interview.
[72] *Raritan Reporter*, January 12, 1933.
[73] Flossye T. Anderson interview.
[74] *Raritan Reporter*, June 11, 1936.
[75] Ibid., May 7, 1936.
[76] *Raritan Reporter*, June 7, 1934.
[77] Ibid., January 26, 1933.
[78] Ibid., April 10, 1941.
[79] Ibid.
[80] Ibid., April 13, 1933.
[81] Ibid., June 15, 1933.
[82] Ibid., June 28, 1934.
[83] Ibid., January 19, 1937.
[84] Nash, *The American People*, v. II, p 817.
[85] Francis Joseph Haney interview.
[86] *Raritan Reporter*, July 13, 1933.

Lomax Canning Factory

Lomax Canning Factory

[87] Ibid., August 6, 1936.
[88] Ibid., September 20, 1934.
[89] Ibid., November 3, 1932.
[90] Ibid., November 3, 1932.
[91] Ibid., November 10, 1932.
[92] Ibid., August 16, 1934.
[93] Ibid., November 8, 1934.
[94] Ibid., September 12, 1936.
[95] Ibid., March 26, 1936.
[96] Ibid., November 5, 1936.
[97] Ibid., November 5, 1936.
[98] Jensen, *Illinois*. p. 138.
[99] *Raritan Reporter,* May 15, 1941.
[100] Morrison, Commager, Leuchtenburg, *American Republic*, v. II, p. 525.

Lock and Dam 18, Gladstone

Fort Stone House, Stronghurst

Evans Stone House, Stronghurst

CHAPTER EIGHT
WORLD WAR II, 1940 - 1947

Just five weeks before Franklin D. Roosevelt was sworn in as President of the United States on March 4, 1933 Adolph Hitler was made Chancellor of Germany. Then in the fall of that same year Hitler became the absolute dictator or *Fuhrer* of all Germany. Next, in a series of bold steps he set out to establish the 1,000 year empire, or the Third Reich, of a Europe under Nazi rule. In 1934, Hitler began to rebuild the German army and navy. In 1935, the *Fuhrer* backed Italy in Mussolini's invasion of Ethiopia. In 1936, he supported the army of the Fascist General Franco in his rise to power in Spain's civil war. In March, 1938 Hitler announced Germany's annexation of Austria. In September of that year he met with the leaders of England and France at Munich, in Bavaria, and afterwards took over onehalf of western Czechoslovakia, called the Southern Part or the Sudetenland. Then, six months later, he announced that he had signed a secret alliance with the Soviet Union. Europe was poised for World War II. It started when, in September, 1939 Poland fell to the Nazi *Wermacht* and by 1940 all of western Europe and Scandinavia was in Hitler's hands. It was called the "lightening-war," the *Blitzkrieg*.[1].

Across a nation preoccupied with the Depression, these events aroused a mixture of fear and pacificism. Initial reaction to Hitler's moves was a dread of the repetition of steps which had gotten the United States into the needless slaughter (as it was thought of by most Americans in the thirties) of World War I. We were, in a word, frightened, and this fear in turn gave way to timidity and solicitude. Many Americans became out-spoken pacifists. A Senate committee revealed that the United States had intervened in World War I not because of a commitment to preserve democracy but because of the maneuverings and intrigues of bankers and arms dealers. Its chairman, Senator Gerald Nye of Wisconsin, advised that if Europeans wanted to fight again, let them.

At the popular level the national mood was reflected in a "peace movement." History books ignored or demoted the role of military heroes. Children were discouraged from playing with guns and war toys. Religious leaders at the 1933 Northern Baptist Annual Meeting vowed that they would "never again" help to kill fellow human beings. The Chicago Federation of Churches publicly resolved that "we declare ourselves as unalterably opposed to war."[2] College students protested the start of Reserve Officers Training Corps on campuses. One college president declared that "war must be banished from civilized society if democratic civilization and culture are to be perpetuated."[3] As news of Hitler's brutal military takeover of eastern Czechoslovakia reached America and then was followed by reports of the internment of thousands of Jews in concentration camps, the public mood shifted only slightly. By 1938, there was a discernible feeling of sympathy for the victims of Nazism, but it was a compassion tempererd by the conviction that Europe had to deal with its own problems.

Roosevelt watched these events and ignored them. His priority, like the nation's, was economic recovery. In his First Inaugural Address he barely mentioned foreign affairs and then it was only in relation to world trade. Clearly, whatever was going to happen in other places took a back seat to the emergency at home. In 1937, after four years, his Second Inaugural

Opposite: Service Flag, WWII

only skirted foreign policy (exclusive of his "Good Neighbor" position toward Latin America). This time he disavowed any American interest overseas. "We shun political commitments which might entangle us in foreign wars," he said, "I hate war."

A similar isolationist reaction came from Congress. In July, 1936 when Hitler and Mussolini plunged into the Spanish Civil War to help Franco, the House passed an arms embargo, under Roosevelt's urging. Between 1937 and 1939 Roosevelt signed the Neutrality Acts. These measures prohibited American loans or credits to belligerents, put an embargo on all arms shipments, forbade Americans from traveling on ships of belligerents and, most importantly, abandoned our historic doctrine of neutral rights. What the President and Congress were saying, explicitly, was that we would take no position on issues of international law and would not distinguish between aggressor and victim nations.

But by the time the President signed these laws he was having grave doubts about America's neutrality. He was beginning to realize that Nazism was a threat to western civilization which the United States ultimately could not avoid. About the same time he ordered a reappraisal of our hands-off policy toward Japanese expansion in Asia. Five years earlier Japan had marched into China and within a short while had taken all of Southeast Asia into it's "Co-Prosperity Sphere." In 1937, Japan and Germany signed a mutual defense alliance. In October, 1937 Roosevelt first spoke out publicly against Japan. In a Chicago speech he warned that America could not escape aggression if aggression went unchecked. He likened it to a disease which must be quarantined lest it spread to the entire community. But the speech had little effect. Two months later Japanese planes sank an American gunboat on the Yangtze River in China. The Japanese government issued a curt apology and we accepted it with relief. A Gallup poll at the time revealed that 70 percent of Americans wanted complete withdrawal from Asia.[4].

When Hitler took over Austria and Czechoslovakia Roosevelt sent him a telegram asking the *Fuhrer* to pledge not to attack the other small countries in Europe. Hitler made a joke of it. That summer, having stronger second thoughts, the President requested Congress to repeal the Neutrality Acts. Congress refused. When Hitler invaded Poland in September, 1939 Roosevelt called Congress back into special session and once again asked for the rescinding of the Neurtality Acts saying that he regretted ever having signed the law. This time, after six weeks of acrimonious debate, because of enormous Presidential pressure, Congress complied. It repealed the earlier legislation and, instead, authorized the sale of military supplies to the Allies on a cash-and-carry basis.

The *Blitzkrieg* destroyed all hopes and illusions of the isolationists. Denmark, early 1940, fell in hours. Norway surrendered in two months. Belgium and the Netherlands succumbed in less than a week. By May, 1940 the British Army was all but obliterated. It barely escaped total disaster by a heroic evacuation called "the miracle of Dunkirk." In June Paris fell. Only England stood, alone. The news stunned everybody. As Samuel Eilot Morrison remembered the summer of 1940:

> "In Boston, crowds on Washington Street bunched in front of placards where the news dispatches were being posted; in New York, they spilled into Times Square to watch bulletins circling the Times Building. The *Blitzkrieg* had shattered America's illusions about the outcome of the European war and its own impregnability. France had capitulated, Britain might soon go under."[5]

The President spoke at the University of Virginia on June tenth. There he pledged to England the "material resources of this nation." Still, only 30 percent of the country agreed with him. Roosevelt then threw out all political considerations. Despite its apparent unpopularity he concluded an arms sale to the Allies and transferred to England fifty American destroyers. Congress, also against the polls, began to come around. After a bitter debate that summer it passed the Selective Service Act which allowed conscription of all men between the ages of twenty-one and thirty-five.

Mail ran nine to one against these meaures. Some Americans were furious. They said Roosevelt was dragging the United States into a war in which we had no business. England was going down anyhow, they said, and there was nothing we could do about the inevitable. Hitler warned that England would surrender by autumn and then Latin America would have to sell all her products to the Third Reich. Draft opposition was vehement. Furthermore, some military experts agrued that a draft was useless in a modern war in which mass armies were outmoded. Others, like Senator George Norris, called the draft the murder of Democracy, Hitler's greatest and cheapest victory.

In Illinois, Chicago mayor Big Bill Thompson said that we had to stay out of the mess. Robert McCormick's *Chicago Tribune* condemned Roosevelt's war-mongering policies. It opposed his military aid to England. It hated conscription. Conservative Republicans warned that any involvement in war would mean dictatorship at home with FDR staying in office, because of another "emergency," until he died. Ethnic groups in the state, like the Germans, wanted no repetition of World War I and its rabid nativism. The Irish had little sympathy for shedding blood for "Johnny Bull." Labor Union leaders said business owners would use the war to raise prices and crack down on organized labor as unpatriotic, just like before.[6]

In the midst of this rancor the national election of 1940 was held on schedule. Part of Roosevelt's reluctance to push for unequivocal Allied aid was grounded in his political instincts. He was willing to buck public opinion polls to help England but he was not willing to lose an election for the benefit of Winston Churchill. Hence his strategy: keep America out of the war until after November. Ironically, the mounting crisis in Europe served to give Roosevelt his party's nomination for an unprecedented third term. He was chosen by acclamation on the first ballot. Republicans, at their convention, turned to Wendell Wilkie of Indiana, a corporate executive who had voted for FDR in 1932. Wilkie, no isolationist, was a personable campaigner who represented his party's "patriotic" wing. The campaign itself never really developed since Wilkie found himself in agreement with FDR on the basic question then before the nation -- both men wanted to help England. His carpings against the New Deal philosophy of "big government" seemed irrelevant and obsolete by the fall of 1940. Roosevelt won twenty-seven million to Wilkie's twenty-two million votes and carried all but ten states.

Democratic Party Ballot 1940

Illinois went for FDR even though he lost the Chicago suburbs and most of the downstate, getting only twenty-eight counties there. But the Republicans won everything else. Dwight H. Green, a district attorney who had gained fame first in successfully prosecuting Al Capone and later as a Chicago mayoral candidate campaigned on a combination of soft-isolationism and anti-Chicago feelings. He agreed with Wilkie about the threat of totalitarianism. He charged that, under the Democrats, the state had actually been run by Chicago aldermen who pulled the strings in the Springfield legislature. Republican Curley Brooks was more outspoken in his bid for the U S Senate. He was an isolationist and would have nothing to do with Roosevelt's warmongering dictatorship. "This is not our war" was Brooks' cry.

The GOP ticket, except for Wilkie, swept the state. It elected Green and Brooks. It got control of both houses of the General Assembly and sent nineteen of the twenty-six Illinois Congressmen to Washington.[7] In Henderson County a Republican victory was in the air. Democrats tried to mount a campaign with rallies at the Court House in October. But they faced strong, sullen, opposition to Roosevelt's "internationalism" and to the idea of another draft. The county returns showed Wilkie over FDR by 3,263 to 1,977. The President took only Bald Bluff and Gladstone this time and his margin of victory in Bald Bluff was only twelve votes. Brooks had no trouble defeating Democrat James M. Slattery by 3,078 to 1,977. Two Republicans won the Congressman-at-large election, one of whom for the first time was young William G. Stratton of Ingleside. In the contested county offices of Circuit Clerk, States Attorney, and Coroner Republicans made a clean sweep.[8]

Early in 1941, however, a change of attitude toward international developments began to appear. In response to FDR's declaration of a "National Defense Week" in February, Edna Barnes Simonson took a decidedly interventionist stand. People everywhere had to awaken to "the present crisis," she warned. "We must...prepare to defend American Rights on land and sea." "United we stand!" she exhorted. She embraced the President. "We must place our confidence in our national leaders and, with our hands in theirs, pledge our support to the National Defense program."[9] The "national defense program," specifically, became the Lend Lease Acts. By this scheme, pushed by Roosevelt immediately after the November election and enacted by Congress, America abandoned any remaining pretense of neutrality. The acts authorized the President to lend or lease equipment, i.e. arms, to any nation he thought vital to the defense of the United States. In obvious terms this allowed FDR to give Britain whatever assistance Churchill needed. It made available, for starters, over $7 billion in armament and foodstuffs. It also pointed the American economy to a dramatic conversion to wartime production.

Events moved fast at the national level. In April, Roosevelt confiscated all German shipping in American harbors. In June, he froze all their assets and broke off diplomatic relations. That same month Hitler, in an astonishing about-face, attacked his ally of 1939, the Soviet Union, and thereby pulled Russia into the war on the side of the Allies. On August 10, Roosevelt and Churchill met aboard a ship off the coast of Newfoundland and drew up the so-called Atlantic Charter. The document contained a list of mutual war goals. These "common principals" included the Four Freedoms, restoration of self-government, and free trade. On September 5, also in the North Atlantic, a German submarine torpedoed the American ship *Greer*. FDR condemned the piracy and authorized the navy to "shoot on sight" any German vessel. Two days later he deployed the Atlantic Fleet to convoy all American shipping to and from Great Britain. At that point the United States was at war, although still unofficially, with the Axis Powers.

Developments in the Far East, however, changed all that. There, Japan continued unchecked her military conquest by expanding east and south to the Philippines, Malaya, and Burma. Our initial reaction was to ignore it. Roosevelt himself seems to have feared the possibility of a two-front war if we interfered with Japanese expansion and so developed what one writer has called "a kind of diplomatic shadow boxing."[10] The United States gave a small loan to China in the summer of 1940. We imposed a weak embargo on American goods to Japan. In July, 1941, after Japan formally annexed all of IndoChina, Roosevelt appointed Douglas MacArthur commander of our Pacific forces and froze Japanese Assets. By that time the Japanese war lords, led by Tojo, had already decided to go to war with Great Britain and the United States to guarantee their gains of empire, or the "Greater East Asia Co-Prosperity Sphere."

The United States, with the aid of the British fleet, had by late summer succeeded in impairing the arrival of Japan of the one commodity Japan had to have -- fuel oil. This impending shortage prompted Tojo to open negotiations with the United States in the fall of that year. But the positions were irreconcilable from the outset because Secretary of State Cordell Hull made it clear that the only way the embargo would be lifted was for Japan to evacuate both IndoChina and the China mainland. Japanese diplomats in Washington responded by presenting the United States, at Tojo's direction, with an ultimatum on November twentieth. Mimicing Hitler's 1938 position at Munich, Tojo said that if the United States would lift the embargo, unfreeze Japanese assets, and stop helping the Chinese and the Philippines he would pledge to occupy no more territory. Assuming, correctly, that Roosevelt would never accept such humiliating terms, even for discussion, Tojo ordered his strike-force out of its rendezvous in the Kurile Islands on November twenty sixth: destination Hawaii.

From all accounts, the United States had no idea that Japan would strike the American naval base at Pearl Harbor. Intelligence reports arriving in Washington that November had warned of Japanese warships off of Formosa and had suggested a possible attack on the Philippines. Hawaii was thought to be too far distant from Japan for any flotilla to get there and back from the standpoint of fuel supply alone. Besides, there was a prevailing attitude that Japan would never do anything to goad America into a war. We were wrong. The Japanese strategic objective at Pearl Harbor was a fatal one: to cripple the Pacific fleet so as to make it impossible for the United States to meddle in Japan's further imperial conquests in Asia. At 7:55 on the morning of December 7, 1941 the attack began. So did World War II.[11]

The people of Henderson County were, like Americans everywhere, shocked but not entirely surprised that the war had started. The signs had been there during the preceding months. For example, in July the county started its first of many "Defense Drives." This one was for collecting metal. Under the direction of the county American Legion Post 765 all towns and villages were asked to turn in their scrap "tin cans" on July 26 and 28 to help bolster the state goal that summer of one million pounds set by Governor Green. The *Raritan Reporter* described the Atlantic Charter for what it really was, despite its guarded language, as the first step to the "final destruction of Nazi tyranny."[12] In November, the AAA contacted county farmers about "the present emergency" and spoke of new price support policies "to permit producers to make a readjustment in production."[13] Soybean loans were extended "to meet defense needs" through the Commodity Credit Corporation.[14] The AAA set new objectives for a "Food For Freedom Program" which called for increases in cattle, hog, sheep, poultry, and barley. A column in the Raritan newspaper in October called attention to a new sight in the county, a draftee hitchhiking a ride along the highway. "Give the Soldier a Lift," the paper said. If you want to get to know something about this "new army" first hand, then pick up the soldier, get acquainted with "the human side of this new army which is building to defend America."[15] The average person in the county, by November, was much like the individual at the bedside of a loved one stricken with a fatal heart attack. They hoped for the best, but prepared for the worst.

The worst happened that Sunday morning in December. The news first came over the radio a little after noon, interrupting regular broadcasts. Later that evening, in a special 8:00 news program, full details of the attack and early casualty reports were given out.[16] And so, among the traditional pre-Christmas advertisements and celebration notices in the *Raritan Reporter* was the grim dissonance of the bold type announcement: **U S DECLARES WAR TO DEFEND DEMOCRATIC RIGHTS**.[17]

The attack, the "dastardly attack" President Roosevelt called it, was followed on December eleventh by a declaration of war on Germany. FDR in his war message to Congress on that day called for a "united effort by all of the peoples of the world who are determined to remain free." The events of the week of December seventh galvanized support behind the President across the nation, in the state, and in the county. There was not a voice of opposition after Pearl Harbor. There was, rather, a sense of relief that the issue had come to a resolution and that the frustation and uncertainties of recent months were over.

The economy of the nation mobilized for war right away. Roosevelt created a War Production Board in December and put the president of Sears-Roebuck, Donald Nelson, in charge of all contracts. Government financing of war-time conversion guaranteed generous profits to businessmen and many who had consistently opposed the New Deal programs of economic regulation now fell in behind FDR's war measures. Another agency established in January, 1942 was the OPA, or Office of Price Administration. Under the direction of Chester Bowles, it set prices and rationed products. Next, the National War Labor Board set wages and hours, supervised safe working conditions, and imposed a no-strike pledge on labor union leaders. Congress passed the Revenue Act of 1942 which raised individual income taxes, and at the same time started regular payroll deduction for the tax, increased corporate taxes to 40 percent, and the excess profit tax to 90 percent.

Across the state people provided full support for the war. In converting to wartime production the last vestiges of the Depression, unemployment and uncertainty, disappeared. An Illinois Council of Defense was set up in April, 1942 along the same lines of operation followed by the Insull committee during World War I. Within a year it was overseeing the local activities of 652 councils that dealt with a variety of wartime measures: civil defense, business loans, farm production, selling war bonds, and rationing. The arsenal at Rock Island moved to colossal production schedules as did the ammunition arsenal at Burlington, Iowa. Caterpillar tractors out of Peoria were sped off production lines to build new airports, roads, and army camps. Food prices soared. Thousands of new workers entered the labor force as essential replacements for men in uniform. Women,

Newspaper Headline, December 11, 1941

teenagers, and the elderly had jobs for the asking. Real per-capita income in Illinois rose to and passed the 1929 base. By war's end Illinoians had three times the income of 1933 although a large portion of the new wealth was diverted to higher taxes and war bonds. All New Deal relief programs were abolished.[18]

The year of 1942 also saw important economic changes in the county. The Lomax Canning Company went into record production of tomatoes on orders from the Department of Agriculture. The federal government, as a part of its support for the company, paid $17.50 a ton toward the purchase of raw tomatoes -- four dollars above the price offered by the company itself the year before. Plant manager Lloyd Sparrow announced in April that canning capacity was to be increased by over one-third of the 1941 level. The plant was expanding its loading-dock facilities. He advertised that his company that summer was employing "a great many men and women of the Lomax community."[19] Other parts of the town saw an abrupt return to prosperity. N.A. Horner's merchandising store, in the older part of Lomax, did a record business in 1942. C.H. Logan's "Red and White" grocery store and Ernie Smith's store likewise did a brisk business. Lee Porter and the Lomax Lumber Company stocked up on inventory. At Gladstone, Fred McKenzie's quarry expanded its excavations on the "coasting hill" south of town. North of the village another quarry was put in full operation under the direction of Robert Thomas and Glenn Lukens. East of Gladstone the Wallbaum quarry worked overtime. The sand pits on the west side, some owned by the CB&Q railroad, dredged limestone, gravel, and clay for cement and plastering work.

Page from Ration Stamp Book

The CB&Q itself, along with the Santa Fe line, experienced a revival of service to freight and passengers. Daily the two companies in 1942 pulled up to 125 train cars towards the Galesburg Terminal. Many cars were loaded with scrap iron directed to the steel mills around Chicago. Oil tankers moved products of the major companies above ground when their pipeline system became overloaded that spring. Neither line had enough open cars to handle the huge grain movements. Passenger service tripled, especially when gas rationing began to take effect late that year. Once more, wrote Hugh Moffet in late 1942, the railroads were "pouring the life blood of freight and passenger business into the arteries which are the main lives of the huge system."[20] Banks flourished for the first time in a decade.

In 1942, two Oquawka institutions, the First State Bank under Robert Moody and the Bank of Oquawka under George Richmond recorded new high resources. By the summer of that year the reserves of the Raritan Bank were up to an all-time high of $2,240,975 with a cash reserve of a unprecedented $851,236.[21] The John La Fond pearl button factory at Oquawka, located near the railroad depot, made thousands of buttons for soldiers' uniforms. By early 1943 it had switched to a second phase of wartime operations, making buttons for uniforms worn by the army nurses. The nearby fresh-water clam shells, the historic source for buttons that had been all but destroyed by the wing-dams built on the Mississippi River by Army engineers, were supplemented by shells from as far away as the Wolf River in South Dakota or the Tennessee River. By then the work force had expanded to a dozen cutters, roughly one-half of its eventual wartime capacity.

While businesses and factories in Illinois were left short handed during the war the state's agriculture benefitted from a draft deferment which

Preparing Silage
Bricker Farm, Raritan

left men on the farm. The federal government encouraged farmers to plant more acres and to grow larger crops than ever before. The state's record was impressive. It ranked first in the nation in soybean production, second in corn and hogs, and fourth in livestock. It was an astonishing turnabout from the Depression years. This agricultural revolution was spurred by technology. New chemical fertilizers increased soil fertility and brought higher yields. Herbicides led to eradication of weeds. Insecticides kept serious insects like the corn borer under control. Hybrid seeds were improved by inbreeding that eliminated detasseling of female corn rows during pollination.

Soybeans replaced oats as the second most marketable crop in the state because of the difficulty during the war of getting natural vegetable oils, from the Pacific Coast, to eastern markets. Margarine replaced butter on many family tables in the early forties signaling the start of a whole new market for soybeans. Old marginal lands had been rejuvenated during the Depression with federal conservation practices such as crop rotation, chemicals, and better drainage. When more workers were needed the farmers hired high school boys and girls during the summer months. In a word, as summarized by Theodore Calvin Pease, "Illinois farmers, numbering more than two hundred thousand, put into operation the greatest program in the state's history."[22]

The war was a bonanza for Henderson County farmers. the hard data tells the story. County land values went from $71.48 to $115.58 an acre between 1940 and 1945. At the start of the war there were just eighty tractors in the entire county. At war's end there were 1,149 tractors in operation. The value of all crops during that five year period doubled: from $1,116,215 to $2,331,484. The aggregate value of livestock products increased almost three fold, from $1,913,979 to $4,871,492.[23] Extraordinary goals for county farmers were in place almost from the first months of the conflict. The AAA established production quota goals for 1942 in soybeans, hogs, and cattle while at the same time it cut out acres planted in oats and wheat. In January, it asked for additional measures. Farmers should watch their topsoil carefully.[24] They should regularly check old machinery and plan to donate any replaced old parts to likely scrap-iron drives.

William L. Forgey, speaking for both the AAA and the Illinois Council of Defense committee in the county, put out a regular series of directives and announcements from his headquarters in Stronghurst. In late January, 1942 he asked farmers to begin to order machinery repair parts immediately and to anticipate likely shortages by the time of spring planting. He noted that the total corn acreage allocated the county for that year's office was increased ten percent, up from 51,444 to 56,587 acres.[25] By February, farmers were meeting to discuss common problems dealing with the war. Labor, despite draft deferments, was in short supply. Machinery dealers posted notice of parts shortages for older model tractors and even new machinery was "very limited, especially combines, tractors, and corn pickers."[26] In March, Forgey said AAA rules for planting soybeans and "other vital war crops" had been significantly relaxed so that farmers now could plant in the 20 percent acreage formerly required as conservation land. Corn, he announced, would be guaranteed a 10¢ per-bushel profit since it could be stored for a cost of only 57¢ a bushel and redeemed at just 61¢ a bushel, including interest.[27]

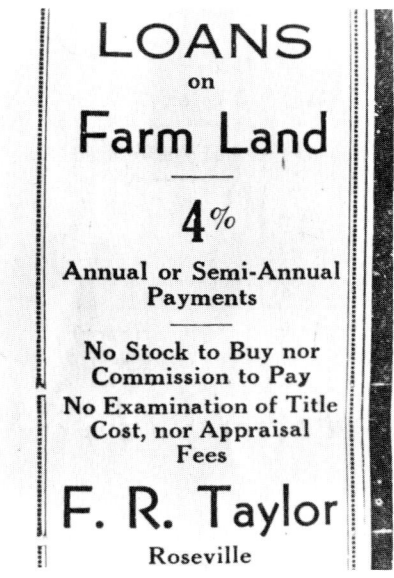

Loan Ad from *Raritan Reporter*

The Farm Bureau, under the direction of A.J. Rehling, farm advisor, did its part. Commenting on the activities of that agency in Henderson County, Moffit boasted: "Show farmers and farm women what they must do to help win the war and they'll do it."[28] The Bureau sponsored regular training meetings for leaders in the high schools at Biggsville and Stronghurst and at town halls in Rozetta and Terre Haute. Rehling sent letters to every farm home to survey what teenage boys might be available as part-time laborers. He was acutely worried about shortages. Rehling was of the opinion that unless the need for "qualified farm labor" was met farmers would not be able to maintain existing production levels let alone meet any increased goals. He expressed concern about the Ordinance Plant in Burlington which seemed likely to compete severely for labor during the upcoming months. Rehling, like Forgey, predicted crippling shortages of machinery unless careful planning was begun immediately. Livestock producers were advised to balance livestock rations with protein supplements so that they could get the most meat, milk, and eggs for the feed used. Other measures were called for. Farmers should use limestone and phosphate. They should keep their rolling land from washing away. They should work harder.

Rehling printed thousands of Farm Bureau pamphlets in the spring of 1942 to dramatize the need for every farmer to get behind Uncle Sam in the crisis. Fighting men, he said, need "plenty of good food to build muscle and produce the energy to do the tough tasks...only the farmer can provide this food." Patriotism was what was needed in the county. "The wartime job of farmers," he said, was to "produce food to feed our own soldiers, sailors and marines; to send our allies all the good substantial food for which we can find ships; and to see to it that the folks here at home are well fed."[29] The response to the patriotic appeals of Rehling and Forgey was encouraging to say the least. By the fall of 1942 over 90 percent of Henderson County farmers had put up AAA signs to show that they were doing their share in the all-out war effort.

Forgey predicted that the county would meet and surpass all the goals. He was correct. In 1943, the AAA and Farm Bureau reported that the demand for increased productivity had met comparatively small problems. That fall the most pressing difficulty was finding adequate storage for the huge crop of soybeans being harvested. Existing elevators and bins accommodated only 29 percent of the crop. The other 71 percent had to stay on the farm until it could be moved. The problem, really, was overcompliance. Farmers, instead of increasing their acreage by 54 percent as requested planted a 100 percent increase instead. So, by 1943, the county harvested an estimated 32,000 acres with a yield of twenty-five bushels an acre for beans. The indications, by September, were for a harvest of 800,000 bushels worth $1.60 a bushel if up to the number-two grade. At that time there was a temporary glut in the market: there just was no place for the soybeans to go, Forgey conceded.

Biggsville Railroad Depot

Despite the glut, the war years were boom times. Biggsville, as a center of the farm economy in that part of the county, did very well indeed. Mileage-gas rationing for farmers forced them to spend more time in town rather than to travel, as some had done before, to Monmouth. Reporters saw Biggsville "customers enter stores and leave with armloads of purchases."[30] Farmers had money to spend and merchants eagerly sought to establish the "farm trade" in their businesses. The "future of Biggsville and other small villages in Henderson," Moffit believed in the summer of 1943, "seems brighter just now than for many years." Merchants heard the jingling of real money. Many farmers "have gone to town with soy-

Oquawka Riverfront, Wayne Elevator in background

beans that brought them from $30 to $40 per acre, paid after delivery and grading."

It was common knowledge, too, that although the price of corn was far less that soybeans, it was realizing a comfortable profit. Yields were up to 145 bushels per acre and all fields had doubled production. The price of corn was over 60¢ and that meant, in Moffit's words, "a lot of money, whether the corn is sold outright or converted into beef and pork in the feed lot."[31] Furthermore, eggs and poultry paid for the farm family grocery bill.

At Oquawka, Wayne Brothers were sending grain shipments out by barge to the bulk of 1,200,000 bushels a year. Carl Wayne, who ran the Oquawka elevator, along with other such operators at Little York and Keithsburg, kept corn traffic flowing down river. Cattle poured into the feed lots. The outlook was described as a "bright one" with cattle and hogs pushing an all-time record. "Never has this country," one writer observed, "had so many meat animals on farms as this year."[32].

Stronghurst, more that any other town benefited from wartime agriculture. It became the main shipping point on the Santa Fe Railroad, according to Moffit, between Kansas City and Chicago. Close to one million dollars of livestock rolled out of here in 1943 under the aegises of the Stronghurst Shipping Association with Otto Steffy as president and C.A. Hartquist as manager. Hartquist regularly handled 300 carloads of cattle, hogs, and sheep there in 1943. Hogs accounted for 70 percent of the volume, cattle for 20 percent, and sheep for the rest. By then Stronghurst had eclipsed both Media and Decorra, former Santa Fe shipping points, because farmers preferred to truck their livestock for shipment at Stronghurst. The Association, listing over 300 members during the war, in 1942 spent $5000 to modernize its stockyards. Stronghurst Grain and Merchandise Company handled the arrival of corn. Glenn Marshall operated the huge double crib near the company's elevator where farmers pulled up with their trucks. Then the corn was quickly lifted to the top of the building where it slid into the appropriate crib. This new structure had a capacity for 8,000 bushels of corn plus 5,400 bushels of small grain, like oats. The corn was left in the ear until spring when it was shelled out for shipment to market. In addition, the older company elevators housed over 11,000 bushels of corn plus oats and wheat. The W.E. Terry lumberyard at Stronghurst could not keep up inventory to meet farmer's needs. They placed order after order with manager Sam Howell only to be told that they would have to wait. But farmers could not wait. They had to have lumber and building supplies to put up storage facilities for their beans until room became available at the shipping terminals. New livestock feeders had to be started. Hog houses had to be constructed. Stronghurst, during the war, was the hub of the county's farm economy. It had offices of the federal agencies, the shipping headquarters, the Farm Loan Association, and Farm Bureau. Because Stronghurst had so many county organization offices the town of about 1,000 people exerted an economic influence on the county comparable to the political clout of Oquawka as the county seat.[33]

Stronghurst Elevator, Built in 1916

Shortages became worse during the war for Henderson County farmers. The two greatest deficiencies continued to be machinery and labor. The central difficulty behind the machinery shortage was the policy of the War Production Board, announced in 1943, to cut the nation's agriculture machinery output to one-fourth of what it had been before the war at a time when farming was mechanized more that ever. Within a year dealers were just not able to sell farmers new machines and those which were available soared in price. A tractor sold in 1943 for $1,435, without a cultivator, compared to a 1941 price of about $1,125 for both tractor and cultivator. A corn planter went for $230 instead of the $140 two years before.[34]

For those farmers willing to pay such prices another hurdle had to be met. They had to apply for "necessary" new machinery at the Henderson County Machinery Rationing Board in Stronghurst. If one expected a purchase in the summer of 1943 the application had to be filed no later than the middle of January. The quotas of new equipment were small and the Board announced clearly that it would not give "purchase certificates" if any existing machinery could be repaired.[35] The strict rationing of purchase certificates continued throughout the duration of the war. Late in 1944, Forgey was still announcing severe restrictions on tractors, pickup balers, side delivery rakes, hay loaders, combines, manure spreaders, corn pickers, corn binders, and corn mowers.[36]

Worse than the frustation of trying to increase production while coping with machine shortages was the farm labor problem. The old rule of thumb then accepted was that one hired hand must be taken on for every additonal forty acres of corn planted. Farm machinery helped to destroy this equation, but because of the crisis in that area most farmers thought about their future capacity in terms of hand labor doing most of the new extra work. From the start of the war there was a keen awareness of a labor shortage, described as a "dark cloud" hanging over the prosperity of the county. Farmers might pool their labor with neighbors. Others could ask their hands to work longer hours, overtime, without extra pay. Perhaps boys and women could be trained to help out. Indeed, in 1943 a local observer wrote of a typical sight of "a group of fifteen or sixteen year old boys, attending high school, hasten home in the afternoon and go directly to the fields to help get in the harvest of corn and soybeans." He saw "women wearing coveralls" working on many farms "running corn elevators, hauling the grain from the fields, and generally taking up the slack wherever possible."[37]

The situation was polled by A.J. Rehling in 1942. He sent out 2,000 questionnaires to every grain farmer, landlord, and tenant on the mailing list of the AAA office. One-fifth of them responded. He asked: "Do you have enough help on your farm now?" Of those who answered, 240 said that they did have enough help while 183 said they were shorthanded. But 279 farmers said they would need more help to harvest the fall crops. Another question read: "Have you had any hired help leave your employ this year to take a job elsewhere?" Farmers answered 164 in the affirmative and 290 in the negative. Most of those who left the farm had gone to work at the Iowa Ordinance Plant at Burlington. Based on current labor conditions, Rehling wanted to know if farmers thought that they could increase their farm production in 1943. Only eighty-six men said they believed an increase possible while 250 declared that it would be inconceivable. A total of 181 farmers even felt that they could not hold 1942 production levels through the next year.[38]

The bottom line of the inquiry showed that Henderson County farmers did not think they had enough farm labor in sight for 1943. A total of 263 respondents said they were short handed and just 117 expressed any confidence about doing what was asked of them. Beef farmers were just as

C.A. (Buck) Hartquist

Weir Fruit Farm, Gladstone

pessimistic as grain farmers. They needed experienced help. Hartquist used an example of one acquaintance who had been feeding out 300 to 350 head of cattle in 1942. In 1943, with his hired hands down in number, this person did not believe he could handle more than 100 head.[39]

The labor shortage had a definite impact upon the draft in Henderson County. Quite simply, because of the acute shortages farmers everywhere wrote to their Selective Service Board asking deferments for their workers, often their own sons. They did not admit, in requesting such deferments, that they were asking for "special favors in this war," as Moffit phrased it. The Board, located in Stronghurst, "helped splendidly" by keeping men on the farm as long as possible.[40] The federal draft law stipulated that every man on the farm who was actually necessary to its operation would be deferred until a replacement could be found. This standard, however, did not apply to a farm that produced subsistence for a single family. Most Henderson County farms, though, fell outside the subsistence category.

By 1945, however, as the draft pools nationwide became shallow the rumor spread throughout the county that all farm workers were about to be inducted. The cause of the speculation, and worry, was a directive by the state draft board which ordered all farm workers between eighteen and twenty-five to report for physical examinations in January of that year. In order to clarify the intent of the physical examination directive, and to allay apprehensions, the state draft director Colonel Paul B. Armstrong, in late February, put out a statement. Armstrong said that the pre-induction physical was to determine only how many men in that group would be physically qualified for service should the need arise. It also was his intent to expedite the induction of young men who were no longer necessary to agricultural production. "Registrants who are helping to produce food and fiber in quantity for general military and civilian use," he said, "will necessarily be given great consideration."[41]

Shortages in farm machinery and labor, and the draft, were only a couple of ways in which World War II altered daily life in Henderson County. There was the rural war-training program, begun in 1943. One of its first objectives was adult training in special agricultural courses in the Food For Freedom Program. Started in Oquawka, classes were open to any person seventeen years of age or older. Admission was free since funds for the classes came from the federal government and were taught by individuals from the vocational agriculture division of the state Department of Education. Some of the popular courses were "Care and Operation of Tractors," "Pork Production," and "The Importance of Fruits in Foods." With minimum enrollments of ten participants they ran from thirty-six to 120 hours in duration and met one night each week.

Another new rural war program was offered by the Extension Service of the University of Illinois College of Agriculture. Its aim was to provide family guidelines during the war and, in theory, to prevent inflation. Each family which enrolled was given a checklist entitled "What Our Family Will Do." Items on the list were specific. It advised to pay cash and not to buy on credit. It said one must spend less for things that were not immediately necessary. It asked participants to invest in War Bonds, pay their taxes promptly, and to operate the rationing program cheerfully.[42] And Christine Pensinger, Chief Home Economist of the state, began a regular newspaper column called "Homemaker For Defense" in which she offered tips from soap conservation to "Defense Recipes" at mealtimes.⁴³ William Forgey told people in 1942 to "eat more fried chicken this summer...because it's the patriotic thing to do." It was "patriotic," he said, "to eat fried chicken and other victory food specials this summer."⁴⁴

Rationing was pervasive. As Forgey's remarks suggested, meat was soon in short supply throughout the county. The general rule during the war was for butchers to count on two and one-half pounds for each person per week. Fish, however, was never restricted and the demand for it proved a real benefit to Oquawka. Sugar rationing began almost immediately. Every family had to register at the nearest grade school in May, 1942 to get a War Rationing Book, Number One. Without the book no sugar could be bought. With it one could get just twenty pounds per person for the entire canning season up to a maximum of 160 pounds for a family.⁴⁵ Coffee rationing began in the fall of 1942. The standard was one pound for every person in the family over fifteen years of age every five weeks, a ration which amounted to a little more than one cup of coffee a day. Some groceries were hard to get by 1943. Merchants complained that folks had more money to buy but they had less to sell. Scarce items included processed vegetables, butter, and cans of pork and beans. Other merchants ran out of buckets, alarm clocks, watches, radios, and so on. Moffit was convinced that it was indeed "tough for a man in a small town to run a store." The difficulties in 1943 were, he said, "innumerable." The "small-town merchants get into the wholesale houses only once or twice a week," he wrote, "and the dribble of stuff the wholesalers receive are quickly snapped up by city merchants who go to the place daily to buy anything that is allowed them."⁴⁶

Oquawka Gas Station

More onerous than anything was the rationing of gas and tires. Usually five gallons a week was the limit, gained through the A-Book stamps, although some individuals, like physicians, had unrestricted prerogatives at the pump. Truck owners had to get an application for "Certificates of War Necessity" from the county Agricultural War Board at Stronghurst. Gas itself sold for 19¢ a gallon or 95¢ for the weekly fillup. Each township had its "tire inspector." Men like W.W. Whaley was the Gladstone representative of the Henderson County War Price and Rationing Board and, like the others in the job, made monthly inspections of tires on cars and trucks to order recapping of those which were wearing dangerously thin. New cars were just not available. Car dealers simply advertised in bold type: NO NEW CARS. Then they went on to push that "your car can *look* like new, *perform* like new with our dependable Dodge-Plymouth Service "with Dick Brown at the Raritan Machinery Company!"⁴⁷ Prices of those commodities—food, fuel, automobiles—were fixed throughout the war by the O.P.A.

Still, people managed to have a good time now and then. Movies filled a void of loneliness and relieved anxiety, much the same as they had during the worst years of the Depression. New movie theaters opened and those which were in business continued the three to four changes of billing every week. The Farm Bureau sponsored War Youth Parties for young singles of high school age or older. Usually dances and square dances were at town halls or Bureau offices and attracted youths from both Henderson, Warren, and McDonough counties. Highlights of Farm Bureau activities, Jim Cook recalled, were the yearly banquets where over 150 people "got acquainted with a number of people from other counties," and each summer, a large July Fourth festival.⁴⁸ Regular weekly dances at Burlington, Macomb, and Galesburg continued despite the gas shortages.

WWII Poster

Savings Stamps to buy Bonds

Places in the county, like the Sunset Gardens at Gulfport, operated by Harold Watson and Fred Webster, did a thriving business.

People accepted the shortages, the frustrations, and the demands of wartime with amazing alacrity. No war experience within memory, certainly not the Spanish American War and not the brief disruptions of World War I, touched the daily lives and personal plans of so many people. Yet, they absorbed the reality of the times. Perhaps the "hard times" of the Depression had steeled their patience, or reduced their expectations, and as a result limited their demands. For whatever the causes, the citizens of Henderson County, just as Americans everywhere then, were patriotic. The prevailing attitude from beginning to end was that "we are all in this together." Self sacrifice was a way of life in those years.

During the first months of the war a fervent patriotism appeared. "There has never been such unity as the country has at present," wrote Mrs. Simonson in early June, 1942. Every American in the county stood solidly behind Roosevelt. The spirit was one of grim, uncompromising determination. She understood, as did most others at the time, "that the home front is as vital to war and to the perpetuation of our way of life as the battlefront."[49] Townships began to display what was called the Service Flag. The flag was a white square bordered with red and blue stars with the names of serviceman in one of the stars.[50] In February, 1943 the *Raritan Reporter* published a poem entitled "Valentines For Victory." A sentimental, poorly written piece, awful as poetry, it appealed to a genuine popular feeling in its closing lines: "Produce more pork; put up more jam/ Save fuel; and give your Uncle Sam/ a Valentine."[51]

The response of the county to war had two sides. On one hand, there was the willing acceptance of the hardships and deprivations of war. The shortages were taken in stride, rationing was a fact of life. When coffee rationing first began in the fall of 1942 the *Raritan Reporter*, echoing a consensus, observed that the practice of rationing was America's historic response to war, going as far back as the Revolution. "The American idea," the paper explained, "is to sacrifice together when the country's welfare needs it."[52] Even when the gap between supply and demand widened during the first year of the conflict and caused retail prices to shoot up an average of 31 percent (twice the rate of World War I) until controls were put on in 1943, no one complained.

On the other hand, the residents of the county responded by taking positive efforts to help the war effort. The best example of this kind of county action was its financial support. The goal was, in the first War Bond Drive, $10,000 and it increased each time throughout the war to twice that amount in 1944. The pitch was always the same: your boys are making the greatest sacrifice so help out. "Back them with your dollars—for it's your dollars that will furnish them with weapons, ammunition, food, and clothing they must have, if they are to whip the enemy."[53]

Sometimes the appeal was blatant. In a February issue of the *Raritan Reporter*, for instance, there was a huge first-page 8 x 14 graphic of a soldier charging a Japanese machine-gun nest. The caption read: "This farm boy stopped bullets intended for you!" Underneath was a story about the death in combat of a Colorado farm boy Joe Mardinec (obviously intended as the soldier in the illustration) and a picture of the Medal of Honor he was awarded. Then the feature concluded with bold type "LET'S *ALL* BACK THE ATTACK!"[54] Other appeals were downright macabre. On the last page of a January, 1944 issue of the *Raritan Reporter* a 12 x 16 sketch showed an eyeless soldier staring out full-faced with guns and bombs exploding in the background with the caption: "I DIED TODAY. WHAT DID YOU DO?" "Back the Attack — Buy More than Before."[55]

War Bond Ad

In addition to War Bonds the county was asked to give to the War Fund. This campaign, according to A.J. Rehling, was primarily to support the U.S.O., the U.S.S., and Red Cross relief packages to captured American soldiers.[56] The method was to send solicitors throughout the county to canvass every family in each school district. It was, like the Bond drive, consistently successful. A 1945 report showed that in a quota for a winter appeal of $4,100 a total of $5,287 was raised, or 129 percent of the expected amount. Rehling complimented the workers on their "splendid job in soliciting funds...the people of the county responded remarkably well."[57]

Scrap drives were another regular feature of home front activity. It gave people a chance to feel that they were doing something for the war on a daily basis rather than just digging into their pockets periodically. Day after day children and adults piled in their barns and garages rusty iron,

Rubber Tire Scrap Pile

rags, paper. The scrap was then collected by men in trucks sent out by the county Agricultural War Board. Usually the pickups were once each month at six designated weighing stations at Gladstone, Biggsville, Stronghurst, Media, Lomax, and Oquawka. The trucks then drove the scrap to a purchaser in Peoria who gave $12.00 a ton for solid scrap. In the August, 1942 drive, for example, the county trucks picked up 358 tons, 687 pounds and received a cash conversion of $3,837.26.[58] Rubber collections were a special scrap effort. In 1943, Oquawka gathered one of the largest piles at the Dixon Service Station, fifty tons of it. The pile had more than ten tons of old tires alone. There, on October 10, 1943 it was loaded onto the CB&Q for shipment to the Rubber Reserve Corporation at Chicago. From Chicago the rubber was transferred to Goodyear Tire mills for use in making "reclaimed tires" for cars.

Advertisements pushed the scrap drives just as they did the bond and fund canvasses, by hyperbole and stereotype. A typical pitch was the one in the March 17, 1942 *Reporter* which announced that in the "SCRAP TO SLAP THE JAPS PROGRAM" the county had gathered 73,926 pounds. "Junk makes Fighting Weapons" another advertisement claimed. It stated that an old field disc meant 210 automatic carbine rifles. One plow made 100 75mm shells. One used tire was turned into gas masks. One old shovel meant four hand grenades.[59]

Ration Book

Civil Defense activities got individuals physically involved in the closest thing to wartime activity. There were two paramilitary defense councils, one for the county as a whole and one for Oquawka. Throughout the county, each town was assigned its chief Air Raid Warden who, in turn, chose his assistants. It was the warden's main responsibility to check to be sure every family complied with a blackout when the siren went off. Every blind had to be lowered, every light turned off. Cars likewise stopped and turned off their lights. At Oquawka, a long blast of the siren followed by five short blasts over a three minute time period was the signal for the blackout. Usually the whole drill lasted about one half hour. There, Gillette B. Dixon and Mayor Russell Manning, the heads of the defense council, made sure that homes were dark and that automobiles were not only stopped but also pulled off Main Street so as to leave it open for emergency vehicles to the river.[60]

At Oquawka, the council took further precautions. They required a written pass for visitors to enter the electric light plant. They placed padlocks on the town's seven well-points and water tower. They placed twenty-two "Block Captains" on each square within the town during blackouts. They stationed eight emergency police in the main part of town and two more at the town's perimeter on the east and south to act as traffic directors. They had three other men on what was called the "bomb and gas squad." Dixon had on hand a telephone list whereby he phoned each block captain during the exercise from his control center in the office of the town clerk. Assisting Dixon on a standby was the chief of the Fire Department, the town Marshall, two physicians, and a nurse.

The county, on a lesser scale in the towns and villages, functioned in the same way as Oquawka. The overall coordinator was Raymond O. Voorhees, Commander of the American Legion Post with his headquarters also at Oquawka. Sheriff E.L. Davenport was in charge of Fire Fighting. Dr. M.J. Babcock was head of Medical Services. E.C. Fort, Superintendent of Highways, was appropriately given responsibility for Public Works and Roads. H.W. Custer of Monmouth had the larger-than-county job of securing public utilities.[61] Other subsidiary activities of the two civil defense councils were to conduct air-raid drills in the schools. These exercises consisted mainly in having children hide under their desks with their hands on their heads. They sponsored for adults a series of First Aid Classes, in cooperation with the county chapter of the American Red Cross, in the gymnasium of the high school at Biggsville every Tuesday evening. The councils also set up county-wide "Patriotic Meeting" days during the summer. The first one was held on Sunday, July 4, 1942 at Oquawka and featured a concert of martial music presented by the Stronghurst Band.[62]

Fred Olson, Bald Bluff
Tank Crew-Anzio

But the grim reality of combat and death was in the war itself not in acting-out civil defense maneuvers. And Henderson County, despite the deferment given many young men on the farm, suffered in the war. It was total war. The nation put over sixteen million soldiers into the fight. Illinois had one million under arms. Almost three times that number, between the ages of eighteen and twenty-five, were registered for the draft in the state. Illinois had a total of 561 local boards. Like the Henderson County board, these were volunteer committees mostly of community leaders who made the thankless judgment of balancing the needs of the military, the community, and the family.[63]

County men were shipped to the state induction centers built by the army at Fort Sheridan on the lakefront of Chicago and at Camp Grant near Rockford. Nearby the army purchased almost 18,000 acres in McDonough County for Camp Ellis as a site for a new training camp for non-combat operations. The naval training center at Great Lakes was inundated by one million men and a $75 million construction program to accommodate them. The Air Force expanded Chanute Field on the south edge of Rantoul and Scott Field near St. Louis.[64]

Henderson County responded well to the draft and the call up. Its first young men registered for conscription just one month after the draft law was passed by Congress. A total of 976 signed their names. Gladstone provided the largest number with 147, then came Stronghurst with 137, and Oquawka with 125 men. The rest came from Lomax (105), Biggsville (101), Raritan (80), Terre Haute (66), Rozetta and Media (each 57), and Bald Bluff (56).[65] The basis of registration was expanded in the winter of 1942 when Governor Green told the state Director, General Armstrong, to sign up all men to the age of forty-five. In the fall of that year Armstrong also announced that the state would no longer grant induction delays because of application for enlistment or application for officer's commission.[66] By war's end the county had registered a total of 2,075 men, 423 of whom were called into the service.

Young men inducted could find comfort in the odds in their favor of survival. Only one-fourth of the military force in World War II was given a combat assignment. The other 75 percent were classified in support roles of skilled and semiskilled jobs or in clerical operations. Aptitude tests, for the first time, played a large role in one's classification. Test scores determined officer candidates. The military started, also for the first time, an extensive program of technical education to meet the urgent need for modern warfare operations. Many men acquired valuable skills which they otherwise would not have had for later civilian life. There was no racial segregation of units, in contrast to the First War. The war experience homogenized men from all walks of life and from all states in the Union.

Reaction in the county to the appearance of young men in uniform, and to their disappearance, was pretty much the same as in all other aspects of the war experience, a combination of stoicism and patriotism. Newspaper accounts, brief biographies, and photos of "Sons in Service" became a standard feature by the spring of 1942. Letters from camp were reprinted and gave folks an overall feeling of reassurance that "things weren't too bad." Hubert Vernoy, for example, wrote about his life at Fort Leonard Wood in Missouri. To him it was all an educational experience that March of 1942. He was taught how to use compressor tools for the first time. He found out how to build bridges out of pontoon boats. The work here, he commented rather casually, "is not so hard, but it is regular."[67] Max Galbraith was a private in the Marine Corp stationed in California. He wrote boasting of the thirteen pounds he had gained due to the "grand meals" he ate since he left home. He gave details of his fascination with visits to "China Town" in San Francisco, although he admitted that the place did seem "creepy" at night.[68]

A more serious tone crept in, however, in letters written the next year. Lowell Cortelyou in April, 1943 wrote about his ship in the North Atlantic. It had been torpedoed and sank. Cortelyou survived the open sea until he was rescued and taken to Iceland. His letters gloss over the harrowing experience but he admitted, "sure glad I'm not still out there floating around in a raft frozen to death." "Think this is about as safe a place as any to be for the duration," he confessed. He was glad to be alive.[69]

Ray Shafer, Biggsville
Battle of the Bulge

John Allaman, Rozetta
Pisa, Italy

Two county residents recalled their wartime experiences twenty years later. John H. Allaman, in February, 1980 remembered his enlisting in the Army Air Corps and being assigned to repair radar equipment in the Signal Corps. He landed at Casablanca on Christmas Day, 1943 and was then stationed at a Repair Base south of Algiers for the next several months. Then he was transferred to Oran, Algeria, then to Naples. Finally he ended up at Pisa shortly after it had been liberated by the Allied armies. Most of all he recalled the poor relations between the Americans and the Italian civilians at the start of the occupation. One incident illustrated the problem. Apparently a church filled with old men, women, and children had been hit during the assault and the Germans convinced the Italians that the Americans had done it deliberately. Another image was the picture of ever-present faces of the hungry children who "hung-out" at trash cans with their tin cups begging for left overs from the GIs. The soldiers, Allaman said, "didn't eat too well" so that "they would have something for them."[70]

John Olson
Guadalcanal, 1945

Bud Haney of Oquawka, in March, 1980 also remembered the war. He was a sergeant in the 69th Infantry Division and saw action at Normandy and subsequent advances through France, Belgium, Luxembourg, Holland, and finally into Germany. He met with Russian troops at Leipzig. There, a Russian officer said something to two enlisted men and "just pulled out a pistol, shot both right through the head, right in the street, and walked off." His other memories are keen. He recalled the bitter winter through the low countries where the wind "cut just like a knife." He lived all the time in the cold. He walked through mud, slush, and slop. He did not wash, even his face or hands, for six weeks that winter of 1945. He never changed his clothes. The dirt "was just ground into you." He ate with his hands.[71]

Some young men came through it all and emerged heroes, decorated with medals, like S/Sgt. Henry Perry who was given a Distinguished Flying Cross for conduct in the Bonin Islands in the South Pacific. Others did not make it. They were the county's war casualties. This news arrived in 1944. In mid-June it was announced, cursorily, that "T.R. Rankin received a message from the U.S. War Department Saturday morning saying search had been discontinued for his son Lt. Ralph Wayne Rankin co-pilot of Liberator Bomber B24 which failed to reach its destination in an overseas flight."[72] Lt. J. Wendell Houtchens was reported missing in action over France on June second. A month later it was confirmed that the twenty-two year old pilot was killed. Private Delbert Wells was severely wounded in the face and shoulders by shrapnel "somewhere in France." PFC Edgar Lee Brown of Biggsville was killed in action on December 29, 1944 in Belgium. The parents of Pvt. Harold S. Schenck received a telegram from Major General J.A. Ulio that their younger son had been killed in action in Germany on November 30, 1944. T/5 William J. Vestal was wounded in action in France on November 19, 1944. John Olson, a Pfc. in the Army was killed in the Pacific Theatre in the summer of 1945. Sergeant Delbert Wells was killed in Germany on March 19, 1945. He was survived by his widow who lived in Dallas City and held a defense job across the river in Ft. Madison. Donald W. Gipe was born at Raritan on the day after Christmas, 1921. He enlisted on September 16, 1942. He was commissioned Second Lieutenant in the Army Air Force on May 23, 1944. He was killed on November 7, 1945. Young Gipe was not buried in the Raritan Cemetery until December, 1948.[73] Even after the war was over the casualty list continued. When it was all finished Illinois lost 10,921 men killed in action, 1,568 died of combat wounds, 57 died of injuries, 4,830 died of non-combat illness, 1,151 were declared missing in action and dead; only 74 were, in June 1946, still thought just missing.[74]

Almost a year before Hiroshima the people of Henderson County were starting to show signs of combat fatigue. They wanted the war to be over. War Bond appeals began to emphasize the beginning of the end. In early November, 1944 one advertisement for the sixth county war bond drive exclaimed: "THEY STARTED IT. LET'S FINISH IT. HELP DEFEAT JAPAN."[75] The shock at the unexpected, sudden death of President Roosevelt in April, 1945 was linked to the impending end of the war. The announcement in the *Raritan Reporter* began with these words: "As the guns of America's fighting forces sounded ever closer the doom of Nazi Germany and Imperial Japan, Franklin Delano Roosevelt died in Warm Springs, Georgia...."[76] A few months earlier local people had started already to look to the world situation after the war. They talked about a "real international organization to keep bandit peoples from again deluging the earth with the blood of innocent people."[77]

Donald Gipe, 1945

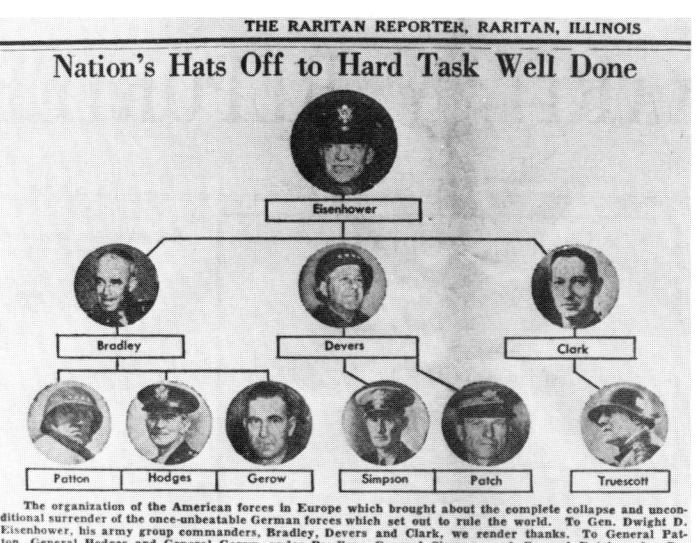

Eisenhower and Group Commanders

The end did come, in the spring of 1945. At the announcement of V-E Day in May the towns held quiet celebrations, usually consisting of home flag displays and a community worship service. Restrained jubilation was the watchword. In contrast, the news of the fall of Japan in August, after Hiroshima and Nagasaki, was met with unabashed festivity. Automobile horns honked continually. Bicycle groups of children tied cans to their fenders while the young riders blared noisemakers about town streets. Still others gave thanks quietly in their churches.

There were other ways to tell that the war was over, and won. A county veterans' party was held in January, 1946 at the High School gymnasium in Stronghurst. Its sole purpose was to honor the "50 or more" returning service men and women. After what was labeled a "bounteous turkey dinner," A.J. Rehling addressed the veterans and their families. Then everyone danced to the music of Bob Thomas and his orchestra which led off with the popular tune, "It's Been A Long, Long, Time...."[78]

World War II had been the longest and costliest foreign war in the nation's history and it required some "reconversion" time, as it was called, back to the routines of peace. Luckily, reconversion created fewer problems than expected. Between 1946 and 1948 twelve million servicemen and women, nationwide were taken back into civilian life. Industry changed, without layoffs and cutbacks, from wartime to peacetime production. Entire new industries appeared and continued on as a consequence of wartime innovations. Synthetic rubber and plastics were two of the most important. There was no post-war depression that many had predicted would repeat the sorry tale of Europe after World War I. There was no political reaction against FDR and the New Deal comparable to the bitterness of the "Normalcy" of the Harding presidency against Wilson and his Progressive reforms.

The figures of reconversion tell the story. Veterans had little difficulty returning to their old jobs (which by law had to be offered back to them) or in finding new opportunities with the skills they had acquired in the service. The economy boomed because of the pent-up consumer demand for goods that had been restricted or inaccessible during the war. National production went from $213 billion to $284 billion. National income increased from $181 billion to $241 billion. Consumer power went from $151 billion to $208 billion. Wages grew. Family income jumped from a yearly average of about $1,000 at the start of the war to just under $3,000 at the end of the reconversion, well above the more gradual rise in the cost of living in those years.

The consumer price index, a measure of living costs taken since 1913, showed that inflation rose from 62 to 72 percent between 1946 and 1948 to just a little above the cost of living for the year of 1920. Farmers, too, for a time saw unprecedented peacetime prosperity, again a contrast to their experience after the last war. An insatiable demand for foods cut short, or off, during the war, aided by government parity programs, increased national farm income between 1946 and 1948 by $5 billion. In 1948, the aggregate farm income was over $30 billion instead of the $11 billion in 1941. The federal government itself cushioned the effects of demobilization. Congress enacted elaborate legislation which gave federal money for all sorts of civilian jobs. It provided veterans with mustering-out pay, insurance, home-loans, subsidies for college education, provisions for health and medical care, and unemployment compensations for one year.

Signs of reconversion could be seen everywhere in the county. Two new county offices were set up in Oquawka and Stronghurst to help veterans take advantage of all the benefits the Federal government was offering. There were some annoying incidents on the part of a few returning men, who felt that the country owed them a job, but they were a minor irritation. Some veterans, a few, were sullen. They felt that the folks back home had had it too easy.[79]

A few disturbing signs of change were found in the passing of old ways. The popular Maddocks Cafe was auctioned off.[80] The Raritan Opera House closed down, except for an occasional benefit dance in the fall of 1945. James Lipes, in announcing his decision to stop showing movies here, explained that he had just put up with too much lately. "Green help" was always "getting things mixed up." But the biggest rub, he complained, was "the young folks who made trouble all the time." They did "everything they could think of to make it unpleasant." It was not the children who were the sore spot. "It was young men and women old enough to act like ladies and gentlemen."[81]

On the positive side, price controls were lifted in the summer of 1946, wiping out the nettlesome reality of federal intrusion into daily life which, to many county adults, had gone on too long, since the Depression. In greeting the good news local merchants pledged publicly that any new higher prices would be due to increased wholesale prices and not because of profit gouging.[82] Men's clothing went up, but only proportional to national increases in retail goods. A suit by 1948 ran between $30 and $60. A man could now purchase a new car and the models were in stock in showrooms by the spring of 1948. Dealers advertised a "fine selection" that was "ready for immediate delivery." A new Pontiac, DeSoto, Plymouth, Mercury, Ford, Frazier, Kaiser, Studebaker all could be had on easy terms. Dealers now pushed their stock instead of sending off frustrated buyers. One businessman advertised that "you may own one of these with or without a trade...we will make a liberal allowance on your old car" and "the balance may be financed at a very low rate of interest."[83] Gas prices either stayed where they were, at 18¢ a gallon for regular or 20¢ a gallon for ethyl, or they decreased because of competition in "gas wars" among station owners.[84]

Membership in the county Farm Bureau hit an all-time high in 1946 at 750 supporters.⁸⁵ The AAA suggested restrictions on post-war production but these measures were intended to stimulate wheat harvests for the recovery of war-torn Europe. They affected mainly the feeders who were asked to limit the amount of corn they accepted from farmers.⁸⁶ The AAA still gave out checks for conservation practices registered with the new chairman Clarence Gibb.⁸⁷ Farmers became a part of an enlarged federal district after the war. Called the FHA or Farmers Home Administration with Arthur M. Brim designated as regional supervisor, the counties of Henderson, Warren, and Knox were consolidated under one office located at 211½ Broadway in Monmouth. The agency was henceforth in charge of agricultural loans (with special emphasis on veteran's assistance), farm improvement loans, and a tenant farm-purchase loan program.⁸⁸ Land prices went up. By 1948, farms were selling at $300 an acre for "good, black land."⁸⁹

Clarence P. Gibb, ASC Chairman

During the war political acrimony all but disappeared in the county and local Democrats capitalized on popular support of F.D.R. For instance, in 1942 the Democrats won a majority of the county offices.⁹⁰ Two years later, at the height of the war, in the presidential election the county returned Democrat Ora Smith of Biggsville to the state legislature by a vote of 325 to 106 over his opponent. That year the Circuit Clerk was also a Democrat. Even though the rest of the offices in 1944 received Republican majorities by almost two-to-one the attitude toward Roosevelt's re-election that year, and toward other Democratic Party victories, was one of calm acceptance of a wartime necessity. There was no partisanship in the 1944 elections either during the campaign or afterwards. All voters seemed glued together by the emotional cement of the war. The only issue mentioned was the prospect of a future United Nations but on that question both county Democrats and Republicans were in agreement in their strong support.⁹¹

But in 1946 the long-festering feud between Oquawka and Stronghurst broke open again. The issue was the proposal to spend $185,000 on a new Court House renovation. The *Raritan Reporter*, echoing the sentiment of down-county townships, stated it might be a "good thing" in theory but "there is a large majority of thinking citizens who realize that this is about as poor a time as could be selected" to start such a project. Materials were still scarce. Labor was "extremely high." The "dollar power to purchase" was at an all-time low.⁹² The vote was decisive. Those opposing registered 1,446 while those in favor numbered just 471 (297 of which came from Oquawka). Stronghurst voters went 277 against and just forty for. Raritan polled 305 against and only six in favor. In 1946 the whole county, with the exception of the popular Ora Smith (and Chris Apt unopposed), came back to the Republican Party. The Republican ascendancy captured state and national offices as well. Republicans won the state treasurers office. Charles Carpentier beat out his Democratic challenger for state Senator by 2,324 to 1,011 votes. Republicans were sent to Congress. Anton J. Johnson and William G. Stratton, both won by two-to-one majorities.⁹³ A popular song of the day caught the political feelings of 1946: "Seems Like Old Times...."

END NOTES FOR CHAPTER EIGHT

¹ The best treatment of Roosevelt and the coming of the war in Europe is Thomas A. Bailey and Paul B. Ryan, *Hitler vs. Roosevelt* (New York, 1979) and James MacGregor Burns award winning study *Roosevelt: the Lion and the Fox* (New York, 1956).

[2] Morison, Commager, Leuchtenburg, *American Republic*, V. II, p529.
[3] Quoted in Nash, *The American People*, V. II, p824.
[4] On the story of Japanese-American relations and the coming of the war in Asia see Charles Neu, *The Troubled Encounter: The United States and Japan* (New York, 1975), Gordon W. Prange, *At Dawn We Slept* (New York, 1981), and John Toland, *Infamy* (New York, 1982).
[5] Morison, Commager, Leuchtenburg, *American Republic*, V. II, p541.
[6] Richard Jensen's provocative interpretation of Illinois in the months before the war is found on pages 142-146 of *Illinois*.
[7] Pease, *Story of Illinois*, p248.
[8] *Raritan Reporter*, November 7, 1940.
[9] Ibid., February 20, 1941.
[10] Nash, *The American People*, V. II, p827.
[11] See Prange, *At Dawn We Slept*, passim.
[12] *Raritan Reporter*, August 28, 1941.
[13] Ibid., November 13, 1941.
[14] Ibid., November 6, 1941.
[15] Ibid., October 23, 1941.
[16] James H. Cook interview.
[17] *Raritan Reporter*, December 11, 1941.
[18] Howard, *Illinois*, pp.522-30.
[19] *Raritan Reporter*, April 23, 1942.
[20] Monmouth *Review Atlas*, November 16, 1942.
[21] *Raritan Reporter* July 6, 1942.
[22] Pease, *Story of Illinois*, p251.
[23] U.S. Department of Commerce, *United States Census of Agriculture: 1945*, Vol. I, pt.5, pp24-25, 44-45, 58-59, 116. See also *Raritan Reporter* June 7, 1945.
[24] *Raritan Reporter*, January 22, 1942.
[25] Ibid., January 22, 1942.
[26] Ibid., February 5, 1942.
[27] Ibid., March 19, 1942.
[28] Monmouth *Review Atlas*, October-November, 1942.
[29] Ibid.
[30] Ibid., "Farm Trade is Something That Will Last After War Ends."
[31] Ibid., December, 1943.
[32] Ibid.
[33] Ibid., "First Load of New Corn Taken to Huge Crib," "Farmers Build Storage Bins for Soybeans."
[34] Ibid., April—June, 1943. See "Farm Machines Soar in Price."
[35] *Raritan Reporter*, December 24, 1942.
[36] Ibid., September 28, 1944.
[37] Monmouth *Review Atlas*, April 1 - June, October, 1943.
[38] Ibid.
[39] Ibid.
[40] Ibid., 1942, 1943, passim.
[41] *Raritan Reporter*, February 25, 1945.
[42] Ibid., August 13, 1943.
[43] Ibid., February 26, 1942.
[44] Ibid., July 16, 1942.
[45] Ibid., April 30, 1942; March 29, 1945.
[46] Monmouth *Review Atlas*, 1943, See "Groceries Hard to Get," "Self Imposed Ration Works."
[47] *Raritan Reporter*, June 14, 1945.
[48] James H. Cook interview.
[49] *Raritan Reporter*, June 8, 1942.
[50] Ibid., December 10, 1942.

[51] Ibid., February 11, 1943.
[52] Ibid., November 28, 1942.
[53] Ibid., April 6, 1943.
[54] Ibid., February 10, 1944.
[55] Ibid., January 29, 1944.
[56] Ibid., October 5, 1944.
[57] Ibid., February 8, 1945.
[58] Ibid., August 20, 1942.
[59] Ibid., March 17, August 29, 1942.
[60] Monmouth *Review Atlas*, January 1942, "Village Ready for Emergency."
[61] *Raritan Reporter*, January 8, 1942.
[62] Ibid., March 17, 1942 first announced the upcoming meeting.
[63] In Illinois neither fathers nor farmers were considered for induction until 1944. Even when this new policy was enacted most boards, looking for men physically fit for invasion combat duty in Europe, passed over the older men. Most of the state's draftees came from a "huge reservoir", in Jensen's words, of unemployed young, unmarried males. See Jensen, *Illinois*, p149.
[64] The distribution of Illinois draftees was: Army, 504,875; Navy, 95,682; Marine Corps, 14,160; Coast Guard, 1,248. Pease, *Story of Illinois*, p252.
[65] *Raritan Reporter*, October 17, 1942.
[66] Ibid., September 17, 1942.
[67] Ibid., March 12, 1942.
[68] Ibid.
[69] Ibid., April 6, 1943.
[70] John H. Allaman tape recorded interview by Rita Souther, February 21, 1980. WIU Archives & Special Collections.
[71] Francis Joseph Haney interview.
[72] *Raritan Reporter*, June 15, 1944.
[73] Ibid., January 6, 1949.
[74] Pease, *Story of Illinois*, p253.
[75] *Raritan Reporter*, November 3, 1944.
[76] Ibid., April 19, 1945.
[77] Ibid., October 28, 1944.
[78] Ibid., January 3, 1946.
[79] Quoted from an interview with Mildred M. Allaman, Raritan, Illinois, November 8, 1945 by John L. Allaman. Typescript "Raritan, Illinois During World War II" in possession of the author.
[80] *Raritan Reporter*, December 13, 1945.
[81] Ibid., November 21, 1945.
[82] Ibid., July 11, 1946.
[83] Ibid., April 29, 1948.
[84] Ibid., December 19, 1946.
[85] Ibid., January 24, 1946.
[86] Ibid., April 18, 1946.
[87] Ibid., September 2, 1948.
[88] Ibid., November 28, 1946.
[89] Ibid., September 30, 1948.
[90] Ibid., November 12, 1942.
[91] Ibid., October 28, November 9, 1944.
[92] Ibid., May 9, 1946.
[93] Ibid., November 7, 1946.

CHAPTER NINE

HENDERSON COUNTY 1948-1984

History is the record of the past and one of the perennial tasks facing all historians is to judge when the past becomes the present. When does the history of Henderson County blend into current events? When does the past end and where does the present begin? There are no easy answers to these questions, although historians who have had to come to grips with it have suggested guidelines. One suggestion is to treat the present as the present generation. But which generation? Should the cutoff point be the writer's own generation? Should events within his or her lifetime be catalogued as current. In this case, the history of Henderson County would terminate in the year of this writer's birth, 1940. Perhaps the notion of a generation should be measurement advocated by Thomas Jefferson when he wrote about the legacy of one generation being passed to its successor. Jefferson stipulated a generation as being about twenty years.

That yardstick would place the period mark at the mid-sixties. Some modern American historians are more daring. They attempt to bring their stories up to the 1980s. The last chapter of Mary Beth Norton's *A People and a Nation*, published in 1986, is entitled "A Sharp Turn to the Right America Since 1981." Gary B. Nash's *The American People Creating a Nation and a Society*, also put out in 1986, in its final chapter deals with "Austerity and the American Dream: The United States Since 1976." I will follow the example set by Norton, Nash, and others and trace the events of Henderson County during the years since its recovery from World War II up to about the time I began work on the county history in the summer of 1983.

Starting in 1948 the people of the county, the state, and the nation tried to make up for lost time. Time lost and opportunities passed by had been the trend of over fifteen years of Depression and war. Ahead was the promise of the abundant life, the American dream of a secure home, healthy family, and sound politics. Nothing that could happen, the feeling was, would be as bad as it had been, nothing would again shatter America's confidence. Now that the devil within and the devil without had been exorcized our self-esteem would never be shaken. We were certain, in those post-years of prosperity and growth, that we had been redeemed by our suffering. We had achieved a sort of national salvation by 1948 and were assured happiness thereafter in the years to come.

A new lifestyle coincided with the new optimism. The economy, pushed by incomes pent up during the war, expanded rapidly and provided employment security for town and farm. Automobile ownership gave nearly everyone, even teenagers, accessible and cheap mobility over a federally-financed system of repaired highways and, later, the interstate highway system. Radio plus television broke down the last vestiges of intellectual and emotional isolation between rural and urban America. They united national and international events with the daily routine of every citizen.

Our society in the 1950s became homogenous. People in Henderson County, for the most part, looked the same as people in Peoria. Everyone lived pretty nearly the same way, within class, and had access to the same medical care, used the same household appliances, wore the same kind of clothes, drove about the same model of car, and drank much the same

Opposite: Henderson County Museum, Raritan

Main Street, Raritan, 1981

brands of beer. High School education became a necessity and a better education a right for all children. Schools were consolidated, more so in Illinois than in any other state. A constitution was brought up to date. The County Court system was modernized. Politicians of both parties embraced as orthodoxy what some had regarded as a fatal heresy just a few years before. No one dismantled the heart of the New Deal welfare program. Social Security was a sacred cow. Federal price supports for farmers were accepted as a "given" in yearly planning. And the role of America in international affairs was that of the unquestioned, most powerful leader of the "free world" against "Communist aggression."

County towns and villages returned to the sort of prosperity they had seen in the twenties. At Lomax, for example, the canning factory at war's end was humming with business. It was filling 100 railroad cars full of tomatoes in 1946 at a valued inventory of $276,426.48. Over the next decade it had a payroll of 200 people working in the plant and another 200 hands in the fields. It produced over 200,000 cases a year.[1] Passenger traffic on the C.B.&Q. and Santa Fe between 1948 and 1958 hit an all-time record. New state highway funds were earmarked for repairs on route 34 and 94. Within a decade there was talk in Springfield of a program to construct a three-corridor network of new highways through the county. One line was to go west from route 67 to Biggsville through Kirkwood and then on to Gladstone on route 34. Another was to run west and parallel to 164 between Oquawka and three miles north of Gladstone. A third was to cross route 67 northeast of Monmouth then head west to hit route 94 north of Biggsville. All construction was to be financed, just as before, by the State Highway Bond Issue. Banks, as a measure of county growth and prosperity, expanded. The Raritan Bank's resources jumped from $2,653,809.98 in 1946 to $3,216,169.13 in 1950, to $4,048,831.44 in 1954.[2] The Bank of Stronghurst went from resources of just $1,885,985.43 in 1954 to $4,725,811.91 in 1961.[3] The Bank of Oquawka likewise quadrupled its assets and along with the Raritan and Stronghurst institutions underwent a vast modern building program in the early sixties as a visible sign of its secure wealth.[4]

Some towns became centers of an interstate commerce in farm products. Stronghurst became a national hog marketing center. On a typical day in 1951 the Livestock Marketing Association there received 1,140 hogs from sixty-three farmers. "Buck" Hartquist shipped out the hogs on two double-deck rail cars (264 hogs to Los Angeles), on single cars to New York City (141 hogs), Bay City, Michigan (129 hogs), two truckloads (110 hogs) were sent to Chicago and another two trucks (228 hogs) pulled out for Milwaukee. In addition, there were the "specialty demands", also filled by Hartquist, placed by several packers and killers from coast to coast.[5] Gulfport river terminal facilities under Everett Harris in 1968 started moving annually over ten million bushels of grain. With easy access to its scales and dumping points farmers could count on almost instant unloading. Harris claimed that it handled 175 trucks each day at the rate of 15,000 and 20,000 bushels an hour. A 50,000 bushel river barge was loaded in under four hours. In order to store the grain unloaded on the barges, eleven round bins 125 feet high held up to 325,000 bushels. The same company that owned the Gulfport operation, the Gladstone Grain Company, also ran a 200,000 bushel capacity elevator business on the mainline of the C.B.&Q. at the town.[6] Beginning in the 1970s the Twomey Company began to supplement the grain storage facilities of the Gladstone operation, then having about a four-million bushel capacity. It built a huge loading dock on the river and put up several steel storage buildings near Gladstone at an estimated capacity of over forty million bushels.

Farm organizations continued to play an important role in the post-war prosperity. The Farm Bureau expanded its activities in the 1950s. It held meetings every month and advertized them with a full-page spread in the newspapers. The Bureau also started a full bi-weekly column on issues and events and discontinued the old monthly bulletin.[7] The column discussed topics such as "Agronomy and Soil Conservation," "Home Economics Extension News," "New Blanket Policy Fire Insurance," "Fertilizers and Blenders," "Lean Hogs Can Be Fast Growing Hogs," and "Family Activities in the Farm Bureau."[8] In 1956, the Bureau entered television with a weekly thirty-minute show put out from Quincy's KHQA channel seven every Sunday afternoon at one-thirty.[9] It embarked on a lobbying program to benefit farmers by legislation in Springfield. The Bureau targeted such measures as exempting farm tractors from automobile licensing, a tax return for upkeep of township roads, a bonding fee for grain buyers, and state funds to expand a cooperative extension service program. It advertised specific measures to assist farmers by providing data on market prices, showing them how to reduce machinery costs, and overall, how to guarantee themselves a fair share to the retail market.[10]

The A.S.C.S. (Agricultural Stabilization and Conservation Service) took over a large part of the old AAA functions. Under Lennie Dannenberg, head of the Henderson County Committee, they inaugurated an ambitious new "set aside" program for area farmers. Advertized as "basically good conservation" it received substantial support during its first years. The plan was to set aside cropland if it had been farmed in the previous three years. These acres, for the next three years, would be planted with rotated crops and legumes. Each farmer was to calculate his expected government reimbursement by multiplying his yield times one-half of his base by thirty-two cents. For example, Dannenburg showed that a 100 bushel yield on a 100 acre base would calculate as 32¢ x 100 bushels x 50 acres to equal $1,600. Paul Stand, another member of the ASC, stressed the fairness of the program. "If the farmer sets aside the percent of acreage from his cropland," he said, "any amount of groups may be planted on the remaining cropland."[11]

No sooner had the program started than Dannenburg told of some changes. When farmers set aside 25 percent of their feed grain base, he announced, they could then rent back the diverted acres as pasture or hay. In 1973, the ASCS made payments without requiring any diversion at all. Farmers only had to limit feed grain to the previous year's plantings and maintain their conserving base. This modification was so attractive that one farmer predicted that "the only farmers who will not sign in either or both programs will be those due to a misunderstanding or just opposed to farm programs."[12]

A new storage plan, as a supplement to the set-aside program, was begun. Farmers could get warehouse and farm-stored grain loans on a 30 or 15 percent option plan. The 30 percent diversion option had the advantage of allowing the farmer to plant any combination of crops without restriction on any individual crop. They would be assured a supplemental payment if the market were broken by overproduction. The 15 percent plan's advantage was in payment per acre. Its initial payment was higher. But there would be a limit to the acres of corn allowed and no reimbursement if the markets were depressed.[13]

The results of these county support programs were impressive. A total of 790 out of 971 farmers, or over 81 percent, signed on to the set-aside measures. It lasted only a year. In the summer of 1974, Dannenburg announced that the set-aside acres were lifted. The goal from then on was a new "Feed Grain and Wheat Program." Farmers were now asked to raise any crop or crops they wanted with a substitution provision to allow credit for base acreage if needed. But at the same time that Dannenburg put out information on this latest innovation he inadvertently signaled the first signs of impending bad times for Henderson County farmers. He mentioned that by late summer of 1973 there were increasing shortages of fuel with which to dry the grain and operators were having trouble transporting grain from their inland elevators to the export areas. The oil crunch was on.

In 1973 farm credit skyrocketed. The warnings came in a statement by John Gilmore, president of Monmouth Production Credit Association. Summarizing a conference he had just attended that winter in St. Louis, he expressed shock and concern at the "rapidly increasing use of farm credit and rising interest rate." The ominous indications, he said, were not just local, they were everywhere. Production Credit Association figures in Arkansas and Missouri, when added to Illinois reports, totaled "nearly a record one billion dollars in 1972" alone! There were alarming increases in new acres under cultivation supported not just with Federal Land Banks loans. Now the commercial banks, for the first time, were jumping into farm mortgages and loans. The projection was disastrous.

Changes in Farming: 1950–1983

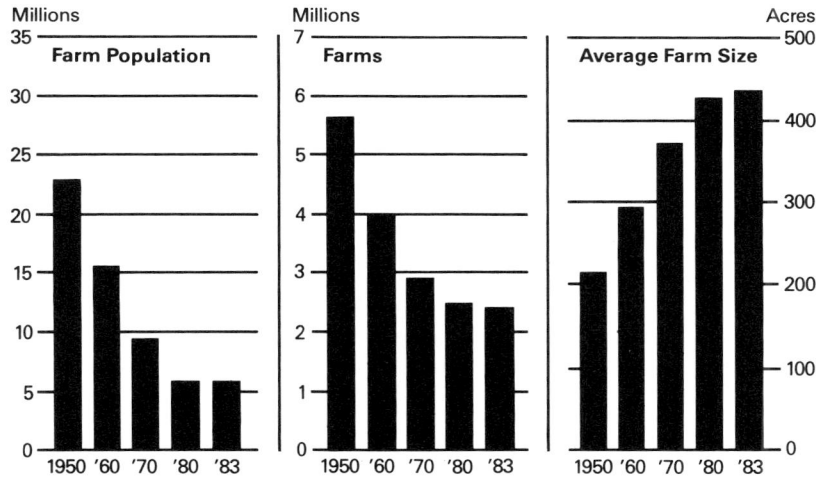

Changes in Farming: 1950-1983

Over expansion would bring lower prices while at the same time farmers had committed themselves to enormously high, fixed, long-term debts. Farm credit and services (insurance, tax assistance) from his Association would double in the next five years, Gilmore said. Farmer's incomes, unfortunately, would go exactly in the opposite direction. A day of reckoning was ahead.[14]

Fuel shortages, a glutted market, and skyrocketing credit were not the only straws in the wind of the agrarian storm that hit the family farm in Illinois. In the early 1950s the figures showed a dangerous erosion of the state's farm population, a two percent drop in ten years. The causes were complicated but were identified even then. Booming post-war industries attracted rural young people to their high wages. Large scale mechanization brought about to meet production demands during the war had resulted in the enormous reduction in the number of field hands. There were, in 1950, larger farms and fewer farm owners. Rural birth rate was only one-half of the urban birth rate.[15] As early as 1951 the average market prices received by Henderson County farmers started going down. The slip was temporary, however, and they still remained four percent above the parity level.[16] Farm land values, for a while, remained relatively steady at about $300 per acre. By the mid-1960s, though, farm close-out sales began to appear with regularity in the county newspapers. They ran about five each week on a seasonal basis, usually announced with: "As I have decided to quit farming I will hold a complete closing out sale" at such and such a time and place.

Unequivocal indications of the negative turn-around in the farm economy came in the fall of 1973. In November, because of the dwindling number of farmers, all agencies in the county were consolidated in one location. Four services were involved: the ASCS, FHA, SCS (Soil Conservation Service), and FCIC (Federal Crop Insurance Corporation).[17] Over the next two years the ASCS, now directed by David Hill, devised new measures to help area farmers. He announced that a "disaster provision" was to be included in loans. New loans on corn and wheat were available at 82 percent of the "target price" of $1.83 and $1.31 a bushel.[18]

The market began to collapse in 1975. Corn went to under $1.15 a bushel.

Gilmore cited the excess in the county elevators combined with a longshoreman's strike over higher pay as the contributing causes. Only corn would be eligible for loans that would be below current market prices anyhow. He nevertheless urged farmers to take advantage of the loans with the hope that the corn market would stabilize and the bean market would recover. By 1977, plans were put in place for farmers in deep trouble. The ASCS office received requests for extra time to redeem last year's corn or to forfeit it to the Commodity Credit Corporation. The grain could be redeemed by paying the principle, interest and storage costs.[19] In 1978, it was announced that the previous year's loans would be eligible for a three year extension or until such time as the natural market prices raised 125 percent of the current loan, or when feed grain reached 140 percent and wheat 175 percent of their respective loan levels.[20] By the fall of 1979 interest rates were hitting 14.5 percent. Loans were then offered only on one-year terms. Bankers began advising farmers to forgo any more loans at that time.[21].

Allaman Implement Company, Stronghurst

In 1980, President Carter's grain embargo hit. Farm Bureau president Harold B. Steele felt the President was discriminating against Illinois farmers. "Please Mr. President," he wrote, "tell me...that I'm not being singled out to bear most of the burden."[22] By October of 1981 many county farmers with maturing loans for the "first time in many years" had to decide whether it was worth requesting another extension or to forfeit their mortgaged grain to the Commodity Credit Corporation. Corn was selling for $2.42 a bushel. The *Quill* reported that most farmers felt it best just to forfeit the grain and start 1981 with another loan in the hope of enrolling in a new reserve program later.[23] Things were getting out of hand. Tractors and combines were consuming enormous amounts of diesel fuel and gasoline at $1.10 and $1.25 a gallon. Herbicides were running up to $20 per acre. Fertilizer costs were hitting about $42 an acre. Costs such as these, when added to soaring interest rates and low grain prices, were prohibitive. County farmers just could not pay their bills. They went out of business. They sold the family farm.

Patterns of daily life were changing. The telephone system, in place since before World War I on a switchboard basis, was made up to date in 1954 when the southern sections of the county were converted to the direct dial system. The project itself was the result of community effort in which $18,000 was raised by subscription and $14,000 by a bonding agency. Elmer Lee Harden, Director of the Telephone Cooperative, placed the first call, as a ceremony, over the new, integrated system.[24] Selling and buying new modern automobiles, until the oil crisis of the mid 1970s, developed into a community participation sport. Newspapers typed the arrival of the next year's models with the fever of a baseball World Series. Three column advertisements in which the various dealers competed for the local dollar became a standard feature of each paper. Just after Christmas the contests began even though the actual new cars were not due to arrive in the showrooms for months. Graphic details, similar to the exaggerated language of the radio sports broadcaster, became the rule. Prices at the time were competitive, with all models except the top of the line within reach of most budgets. For example, in 1956, a Buick V-8 at Neff Implement Company in Stronghurst, ran just $2,297.88 and at Bennett Motor Company a man could get a Pontiac for exactly the same price.[25]

New Car Ad from Newspaper

The same space commitment which the newspapers gave to area automobile dealers they devoted, more than ever before, to local events.

Floods and other disasters were front page feature stories. In the spring of 1950 the county experienced, wrote the editor of the *Raritan Reporter,* the "most severe flood in history along the Mississippi." In late April both Oquawka and Gladstone areas were ravaged. Livestock drowned. Route 164 was inundated. Railroad tracks were washed out. No mail was delivered in the area. Even the old covered bridge over Henderson Creek was flooded.[26] In 1965, over 28,000 acres flooded when the levee north of Gladstone broke followed the next day by a rupture of a second levee west of Crystal Lake Club House. Water spilled over the viaduct on Route 34 and cars were stranded with flood rising to thirty-four feet on the highway at some places. Then a third levee gave way at Henderson and Ellison Creek and only twenty-four hour work on sand bags prevented a break near the county seat itself. Red Cross emergency aid stations were set up at the Union High School and the postoffice at Biggsville. The Council of Churches provided clothing. FHA made agricultural loans on twenty-year terms with no limit to the amount that could be requested.[27] In 1973, the Mississippi crested at twenty-five feet near Oquawka, higher than the 1965 disaster. This time President Nixon declared the county a disaster area and thereby allowed financial help to be secured by application to the state division of Unemployed Compensation for loans at only five percent interest.[28]

Corner of US 34 and Carman Road, 1965

Automobile wrecks and fatalities appeared, along with photographs, with depressing regularity in the newspapers. Now and then train wrecks captured their attention, such as the 1954 derailment of the Sante Fe near Lomax. There, on August 20, a passenger train running at eighty-five miles per hour jumped the track. Eleven cars were overturned and the wreck tore up the track for more than a quarter of a mile. Four people died in the tragedy and a number of others were taken to nearby hospitals. Speculation about the cause of the disaster pointed to a broken equalizer on a rear truck of the forward lounge car.[29]

One of the most interesting developments to surface during the 1960s was an increasing sensitivity to, and awareness of, what had happened in the county in the nineteenth century. The people developed, and nurtured, a strong sense of their own history. Signs of this new historical awareness were everywhere. Foremost was the creation of a county Historical Society. Officially formed in 1975 in conjuction with the upcoming American bi-centennial, efforts to create such a group extended back to the summer of 1962. In late summer of that year a preliminary meeting of interested persons was held at Stronghurst where, at 8:00 on Monday evening, August 12, about a dozen people gathered at the M.S.T. Fire Station. The Stronghurst Booster Club, from the start, backed the idea with its endorsement. At the meeting, Mrs. Boyd Finch of Aledo, an officer of the Mercer County Historical Society, spoke about the steps needed to organize such a society in Henderson County and commented generally on the work such societies carry on throughout the state. She announced that the Executive Director of the Illinois State Historical Society in Springfield, Dr. Clyde Walton, wished to have an opportunity to talk with the group. A week later at another meeting, John Bigger was elected as temporary chairman and William L. Finch was chosen temporary secretary. At this second gathering of about thirty people the vote was passed formally to organize a historical society at a meeting set for September at the Union High School.[30]

Two September meetings were convened at the High School. At the second meeting Clyde Walton spoke. He explained that the basic aim of every

Above: Jacob Allaman, Bridge Builder

Above Right: Allaman Covered Bridge before

Restoring Covered Bridge, 1984

county society was to "gather, compile, and preserve" its history. He gave specific guidelines as to how to incorporate. A membership fee schedule was adopted: $2.00 for individuals and $5.00 for a family. Newspaper editor and publisher Paul Bell of Stronghurst volunteered to furnish membership cards free of charge. A Planning Committee with E.A. Fort, Jr. as chairman was appointed. Another meeting was held at the Circuit Court room of the Courthouse on Thursday evening, October 18, 1962. At that time, after James T. Hickey, the Lincoln expert from the State Historical Society, spoke on "Mary Lincoln: A Tragic Portrait," a permanent list of officers was elected.[31]

Other signs of historical activity were the various restoration projects begun throughout the county. South of Oquawka the covered bridge was rebuilt. Although interest in preserving the 104 foot long structure, erected in 1866, was expressed as early as 1957 when the state Division of Highways repaired most of the heavy part of the roadway, little was done toward rebuilding the entire structure until the 1970s. Through efforts of the Historical Society, the bridge was listed on the National Register of Historic Places. It became a landmark.[32] The Society's plans were set back considerably when in June, 1982 a flood washed out the bridge from its footings.[33] Citizens rescued much of the original lumber from Henderson Creek and were able to get financial aid from the state Department of Transportation to help in completing its restoration. Also D.O.T. Maintenance Engineer Charles Glick from Peoria was placed in charge of the project.[34].

In the summer of 1984 the rebuilding was begun. Working closely with John H. Allaman who represented the Society, the wooden framework was first precut and assembled on the Allaman farm. About 75 percent of the woodwork was original salvaged timber from the earlier flood. Steel was used to roll the bridge across the creek and left to protect it from future floods. The wooden frame was built as originally designed. By then the state, through the efforts of Representative Clarence Neff, had put up $60,000 in a restoration grant to which were added funds raised in drives sponsored by the Historical Society. By mid-summer Glick had constructed a scale model of the restoration. By September the covered bridge was back in place. The thirty-ton structure was placed on the two steel beams. The original sign was put over the entrance: "Five Dollar Fine For Leading or Driving Any Beast Faster than a Walk, or Driving More than 30 Head of Cattle, Mules or Horses at a time in or Across the Bridge."[35]

Raritan Opera House, 1981

Other restoration projects were started. The Raritan Opera House, built in 1903 and remodeled slightly in 1954, was by the early 1980s in need of fundamental rebuilding. It required a new roof and new electrical wiring, a new lighting system, and new furniture. As a starter, the building, like the covered bridge, was registered as a historic landmark. Then the Historical Society, in September of 1983, donated $800 toward the restoration. It helped put on a benefit production entitled "Vaudeville Is My Home," a slapstick comedy by the Henderson County Arts Council directed by Connie Duncan of Macomb.[36] A year later another production was staged to raise more money for the house.[37] The Alexis Phelps home in Oquawka was another restoration goal. Having been vandalized in the winter of 1978, the structure, located north of Schuyler Street and started in 1832 by Alexis Phelps, was the site of the first county government. Later it provided hospitality for Stephen Doulgas and Abraham Lincoln. In 1980, the house was recognized by the state as a historic structure and two years later was placed on the National Register of Historic Places.[38] The South Henderson Church and Cemetery, built in 1854, was another concern. In dilapidated condition by the 1970s, the U.S. Department of Interior awarded a grant of $6,397, to be matched by state funds, for historic preservation. The plan was to stabilize the roof and install new shingles and rennovate the interior.[39]

Alexis Phelps Home, Oquawka

Brochure from Heritage Tour, 1987

Historical endeavors also included the creation of a county museum, the production of historical dramas, the development of annual "Heritage Days" celebrations, an oral history program, and the writing of the county's history. The first advertisement for the building of a county museum appeared in the September 10, 1975 issue of the *Quill*. A two paragraph article announced a county-wide meeting at the Bank of Stronghurst on October 2, at 7:30 where Clarence Neff would lead a community discussion about establishing a museum. John H. Allaman of the Historical Society chaired the meeting. That November a group formed a Planning Committee of about twenty members and set to work. By the next summer they had started a "temporary" museum in the grade school building at Raritan. And, on July 4 of that year, they hosted a large opening celebration at which an estimated 4,500 people attended.[40] By the summer of 1977 the museum was holding regular visitor's hours every afternoon under the direction of Rita Souther.[41] Later, James Cook of Raritan took over primary responsibility for the museum's exhibits and operations. In 1981, a charming historical drama "Memories of the Prairie" was produced. The play consisted of folk music and readings from historical sources adapted from collections of the Western Illinois University Libraries.[42] Marjory Dreher in the spring of 1975 began collecting tape recordings as a part of an oral history program to preserve the county's past, a project later continued and expanded by Rita Souther's interviews with numerous senior citizens of the county.[43]

Heritage Trail celebrations were started in October 1978. It turned into an annual event with a two-day schedule of tours to various sites throughout the county. Also featured were county art, needlework, weaving and other crafts, antique displays, museum exhibits at Stronghurst, Oquawka, and Raritan, games (waterwitching and horseshoes, volleyball) and a series of breakfasts, lunches, and chicken dinners. Towns celebrated their historic birthdays on their own. Lomax, for example, in 1983 had its 101st celebration when over 1,000 attended for a time of a parade, a chicken fry and streetdancing.[44] To preserve the entire sweep of the county's development the Historical Society in 1977 began laying plans for the writing and publication of a new county history.

Things historical were not the only means of entertainment. Farmer's Picnics and County Fairs continued just as before the war. Usually held in August they featured free entertainment and band concerts. Often they became stomping grounds for local and state politicians who used them as a convenient vehicle to meet with large numbers of voters without having to endure much traveling from one village to the next.[45] The Henderson County Fair of 1953 was headlined "The Biggest Attraction in the History of Your County Fairs." It had five consecutive evenings of activities on the fair grounds at Stronghurst. There one could see "Hell Drivers" in a cavalcade of crashing cars and motorcyles or a horse show on Wednesday night, or the clown "Don Adams and his ding dandy bicycle" on Monday.[46] There were, for a time anyhow, annual "Soldiers and Sailors Reunions." Typical was the one which took place in Oquawka in September 1952. Advertised as "unusually fine free entertainment" at the "Bank Corner" for "four nights in a row." There one could hear barber shop quartets, watch a local talent program, and take some of the "Port City Rides" which were set up on streets in the business section. All events were sponsored by the Veterans of Foreign Wars.[47] High School students presented their annual plays in the opera houses at Oquawka, renovated in 1950, and Raritan. National entertainment figures came to the area from time to time. For example, in January 1951 Gene Autry

County Fair, 1957

starred in a three hour stage show, along with Smiley Burnette, at the Memorial Auditorium in Burlington.[48] The American Legion presented the "1952 Minstrel Revue" on two nights in November at the High School Gymnasium in Stronghurst.[49]

In another area of what people did for amusement, the county after the Second World War became a mecca for outdoor recreational activities. It was especially noted for its duck hunting refuges along the Mississippi River. Under the operation of the state Department of Conservation, hunters traveled from a three-state region to draw for duck blinds in selected sites. In the northern edge of the county the Big River State Forest became a popular location for finding deer, wild turkey, and doves. In spots all along the Mississippi, at Gladstone Lake, and on the North and South Henderson Creeks amateur fishermen casted and spun for a variety of fresh water catch while commercial fishermen thrived between Dallas City and Oquawka. The big river became a new focal point for campers, boaters, and swimmers who thronged to its public access areas and to the state parks located just north of Oquawka. Delbar State Park, built on land donated by the Delbar family and pushed through the legislature by Clarence Neff, attracted weekend picnickers from May through September. During the colder months folks ran the trails in snowmobiles or skimmed through the parks on cross-country skiis.

Dances continued to be a popular diversion, at least for about a decade after the end of the war. The V.F.W. sponsored Saturday night dances at Gladstone, "both round and square dancing," for only 50¢ admission. Burlington, more than ever though, picked up the young crowd with their "live bands" at the city's auditorium. Sammy Kaye played there in October, 1952. In February, 1953, Spike Jones and his New Musical Depreciation Revue of 53 came to town.[51] Lesser names, like Skinny Ennis and his Orchestra, filled in between the more famous bands for just $2.00 a person at the door.[52]

Movies, like dances, were a mainstream of entertainment until their eclipse, like the big bands, in the 1950s. Almost every movie theater in the county by the late forties was advertising a change in attractions three times every week. Often double-features were on the bill. Admissions were still modest, only 40¢ for adults and 12¢ for children. Some of the movie titles were risque. The Bland Theatre in Blandinsville advertised in the *Raritan Reporter* in July 24, 1952, the one-night only showing of *A Night At The Follies*. "See Big Time Burlesque featuring Evelyn West, Adults only! All Seats 74¢" the caption read.

By 1958, however, the demise of the movies was everywhere. Theaters simply stopped operation without announcement or fanfare. Other places tried to hold on to their audiences. The Cawson Theater in Stronghurst was one of these diehards. It advertised "Help Keep a Movie in Stronghurst" or "Get More Out of Life--Go Out to a Movie." People could not go out as often as before though. Theaters were by then open only on Wednesday evenings and on Friday and Saturday nights.[53] By 1959 the Stronghurst theater had closed its doors and the only movie house in the county still running was the State Theater in Oquawka.[54] It continued for a while longer under Robert Jern who advertised for "the latest pictures with good sound in an air conditioned building...."[55] It did not last. Movies as entertainment were on their last legs. They had been replaced by television.

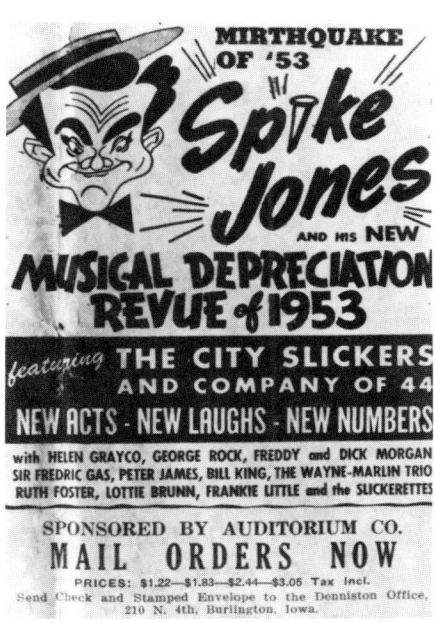

Entertainment Ad from Newspaper

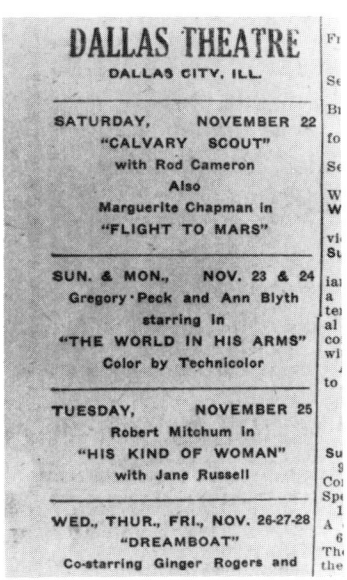

Movie Listing from Newspaper

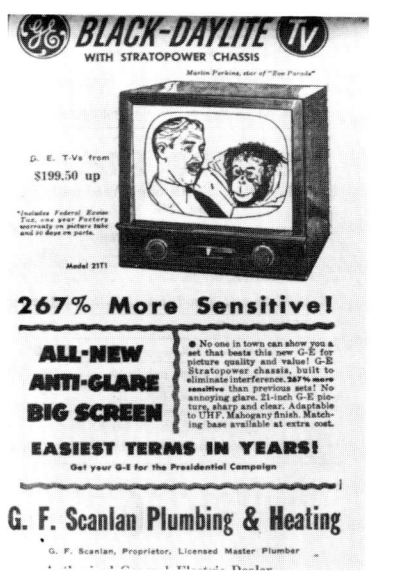

TV Ad from *Raritan Reporter*, 1950's

Christmas 1950 was the debut of television in Henderson County. At that shopping season, for the first time, newspapers advertised both console radios (a standard holiday item since the thirties) and television sets. By the next season radios had disappeared from the layouts and instead just televisions were pushed. Sylvania was the predominant model. Typical was the advertisement for a seventeen-inch "mahogany finish table model" Sylvania for only $239.95 or a seventeen-inch walnut console for just $322.95 at Larson Furniture Mart in Stronghurst. New business sprang up around the technology. Knutstrom TV business appeared in the show room of the Knutstrom Chevrolet Building in Stronghurst.[56] Richard Knutstrom was the subject of a front page picture article in the *Graphic-Reporter* which touted him as having just completed a thirty-six week residential training program at DeVry Technical Institute in Chicago.[57]

More traditional means of entertainment tried to compete with television. The fairs came each summer, although they were much smaller than before. Oquawka constructed a new boat ramp at an estimated cost of $95,000 sponsored by the "Riverfront Improvement Committee" and its grant from the Illinois Department of Conservation.[58] In 1967, a Youth Center opened at Oquawka. It had billboards and table tennis, a snack bar operated by members of the Kiwanis Club, a reading lounge on the first floor and upstairs was a juke box, a record player, and a dance floor. The Center was open every Friday and Saturday night from 8:00 till 11:00 for teenagers and on Thursday nights for the seventh and eighth graders.[59] But by then almost everybody else either stayed home, glued to their televisions, or drove out of the county for entertainment on weekends. The older era, when the county had been both a place to work and play, had passed away.

Henderson County Jail, current photo

Some things never changed. Crime, for instance, seemed largely uneffected by post-war alterations in the economy and social life. A new jail, with cell video monitoring equipment, was constructed in the 1980s. In the modern building the sheriff's deputies incarcerated and watched over petty thieves such as the person who stole all of the women's clothing from the car of a Des Moines salesman while the man was drinking inside the Western Club late one Saturday night in October, 1951.[60] A typical docket before Judge Earl Knox was published in the summer of 1956. Arraigned before the judge were men accused of driving a motor vehicle without a license, driving while intoxicated and reckless driving, aggravated assault and battery, larceny, stealing gasoline (sentenced to one year probation and court costs), and child abandonment (released when wife refused to testify).[61] The bank at Biggsville was robbed in the spring of 1961 and the culprit, Richard Anderson of LeMars, Iowa, was apprehended and turned over to the custody of the Federal Marshall from Peoria.[62] Unknown bandits sprang in upon a private poker game in the second floor of the Blue Goose tavern in Oquawka in October, 1963. There, at gunpoint, they lifted over $4,000 from the people around the table. The newspaper discreetly reported that "names of the seven men who were in the game were not disclosed by the sheriff." There were two murders. A stabbing at the Upton Tavern in Gulfport took place in November, 1965 when Gary Norris attacked Chuck Lawler during a fight in the parking lot of the bar. Lawler later died of his wounds. A migrant worker, Pablo Gonzales, who worked at Camp Number Two near Lomax, was stabbed to death during a drinking bout with another worker, Jesus Garcia. Louis Bondaldi stabbed John F. Phelan, a University of Illinois undergraduate from Fort Madison, in the parking lot of a liquor store after both men had left Grandinetti's Supper Club. Bonaldi was sentenced to twenty years in the state penitentiary.⁶⁴ The annual crime report for the county in 1983 listed thirty-two felonies (burglary, theft, deceptive practices, property damage, battery) of which eight individuals were sentenced to the Illiniois Department of Correction.⁶⁵

There was a new development in the history of crime in the county, however, drugs. The first public sign of concern with the problem surfaced in the late sixties. In 1969, the United States Department of Justice selected Henderson County as one of eleven counties in the entire nation targeted for systematic destruction, by plowing or spraying, of marijuana plants. Two men and two women were arrested at that time in a cornfield one mile west of Gladstone on drug growing charges.⁶⁶ A county youth was caught in a drug raid at Monmouth College in the spring of 1972.⁶⁷

Stronghurst School

While some things remained pretty much the same and other aspects of county life changed many for the better. The perspective of the community toward education, for example, saw a pronounced and progressive alteration. Basically, the one-room school house disappeared. The unequal system of high school education, where some parts of the county had opportunities within easy reach and others did not, was replaced by an integrated, consolidated high school system. In 1948, there were still twenty-five rural schools, four village grade schools, and three high schools in the county. That same year under L.C. Kerley the first District Superintendent, steps of consolidation (already suggested in 1945 by Chris Apt), began. Sixteen of the rural schools were shut down. The high school children from Oquawka were transferred to Gladstone to form a Gladstone-Oquawka High School. In 1950, voters approved by 228 to fourteen the formation of a Unit High School District.⁶⁸ And in 1953 they approved, again by a large majority, the creation of seven Grade School Districts.⁶⁹

By 1954, the old non-high school district (#200) was abolished.⁷⁰ In March of that year the Henderson County Board of School Trustees was organized. It would henceforth have control of all finances and have jurisdiction over intra-county school boundaries.⁷¹ The State Superintendent of Public Instruction visited the county and recommended specific improvements. He and his staff of five assistants discovered a critical need for additional building facilities because of the crowded conditions at both elementary and high school levels, especially at Oquawka, Biggsville, and Gladstone. He recommended that all children ages nine to

Biggsville High School

twelve be placed "under one roof." Lastly, he expressed the need for more and better instructional equipment.[72]

During the following years specific measures were undertaken to upgrade the system. A "School Support" program was pushed by the newspapers and a series of public meetings to discuss problems and solutions were announced. A bond issue of $850,000, however, was rejected in November, 1957 by 663 to 498 votes.[73] Undaunted, an Advisory Council was organized to focus on needed changes in the county and to "come up with an answer that will meet both state specifications and the voters approval."[74] The Council held meetings to show the public how adjacent areas at Carthage, Camp Point, and Warsaw had met their problems.[75] It developed a specific plan of consolidation.[76] A vote on consolidation of District 115 was taken in November and the voters of Oquawka, Biggsville, Gladstone, Rozetta, and Gulfport precincts approved by 767 to 531.[77] Impetus for consolidation in the southern part of the county came the following year from Stronghurst. The *Graphic Reporter* led the fight for support. In the winter of 1959, a petition for consolidation "to enhance the educational opportunities, the administrative facilities, and the economic stability of the community's school system" was presented to the Circuit Court.[78] A public hearing on the petition was held and in May the referendum was taken. The proposal was approved by 307 in favor to just fifty against.[79] The new Unit #116 school board was, accordingly, chosen that summer. Then, in August, a new County Superintendent elected that spring, Leman A. Dennison, took over his office at Oquawka.

By the early 1960s the county school system had envolved into two major districts each with its high school and seven grade schools.[80] Media-Wever functioned as a third district with a small high school. In the fall of that year there were 1,271 students enrolled in the elementary attendance centers and 445 pupils in the three high schools (just seventy-eight at Media).[81] There were seventy-one teachers on contract. Building programs accompanied administrative consolidation. Stronghurst expanded its high school in 1954. A new building, "Union High School" as it was to be called, was started in 1959. In 1964, District 116 voters approved a $60,000 bond issue. In 1969, voters sanctioned a $682,000 bond issue for alterations and additions at Biggsville, Gladstone, and Oquawka.[82] Ad-

Media High School

ministration was further refined. In compliance with state law the office of county superintendent was discontinued in 1969 and was replaced with a Regional Superintendent of Education, each region with a specified minimum number of inhabitants.[83]

Talks were begun in 1969 toward the joining of Units 116 and 103, Media-Wever, and the next year, after a series of public hearings, the vote was taken. The measure was approved overall by 779 to 433. But the rural precinct of Media voted 262 to 98 against the merger as did both the villages of Media (forty-two no, thirty-two yes) and Raritan (seventy-six no, twenty-three yes).[84] By the late sixties further innovations were seen in the development of an adult education program for the county. Approved by the Office of Public Instruction, courses were on a twelve week basis with classes of three hours once a week for high school credit. Tuition was only six dollars per class.[85] The county joined into a Junior College District with Hancock County and opened the doors to higher education to any student with a high school diploma.

By the mid 1970s the momentum for educational expansion stopped. Enrollments, following a steady decline of population in the county, fell off. State aid, accordingly, was cut. In 1977, the districts faced major budget slashes. Southern was reduced by $185,000 and Union by $85,000.[86] Teacher unrest appeared. As early as 1964 they had decried their salary schedule. Data then showed that teachers were receiving much less than the state or national average of $4,997 a year.[87] By the late seventies some teachers demanded union recognition. In 1981, the Board told the teachers in the Union District that a union was not acceptable. They informed Lee Wiggins, spokesman for the teachers union, that there could be no further discussions with the Board until teachers "dropped the idea of a union and collective bargaining."[88] Wiggins, who spoke for fifty of the sixty-four teachers in the Union Disrtict, demanded in turn, union recognition and a written contract on plant conditions and salaries. By the fall of 1984 the issue of a teachers' union and the school board came to a head. Early in September, the teachers of Unit 115 went on strike. The Union High School was shut down as were schools at Gladstone, Biggsville, and Oquawka. On October 10, the fifty teachers pledged to stand firm and to remain out of the classroom for the fifth consecutive day. The Board made the union an offer. A six-day negotiating

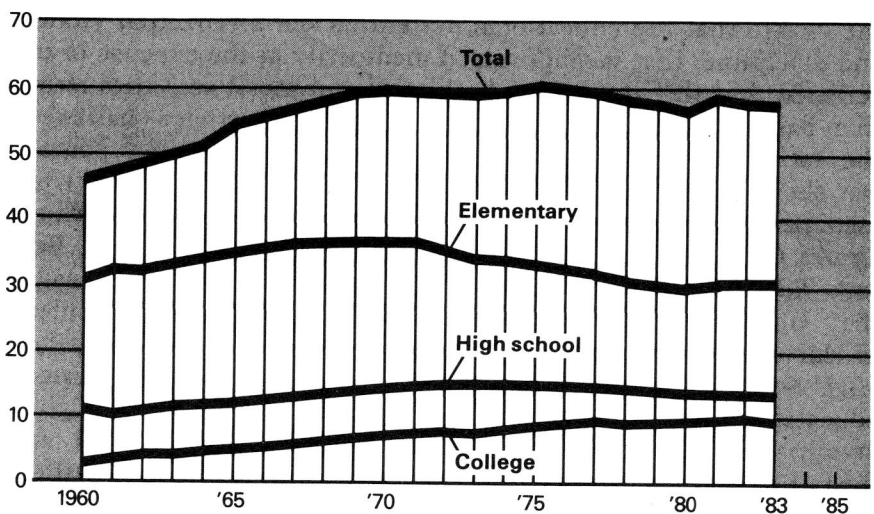

School Enrollment, by Level of Instruction: 1960-1983

School Enrollment Chart

Henderson County Courthouse

marathon began. Both sides called in mediators in the persons of Stephen G. Evans, Circuit Judge of the Ninth Judicial Circuit, and John Alexander. Finally, mediator Judge Evans announced an agreement. The teachers voted approval and on Wednesday, October 17, with a new contract, schools were reopened.

Like education, much of the voter's energy in the 1950s and 1960s was directed toward legal reform and improvements. The entire system of county justice was altered by changes in the local courts. And, looking at Springfield, Henderson county residents saw its delegates rewrite the state's fundamental law to adopt other modifications that would affect their daily lives for the rest of the century.

The County Court, established in 1848, was set up as trial and circuit court of procedure. Then, in 1870, it became a court of record as well. In 1939, the legislature increased the civil jurisdiction of county courts from $1,000 to $2,000. Until the 1960s there were two principle divisions in the system. One division called "law" dealt with civil and criminal matters. The other half was probate. The County Court then had concurrent jurisdiction with the Circuit Courts in all civil cases not over $2,000. The same overlap occurred in criminal matters where the punishment was not "in the penitentiary or death." It had sole control over probate settlements. Judges of the County Court were appointed by the elected judges of the Circuit Court and served as Associate Judges of the Circuit Court while serving on the county bench.

All this was reorganized in 1963 by statute. There would be no more Justices of the Peace, all misdemeanors and petty civil actions went to the Circuit Court Magistrate with five magistrates (paid a salary of $10,000) for each circuit. All court records were transferred to the Circuit Clerk's office. Most importantly, all County Courts in the state were terminated at the end of 1964 and all their functions were transferred to the Circuit Court. There would be only one local court for the citizens of Henderson County from then on, the Circuit Court of the Ninth Judicial Circuit, a jurisdiction that embraced not only Henderson County but the counties of Warren, Knox, Fulton, McDonough, and Hancock. Sitting county judges became one of seven Associate Judges of the Circuit Court and existing Justices of the Peace became Magistrates of the same circuit.

In 1970 Illinois received a new constitution and this document, among other important things, again revised the court system. The constitution was the fourth such fundamental law for the state and its sixth such convention to write one. By the Seventies there were demands for basic changes in the century-old document even though one of the most glaring problems, that of apportionment in the legislature, had been handled by amendment. The United States Supreme Court also had settled another problem, the constitutionality of the recent income tax law. Still the prevailing feeling was that after a century the whole framework needed re-examination. An election in 1968 on whether to call a convention, or Con-Con, was low-keyed and received two-to-one support.[89] Delegates to the convention were selected the following year. Each Senate District sent the top four people on a listing of up to ten candidates. Most delegates were unknown. Henderson County selected Lewis D. Wilson, Seymour Golden of Rock Island, and local men Kirk Johnson and William A. Armstrong.[90]

Circuit Courtroom, Oquawka

At Springfield, the 116 delegates first began work in the House of Representatives on December 8, 1969. Republicans controlled a majority, but lacked any political discipline. Soon they decided to continue deliberations in the historic setting of the restored Old Capitol Building. There they became balkanized into regional and local interest factions. Fortunately, though, because of a general feeling of temporary cohesiveness, or shared frustration, between the Chicago area and downstate delegates the interminable procrastinations of the 1920 Constitutional Convention were avoided. A new document was ready to be submitted for ratification by the late summer of 1970 and the ratification procedure was organized so as to weight the outcome in its favor. The constitution modernized the courts. Under the new law all former magistrates became associate judges and county associate judges became resident circuit judges. Henderson County though, was still designated as part of the Ninth Judicial Circuit. Four of the more debatable provisions were listed apart from the main document for approval or rejection. These issues were: (1) voting age lowered from twenty-one to eighteen years, (2) death penalty abolished, (3) status quo on election of judges, (4) state representatives continued from multimember districts.

The ratification vote was taken on November eighteenth. Of the four separate propositions the first two were defeated. The people, however, decided to keep their judges as elected officials. The old system of three representatives from each district also won approval. The new constitution itself was ratified by a state-wide vote of 1,122,425 to 838,168.[91] Henderson County residents were kept abreast of the details on the "Con Con" by a regular series of reports published in the *Graphic Reporter* by J. Otto Mees whose first article began in December 17, 1969, and continued almost weekly for the following eight months. Despite being fully informed, or because of the information, the voters went in the opposite direction of the state and other counties of western Illinois. They voted it down. The primary objection seems to have been the projected fear that the new constitution, by giving "unlimited power" to the legislature to increase taxes in the words of the *Graphic Reporter*, would certainly allow new state expenditures without the people's consent. The county vote was 1,270 against and just 465 in favor. Not one precinct in the county accepted the new document. Like the rest of the state, however, the county rejected the lowering of the voting age (1,162 no, 520 yes) and the abolishing of the death penalty (1,262 no, 402 yes).[92]

Despite county opposition the state had a new fundamental law which required a number of important changes in government. The legislature, by the new constitution, levied a new sales tax. All personal property taxes had to be eliminated within ten years. The legislature was now required to meet at least once every year. The executive branch had to be chosen from the same party. All secondary and primary schools were under the same board. The governor was given line-item veto authority over the budget. An expanded Bill of Rights required non-discrimination in employment practices and housing on the basis of race, sex or physical handicap.

The issues of changing the County Court or approving the new constitution were bi-partisan and, as such, were the exception to the pulse of county politics, which alligned itself along traditional party lines. By 1950, both parties campaigned vigorously although they started late in the political season, in September. The Democrats launched a motor caravan on September 5 and for the next seven weeks stopped at places throughout the county. Frequently, U.S. Senate minority leader Scott W. Lucas led the entourage. Biggsville's Ora Smith, then the state Treasurer, ran for Clerk of the Illinois Supreme Court and Michael Howlett ran for Smith's job.[94] The Republicans started about the same time with a "handshaking tour" of the towns and villages. Their man was the party's candidate for state Treasurer against Howlett, William G. Stratton. Also traveling throughout the county were Congressman Robert Chipperfield and state Senator Charles F. Carpentier.[95] On October 3, William McKinley Dirksen, candidate for the United States Senate, spoke at Stronghurst.

On Tuesday evening at 7:00 Dirksen addressed a large and enthusiastic crowd. He deplored the high taxes and high federal deficits which the Democratic party had laid on the nation. He heartily approved the new Taft-Hartley law and its anti-union provisions of requiring federal intervention to stop and prevent a strike. His address was pedagogical though. It "took the form of a lecture in elementary economics" the *Raritan Reporter* quipped.[96] On the crisis in Korea, then just underway, Dirksen's only comment was his concern that our intervention might result in increased federal income taxes.

The 1950 vote showed the resurrection of the Republican party. They swept into office both in the county and the nation. Only two Democrats were given pluralities in the county, Chris Apt for Superintendent of Schools, and George Voorhees for Sheriff. This time there was an amazing upswing in voter participation: 80 percent of the registered voters, an astonishingly high percentage of turnout in any recorded election.[97] Dirksen defeated Democrat Lucas by 2,310 to 1,534. Stratton topped Howlett by 2,351 to 1,328, and Smith lost the Clerkship by thirty votes. Charles Carpentier surged to victory over Virgil Bozeman of Moline by 2,230 to 1,468 in the county and by a majority of 7,500 in the district as a whole. Chipperfield won a seat in Congress from the 19th District by 2,275 to 1,398 in the county returns and in the district vote by 69,128 over his opponent, Jack Kerwin of Moline, 40,201.[98]

The Republican momentum continued in the presidential election of 1952. That year Clarence Neff entered politics by taking an appointment to fill the unexpired term of representative John McGovern as president of the Stronghurst Village Board.⁹⁹ Republicans were sent from the county to attend the state party convention in June at the State Armory in Springfield. Ben Hill, county chairman, went as a member of the Platform Committee. Other delegates included Loren Van Doren and Waldo Erickson of Raritan, Fred Gibb of Media, Fred Welch of Rozetta, Mark Moore of Bald Bluff, and from Oquawka Charles Brooks and Peter Hoskins.¹⁰⁰ The Democrats invited Governor Adali Stevenson to visit the county. In the summer of 1951 he addressed 1,500 people at a Friday evening fish fry at Shokokon.¹⁰¹ Some Democrats, the following summer, watched their governor receive the nomination of his party, for the first time, on their television sets.

The election was another Republican landslide. Eisenhower, the Republican nominee, carried every county precinct for a majority of 2,839 to 1,458 over Stevenson. Stratton won the governorship by a 1,134 majority and served in that office until he lost to Democrat Otto Kerner in 1960.¹⁰² Twice Stratton visited Henderson county. In September, 1956 he arrived at Stronghurst on a Friday afternoon and led a motorcade throughout the county. At Stronghurst he was introduced by Clarence Neff who by then was Republican Party County Chairman. In his remarks Stratton stressed his accomplishments as governor. In particular he noted that the county had received $889,000 for construction of roads and bridges. He stressed his commitment to improvement of all state institutions, especially in the care of the mentally ill.¹⁰³ In the fall of 1960 he conducted what was called a "Helicopter Campaign" of the county. In just one afternoon he personally visited Oquawka (at 12:20), Stronghurst (at 1:15) and Lomax (at 1:50).¹⁰⁴

The year of Stratton's helicopter campaign was the year of the presidential contest between John F. Kennedy and Richard M. Nixon. Little information survives about local reaction to these two candidates for by then television was the electioneering vehicle instead of the personal tours and public stand-in spokesmen. There was one expedition of Henderson County Republicans to Springfield to see Nixon in an October parade. John Richey and Clarence Neff organized the group which traveled to the Parade Grounds in the southern part of the capital.¹⁰⁵ The results of the November election gave the county to the Republicans, as expected. Nixon received 2,592 to Kennedy's 1,677 with only Carman and Gladstone going for the Democrat. Samuel W. Witwer won over Democrat Paul Douglas in the Senate contest by 3,196 to 1,869. And, against the statewide trend, Stratton got 2,250 votes to Kerner's 1,958.¹⁰⁶

The Sixties were a time of Republican consolidation of power in the county. Clarence Neff, with sure attention to details, became a leading party official, both in the county and at Springfield. In the 1962 primary he came in first for election as representative for the 15th District in a field of eight candidates. Neff swamped all opponents. He tallied 5,116 votes to his closest rival's 204. Dirksen, that year, clobbered his opponent 1,673 to 180. Overall, the general primary total Republican vote saw 2,098 registrants to 779 for the Democrats.¹⁰⁷ Neff received five significant committee assignments in Springfield and started a regular column in county newspapers called "Capitol News."¹⁰⁸ His main pitch to voters was the pledge to "fight overspending of taxpayers money and sound practices in state government." He helped form the "Economy Bloc" in the legislature. He plugged loopholes in the collection of state taxes.¹⁰⁹ In his third term in office he escalated opposition to state spending. He condemned "the state going into debt for the purposes [of bond issues] and

Charles Percy, Republican Candidate for Governor with Clarence E. Neff, State Representative

paying huge sums in interest to build buildings on the time payment plan."[110] He introduced bills to require motorcycle operators to wear crash helmets and to have automobile drivers charged with D.W.I. submit to a blood test or forfeit their license. By 1968, Neff was chairman of the powerful Banking and Savings & Loan Committee and chairman of the Legislative Republican Caucus.[111] He favored firearms control by requiring an owner's identification card to prevent criminals from buying firearms or ammunition. In 1964, Charles Percy came to the area to endorse Neff's re-election along with Percy's own bid, unsuccessful it turned out, for governor.

But 1964 was an off-year for the Republican party. President Kennedy had been assassinated in Dallas the previous fall.[112] President Johnson's Great Society program had captured a groundswell of sympathy for the fallen president and the Texan translated that feeling in Congress into a bipartisan support for liberal Democratic programs. Barry Goldwater came to the county and was photographed alongside Neff on the "Goldwater Special Train" in early October.[113] Percy spoke at Grandinetti's Supper Club and shared the head table with Earl Eisenhower, Ike's brother, and Robert McLoskey of Monmouth. Before the dinner Percy mingled with the crowd of about 600 people and gave a "concise explanation of his goals for Illinois" challenging incumbent Kerner on education, taxes, the economy, and of course, the political domination of Chicago in the legislature.[114] He lost anyhow. Percy did carry Henderson County by 2,118 to 1,858 but Kerner carried the state. McLoskey lost to Gale Schisler by 74,210 to 81,886 in the 19th District although, like Percy, McLoskey carried the county by a narrow margin of 2,099 to 1,949.

Goldwater lost the county, the state, and the nation. The stalwart Republican newspaper the *Graphic Reporter* was infuriated at the loss and blamed it all on the Senator from Arizona. "As the Republican candidate for president," it wrote, "he not only upset himself but also hundreds of other Republican candidates from county to national levels."[115] The county was Johnson's that year. He defeated Goldwater by 2,271 to 1,867 votes. It was an "all time straight Democratic vote."[116]

Two years later, on the off-year elections, the Republicans revived. Richard Nixon tried to help. He set up a large rally in Rock Island in hopes of aiding young Thomas Railsback in his first bid for Congress against Democrat Gal Schisler. Nixon, in earlier remarks at Macomb, referred to Railsback's fine qualifications for that office.[117] County Young Republicans chartered a bus for the Rock Island visit. Nixon never showed up. Railsback won on his own. He spoke throughout the district, from early spring on, at women's clubs, Rotaries, picnics, and party rallies. From the start he stressed his independence. He claimed to have voted independently "while serving as state Representative." He said that he "tried to consider each issue independently, giving due consideration to what will best serve the people of his district." "If elected Congressman," he promised, "I will do the same."[118] He defeated Schisler in the county returns by 1,949 to 1,735. In that same election Charles Percy captured the Senate seat held by Paul Douglas and carried the county by 2,183 to 1,501 votes.[119]

The Republican momentum continued through the 1968 presidential contest. Nixon defeated Humphrey in the county by 2,224 to 1,635, Ogilvie won the governorship race by 2,355 votes over Democrat S. Shapiro. Dirksen trounced William Clark by 2,530 to 1,516. Railsback won a second term over a challenge from Craig Lovitt by 2,488 to 1,538 and Neff was victorious by 4,337 in the county and was first of the three candidates in the 19th legislative district, polling over 70,000 votes.[120]

The year 1972 saw Governor Richard B. Ogilvie come to Delabar State Park for a Sunday afternoon fish fry. Addressing a crowd of over 3,000 persons he promised that "this area will soon have the best and finest and most improved roads of any area in the state." The people, believing what he promised, applauded enthusiastically.[121] The reapportionment of the 47th District in 1972 to include Hancock, McDonough, Henderson, Warren, and parts of Henry and Knox counties pulled Senator Clifford Latherow, a popular Republican from Fountain Green, into the ranks.[122]

Delabar State Park, current photo

Democrats in 1972 awakened, organized, and in the spring election of that year, under a new law in which members of the County Board were elected at large instead of from each township, captured control of the Board for the first time since the Depression.[123] At their initial meeting they chose Democrat D. Donald Pence of Lomax as Chairman. Governor Ogilvie headlined another fish fry in September and spoke in front of a crowd almost twice the size of the spring rally. The governor led a "parade of Republican candidates for state and district office across the speaker's platform for brief remarks.[124] Congressman Tom Railsback was master of ceremonies. In October a motor caravan of Republican candidates, headed by Clarence Neff and Clifford Latherow, toured the county stumping for their party and for the re-election of President Nixon.[125] On November first the *Graphic Reporter*, in bold headlines, predicted a high voter turnout: "Henderson County Out to Beat World Records on Nov. 7." They reported 5,300 registered voters in the county with only slightly more Republicans than Democrats.[126]

The turnout was unusually high, 85 percent of Henderson County voters went to the polls. They overwhelmingly, with many Democratic crossovers, voted for Nixon over George McGovern, by 2,681 to 1,744. Only Gladstone, Lomax, and Oquawka #2 stayed Democratic. Percy defeated Roman Puchinski by about the same ratio or 2,822 to 1,536. Ogilvie, however, lost to "Walkin" Dan Walker in a close race for governor, 2,119 to 2,328. Neff still outdistanced all other candidates by almost 1,800 votes ahead of his closest rival, Carrol Wilson.[127]

In 1972, the Republican ascendency in Henderson County had peaked. By that time a number of historic developments, some long-term and festering, others rather immediate in time, began to erode the sense of confidence in the political system and, in turn, cut away, by dissillusionment and apathy, in participation in the political process. Cynicism replaced the confidence of the previous decade. The two catalysts for the reversal of attitudes were the weariness of war and shock of Watergate.

War had been an unwanted intrusion, at best, on the people of the county since Korea. Simply put, most people in the county (and nation) felt that the sacrifices of World War II had purged the world of tyranny once and for all. Many veterans, when called upon just five years after being mustered out in 1945 to don the uniform again responded with patriotism but with little enthusiasm.

The Korean War began on June 25, 1950 when North Korean forces invaded South Korea across the 38th parallel, a Soviet-American line drawn after World War II dividing the country into Communist and Democratic zones. By August, the North Korean army occupied all of the southern half of the country except a small enclave in the southeast around the city of Pusan. America was taken by surprise. President Truman, already stung by the recent fall of China to the Communists, was determined to halt any further advances in Asia. Recalling England's reluctance to face up to Nazi advances in Europe in the 1930s, the President adopted a Churchillian pose. He would not back down. If unchallenged, this new threat of Communist tyranny, he said, would lead to another World War.[128]

Truman placed General MacArthur, then in Japan, in full command. He got the Security Council of the United Nations, when the Soviet Union with its potential veto was absent, to approve America's "peace keeping" action in Korea to "repel aggression and restore Peace." He ordered naval and air forces into battle. Then the Marines landed in amphibious assaults behind North Korean lines. Army troops were committed. By October, after a daring invasion by MacArthur at Inchon, the North Koreans retreated to the Chinese border. The next month, however, the Chinese invaded in a massive counter-attack. Americans were pushed below the 38th parallel and the war settled into a stalemate.

MacArthur bridled under restraints of Truman's orders not to invade China and publicly challenged the President's ability. Truman, as Commander-in-Chief, fired him.[129] Truce talks started in 1953 but bogged down while the fighting continued, without purpose it seemed. At last, on July 27, 1953, an armistice was signed. In the previous three years 34,000 Americans had died. Military expenditures soared from $13 billion in 1950 to $60 billion in 1953. The war caused budget priorities to reverse: more money for the military and less for the needs of the American people. New questions were asked which had never been asked before. Why could we not win the war? What was wrong with us, the strongest nation on earth, that we could not subdue a small insurrection in a backward little country in Asia? Who, or what, was undermining the American cause at home?

The initial reaction to the protracted war was for voters to kick out the person responsible for it. In 1952, the Republicans ran Dwight Eisenhower on a campaign that focused on Korea. Indeed, they had a contradictory pitch. On one hand, they blamed the Democrats for the war and Ike pledged that, if elected, he would end it. "I shall go to Korea," was his slogan. On the other hand, Republicans charged that the Democrats were "soft on Communism" at home and that some Democrats themselves had a historic sympathy with Socialism and other dangerous "un-American" ideas.

The Democrats met in Chicago and, with Truman refusing to run, chose Illinois Governor Adali Stevenson as their standard bearer. Stevenson, unlike Truman in 1948, seemed not to know what to do with these charges. He appeared uncertain as to how to deal with being called a war monger against Communism in Korea and the leader, or at least tolerant, of Communist subversion at home. Ike won in a landslide. He captured 55 percent of the popular vote, thirty-nine states, and 442 electoral votes. Stevenson carried just nine states, and eighty-nine electoral votes. The Republicans, for the first time since before the Depression, got control of the House of Representatives and tied for control of the Senate. Henderson County, like the nation, gave Ike an overwhelming majority even against their own favorite son. Eisenhower received 2,839 to Stevenson's 1,458 votes.[130]

The news about Korea, to Henderson County, meant news of casualties. There was little in the newspapers about events of the fighting itself and only veiled references to a potential "victory," in marked contrast to the jingoistic rhetoric of a decade before. For almost a year there was nothing about the war except a few notices, and photographs, of men in the service. But by the fall of 1951, the grimmer news appeared. On September 27, 1951 the *Raritan Reporter* wrote that Wade Meloan had received a telegram that his son Don had been wounded. Robert Norville of Stronghurst lost the use of his left hand and suffered bodily injuries in an exploding booby trap. Dean McIntyre was killed on October 17, 1952. On October 30, his wife gave birth to his son, Dean Ivan Jr. at a Burlington hospital.[131] Harry L. Alecock, Jr., of Rozetta was killed in September, 1952. He had graduated from the Biggsville High School in May, 1950. Others were more fortunate. PFC James H. Cook of Raritan, who enlisted in June, 1951, was selected as "Today's Serviceman" by the *Raritan Reporter* and, in June of 1953 returned home uninjured from Saseto, Japan.[132]

Indochina became another Asian battlefield, Almost as soon as Americans had extricated themselves from Korea they became entangled in the politics of war in Vietnam. That country had long been a colony of France and France, seriously weakened by World War II, could not hold on to power against the rising forces of nationalism led by Ho Chi Minh. Truman was the first President to become concerned with the outcome of these developments. To him, the fall of France in Southeast Asia meant the spread of Communism and the replacement of a western power in that region with a government linked to Moscow. Truman saw Communism as monolithic. If a piece of Southeast Asia succumbed to it the whole of the subcontinent would fall. He gave the French economic aid but refused to provide any direct military help.

Eisenhower saw the French lose Vietnam. In 1954, their main fortress at Dien Bien Phu fell and France pulled out of Saigon. Ike saw all Southeast Asia falling like a row of dominos. Burma and Indonesia were, in his mind, to be followed soon afterwards by Japan, the Philippines, Australia, and New Zealand. Yet Ike was not prepared to have America rescue Vietnam. He believed that only a "sudden, unforseen emergency" could justify unilateral military intervention. In 1956, with Vietnam divided in half by a Geneva Convention, the problem seemed temporarily under control. The Convention, however, required national elections to be held the following year. The Diem government in South Vietnam, supported by President Eisenhower, refused to hold them.

By the time Kennedy was elected President, American economic aid to Diem had increased and Ike had sent the first 675 military advisors to Saigon. Eisenhower told Kennedy, privately in the Oval Office on Inauguration Day, 1961 of his fears. Pointing to a global map he noted Southeast Asia and said to Kennedy, "This is one of the problems I'm leaving you that I'm not happy about. We may have to fight."[133] Kennedy, despite later doubts, sent in American troops to help the Diem Regime, over 16,000 of them.

After Kennedy's death Lyndon Johnson drew the line. He, like Truman, believed that the Communists had to be stopped in South Vietnam or we would have a World War III. Like Ike, he believed, too, in the domino theory of Communist advance in the South Pacific. But Johnson, unlike Presidents before him, expanded the American commitment in Vietnam enormously. Johnson "took the Vietnam War and made it his own."[134] In August, 1964 he got Congress to approve a cleverly-worded statement, the Gulf of Tonkin Resolution, allowing the President to deploy military force to defend American ships against aggression. He said of the Resolution that it was "like Grandma's nightshirt—it covered everything."[135]

Military escalation followed. By 1965 there were 184,000 ground troops in Vietnam and American planes were bombing targets in the northern part of the country. By 1966, there were 485,000 American troops there and in 1968 the figure went over one-half million. Massive American supplies were sent. Saturation bombing was begun. The North Vietnamese, in 1968, counterattacked. In a January offensive they overran provincial capitals and struck at the American embassy in Saigon. They attacked the American air base and the Presidential palace in the capital. At home, over evening television news, Americans saw for the first time the awful reality of the combat. They also saw that the war could not be won. They became disillusioned.

The earliest signs of the war in Henderson County appeared in 1966 in speeches by Senators Dirkson and Percy. In February of that year, Dirkson, addressing a Republican dinner, asserted that America "must win in Vietnam." "If Vietnam falls," he warned, "so will fall other countries and the defenses of this country will become closer and closer to our coast."[136] Percy had a different perspective. Addressing an audience at Grandinetti's Supper Club that August he called for "a way to bring this tragic conflict to an honorable solution." He suggested that the "Asiatic powers" get together to work out a settlement.[137]

In general, newspaper coverage of the war in the beginning was exaggerated patriotism. Stories of the suffering of the Vietnamese people at "the hands of cruel invading Communists" were regular features.[138] A Henderson County TRAIN Committee, a right-wing pro-victory group, showed films portraying the "method by which the Communists came to power in China, Algeria, and Cuba with the same strategy being implemented here in the U.S. today."[139] Other people, like Quincy editor and minister Richard Hurley, told forty persons in a Stronghurst fire station that "we could win the war in six weeks" if the restrictions on American military power were removed." We had to stop "the present trade and aid to European Communist countries because they were providing eighty percent of the war material to North Vietnam."[140] Green Beret veteran Tom Hollingsworth told a large audience in the LaHarpe Club House in June, 1968 that "the Communist strategy of divide and conquer, so successful in Vietnam, was now seen in operation in the United States."[141] In March, 1969, Lt. Colonel Jack Mohr, in a month-long tour of the area, spoke for a half-hour on "The Missing Alternative is Victory." Mohr told of his capture, torture, and "miraculous escape" from the "Korea Communists." He denounced restrictions on the military such as those that, he said, had prolonged the Korean conflict.[142]

Henderson County saw the effects of war not only on their television sets but in their newspapers. At first the news was positive, a pride in local boys who were fighting there. Featured articles appeared, for example, on Airman Harold Goff or Seaman Arnols.[143] Exaggerated reports of enemy casualties were reprinted without question. But in January, 1968 the bad news started. On January 25, the *Graphic Reporter* told that Sergeant Herley Ayers Jr., brother of Mrs. Marjorie Laws of Stronghurst, was killed.[144] Lt. Milford Don Isaacson, also of Stronghurst, was killed in

Don Isaacson, Stronghurst, 1970

combat early in 1970. Lance Corporal John O. Waterman of Biggsville was wounded in the left groin and pelvic area.[145] Sergeant Richard H. Jamison also received a Purple Heart for severe wounds in both legs.[146] PFC Michael Robbins of Oquawka was seriously wounded in the abdomen.[147]

About the same time as the casualty reports filtered back to the county there was a noticeable change in the attitude toward the war. By 1970, the demand for a quick victory had stopped. The name-calling of "communist sympathizer" had disappeared. President Nixon himself reflected the new perspective when in November, 1969 he approved of the withdrawal of American forces as the first step to end the war. "The majority of the residents of Henderson County," wrote the *Graphic Reporter*, "approve of the gradual withdrawal Vietnam peace plan as outlined by President Nixon." It was, overall, a "safe, sane, and honorable plan."[148] Nixon asserted that the South Vietnamese themselves should take over the fighting. The shocking episode of American's massacring innocent women and children at My Lai further caused many Americans to wonder about our conduct of the war. Nixon, though, in 1970, tried one last offensive, an invasion of Cambodia. It, too, failed to bring North Vietnam to terms. In 1971, the overall Vietnamese war policy was seriously undermined by the publication of the Pentagon Papers. The material gave documented proof of fabrications about the conduct of the war and the faulty assumptions which had escalated the United State's involvement.

By 1972, the war had become a political albatross, a serious problem in Nixon's upcoming re-election campaign. Accordingly, diplomatic peace moves under Nixon's National Security Advisor Henry Kissinger were intensified. Kissinger was able to announce just before the fall elections: "Peace is at hand." For a while the North Vietnamese balked but early in 1973 the talks in Paris began and by the end of the year a cease-fire was agreed upon and signed. Kissinger, for his efforts, was awarded the Nobel Peace Prize.

The longest war in American history was over. Fifty-seven thousand Americans were dead and more than 300,000 wounded or maimed for life. It cost the nation $150 billion. Congressman Railsback, in his "Railsback Speaks from Washington" column, echoed a sense of many of his constituents, and of the nation itself, when in February 1973, he wrote:

> "In my opinion, no one in this country would ever want to be involved in another war like Vietnam. We paid a terribly high price. It is imperative that Congress act now to reassert its constitutional perogatives and establish firm guidelines to be followed if future hostilities should occur. I believe most members of Congress, be they conservative, liberal, or moderate, would subscribe to this policy."[149]

They did subscribe and Congress passed the War Powers Act of 1973 which, by law, prevented any future President from commiting America to war without the approval of Congress in its legitimate and sole power to declare war.

At the same time that the Congress, in the War Powers Act, was reasserting its historic role in foreign policy it had also set out on a course of action designed to offset a dangerous increase in Presidential power in domestic affairs. It had started to investigate what became known shortly as "Watergate." President Nixon, by 1972, felt beseiged. Frustrated by

Congressman Railsback, c. 1970

the course of events in Vietnam and by mounting criticism of the war at home he felt ever more put upon by his enemies. People did not seem to understand that he wanted out of that war, not to increase the casualty lists. It was the Vietnamese themselves, in both the North and the South, who were prolonging the agony. No one seemed to understand, he felt, that he was doing his best. No one seemed to understand, in Nixon's mind, except a loyal group of close friends. It was this almost paranoid attitude of the President, fully ripened by 1972, combined with the fanatic loyalty of his aids that brought about Watergate. And it was Watergate which brought down Richard M. Nixon.

The President asked his close advisers to organize his campaign for re-election in 1972. Headed by men such as Attorney General John Mitchell, Special Counsel Charles W. Colson and John Dean, and employing specialists like E. Howard Hunt and G. Gordon Liddy (former operatives for the CIA and FBI) they set in motion a series of steps to sabotage the Democratic Party in the upcoming contest. The Committee to ReElect the President, known as CREEP, drew up an inventory of prominent individuals who had opposed policies of the Nixon Administration. This was the "enemies list." They organized a group of men to seek out and stop what were labeled as security leaks such as the Pentagon Papers. The group called themselves the Plumbers. CREEP launched a massive campaign fund-raising drive to beat the new federal law which would soon demand public disclosure and limitation of all such money. The Plumbers installed wiretaps on various Democrats and considered a bizarre plan to disrupt their nominating convention with bribes and prostitutes. Early in June, 1972 Attorney General Mitchell authorized the wiretapping of the Democratic national headquarters in the Watergate apartment complex in Washington. On June 16, the nightwatchman at the building, Frank Wills, noticed that two doors leading to an underground garage had been taped to keep them from locking shut. He telephoned the police. At 2:20 in the morning five men were arrested.

In the following summer months the story began to develop. It was established that the Plumbers were in charge of the break-in. CREEP had raised the money to pay them not only before the break-in but afterwards as well to keep them from disclosing information. The White House covered up. E. Howard Hunt's name was removed from all White House directories. Nixon's chief of staff, H.R. Haldeman, told the FBI to cut back on the investigation because of "matters of national security." President Nixon said that John Dean's complete investigation had revealed that no one in his administration was involved in the break-in. Early in 1973, Federal District Judge John Sirica tried the burglars. At the hearing, one of the burglars, James McCord, implicated CREEP. In May, the Senate Select Committee on Campaign Practices, chaired by Senator Sam Ervin, began its investigation. In front of television cameras John Dean said there had been a White House coverup. Another administration aid, Alexander Butterfield, told about a secret taping system in Nixon's office where discussions about Watergate had been recorded.

Nixon stonewalled. He fired his two top aides, Haldeman and Ehrlichman, and told a television audience: "There will be no whitewash at the White House." He appointed a Special Prosecutor, Archibald Cox of Harvard Law School, to look into the matter. Cox asked to hear the tapes. Nixon fired him. He named another Special Prosecutor, Leon Jaworski, and at the same time fired Elliot Richardson, the new Attorney General who had chosen Cox in the first place, and his deputy William Ruckelshaus, in the

"Saturday Night Massacre." Vice President Agnew resigned that same month, pleading no-contest to charges of accepting bribes and tax evasion.

Newspaper reporters, especially from the *Washington Post*, dug for more information which they got from an anonymous White House informant called "Deep Throat." He implicated Nixon himself. Nixon, the next spring, finally released part of the tapes but again denied any knowledge of the cover-up. But the tapes were edited and full of crucial gaps. The Judiciary Committee of the House began to draft articles of impeachment. On July 24, 1974, the Supreme Court ordered Nixon to turn over all of the tapes to Judge Sirica. The House Committee voted for impeachment of the President. On August 5, Nixon gave Sirica the tapes. On August 9, 1974, the President resigned.[150]

Reaction to the events of Watergate in Henderson County was a sparse embarrassment. Only Congressman Railsback issued public statements. At first he was simply "appalled" by the events of the bizarre case. He felt that Nixon would rise to the responsibility of initiating necessary "action to open this case to the public to restore their confidence...." He cautioned restraint. "It is of paramount importance," he wrote in May, 1973, "that we avoid extremes and maintain a balanced perspective." "Until all the facts are available to us," he concluded, "it is imperative that we reserve judgment on all those implicated or associated with the Watergate scandal."[151] Railsback reported in the fall that "many of my constituents" wanted a quick resolution to the affair and prosecution of the guilty parties.[152] By the fall of 1973 Railsback was talking about a "shaken" and "disillusioned" American people.[153] On the "Saturday Night Massacre" he wrote of a "public outrage and outcry." He stated flatly that he would "accept nothing less" than a "totally independent prosecutor." He sensed by then that "our government stands at an important crossroads."[154] On television, the following summer, Railsback voted in favor of Nixon's impeachment. When the President quit, Railsback was relieved. His resignation was unavoidable and served to "short circuit the inevitable result of removal." Railsback ended with the hope that "we will see a united effort behind the new President Gerald Ford and direct attention to the urgent problems that confront us...."[155]

A week after Nixon resigned the Democrats in Henderson County held a fish fry at Delabar Park. The next month Republicans did the same thing at the same place. Politics returned to normal.[156] In that fall's off-year elections Railsback was returned to Washington with a sizeable county majority of 2,146 votes over his opponent Jim Gerdel's 1,543. Neff's voting plurality shrank, however. He received a total district vote of 3,603 with Democrat Sam McGrew of Galesburg, running 3,006 and fellow-Republican McMaster coming in with 2,337.[157] Democrats controlled the county board by six to five members. In 1976, Kenny McMillan replaced Clifford A. Latherow in the Illinois Senate.[158] In 1976, Jimmy Carter replaced Ford as President and Ford barely carried the county with his 2,210 to Carter's 2,152 vote.[159] Governor Thompson began his terms as governor that year and on the following years twice visited the county to stump for Neff, McMillan, and Railsback.[160] President Carter, too, passed by the county in the summer of 1979 on a steamboat trip on the Mississippi and at Burlington he shook hands with leading county Democrats.[161]

Oquawka Mayor Barbara Lumbeck presenting basket of Oquawka melons to President Carter, 1979

Carter's sojourn did him no good in the upcoming election. He lost the county to Ronald Reagan by 1,609 to 2,443. That year Railsback was still

Levee and Drainage Ditch, current photo
The draining of the Mississippi River bottoms in Henderson County began in 1912. Drainage District #1 consisting of 6034 acres lies north of the Burlington railroad tracks; District #2 (6427 acres) lies south of the tracks and District #3 (2186 acres) is south of Oquawka. Land that went begging at $15 per acre before draining sold for $100 per acre two years later. Draining the swamp land east of Burlington permitted construction of present Route 34 and the building of the MacArthur bridge which was completed March 29, 1917.

MacArthur Bridge, current photo

popular with over 70 percent of the voters casting their ballot for him. The next election year, though, he lost the Republican primary to Ken McMillan and McMillan, in the 1980 election, lost the House of Representatives seat to a Democrat, Lane Evans of Rock Island. In 1983, Clarence Neff retired from politics.[162] Zack Stamp, a Republican protege of Governor Thompson, tried to take his place in Springfield but in 1984 he was defeated by Macomb attorney Kent Slater.[163]

And so, basic rhythms of life returned to Henderson County. Within memory its people had gone through World War I, the Great Depression, three more wars, a technological revolution, and Watergate. They had endured. To be sure, problems remained. A farm crisis of major proportions loomed with few solutions in sight. The Lomax Canning Company had gone out of business. All the movie houses were shut down. Population overall was declining steadily except for an unusual spurt of growth west of Gladstone due to the immigration of Burlington families seeking lower real estate taxes in Illinois. A few changes dotted the landscape. There was a modernized courthouse, one of the two oldest such buildings in Illinois still in continuous operation. The first additions to the structure were put on in 1965 and in 1978 the courtroom was extensively refurbished. Oquawka had a new paper, the *Current*, which began its publication that same year. Centering attention on local features the editor, Gus Hart, brought a heightened awareness to his readers of the heritage, both present and past, of their county.

But as this historian crisscrossed Henderson County in the summer of 1983 a sense of deja vu came over him. There was, at first, a feeling of melancholy as I looked out of my car window at acres and acres of corn and beans and no homes, no farm buildings, no livestock, no fences. If I stopped and got out of the car on almost any blacktop there was the silence. A redwing blackbird might protest my presence but the crickets, unaware, hummed their ritual in the soaring August heat. No one was around. It was as if the landscape were returning, gradually, to the way it had been 150 years ago.

The melancholy turned more often than not to reverence. I saw the county as it had once appeared in the eyes of its first settlers. Then the treeless lands had inspired a promise of a new life for those who had come west. Then Henderson County held an inspiration equal to man's capacity to wonder. Now, of course, the prairie grass was replaced by corn and beans. Yet, the great green fields of the Republic spread out, as always, forever.

END NOTES FOR CHAPTER NINE

[1] *Henderson County Graphic* July, 1962.
[2] *Raritan Reporter*, July 11, 1946; March 23, 1950; January 9, 1954.
[3] Ibid., July 7, 1954; October 12, 1961; *Henderson County Graphic Reporter*, September 26, 1963.
[4] Henderson County *Quill*, September 25, 1974.
[5] *Raritan Reporter*, April 26, 1951.
[6] Ibid., September 10, 1969.
[7] *Henderson County Graphic Reporter*, February 16, 1956.
[8] Ibid.
[9] Ibid., March 15, 1956.
[10] Ibid., May 22, 1968.
[11] Ibid., January 20, 1971.
[12] Ibid., February 7, 1973.
[13] Ibid., December 27, 1973.

[14] Ibid., January 31, 1973.
[15] *Raritan Reporter,* August 10, 1950.
[16] Ibid., October 4, 1951.
[17] *Quill,* November 28, 1973.
[18] *Raritan Reporter,* March 5, April 9, 1975.
[19] *Quill,* November 2, 1977.
[20] Ibid., January 4, 1978.
[21] Ibid., October 21, 1979.
[22] Ibid., January 30, 1980.
[23] Ibid., October 7, 1981.
[24] *Henderson County Graphic,* September 23, 1954.
[25] *Henderson Graphic Reporter,* March 15, 1956.
[26] *Raritan Reporter,* April 27, 1956.
[27] *Henderson County Journal,* May 6, 1965.
[28] *Graphic Reporter,* May 2, 1973.
[29] *Graphic,* September 20, 1954.
[30] *Graphic Reporter,* August 2, 16, 1962.
[31] Ibid., September 20, October 11, 1962.
[32] *Quill,* March 19, 1975 Keith A. Schulle, "Jacob Allaman, Covered Bridge Builder: A Case Study," Journal of the Illinois State Historical Society (Summer 1983) pp 139-49.
[33] Ibid., June 14, 1982.
[34] Ibid., August 30, 1983.
[35] Ibid., September 12, 1984. In 1986 the Illinois Department of Transportation was given a First Place Award by the Federal Highway Administration for their work in "Historical Preservation and Cultural Enhancement." The restoration of the covered bridge was cited as instrumental in the achievements meeting the federal requirements.
[36] Ibid., September 28, 1983.
[37] Ibid., September 27, 1984.
[38] Ibid., February 12, 1978.
[39] Ibid., March 19, 1980.
[40] Ibid., July 7, 1976.
[41] Ibid., June 1, 1977.
[42] Ibid., September 9, 1981.
[43] Ibid., May 28, 1975.
[44] Ibid., May 18, 1983.
[45] *Raritan Reporter,* August 8,9,16, 1946; July 3, 1954.
[46] Ibid., July 23, 1953.
[47] Ibid., September 11, 1952.
[48] Ibid., January 11, 1951.
[49] Ibid., November 20, 1952.
[50] Ibid., June 19, 1951.
[51] Ibid., February 9, 1953.
[52] *Graphic,* January 24, 1954.
[53] *Graphic Reporter,* June 16, 1958.
[54] Ibid., October 12, 1959.
[55] Ibid., June 8, 1961.
[56] *Raritan Reporter,* October 11, 1951.
[57] *Graphic Reporter,* May 6, 1954.
[58] Ibid., August 19, 1970.
[59] Ibid., September 21, 1967.
[60] *Raritan Reporter,* October 9, 1951.
[61] *Graphic Reporter,* August 20, 1956.
[62] Ibid., May 4, 1961.
[63] Ibid., October 17, 1963.
[64] Ibid., September 1, 1966; March 16, 1967.

Carthage Lake Pumping Station, current photo

River Bottom Irrigation System, current photo

Biggsville Quarry, current photo

Laying 36" pipeline for Galesburg water supply, 1958

[65] *Quill,* August 15, 1984.
[66] *Graphic Reporter,* May 19, 1971.
[67] Ibid., April 5, 1972.
[68] *Raritan Reporter,* March 23, 1956.
[69] Ibid., May 21, 1953.
[70] *Graphic,* February 11, 1954.
[71] Ibid., March 18, 1954.
[72] *Graphic Reporter,* June 10, 1956.
[73] Ibid.
[74] Ibid., February 28, 1958.
[75] Ibid., May 1, 1958.
[76] Ibid., July 24, 1958.
[77] Ibid., November 20, 1958.
[78] Ibid., February 2, 1959.
[80] The High School at Terre Haute had been closed and its students bused to the La Harpe High School in Hancock County. See Ibid., November 3, 1960.
[81] Ibid., November 17, 1960.
[82] Ibid., May 21, 1969.
[83] Ibid., September 17, 1969.
[84] Ibid., March 10, 1971.
[85] Ibid., December 28, 1967.
[86] *Quill,* November 9, 1977.
[87] *Graphic Reporter,* January 30, 1964.
[88] *Quill,* July 1, 1981.
[89] Howard, *Illinois,* pp 563-67.
[90] *Graphic Reporter,* September 17, 23, 1969.
[91] Howard, *Illinois,* p. 564.
[92] *Graphic Reporter,* December 9, 1970.
[93] *Raritan Reporter,* April 6, 1950 showed a low point in party battles in the county when only 25 percent of the registered voters bothered to turn out for the primary.
[94] Ibid., September 7, 1950.
[95] Ibid.
[96] Ibid., September 21, 1950.
[97] Ibid., November 7, 1950.
[98] Ibid.
[99] Ibid., April 10, 1952.
[100] Ibid., June 26, 1952.
[101] Ibid., July 19, 1951.
[102] Ibid., November 17, 1952.
[103] *Graphic Reporter,* September 28, 1956.
[104] Ibid., October 13, 1956.
[105] Ibid., October 13, 1960.
[106] Ibid., November 11, 1960.
[107] Ibid., April 12, 1962.
[108] Ibid., February 7, 1963.
[109] Ibid., January 9, 1969.
[110] Ibid., January 27, 1965.
[111] Ibid., February 15, 1968.
[112] Ibid., November 28, 1964.
[113] Ibid., October 8, 1964.
[114] Ibid., October 26, 1964.
[115] Ibid., November 5, 1964.
[116] Ibid.
[117]
[118] Ibid., May 12, 1966.

[119] Ibid., November 9, 1966.
[120] Ibid., November 10, 1968.
[121] Ibid., October 19, 1969.
[122] Ibid., March 15, 1972.
[123] Ibid., April 5, 1972.
[124] Ibid., September 20, 1972.
[125] Ibid., October 23, 1972.
[126] Ibid., November 1, 1972.
[127] Ibid., November 8, 1972.
[128] For further details see Bruce Cummings, *The Origins of the Korean War* (New York, 1980) and Glenn D. Paige, *The Korean Decision* (New York, 1968).
[129] John W. Spaniel, *The Truman-MacArthur Controversy and the Korean War* (New York, 1959) gives the first full account of this constitutional crisis.
[130] Elmo Richardson, *The Presidency of Dwight D. Eisenhower* (New York, 1979).
[131] *Raritan Reporter,* October 30, 1952.
[132] Ibid., January 19, June 4, 1953.
[133] Quoted in Morrison, Commager, Leuchtenburg *American Republic,* v. II, p. 756.
[134] Wash, *American People,* v. II, p. 936.
[135] Ibid., p. 937.
[136] *Graphic Reporter,* February 10, 17, 1966.
[137] Ibid., August 18, 1966.
[138] Ibid., February 10, 1966; March 2, 1967; May 1, June 19, 1968.
[139] Ibid., July 17, 1968.
[140] Ibid., May 1, 1968.
[141] Ibid., June 19, 1968.
[142] Ibid., March 12, 1969.
[143] Ibid., March 10, 1966.
[144] Ibid., January 25, 1968.
[145] Ibid., March 18, 1970.
[146] Ibid., November 18, 1970.
[147] Ibid., November 19, 1969.
[148] Ibid., November 5, 1969.
[149] Ibid., February 21, 1973.
[150] Watergate literature includes John W. Dean, *Blind Ambition* (New York, 1976) Jim Hougan, *Secret Agenda* (New York, 1984); J. Anthony Lukas, *Nightmare: The Underside of the Nixon Years* (New York, 1976). Theodore White, *Breach of Faith* (New York, 1975) gives the most sympathetic account of Nixon's conduct. Bob Woodward and Carl Bernstein, *The Final Days* (New York, 1976) write of the story from the other perspective.
[151] *Quill,* May 9, 1973.
[152] Ibid., September 19, 1973.
[153] Ibid., October 24, 1973.
[154] Ibid., November 7, 1973.
[155] Ibid., August 14, 1974.
[156] Ibid., August 21, September 18, 1974.
[157] Ibid., November 6, 1974.
[158] Ibid., November 19, 1975.
[159] Ibid., November 7, 1976.
[160] Ibid., September 21, 1976; September 27, 1978.
[161] Ibid., August 22, 1979.
[162] Ibid., November 16, 1983.
[163] Ibid., November 23, 1983; Feb. 8, March 14, 1984.

Jinks Hollow, Oquawka, current photo

Hog Thief Hollow, Gladstone, current photo

Lock and Dam 18 - Completed in September 1937
One of 12 navigation structures operated by the Rock Island District.

Twomey Company 35,000,000 bushel grain storage faility at Gladstone.
Total company storage capacity in Henderson-Warren Counties is 48,000,000 bushels

Remaining concrete base of tower at Walbaum Quarry East of Gladstone

LIST OF ILLUSTRATIONS
Unless otherwise noted all illustrations are the property of the Henderson County Historical Society.

Title	Page
Military Tract — Reproduced from *Illinois: A History of the Prairie State* with permission of Robert P. Howard	4
Land Grant Document — Reproduced from *A Commemorative History of Champaign County* with permission	7
Map of Black Hawk War — Reproduced from *Illinois: A History of the Prairie State* with permission of Robert P. Howard	19
Jack's Mill Bridge — Reproduced with permission of Glen Meyer	32
Jack's Mill — Reproduced with permission of Glen Meyer	33
Slaon Hall — Reproduced with permission of Louise Milligan	40
Biggsville Methodist Church — Reproduced with permission of Louise Milligan	42
J.B. Patterson — Reproduced with permission of Henderson County Quill	44
Union Army Soldier — Reproduced with permission of Francis Haney	50
Packet Steamboat — Reproduced with permission of Eileen Nolan	52
Union Army Veterans, Raritan — Reproduced with permission of Joyce Arnold	56
Olena Cornet Band — Reproduced with permission of Raymond Johnson	94
William 'Billy' Lee — Reproduced with permission of John L. Allaman	98
Jessie McCarty — Reproduced with permission of John L. Allaman	99
E.O. Barnes — Reproduced with permission of John L. Allaman	107
Oquawka Button Factory — Reproduced with permission of Chauncey Peters	114
Button Factory Workers — Reproduced with permission of Eileen Nolan	114
Button Blanks — Reproduced with permission of Robert Reeder	114
Biggsville - Early Scene — Reproduced with permission of Louise Milligan	115
One Horse Saloon — Reproduced with permission of Gillette Dixon	115
Raritan Opera House — Reproduced with permission of Mary Overstreet	117
Sterling L. Morelock — Reproduced with permission of John L. Allaman	120
Men leaving for Army — Reproduced with permission of Charles Allaman	122
Burg Auto — Reproduced with permission of John Haigh	127
Lomax Airplane — Reproduced with permission of J.D. Brand	128
August Wiegand — Reproduced with permission of Louise Milligan	135
Media State Bank — Reproduced with permission of Wayne Gearhart	136
Wever Academy burning — Reproduced with permission of Frank Butler	138
Oquawka Light Plant — Reproduced with permission of Eileen Nolan	142
Governor Small — Reproduced with permission of Louise Milligan	148
Paving Rt. 8 — Reproduced with permission of Louise Milligan	149
Chris Apt — Reproduced with permission of Mrs. Hugh Yaley	151
Lynn Hotel — Reproduced with permission of Louise Milligan	153
Olson Farm — Reproduced with permission of Fred Olson	158
Stronghurst Bank — Reproduced with permission of Helen Ryan	163
Bank of Oquawka — Reproduced with permission of Gillette Dixon	167
Burkett Harware Store — Reproduced with permission of Louise Milligan	168
Edna Barnes Simonson — Reproduced with permission of Bob and Marcia Simonson	169
Business Section - Media — Reproduced with permission of Arthur Kane	174
Oquawka Riverfront — Reproduced with permission of Robert Reeder	194
C.A. Hartquist — Reproduced with permission of Jan Rehm	195
Oquawka Gas Station — Reproduced with permission of Gillette Dixon	197
Rubber Tire Collection — Reproduced with permission of Gillette Dixon	200
Fred Olson crew — Reproduced with permission of Fred Olson	202
Ray Shafer — Reproduced with permission of Ray Shafer	203
John Allaman — Reproduced with permission of John H. Allaman	203
John Olson — Reproduced with permission of Fred Olson	204
Donald Gipe — Reproduced with permission of Dwain Gipe	204
Clarence Gibb — Reproduced with permission of Lucille Fort	207
Covered Bridge — Reproduced with permission of Eileen Nolan	218
Restoring Covered Bridge — Reproduced with permission of Robert Reeder	218
Neff & Percy — Reproduced with permission of Clarence E. Neff	229
Donald Isaacson — Reproduced with permission of Mrs. Agnes Sanderson	233
President Carter — Reproduced with permission of *The Burlington Hawk-Eye*	237
Twomey Company — Reproduced with permission of Twomey Company	243
Evans and Ross — Reproduced with permission of Jane Evans	244

Jane Evans and Virginia Ross platting Olena Cemetery for their publication.

INDEX

A

A.S.C.S. (AGRICULTURAL STABILIZATION AND CONSERVATION SERVICE) 213, 214, 216
AAA 169, 170, 171, 172, 174, 178, 189, 190, 192, 193, 195, 207, 213
ABBEY, Frank E. 144
ADAMS, John Quincy 1
AGNEW, Vice President 237
ALECOCK, Harry L., JR. 233
ALLAMAN, Jacob 218
   John 203
   John H. 0, 203, 218, 220
   John Lee 0
ANDERSON, Mildred 0
APT, Chris 207, 223, 228
   Chris A. 151
   Chris S. 177
ARMSTRONG, Colonel Paul B. 196
   William A. 227
ASTOR, John Jacob 12
AYERS, Herley, JR. 234
ABOLITIONISM 65
ABOLITIONIST 34
ADULT EDUCATION 225
AGE OF JACKSON 3
AGRIBUSINESSMAN 133
AGRICULTURAL 58
AGRICULTURAL MARKETING ACT OF 1929 160
AGRICULTURAL WAR BOARD 200
AGRICULTURE 26, 77, 79, 132
AGRICULTURE WITH CRAFTS AND PROFESSIONS 27
AIR RAID WARDEN 201
AIRPLANE ASSEMBLY PLANT 157
ALEXIS PHELPS HOME 219
AMERICAN FUR COMPANY 5, 12, 31
AMERICAN HOUSE 33
AMERICAN LEGION 221
AMUSEMENT 221
AMUSEMENTS 105, 176
ATLANTA 70, 73
ATLANTIC CHARTER 188
AUCTIONS 168
AUSTRALIAN BALLOT 152
AUTO EXCURSIONS 113
AUTOMOBILE 112, 113, 147
AUTOMOBILES 127, 154, 175, 216

B

BABCOCK, Dr. M. J. 201
BACHELORS 25
BAD AXE CREEK 20
BALD BLUFF 26
BAND CONCERTS 141
BANK CLOSINGS 161
BANK OF OQUAWKA 167, 191, 213
BANK OF STRONGHURST 213
BANK OF SWAN CREEK 163
BANKERS 179, 216
BANKS 136, 137, 159, 160, 162, 163, 166, 167, 168, 169, 191, 212, 214
BAPTISTS 39, 40, 91, 92
BARNES, Edward O. 87, 100, 110, 114, 131, 139, 153, 164
   Robert 87
BATTLE OF MURFREESBORO 68
BATTLE OF BAD AXE CREEK 20
BEALL, A. L. 110, 138
BEARDSTOWN 7, 18
BEATY, Captain William 13
   William 13
BEAUREGARD, P.G.T. 57
BEDFORD TOWNSHIP 37
BELL, Charles M. 88
   Paul 218
BEVERIDGE, John L. 100
BIG BANDS 175
BIG RIVER STATE FOREST 221
BIGGER, John 217
BIGGS' MILL 35
BIGGS, John 35
BIGGSVILLE 26, 27, 30, 35, 36, 39, 58, 59, 67, 82, 87, 88, 89, 90, 92, 95, 96, 97, 105, 111, 114, 151, 167, 168, 193, 201, 204, 212, 223
BIGGSVILLE CLIPPER 87, 89, 102
BIGGSVILLE HIGH SCHOOL 89, 134
BIGGSVILLE TOWNSHIP 14, 26
BILLY LEE MURDER 98
BIRTH 25
BIRTH RATE 28, 162, 215
BIRTHRATE 81
BLACK HAWK 12, 15, 16, 17, 18, 20, 21, 25
BLACK HAWK WAR 15, 19
BLACK, William 34
BLACKHAWK CAVALRY 66
BLANDINSVILLE 163
BLITZKRIEG 185, 186
BOGUS HOLLOW 45
BOLSHEVIKS 131
BONUS MARCHERS 161
BOOTLEGGER 146
BOOTLEGGING 130, 144, 145
BOUNTY LAND 3
BRAGG, General 68
BRENNEN, Martin A. 177
BROKAW, Cornelius 109
   Joshia 36
   Josiah 37
BROOKS, Curley 188
BROWN, Barnum 99
   Edgar Lee 204
BRYAN, William Jennings 151
   William P. 35
BUCHANAN, James 55
BURLINGTON 58
BUSINESS 58
BUSINESSES 136, 163, 191
BUSINESSMEN 27
BUTLER, George H. 87

C

C.B.&Q. 212, 213
CAMBODIA 235
CAMP BUTLER 66, 67
CAMP ELLIS 202
CAMP GRANT 202
CAMP LIFE 72
CAMP ZACHARY TAYLOR 121
CAMPBELL, John 14, 31
CAMPERS 221
CAR DEALERS 197
CAR PRICES 149, 206
CARMAN 65, 82, 83, 101, 151
CARMAN, Joseph 85
CAROTHERS, Andrew 34
CARPENTER, Charles F. 228
CARPENTIER, Charles 207
CARS 123, 148, 197, 216
CARTER, Jimmy 237
CARTHAGE 7, 11
CARTHAGE AND BURLINGTON RAILROAD 84
CASUALTIES 68, 69, 72, 73, 122, 124, 204, 233, 234, 235
CATFISH HOUSE 33
CATHOLIC 39, 48
CATHOLICS 93
CB & Q 35
CB&Q 36, 39, 83, 91, 92, 101, 113, 115, 140, 191, 200
CB&Q LINE 58, 85
CEDAR CREEK 39
CENSUS 2
CENSUS DATA 108
CENSUS MARSHALS 25, 28
CENSUS OF 1840 25
CENSUS, UNITED STATES, (1840) 25, 26, 27, 28
   UNITED STATES, (1850) 26, 27
   UNITED STATES, (1860) 77, 78, 79, 80, 81, 82, 83
   UNITED STATES, (1870) 77, 78, 79, 80, 81, 82, 83
   UNITED STATES, (1880) 81, 82, 83
CHANT, George 169
CHANUTE FIELD 202
CHASE, Salmon P. 53
CHATAUQUA 151
CHATTANOOGA 68, 69, 70
CHAUTAUQUA 117, 141
CHEMICAL FERTILIZERS 192
CHICAGO TRIBUNE 187
CHICAGO, BURLINGTON AND QUINCY RAILROAD 36
CHIPPERFIELD, Robert 228
CHURCHES 37, 39, 40, 41, 42, 43, 44, 91, 92, 93, 94, 95, 153
CHURCHILL, Winston 187, 188
CIRCUIT COURT MAGISTRATE 226
CIRCUIT COURTS 226
CIRCUSES 117
CIVIL DEFENSE 201
CIVILIAN CONSERVATION CORP. 166, 172
CLARK, William 230
CLAY, Henry 47
CLEVELAND, Emmett 122
   Grover 95
CLOSE-OUT SALES 215
CLOTHING 9, 112, 136, 174
COCHRAN, John D. 142
COLLECTIVE BARGAINING 225
COLLEGE EDUCATION 110
COLSON, Charles W. 236
COMMERCE 7, 11, 78, 84
COMMERCIAL HOUSE 36
COMMODITY CREDIT CORPORATION 190, 216
COMMUNIST PARTY 130
CON CON 152, 227
CONSOLIDATED HIGH SCHOOL SYSTEM 223
CONSOLIDATION 224
CONSTITUTION OF 1848 88
CONSTITUTION, ILLINOIS 151, 152, 227, 228
CONSTITUTIONAL CONVENTION 151, 152
Constitutional Convention, 1920 227
COOK'S GARAGE 146
COOK, James 220
   James H. 233
   Jim 197
COOLIDGE, Calvin 129, 133
COPPERHEAD 61, 64, 96
COPPERHEADS 57, 61, 62, 63, 64, 65
CORK SCHOOL 137
CORNET BAND 141
CORTELYOU, Lowell 203
COST OF LIVING 174
COUNCIL OF DEFENSE 121, 129
COUNTY BOARD OF EDUCATION 174
COUNTY CENSUS 25
COUNTY COURT 226, 228
COUNTY COURT SYSTEM 212
COUNTY COURTS 226
COUNTY FAIRS 175, 220
COUNTY FARMERS 168
COUNTY ILLINOIS EMERGENCY RELIEF COMMISSION OFFICE 172
COUNTY JAIL 172, 177, 222
COUNTY JAILHOUSE 46
COUNTY MUSEUM 220
COUNTY POOR FARM 97
COUNTY POOR FARM-JAIL 173
COUNTY SEAT 177
COUNTY SEAT CONTEST 105
COURT HOUSE RENOVATION 207
COURTHOUSE 177, 218
COVERED BRIDGE 218
COWAN, John 84
COX, Archibald 236
   James 129
COXEY'S ARMY 100, 101
CRAFTSMAN 80
CRANE, Michael 34, 84
CREEP 236
CRESWELL, Samuel 61
CRIME 44, 45, 97, 98, 99, 100, 114, 146, 174, 222
CRIMES 115
CROSS GABLE BARNS 108
CROSTHWAIT, H. W. 36
CULTIVATOR 1
CURRY, Alanzo 73
CURTS, John 34
CUSTER, H. W. 201

D

DAILY LIFE 2, 8, 9, 10, 13, 173, 216
DALLAS CITY 30, 35, 54, 82, 83, 85, 109, 113, 117, 118, 204, 221
DALLAS, George M. 35
DALTON, John 84
DANCES 197, 221
DANNENBERG, LENNIE 213
DAVENPORT, Colonel George 45
   E. L. 201
   George 18
   John 12, 31
DAVIDSON, Francis 84
DAVIS, Abner 34
   Jefferson 57
DEAN, John 236
DEBS, Eugene V. 124
DECLARATION OF LOYALTY

124
DECORRA 83, 100, 132, 194
DEFENSE DRIVES 189
DELABAR PARK 237
DELABAR STATE PARK 231
DELBAR STATE PARK 221
DEMOCRAT 152, 177, 188
DEMOCRATIC 150
DEMOCRATIC CANDIDATES 177
DEMOCRATIC PARTY 53, 60, 61, 62, 63, 146, 150, 176, 178
DEMOCRATIC PARTY BALLOT 1940 187
DEMOCRATS 47, 51, 52, 53, 54, 55, 65, 66, 86, 107, 129, 146, 149, 150, 151, 177, 188, 207, 228, 229, 231, 232, 237
DENEEN, Charles 152
DENNISON, Leman A. 224
DEPARTMENT OF PUBLIC WELFARE 167, 172
DEPRESSION OF 1893 100
DIRKSEN, Everett 178
   William McKinley 228
DIRKSON, Everett 234
DIRT ROADS 147, 172
DISTILLERY 34
DIXON'S FERRY 20
DIXON, Gillette B. 201
   Joseph 83
DIXSON, Joseph 82
DOUGLAS, Paul 229
   Stephen 47, 51, 52, 219
   Stephen A. 47, 48, 54, 57, 62
DRAFT 121, 196, 202
DRAFT BOARD 121
DRAFT DEFERMENT 191
DRAFT DEFERMENTS 192
DRAFT LAW 121
DRAFT OPPOSITION 187
DRAFTEES 121
DRED SCOTT DECISION 65
DREHER, Marjorie 0
   Marjory 220
DRUGS 223
DUCK HUNTING 221
DUGOUT CREEK 25
DUNCAN, Joseph 31
DUNN, John 34
DUNNE, Edward F. 152
   Governor Edward F. 147
DUTCH REFORMED 39, 91
DUTCH REFORMED CHURCH 40

E
EAGLE HOTEL 58
EAGLE HOUSE 33
EARLY WAGON TRAILS 22
EDUCATION 43, 44, 84, 88, 89, 90, 109, 110, 111, 137, 138, 139, 173, 174, 212, 223, 224, 225, 226
EIGHTEENTH AMENDMENT 144, 146, 161
EISENHOWER, Dwight 232
   Dwight D. 205, 229, 233
ELECTIONS, COUNTY 46, 47, 176, 177, 207
   ILLINOIS 51, 52, 62, 107, 150, 151, 178, 187, 188, 228, 229, 230, 231, 237, 238
   NATIONAL 54, 107, 119, 120, 129, 130, 150, 151, 178, 187, 188, 228, 229, 230, 231, 237
ELECTRIC POWER 142
ELECTRICITY 141
ELECTRIFICATION 142, 143

ELLISON CREEK 8, 14, 25, 34, 64
ELLISON CREEK CHURCH 93
ELLISON RIVER 33
EMANCIPATION PROCLAMATION 63
EMERGENCY BANKING RELIEF ACT 166
EMERGENCY RELIEF COMMISSION 171
EMMERSON, Governor Louis L. 162
   Lewis L. 148
ENERGY CRISIS 123
ENTERTAINMENT 140
ENTERTAINMENTS 176
ERICKSON, Waldo 168
   Waldo M. 168
ERNST, Ferdinand 9
ERVIN, Senator Sam 236
ESPIONAGE ACT 124
ETHNIC GROUPS 60
ETHNIC MAKE UP 59
EVANGELICAL SECTS 94
EVANS, Lane 238
   Stephen G. 0, 226
EXTENSION SERVICE 196

F
FAIRS 140
FALL CREEK 25
FAMILY FARM 79, 108, 132, 159, 215, 216
FAMILY INCOME 168, 205
FAMILY LIFE 2, 10, 13, 15, 20, 25, 26, 27, 105, 108, 109, 134, 135, 136, 162, 172, 173, 174, 175, 176, 216, 217
FAMILY SIZE 28, 81
FAMILY STRUCTURE 81
FARM 34, 109, 133, 175, 192
FARM ACREAGE 132
FARM BUREAU 140, 169, 170, 171, 173, 174, 176, 192, 193, 194, 197, 206, 213
FARM ECONOMY 132, 134, 159, 193, 215
FARM FAMILIES 1, 35
FARM FAMILY 135
FARM FORECLOSURES 163
FARM INCOME 132, 160, 161, 171, 206
FARM LABOR 193, 195
FARM LAND 108
FARM LAND VALUES 215
FARM LOAN ASSOCIATION 194
FARM MACHINERY 77, 195
FARM PRODUCTS 36
FARM PROFITS 109
FARM SALES 109
FARM WORKERS 133, 196
FARMER 6, 108, 214
FARMER'S PICNICS 220
FARMER'S REGISTER 1
FARMERS 1, 2, 3, 5, 14, 25, 26, 27, 35, 36, 39, 46, 77, 78, 88, 89, 101, 131, 132, 134, 162, 163, 166, 169, 171, 174, 177, 179, 189, 192, 193, 194, 195, 206, 207, 212, 213, 214, 215, 216
FARMERS AND MERCHANTS STATE BANK 137
FARMERS HOME ADMINISTRATION 207
FARMERS INSTITUTE 134
FARMERS' PICNIC 140
FARMING 34, 80, 159

FARMS 77, 79, 136, 196, 207
FEDERAL CROP INSURANCE CORPORATION 215
FEDERAL DEPOSIT INSURANCE CORPORATION 168
FEDERAL EMERGENCY RELIEF ASSOCIATION 166
FEDERAL FARM BOARD 160
FEDERAL LAND OFFICES 5
FEDERAL LAND RECORDS 0
FEDERAL PRICE SUPPORTS 212
FIELD HAND 80
FIELD HANDS 79
FINCH, John M. 35
   William L. 217
FIRST NATIONAL, THE 168
FIRST STATE BANK 191
FIRST STATE BANK OF STRONGHURST 134
FLOODS 217
FOOD ADMINISTRATION 132
FOOD FOR FREEDOM PROGRAM 190, 196
FOOD PRICES 123, 190
FORD, Gerald 237
FORECLOSURES 161
FOREIGN ADULTS 82
FOREIGN-BORN 59, 60, 124
FOREIGN-BORN ADULTS 29, 82
FOREIGN-BORN CHILDREN 30
FOREIGNERS 48, 59, 60, 130, 131
FORESMAN, Merlin 109
FORGEY, William 197
   William L. 169, 192
FORT ARMSTRONG 10
FORT LEONARD WOOD 203
FORT SHERIDAN 121, 202
FORT, E. A., Jr. 218
   E. C. 201
FORWARD, I. F. 123
FOSTER, John 145
   John M. 1¹6, 175
FOURTH PRINCIPLE MERIDIAN 5
FRATERNAL 94
FRATERNAL ORGANIZATIONS 94, 116
FREE SOIL PARTY 48
FREEPORT 51
FRONTIER FOOD 9, 10
FT. ARMSTRONG 10, 12, 18
FT. DONALDSON 67
FT. MADISON 5, 17, 34
FT. SUMTER 56, 57
FUEL SHORTAGES 123, 214, 215
FUR TRADE 12
FUR TRADER 11

G
GAINES, General Edmund P. 16
GALBRAITH, Max 203
   Raymond 147
GALENA 11, 14, 31
GALESBURG 52
GALLAND, Dr. 12
   Dr. Isaac 11
GAS PRICES 206
GAS RATIONING 193
GENUNG, Joseph 35
GIBB, Clarence P. 169, 207
GIBSON, John 13, 14, 34
GILMORE, John 214, 216
   W. W. 64
GIPE'S CAFE 136
GIPE, Donald 204
   Donald W. 204

GLADSTONE 30, 36, 39, 58, 59, 82, 84, 85, 93, 94, 95, 99, 100, 105, 191, 212, 213, 217, 221, 223
GLADSTONE CATHOLIC CHURCH 93
GLADSTONE DEPOT 84
GLADSTONE GRAIN COMPANY 213
GLADSTONE LAKE 221
GLADSTONE REFINERY 85
GLADSTONE TOWNSHIP 27, 28, 35
GLADSTONE-OQUAWKA HIGH SCHOOL 223
GLICK, Charles 218
GOLDEN, Seymour 227
GOLDWATER SPECIAL TRAIN 230
GOLDWATER, Barry 230
GORDEN, James W. 177
GORDON, James 88
   James W. 123
GOVERNMENT, COUNTY 46, 47, 105, 106, 107, 176, 207, 226, 227
GRADE SCHOOL 220
GRADE SCHOOL DISTRICTS 223
GRAMMAR SCHOOL 90
GRAND ARMY OF THE REPUBLIC 94, 95
GRANDINETTI'S SUPPER CLUB 230, 234
GRANT, Ulysses S. 70, 73
GRAVES, Judson 87
GRAY, Judge John A. 106
GREAT LAKES NAVAL TRAINING CAMP 122
GREAT LAKES TRAINING CENTER 121
GREEN, Dwight H. 187
GULF OF TONKIN RESOLUTION 234
GULFPORT 30, 85, 97, 98, 145, 213
GUNBOAT 97, 98
GYPSIES 114

H
HAGEMAN, James 37
HAIL, Eugene A. 87, 107
HAINES, James 9
HALDEMAN, H. R. 236
HAMLIN, Hannibal 53
HANEY, Bud 175, 204
HARD ROADS 175
HARDEN, Elmer Lee 216
   Robert 146
HARDING, Warren Gamaliel 129
HARRIS, Charles M. 65
   Daniel 45
   Everett 213
HARRISON, Benjamin 95
   William Henry 47
HART, Gus 238
HARTQUIST, Buck 213
   C. A. 194
   Clarence A. 169
HAWK-EYE 12
HAY, John 102
HENDERSON COUNTY ARTS COUNCIL 219
HENDERSON COUNTY COURTHOUSE 106
HENDERSON COUNTY DEMOCRAT 87
HENDERSON COUNTY FAIR 175, 220
HENDERSON COUNTY FARM

BUREAU 134
HENDERSON COUNTY FARM LOAN ASSOCIATION 169
HENDERSON COUNTY HISTORICAL SOCIETY 0, 217, 218, 219, 220
HENDERSON COUNTY JOURNAL 87, 107
HENDERSON COUNTY MACHINERY RATIONING BOARD 195
HENDERSON COUNTY MUSEUM 211
HENDERSON COUNTY MUSIC AND DRAMA SOCIETY 176
HENDERSON COUNTY VIGILANCE COMMITTEE 96
HENDERSON COUNTY VIGILANTIES 96
HENDERSON COUNTY WAR PRICE AND RATIONING BOARD 197
HENDERSON COUNTY WAR SAVINGS LEAGUE 124
HENDERSON CREEK 7, 13, 14, 18
HENDERSON PLAINDEALER 87
HENRY, General James D. 21
HERBERTZ, Herman 87
  William 87
HERITAGE TRAIL 220
HIGH SCHOOL 88, 89, 90, 110, 111, 139, 205
HIGH SCHOOL EDUCATION 223
HIGH SCHOOLS 138, 139, 173
HIGH-SCHOOL 138
HIGHWAY 212
HIGHWAY EMBLEMS 148
HIGHWAYS 149, 152, 212
HILL, David 215
HIRED MEN 135
HIROSHIMA 205
HISTORICAL DRAMAS 220
HITLER, Adolph 185, 186
HOLLY, George W. 99
HOME BREW 145
HONEY AND DUGOUT CREEK 8
HONEY CREEK 10, 25, 98
HONEY CREEK TOWNSHIP 33
HOOD, General John B. 71
HOOVER, Herbert 123, 132, 160
HOOVERISM 164
HOPPER MILL 35
HOPPER'S MILL 99
HOPPER, John 35
  Lambert 34
HORIZONTAL MOBILITY 26, 80
HORNER, Governor 177
  Governor Henry 166
HOUCHINS, John 34
HOUSE DIVIDED SPEECH 51
HOUSTON BANK 163
HOUSTON BANK OF BLANDINSVILLE 163
HOUTCHENS, J. Wendell 204
HOWLETT, Michael 228
HULL, Cordell 189
HUMPHREY, Hubert 230
HUNT, E. Howard 236
HUSTON, Joel 37
HUTCHINSON, Samuel 64

I

IGOE, Michael L. 177
ILLINOIS BELL TELEPHONE COMPANY 112
ILLINOIS COUNCIL OF DEFENSE 190, 192
ILLINOIS EMERGENCY RELIEF COMMISSION 178
ILLINOIS EMERGENCY RELIEF COMPANY 162
ILLINOIS FARMERS INSTITUTE 115
ILLINOIS FRONTIER 6, 9
ILLINOIS HIGHWAY COMMITTEE 147
ILLINOIS HIGHWAY IMPROVEMENT ASSOCIATION 147
ILLINOIS HISTORICAL RECORDS SURVEY 166
ILLINOIS IN 1837 31
ILLINOIS STATE ARCHIVES
ILLINOIS STATE HISTORICAL SOCIETY 217
IMMIGRANTS 28, 29, 30, 36, 59, 130
IMMIGRATION 81, 82
INFLATION 206
INSULL, Samuel 121
IOWA ORDINANCE PLANT 195
ISAACSON, Don 234
  Milford Don 234

J

JACK'S MILL 33, 34
JACKSON, Andrew 1
JAMISON SETTLEMENT 39
JAMISON, John 14
  M. N. 87
  Richard H. 235
  Samuel 14
  W. R. 33
  William 31
JAPAN 186, 189, 204, 205
JAWORSKI, Leon 236
JAZZ 143
JEFFERSON, Thomas 3
JIMMY CARTER'S GRAIN EMBARGO 216
JOB'S LANDING 7
JOHNSON, Andrew 65
  Anton J. 207
  Edythe C. 110
  Hiram 129
  Kirk 227
  Lyndon 233
JOHNSTON, General Joseph E. 70
JUNE 1917 124
JUNIOR COLLEGE DISTRICT 225

K

KEITHSBURG 83
KENDALL, Wilson 34
KENNEDY, John F. 229, 233
KEOKUK 12, 15, 17, 18, 21, 32, 44, 45
KEOKUK, Chief 15
KERLEY, L. C. 223
KERNER, Otto 229
KERSHAW, Andrew 88
KINSLOE, T. W. 66
KISSINGER, Henry 235
KNAPP, Yvonne 0
KNOW NOTHING PARTY 48
KOREA 231, 232, 233

L

LABOR 160
LABOR FORCE 78
LABOR SHORTAGE 195, 196
LABORER 35, 80
LABORERS 27, 79, 80
LAMOINE RIVER 18
LAND ACT OF 1796 5
LAND OFFICE TOWNS OF QUINCY 7
LAND OFFICE WARRANT 7
LAND PRICES 134, 168, 207
LAND VALUES 192
LANDON, Alfred 177
LATHEROW, Clifford 231
  Clifford A. 237
LEE, William "Billy" W. 98
LEGAL REFORM 226
LEWISTOWN 11, 12
LIBERTY BOARD 122
LIBERTY BONDS 129
LIDDY, G. Gordon 236
LINCOLN HIGHWAY 148
LINCOLN, Abraham 18, 34, 48, 51, 52, 53, 54, 55, 56, 57, 60, 61, 62, 63, 65, 66, 70, 71, 73, 219
LINCOLN-DOUGLAS DEBATES 51, 52
LINK'S GARAGE 147
LITTON, W. P. 98
LIVESTOCK MARKETING ASSOCIATION 213
LOG CABIN 5, 6, 8, 10, 11, 12, 14, 31, 33, 34, 37, 45
LOG CABIN SCHOOL 43
LOG CABIN SCHOOLS 42
LOG CABINS 8, 9, 21
LOMAX 77, 83, 85, 94, 99, 151, 167, 168, 191, 212, 220
LOMAX CANNING COMPANY 191
LOMAX CANNING FACTORY 181
LOMAX INDUSTRIAL CORPORATION 136
LOMAX LUMBER COMPANY 191
LOMAX TOWNSHIP 7, 25, 26, 59, 81, 83
LOMAX, Robert 85
LONG, Huey 166
LONGWORTH, Alice Roosevelt 130
LOOKOUT MOUNTAIN 69, 70
LOWDEN, Frank 152
  Governor Frank O. 121, 147
LOYALTY CARD 124
LUCAS, Scott W. 228
LUMBECK, Barbara 237

M

MACARTHUR, Douglas 189
  General 232
  General Douglas 161
MACOMB 18
MADDOCK'S CAFE 143, 206
MADDOCK, Clarence 143
MADISON COUNTY 5
MAINS, John F. 88
MANILA 102
MANNING, Russell 201
MANUFACTURING 33
MARKET-FARMER 15
MARSHALL, Alexander 34
MARTIN, B. H. 88
  Nathaniel 34
  Preston 39
MASONS 94
MCCARTY, Jessie 98, 99
MCCLELLAN CLUB 65
MCCLELLAN, George 65
MCCORD, James 236
MCCORMICK, Robert 187
MCELHINNEY, A. S. 172
MCGOVERN, George 231
MCGREW, SAM 237
MCINTYRE, DEAN 233
MCKEE, John 36
MCKINLEY, William 102
MCKINNEY, John 13, 14, 39, 43
MCMILLAN, Ken 238
  Kenny 237
MCNARY-HAUGEN FARM RELIEF BILL 133
MCQUEEN, Robert 33, 84
MECHANIZATION 215
MECHANIZED FARMING 195
MEDIA 77, 83, 84, 87, 90, 95, 114, 132, 134, 138, 168, 194
MEDIA BANK 163, 168
MEDIA RECORD 87
MEDIA STATE BANK DIRECTORS 136
MEDIA TOWNSHIP 83, 89
MEES, J. Otto 227
MELLON, Andrew 160
MELOAN, Don 233
MELVIN, Leon 122
MEMPHIS, T. O. 72
MEN'S CLOTHING 123, 206
MENDENHALL, Jacob 34
MERCHANT 36
MERCHANTS 27, 33, 35, 77, 78, 79, 80, 163, 164
MERCHANTS' 153
METHODIST 91
METHODIST CAMP REVIVALS 91
METHODISTS 39, 40, 92
MEYERS, Henry S. 163
MILITARY PATENT 34
MILITARY TRACT 3, 5, 18, 22
MISSIONARY RIDGE 69, 70
MITCHELL, John 236
MODERN WOODMEN 95
MOIR, James 33
  William 3?
MONEY 162
MONMOUTH PRODUCTION CREDIT ASSOCIATION 169, 214
MONROE, James 3
  President James 3
MORELOCK, Sterling L. 120
MORRIS, Captain William 62
  I. N. 52
  William 66
MOVIES 118, 142, 143, 153, 159, 175, 197, 221

N

NAGASAKI 205
NASHVILLE 67
NATIONAL REGISTER OF HISTORIC PLACES 218, 219
NATIONAL WAR LABOR BOARD 190
NATIVISM 130, 131
NEFF IMPLEMENT COMPANY 216
NEFF, Clarence 218, 220, 221, 228, 229, 231
  Clarence E. 229
NEGRO QUESTION 65
NEUTRALITY ACTS 186
NEW CAR 206
NEW DEAL 165, 166, 167, 171, 172, 176, 177, 178, 179
NEW YORK STOCK EXCHANGE 159
NICHOL, Peter 34

249

NICHOLS, Thomas 34
NINTH JUDICIAL CIRCUIT 226, 227
NIRA CODES 171
NIXON, Richard 230, 235
   Richard M. 229, 236, 237
NOBLE, John 145
NON-HIGH SCHOOL DISTRICT 223
NON-HIGH SCHOOL UNITS 110
NORMALCY 129
NORRIS, George 187
NORTH HENDERSON CREEK 25
NORVILLE, ROBERT 233

O

OCCUPATIONAL PROFILE 26, 27, 35, 58, 78, 79, 80, 108, 133, 163, 168, 169, 172, 193, 194, 195, 213
OCEAN-TO-OCEAN HIGHWAY 148
ODD FELLOWS 94, 116
OFFICE OF PRICE ADMINISTRATION 190
OGILVIE, Richard 230
   Richard B. 231
OLD CAPITOL BUILDING 227
OLENA 26, 27, 34, 82, 93, 94
OLENA AND HOPPER 30
OLENA CORNET BAND 94
OLENA TOWNSHIP 26, 34
OLENA TRAGEDY 98
OLSON, John 204
ONE HUNDRED DAYS 165
OPERA HOUSE 141, 173
OPERA HOUSES 116, 141, 142, 220
OQUAWKA 13, 15, 17, 18, 25, 26, 27, 29, 30, 31, 32, 33, 34, 38, 39, 41, 42, 44, 46, 52, 54, 58, 59, 60, 64, 65, 66, 67, 72, 78, 79, 80, 82, 83, 85, 87, 88, 90, 92, 93, 94, 95, 96, 97, 99, 100, 105, 106, 111, 112, 113, 116, 118, 136, 137, 138, 141, 143, 144, 145, 150, 151, 167, 168, 172, 173, 175, 177, 191, 194, 196, 201, 206, 207, 212, 217, 218, 219, 220, 221, 222, 223
OQUAWKA AND SHOKOKON 30
OQUAWKA BRASS BAND 53, 57, 72
OQUAWKA BUTTON FACTORY 114
OQUAWKA JUNCTION 59
OQUAWKA PLAINDEALER 44, 87
OQUAWKA SPECTATOR 102
OQUAWKICK 11
OQUAWKIEK 31
ORDERS 94
OVER EXPANSION 215

P

P & O 39
PALMER, John M. 100
   Mitchell 131
PANIC OF 1837 32
PATENTS 3
PATTERSON, E. M. 58
   E.H.N. 42, 44, 53
   Edwin (E.H.N.) 86
   Harry N. 86
   J. B. 47
   John B. 25, 31, 44
   Robert M. 39
PAVED ROAD 148, 173
PAVED ROADS 147, 153, 159

PEARL BUTTON FACTORY 191
PEARL HARBOR 189, 190
PENCE'S FORT 13
PENCE, D. Donald 231
   John 13, 20, 31, 33, 66
PEORIA AND OQUAWKA PROJECT 39
PERCY, Charles 229, 230, 234
PERRINE, I. 146
PERRY, Henry 204
PHELPS BROTHERS 11, 12, 13
PHELPS, Alexis 11, 31, 47
   Stephen S. 99
   Sumner 11, 12, 13, 17, 18, 20, 31, 52, 58, 99
   William 12
   William H. 42
PHYSICIAN 43, 79
PHYSICIANS 33, 58, 86
PICNICS 153
PIKE COUNTY 5
PIONEER 10, 21
PIONEER'S 6
PIONEERS 1, 8, 10, 14, 25
PLACES OF BIRTH 30
PLUMBERS 236
POE, Edgar Allen 31, 44
POLITICAL PARTIES 46, 47, 51
POPULATION 3, 154
POPULATION DECLINE 130
POPULATION GROWTH 77
POPULATION PROFILE 79
POSTMASTER 44
PRESBYTERIAN 40, 91, 93
PRESBYTERIANS 39, 92
PRICE CONTROLS 206
PRICES AND WAGES 160
PROFESSIONS 78, 79
PROHIBITION 100, 144, 145, 146
PROHIBITION ERA STILL 145
PROHIBITIONIST PARTY 86
PROSTITUTES 79, 97
PUBLIC WORKS ADMINISTRATION 166
PULLED OUT OF ATLANTA 71

Q

QUINCY 67
QUINCY FEDERAL LAND OFFICE 33

R

RADIO 142, 143, 175
RADIOS 154
RAILROAD 1, 33, 36, 39, 82, 84, 86
RAILROAD DEPOT 35
RAILROAD TOWNS 77
RAILROADS 1, 35, 77, 83, 84, 85, 86, 162, 191
RAILSBACK, Thomas 230, 237
   Tom 231
RALSTON, James 45
RANKIN, Alex 84
   Ralph Wayne 204
   Robert A. 99
RARITAN 30, 36, 67, 82, 86, 87, 92, 95, 100, 109, 116, 122, 136, 142, 154, 167, 168, 177, 220
RARITAN BANK 163, 191, 213
RARITAN BULLETIN 87
RARITAN OPERA HOUSE 117, 118, 143, 206, 219
RARITAN REPORTER 87, 100, 102, 105
RARITAN STATE BANK 137, 168
RARITAN TOWNSHIP 26, 29, 137

RATION STAMP BOOK 191
RATIONING 123, 195, 197
RECONSTRUCTION FINANCE CORPORATION 161
RECONVERSION 205, 206
RECREATION 140
"Red Ball" Road 148
RED SCARE 130
REDMAN, Captain Rezin 10
REFORMED 39, 91
REHLING, A. J. 192, 195, 199, 205
   F. 123
REPUBLICAN 52, 54, 66, 95, 121, 149, 150, 151, 177, 207
REPUBLICAN PARTY 48, 146, 229, 230
REPUBLICANS 53, 62, 63, 65, 107, 129, 150, 152, 159, 176, 178, 187, 188, 228, 230, 231, 232, 237
RESTORATION PROJECTS 219
REVENUE ACT OF 1942 190
REYNOLDS, Governor John 15
RICE, William 86
   William C. 35
RICHEY, John 229
RIGG, Romelius 14
RINGLING BROTHERS CIRCUS 117
RITCHEY, Thomas G. 96
RITCHIE SETTLEMENT 39
RITCHIE, James 13, 14
RIVERFRONT IMPROVEMENT COMMITTEE 222
ROAD IMPROVEMENTS 113
ROADS 148
ROBBINS, Michael 235
ROBERSON, David 35
ROBINSON, Rufus 106
ROCK ISLAND 17
ROCKFORD, ROCK ISLAND, AND ST. LOUIS RAILROAD COMPANY 83
RODMAN, William 34
ROLLOSON, William H. 35
ROLLOSSIN, William H. 54
ROMAN CATHOLIC 42
ROMLEY, Mercellies M. 87
ROOSEVELT, Franklin D. 129, 165, 176, 178, 179, 185, 186, 187, 188, 190
   Franklin Delano 204
   President Theodore 102
   Theodore 105, 119
ROSE, Jeremiah 84
ROSECRANS, General 68
ROZETTA 172
ROZETTA TOWNSHIP 26, 28, 29, 93
RURAL ELECTRIFICATION 174
RUSHVILLE 7, 18
RUSSIAN REVOLUTION 130
RYSON, James 13, 14

S

SADIE MCCOY 94
SAGE, Gideon 36
SAGETOWN 27, 36, 105
SALE-WARS 163
SALES TAX 166
SALOON 47, 115
SALOONS 36
SANDERSON, Mabelle 134, 135
SANT, George D. 96
SANTA FE 83, 85, 91, 113, 117, 169, 191, 194, 212, 217
SANTA FE RAILROAD 113

SAUK AND FOX INDIANS 7
SAUK OR FOX 10
SAUK-FOX 5, 12, 17, 21, 32
SAUK-FOX INDIANS 1, 10, 15
SAUK-FOX TRIBES 20
SAW AND GRIST MILL 34
SCHENCK, Harold S. 204
SCHISLER, Gale 230
SCHOOL 88, 90, 116
SCHOOL DISTRICTS 109
SCHOOL HOUSE 223
SCHOOL SUPPORT PROGRAM 224
SCHOOLHOUSES 137, 174
SCHOOLS 44, 110, 137, 212, 228
SCHWEITZER, H. H. 170
SCOTT FIELD 202
SCRAP DRIVES 199, 200
SCROGGINS, John 36
SECESSION CRISIS 55, 56, 57
SEDITION ACT OF 1918 124
SELECTIVE SERVICE BOARD 196
SENATE SELECT COMMITTEE ON CAMPAIGN PRACTICES 236
SET-ASIDE PROGRAM 214
SEWARD, William 53
SEX 112
SEX BIAS 27
SEX RATIO 26, 28, 46, 78, 81
SEXUAL DISCRIMINATION 138
SHAFER, Ray 203
SHALLENBERGER, Alfred L. 177
SHAPIRO, S. 230
SHERMAN, William T. 70, 71
SHOKOKANON 33
SHOKOKON 33, 82, 84
SHOQUOKON 33
SHORT, Abner 14
   Gabriel 13, 14
SIMONSON, Edna Barnes 169, 188
   Ralph 122
SIMPSON'S ACADEMY 42
SIMPSON, Fred A. 87
SIRICA, Judge John 236
SLATER, Kent 238
SLAVE-SOCIETY BACKGROUNDS 30
SLAVERY 2, 12, 47, 48, 51, 52, 53, 62, 63
SLAVES 63, 64
SMALL, Governor Len 148
   Len 150, 176
SMITH, Jeremiah 13, 20
   Joseph 11, 84, 85
   Ora 207, 228
SOCIAL LIFE 59, 94, 95, 111, 112, 113, 114, 116, 117, 118, 140, 141, 142, 143, 144, 145, 146, 147, 152, 153, 154, 155, 173, 174, 175, 176, 197, 198, 206, 211, 212, 220, 221, 222
SOCIAL SECURITY 172
SOCIAL SECURITY ACT 166
SOCIAL STRUCTURE 28
SOCIAL VALUES 153
SOIL CONSERVATION SERVICE 215
SOUP KITCHEN 161
SOUTH HENDERSON 14, 25
SOUTH HENDERSON CHURCH 39, 40, 92
SOUTH HENDERSON CHURCH AND CEMETERY 219
SOUTH HENDERSON CREEK 7, 13, 35, 85

SOUTHER, Rita 220
SPANISH CIVIL WAR 186
SPANISH-AMERICAN WAR 101, 105
SPARROW, Lloyd 191
SPECTATOR 44
SPECULATORS 5
ST. PATRICKS CHURCH 118
STAGE COACH LINE 38
STAMP, Zack 238
STAND, Paul 214
STAR HOUSE 36
STATE BANK OF STRONGHURST 167
STATE HIGHWAY BOND ISSUE 212
STATE HIGHWAY COMMITTEE 147
STATE INDUCTION CENTERS 202
STATE MOUNTED POLICE SYSTEM 149
STEAMBOAT 32, 52
STEAMBOATS 33, 52
STEELE, Harold B. 216
STEFFY, Otto 194
STEVENSON, Governor Adali 229
STOCKMARKET CRASH 159
STRATTON, William G. 188, 207, 228, 229
STRIKES 130, 131
STRONGHURST 77, 83, 90, 101, 106, 111, 114, 115, 116, 117, 118, 134, 135, 137, 140, 141, 151, 167, 174, 175, 177, 192, 193, 194, 195, 196, 205, 206, 207, 213, 216, 217, 220, 221
STRONGHURST BAND 201
STRONGHURST BANK 163, 168
STRONGHURST CANNING FACTORY 163
STRONGHURST COOPERATIVE SHIPPING ASSOCIATION 132
STRONGHURST DEPOT 83
STRONGHURST GRAIN AND MERCHANDISE COMPANY 169, 194
STRONGHURST GRAPHIC 88
STRONGHURST SHIPPERS ASSOCIATION 169
STRONGHURST SHIPPING ASSOCIATION 194
STRONGHURST TOWNSHIP 28, 90
SUNSET GARDENS 198
SWAN CREEK BANK 115
SWANSON, Carl 121
SWEDLUND, Marie 137, 138

T

TALCOTT'S HOTEL 36
TAMA 12, 15, 18, 20
TANNER, John R. 102
TEACHER'S ASSOCIATION 173
TEACHERS 42, 111, 138, 173, 224, 225
TEACHERS' INSTITUTE 138
TELEPHONE 112, 173
TELEPHONE SYSTEM 216
TELEVISION 221, 222
TENANTS 133
TERRE HAUTE 30, 35, 82, 86, 92, 95
TERRE HAUTE TOWNSHIP 137
THARP, Peter 36, 37, 43
THIRD REICH 185, 187
THOMAS, General 71
THOMPSON, Big Bill 140, 187
  Chester 177
  Governor William 237
THORP, Jacob 36
TOLEDO, PEORIA, AND WARSAW RAILROAD 83
TOM CREEK 14, 25
TOWN 80
TOWN DIES 153
TOWN LOTS 33
TOWNS 30, 37, 77, 86, 136, 163, 212, 213
TOWNSEND, Dr. Francis E. 166
TRACTOR 195
TRACTORS 132, 192
TRADERS 5
TRAMPS 113
TRUMAN, Harry S. 232, 233
TURNER'S HALL 145
TWENTY-FIRST AMENDMENT 146
TWOMEY COMPANY 213

U

U. S. MAINE 102
UNEMPLOYMENT 26, 80, 160, 161, 162, 179
UNEMPLOYMENT RATIO 27
UNION HIGH SCHOOL 217, 224, 225
UNIT HIGH SCHOOL DISTRICT 223
USED-CAR BUSINESS 149

V

V-E DAY 205
VAN ARSDALE, S. B. 36, 37
  William H. 109
VERNOY, Herbert 203
VESTAL, William J. 204
VETERANS 206
VIETNAM 233, 234, 235, 236
VIGILANCE COMMITTEE 96, 97, 98, 99
VILLAGES 212
VOORHEES, Frank 122
  George 177, 228
  Gilbert 109
  Harry 122
  Henry 37
  Jacques 36, 40
  Raymond O. 201

W

WALKER, Dan 231
WALLACE, Henry 123, 169
  William 96
WALTON, Clyde 217
WAR BOND 204
WAR BOND DRIVE 198
WAR OF 1812 2, 10, 11
WAR POWERS ACT 235
WAR PRODUCTION BOARD 190, 194
WAR SAVINGS STAMPS 122
WAR WITH MEXICO 47
WAR YOUTH PARTIES 197
WARNER INCIDENT 15
WARREN 34, 82, 94, 97
WARSAW & ROCKFORD COMPANY 39
WARSAW AND ROCKFORD RAILROAD 58
WATERGATE 236, 237
WATERMAN, John O. 235
WAYNE, Carl 194
WEIR FRUIT FARM 195
WEIR, William 174
  William T. 109
WELLS, Delbert 204
WERTS, Everett L. 107, 144
  Evert L. 121
  Larry 143
WESTERN ILLINOIS STATE NORMAL SCHOOL 116
WESTERN ILLINOIS UNIVERSITY 0
WESTERN ILLINOIS UNIVERSITY LIBRARIES 0, 220
WEVER ACADEMY 84, 89, 90, 138
WEVER, Nathan 83, 89
WHIG PARTY 48, 51
WHIGS 47
WHITMAN, George B. 170
WIGGINS, Lee 225
WILCOX, Samuel 64
WILKIE, Wendell 187, 188
WILSON'S WAR MESSAGE 120
WILSON, Carrol 231
  Lewis D. 227
  Woodrow 105, 107, 119, 120, 124, 129
WITWER, Samuel W. 229
WOLF CREEK 14, 25, 34
WOMAN 112
WOMEN 2, 9, 10, 13, 25, 27, 77, 78, 134, 135, 137, 138, 150, 190
WORKERS 130
WORKS PROJECTS ADMINISTRATION 166
WORLD WAR I 105, 118, 119, 121, 122, 130

Y

YANKEE 28
YATES, Governor Richard 54, 57
YELLOW BANKS 11, 12, 13, 14, 18, 31, 45, 46
YELLOW JOURNALISM 101
YOUNG AMERICA 64
YOUNG REPUBLICANS 230
YOUTH CENTER 222

Z

ZINK, Soloman 99

This book was set in Century Book type
Endleaves 90# Mead; Cover, Mulberry Crush Grain Kivar
Text sheets printed on 70# Mead Moistrite Matte and
bound by Walsworth Publishing Company, Marceline, MO